"There are few people who know China in the way that Steve Mosher does, or have experienced it as he did. For decades, Mosher has been on the literal front line watching Chinese communists execute their Culture of Death. He saw it firsthand and has continued to chronicle it like few others. He saw bullying by the Chinese communists intimately and personally, beginning with their assault on a group of village women who dared to want to bring a second child into their world. Now, he's digging still deeper to tell us more about this Bully of Asia and its plans against a much larger population. I'm pleased that Steve Mosher has undertaken this book."

> —**PAUL KENGOR**, professor at Grove City College and author of *God and Ronald Reagan* and *The Politically Incorrect Guide® to Communism*

BULLY OF ASIA

BULLY
OF ASIA

WHY CHINA'S DREAM IS THE NEW THREAT TO WORLD ORDER

STEVEN W. MOSHER

REGNERY
PUBLISHING
A Division of Salem Media Group

Regnery® is a registered trademark of Salem Communications Holding Corporation

Cataloging-in-Publication data on file with the Library of Congress

ISBN 978-1-62157-696-9
e-book ISBN 978-1-62157-705-8

Published in the United States by
Regnery Publishing
A Division of Salem Media Group
300 New Jersey Ave NW
Washington, DC 20001
www.Regnery.com

Manufactured in the United States of America

10 9 8 7 6 5 4 3

Books are available in quantity for promotional or premium use. For information on discounts and terms, please visit our website: www. Regnery.com.

*For the officers and men
of the U.S. Seventh Fleet, with whom I once served,
as they guard the frontiers of freedom*

CONTENTS

INTRODUCTION

THE GRAND UNIFICATION:
CHINA'S ZERO-SUM VIEW OF THE WORLD

*"What made war inevitable was the growth of Athenian
power and the fear in Sparta this provoked."*
–THUCYDIDES, *History of the Peloponnesian War*[1]

*"The Grand Unification of All Under Heaven is the paramount
law and a general rule from antiquity to the present."*
–DONG ZHONGSHU, *Han dynasty Scholar (179–104 B.C.)*[2]

In 431 B.C., fearful of a rising Athenian empire, Sparta assembled its army of about four thousand hoplites and marched on Athens. Its leaders were determined to subjugate the rival city-state and disperse its growing empire. The Peloponnesian War that followed dragged on for almost three decades. It ended only after the Athenian fleet—the city-state's lifeline to its empire of islands—was destroyed in 404 B.C.

The war was the longest and costliest in Greek history, yet in victory the Spartans were not vindictive but magnanimous. While they stripped Athens of its defensive walls, its overseas possessions, and what remained of its fleet, they rejected calls by Corinth and Thebes that the city itself be leveled and its population enslaved. Instead, they accepted the Athenians as allies. Even when the city overthrew its newly appointed Spartan governors a year later and restored democratic rule, Sparta did not intervene.

Sparta had gone to war with the goal of "liberating the Greeks" and it had achieved its aim. Despite its fearsome, warlike reputation, ancient Sparta had established a just peace. It had weakened (but not destroyed) a dangerous rival, freed other city-states from Athenian rule, and established the mildest of hegemonies. To its credit, it did not establish a Spartan despotism.

Five thousand miles to the East, a similar struggle for dominance—sparked by similar fears—had long been underway. But it ended not in freedom but in tyranny. Even during the early stages of China's Spring and Autumn period (772–481 B.C.) the local Chinese dukes and marquis, despots all, had little enough in common with Spartan oligarchs or Athenian democrats. Indeed, the Greek wars, limited in time and space and—one must add—cruelty, seem almost quaint in comparison to the bloodletting that was already taking place in north and central China, where vast hordes of soldiers and chariots clashed on a continent-sized landscape.

Perhaps the growing inhumanity shown by the Chinese dukes and their generals was inevitable, given the three centuries of constant warfare that they and their peoples had already endured. In any event, by the beginning of the Warring States period (475–221 B.C.), a half century before the beginning of the Peloponnesian War, all the civilized conventions that had once governed warfare in the Orient had been stripped away, leaving only deceitful stratagems and the bare, bloody conflicts that followed when these failed. And when they succeeded, the butchery was oftentimes even worse.

In the two and a half centuries that followed, the surviving rulers became ever more adept at regimenting and mobilizing the societies that they governed. As we will see in chapter two, the end result was the virtual abolition of civil society, as the state commandeered every available societal and economic resource for total war.

THE "GRAND UNIFICATION" OF "ALL UNDER HEAVEN"

The ruler who emerged victorious from this centuries-long carnage was the one who had best perfected his totalitarian control of society in the name of the state. If Sparta had gone to war to "liberate the Greeks" by freeing their city-states from Athenian domination, the goal of the first emperor of the Qin dynasty, Qin Shihuangdi, was the opposite: he wanted to enslave the Chinese by subjugating their independent kingdoms to his own rule. Utterly ruthless in his pursuit of power, he was known for slaughtering surrendering armies—as well as Confucian scholars—to the last man.

As the greatest tyrants have ever done, Qin Shihuangdi found it useful to declare his divinity. Thus he could insist that craven submission was the only proper response to his godhead. He invented his own title, which signifies that he was the founding (*shi*) emperor (*huang*) and god (*di*) of the Qin Empire. Upon unifying China in 221 B.C., not only did he demand absolute obedience as *huangdi*, or god-emperor, he ensured that he got it by establishing the closest thing to a totalitarian regime the world had yet seen. In chapter two we will take a detailed look at the Qin political order, which, significantly, as the late Chairman Mao Zedong himself affirmed, has endured down through the ages to the present day. The ghost of Qin Shihuangdi continues to lurk behind every Chinese ruler today.

Great Han chauvinists tend to overlook Qin Shihuangdi's crimes against humanity. After all, they say, he accomplished the "Grand Unification" of China, ending the fearful "chaos and disorder" of the Warring States period and ushering in "peace under Heaven." That it was the "peace" of a police state matters less to them than that it put an end to centuries of conflict by incorporating "All Under Heaven" (*tianxia*) into a single tightly controlled polity.

The phrase the "Grand Unification" (*datong*)—or, as it is sometimes translated, the "Great Uniformity"—comes originally from the *Book of Rites* (*Liji*), where Confucius writes, "When the Great Way prevails, the world will belong to all. They chose people of talent and ability whose words were sincere, and they cultivated harmony. Thus people did not only love their own parents, not only nurture their own children.... In this selfish schemes did not arise. Robbers, thieves, rebels, and traitors had no place, and thus outer doors were not closed. This is called the Great Uniformity."[3]

But it is not the lofty Confucian ideal of a society that is public spirited, crime free, and even vaguely democratic that China rulers have pursued down the centuries. Like Confucianism itself, as we will learn later, the Great Uniformity that the Sage described has been twisted into something nearly resembling its opposite.[4]

But even in its original iteration by Confucius, the Great Uniformity is not a call for free men to liberate themselves from tyranny, but rather a celebration of national unity (no rebels or traitors), of social conformity (no robbers and thieves), and implicitly of the state itself, which is viewed as the iron scaffolding that locks everyone firmly in place. The Great Uniformity, in other words, is a literal *uniformity* of thought and action that does not arise from below but is instead imposed from above. Societal conformity is seen as essential for maintaining political unity. From the very beginning of China's existence as a unified state, dissent has *always* been strictly limited.

The Qin state of Qin Shihuangdi crushed all of China's other kingdoms before it was replaced by the Han dynasty, which then continued to expand, imposing the Qin political order wherever it went. Dynasties rose and fell in the centuries that followed, and China often splintered. But the brutal and incessant wars that followed these break-ups ensured that the societal ideal remained the "Grand Unification." Sparta may have been content to let other city-states in the Greek union rule themselves according to their own lights, but no Chinese ruler would willingly allow any part of the Chinese polity to remain outside of his grasp.

The latest iteration of the ancient Qin political culture—the People's Republic of China (PRC)—similarly longs to bring All Under Heaven (*tianxia*) under its sway. That is why it is so intransigent on Taiwan. And that is why it continues to make territorial demands in the South China Sea, in the East China Sea, on the Tibetan Plateau, and elsewhere. Only through continuous expansion can the ideal of the "Great Uniformity" ultimately be realized.

China is ambitious to extend its "benevolent rule" even farther. Other translations of *datong* favored by Chinese scholars, such as the "Great Tranquility," and the "Great Harmony," better convey the more chauvinistic connotations of the phrase. They suggest a future world that lies happily quiescent under a dominant Chinese order.

Modern Chinese thinkers such as Hu Angang not only embrace the idea of a future *Pax Sinica*; they argue that it will bring peace, harmony and brotherhood to all peoples. In fact, Hu has declared that China will soon establish just such a "World of Great Harmony" (*shijie datong*, or *tianxia datong*). He claims that the World of Great Harmony is not only "China's dream" but is also the "world's dream."[5]

Francis Fukuyama may have declared the end of history following the collapse of the Soviet Union, but the Chinese leadership elite beg to differ. The *true* end of history, they say, will only arrive when China ushers in the World of Great Harmony, when all the world lies supine under the benevolent direction of the Chinese party-state.

AMERICA, CHINA, AND THE THUCYDIDES TRAP

Thucydides' sobering reflection on the causes of the Peloponnesian War has recently gotten a lot of attention—at least among students of international relations—because of Graham Allison. The Harvard University scholar coined the phrase "Thucydides Trap" to suggest that the most likely outcome of an encounter between a rising power and an existing power is armed conflict. "In 12 of 16 cases [we examined] over the past 500 years," Allison writes, "the result was war."[6]

So is the Greek tragedy that locked Sparta and Athens in combat in the third century B.C. about to repeat itself between America and China in the twenty-first century? Or, as Peter Navarro has put the question, "Will a rapidly rising China play the upstart Athens to America's wary Sparta as both plunge headlong into the infamous 'Thucydides Trap'?"[7]

The two countries certainly have radically different views of how the world of the future should look.

America fully intends to maintain the commanding position in the global order that it created for itself following World War II and maintained following the collapse of the Soviet Union. From the first Bush administration's 1992 "Defense Guidance" through the 2002 "National Security Strategy" of the second Bush administration, it has been the continuing policy of the United States to maintain its global preeminence and check rising powers. Perpetuating that preeminence remains the goal today under the "America First" policy of the Trump administration.

China, on the other hand, sees America as a power in terminal decline, exhausted from decades of imperial overstretch and war. It looks forward to building its World of Great Harmony on the ashes of the existing world order. By the middle of this century, when the PRC finishes running its hundred-year marathon—to borrow Michael Pillsbury's phrase—it imagines that it will be the dominant power on the planet. And it has made no secret of the fact that it is prepared to fight wars to achieve this end.

There is no room in either country's conception of the future global order for the other—at least as a peer competitor.

That the story of Athens and Sparta has, mutatis mutandis, been repeated again and again down through time is hardly surprising. "Offensive realists"—among whom I count myself—see the world as an anarchic system in which force is the ultimate arbiter. As the leading proponent of offensive realism, John Mearsheimer, has pointed out, in this world of insecurity—a world in which states can never be certain what the intentions of other states are—the only rational course of action for a great power is to attempt to achieve security through hegemony.

Other Western students of international relations, however, especially those of an "idealist" bent, reject the notion that conflict between great powers is somehow inevitable. They prefer to believe that open conflict between states can *always* be avoided through a proper combination of concessions, compromises, and confidence-building measures. They believe that cleverly designed international institutions and norms, craftily worded treaties and trading relationships and, above all, a willingness to negotiate until the cows come home, can prevent the deadly Thucydides Trap from ever being sprung.

In the case of the United States and China in particular, the idealists are convinced that the growing tensions can be defused, or at least contained, by keeping the focus on what we supposedly have in common. Thus they speak of our shared interest in combating "climate change" or of containing the threat from North Korea, or of our massive (if one-sided) trading relationship and mutual investments. If only America does not allow itself to fall prey to irrational fears over China's rise, they say, conflict can be permanently avoided. Far better to allow China to carve out its own sphere of influence as Asia's regional hegemon than attempt to contain it through a growing network of alliances. Any attempt to check China's designs will only increase tension between our two countries and potentially lead to events spiraling out of control. Armed clashes must be avoided at all costs, even if this means that the United States must preemptively stand down.

Although idealists tend to dominate academic discourse at Western universities, they are exceedingly thin on the ground in China. The overwhelming majority of Chinese strategists are, like Mearsheimer and myself, offensive realists. As such, they are convinced that "the world is condemned to perpetual great power competition."[8] And, as Great Han chauvinists all, they are determined to maximize China's power and influence in order to win that competition.

It is critically important to realize not only that Chinese strategists are offensive realists, but also that they have been offensive realists for a *very, very long time.*

Several hundred years before Thucydides put pen to parchment, battles were raging on the North China plain. As we will see in chapter two, during the centuries of the Eastern Zhou dynasty (770–221 B.C.) nascent China was in the throes of almost constant warfare. While the Peloponnesian War lasted a mere quarter century, China's states warred for more than *half a millennium.* Indeed, the entire period from the Spring and Autumn Annals through the Warring States period might accurately be called China's "Five Hundred Years' War." This war not only lasted far longer than any contemporaneous Western conflict, it also drew in a far greater number of state actors, who deployed far larger armies over a far larger map than any conflict the world had yet seen.

In the course of these centuries of incessant conflict, the various Chinese rulers and their advisors tried every imaginable arrangement to keep the peace. They held peace conferences, signed treaties, and negotiated defensive alliances. They held disarmament conferences and agreed to limit their military strength. They tried to maintain the status quo by maintaining a balance of power among their number. They even organized a kind of proto–League of Nations, under the terms of which the Zhou king, or the local rulers themselves, appointed one of their number as "hegemon" (*ba*)—roughly equivalent to "defender of the realm" in those days, rather than an all-dominant power, as today[9]—to keep the peace among the many states.

Some of these maneuvers purchased a few years, even a few decades, of peace, but they *all eventually failed.* Those states that sought security by treaties, alliances, and champions were eventually absorbed. Those states that relied upon their own might, judiciously building up their strength and opportunistically expanding through conquest, were rewarded over time with increasing territory, population, and power.

All this is to say that Chinese strategists do not need to be convinced that they are living in an anarchic international system, since for centuries China had the most anarchic system the world has ever seen *within its very borders*.[10] Nor do they need to be convinced that the security of the PRC can only be secured by relentlessly increasing state power vis-à-vis its competitors. Although this does not necessarily mean aggressive territorial expansion, it certainly did in China's past. And this is why China today, as it seeks to become Asia's regional hegemon, is vigorously asserting ambitious territorial claims in all directions of the compass.

Chinese intentions are evident everywhere you look, hiding in plain sight. China's humiliation at the hands of Western barbarians breeds a desire for revenge, (as we shall see in chapter one), which is all the more vigorously pursued because China's long centuries of regional hegemony suggest to its leaders that they are owed deference (chapter two). The founding of the PRC was driven by a desire to once again bestride Asia (chapter three), while Deng Xiaoping's "second revolution" was launched precisely because Maoism failed to restore national greatness (chapter four). Under Jiang Zemin the Chinese Communist Party (CCP), in accepting the new rich into its ranks, came to resemble a "national socialist" party (chapter five). Xi Jinping's "China dream" is a world under Chinese hegemony (chapter six), while his propaganda apparatus relentlessly stokes national narcissism to create a sense of cultural, economic, and even territorial entitlement among the population (chapter seven). The Chinese are taught that only America still stands in the way of the achievement of the "China dream" (chapter eight), a claim that the Chinese party-state uses to justify "unrestricted warfare" against the reigning hegemon, the United States. China is determined to bring this conflict to a successful conclusion and usher in the World of Great Harmony (chapter nine). In the final chapter I will discuss ways that America can meet the challenge posed by China's rise (chapter ten).

The roots of China's current behavior are buried deep in its five-thousand-year history. The leaders of the world's only surviving civilizational empire quite naturally view the present through the looking glass of the past—and see themselves reflected in the imperial bureaucracies of a dozen dynasties past. But the modern Chinese party-state, in order to maintain social cohesion, is also deliberately stoking the fires of national narcissism and super-patriotism using any and all means at its disposal, including glorifying China's long history. While we in the West seem determined to forget our own unique history—even denigrating the most successful civilization the world has ever seen in the name of multiculturalism—China is busy not only remembering but celebrating and embellishing its own.

With China, more than any other country, what's past is necessarily prologue. So it is there, in the formative years of Chinese civilization, that we begin our efforts to understand China's relentless drive for dominance.

1

A **DISEASE** OF THE **HEART**

"The Japanese are like a disease of the skin,
but the Communists are like a disease of the heart."
—CHIANG KAI-SHEK[1]

"There is only one challenge that today represents a clear
and existential threat to America's national interests....
The rise of the People's Republic of China."
—HARRY J. KAZIANIS[2]

"China had a very high opinion of its own achievements
and had nothing but disdain for other countries.
This became a habit and was considered quite natural."
—SUN YAT-SEN[3]

The political leader with the most experience fighting the Chinese Communist Party—first successfully and later much less so—was Nationalist leader Chiang Kai-shek. After the Japanese invasion of Manchuria in 1931, Chiang was under enormous pressure to declare war on the Empire of the Rising Sun. He refused, arguing that before the Japanese could be driven out of China, the Communist rebellion must first be put down. "First internal pacification, then external resistance," he insisted. Even when the Japanese launched a major offensive in Shanghai in 1932, he threw his best divisions into the fray but in the end refused to be drawn into an all-out conflict.

"The Japanese are like a disease of the skin," Chiang later explained to his restless army commanders, "but the Communists are like a disease of the heart." By this he meant that the Japanese, with their powerful navy, could seize China's coastal cities almost at will, but they simply did not have the manpower or resources to take and hold the vast and heavily populated interior of China over time. He knew they would eventually be forced by time or circumstances to leave, although he could not have known that China's liberation would not be accomplished until 1945, only after the blood of nearly a half million Americans, and many times that number of Chinese, had been spilled.

The Communists, on the other hand, already controlled vast stretches of the Chinese heartland. And Chiang was familiar enough with their fanaticism to know that, unless their red armies were completely annihilated, they would continue their struggle until they were victorious. It was to be a battle to the death—"you die, I live," as the Chinese say—for the very heart of China. In the end the "disease of the heart" that Chiang had warned about did indeed prove fatal to his own Nationalist government, and with its retreat to the island of Taiwan died the dream of a free and democratic China.

Chiang Kai-shek's remarkable metaphor can be used to illustrate the severity of the threats that America faces today. There are, as it turns out, a range of dangers that qualify as diseases of the skin. The radical Islamists clearly fall into this category. They will indeed fight to the death, but with their failing caliphates and their limited appeal even within the Muslim world itself, it is they who will die. Terror attacks—however much fear they may sporadically generate among the population—are a sign of weakness, not of strength. (Any tactic that results in the death of your most committed followers is ultimately self-defeating.) At the end of the day such attacks, however deadly they prove to innocent bystanders, pose no real danger to the world order America and the West have built.

Iran and North Korea are greater threats. A nuclear-armed Iran would threaten the Sunni Arab nations and jeopardize the very existence of Israel. In fact, the mullahs openly speak of using nuclear weapons to usher in the reign of the Twelfth Imam. As far as North Korea's nukes and missiles are concerned, these already constitute a serious threat to our allies in East Asia. That Kim Jong Un is additionally seeking, with help from across his country's border with China, to acquire the ability to strike at the American homeland should give us all pause. But it would be a mistake to write off the Madman of Pyongyang as criminally insane, since he may be banking on his new weapons systems to intimidate the United States and its allies into trying to buy him off again, a ploy that his father successfully used against both the Clinton and Bush II administrations.[4] Neither country, however, constitutes an existential threat to the continued existence of the Republic. Both are clearly diseases of the skin, both are able to inflict serious injury on their near neighbors, to be sure, but not to the world as currently constituted.

The question of whether Russia is a disease of the skin or of the heart is considerably more controversial. Obviously, if Putin were to launch his nuclear-tipped missiles against the West they would cause tremendous devastation. Yet the death of tens of millions of Westerners would not mean the end of Western civilization any more than the Holocaust, with its six million victims, meant the end of Jewish civilization. Civilizations are far more difficult to destroy than cities. They exist in the minds of men, in their values and beliefs, in their cultures and institutions. Moreover, Putin knows that Russia would be a smoldering ruin less than an hour after he ordered such an attack. Presumably he is no less afraid of mutually assured destruction than his Soviet predecessors were.

Only an alternative ideology could pose a real danger to the United States and to the civilization of which it is the principal defender. In "scientific" Marxism, the Soviets had just such an ideology—the appeal of communism far transcended their own country's borders—and they vigorously promoted it for decades. While they were not successful in remaking the world in their own image, they were able to spread their errors to many countries around the globe.

Today's Russia has little to offer in this regard. The autocratic rule practiced by Putin is neither a system of belief nor a civilizational advance. Rather, it is a retreat into Russia's Tsarist past.[5] Today's Russia conceives of itself, as it has throughout much of its history, not as an alternative to Western civilization, but as its easternmost outpost.[6] The Russian government may be no friend to free speech and democratic rule but, supported by the Russian Orthodox Church, it fervently promotes the family and traditional values, opposes mass immigration, and mocks multiculturalism.[7] For this, of course, it is roundly reviled by the secular Left.

While the Soviets dreamed of a world under communism, the current occupants of the Kremlin have far more limited objectives. They have neither the means nor the will to pose a serious threat to the existing world order, much less to undertake to build a new one. Rather, they merely want the country they lead to once again be respected as a great power, as it was in centuries past. More worrisomely, they want to gather scattered Russian minorities—stranded in the various Soviet Republics by the dissolution of the USSR—back into the bosom of Mother Russia. The continual expansion of NATO eastward is greatly resented, since it is seen as encroaching upon Russia's traditional sphere of influence. The 2004 incorporation of Estonia, Latvia, and Lithuania into the Western alliance was a particular blow to Russian pride, since these countries were once Soviet Republics and each has a sizable Russian minority.

The Russians woke up on December 26, 1991, to find half their country gone. Putin's goal is to piece back together as much of the Russian Empire as possible, beginning with Russian-speaking territories adjacent to his current borders. The seizure of Crimea and the proxy war in eastern Ukraine are pure irredentism, not a prelude to an invasion of Eastern Europe. This is not to say that the covert war that Russia is conducting in the eastern Ukraine is justifiable. Clearly it is not. Russia should be made to pay a heavy price for violating the territorial integrity of that country to ensure that it does not continue its aggressive, destabilizing behavior. At the same time, we should not lose sight of the larger strategic picture, in which Russia is, at best, a second-tier player.

Outside of its "near abroad" Russia's foreign policy seems to be simply reductionist: whenever and wherever Putin can thumb his nose at the United States and NATO—by holding joint naval exercises with China in the South China Sea and the Baltic, for example—he will do so. At the same time, Russia has its own worries about China's rise, a country with which it shares a forty-two-hundred-kilometer-long border, and that now competes for influence in the former Soviet Republics of Central Asia. Russia does not want to end up as "China's Canada," and even less as the junior partner in a reconstituted Sino-Russian bloc.

There is no reason to believe Tsar Vladimir Putin dreams that his own power will one day eclipse America's, much less that he harbors the secret ambition to remake the world in Russia's image. Under Putin, Soviet expansionism has given way to a much more parochial project that we might call, for want of a better term, *making Russia great again*. I grant that even this limited goal constitutes an existential threat to some of the newly independent states of Eastern Europe, whose security we have now guaranteed by treaty. But it is clearly not fatal to the United States itself, nor particularly threatening to the world order that America has created.

Loud and insistent voices continue to demand that we declare eternal enmity towards Moscow. They tell us that the clumsy Russian bear is our most dangerous adversary, and that it must be beaten down and brought to heel. There are many problems with this overblown analysis, not least of which is that Russia's economy is less than one-tenth the size of our own. Moreover, whatever else Russia is, she remains a part of Western civilization, within whose ambit she lives, thinks, and has her spiritual roots. It is not unlikely that democratic rule may one day be restored in Russia, which means that she has the potential to be our friend. But even while she remains under the dictatorial rule of the thuggish Vladimir

Putin, we can surely find an amicable resolution to our differences. And this we must do. The present fixation with Russia, which does not pose a deadly threat to America and the West, unnecessarily distracts us from the one country that does.

In all the world there is only one threat to the United States that must be classified as a disease of the heart. This is a country

- That long ago invented totalitarianism—the total subjugation of the individual to the state—and that still practices a modified form of this all-embracing political tyranny today
- That produced its own high civilization, which it imagines surpasses anything the West, or the rest of the world, has to offer
- That is persuaded that, by reason of this superior culture, it is owed universal deference
- Whose leaders govern an ethnic-based empire and tout the racial superiority of their race over all others
- That concludes from its long centuries of regional hegemony that it has a natural right to once again bestride the region
- Whose humiliation, real or imagined, at the hands of the West has been used to foster a deep desire for revenge in everyone from the top leaders on down to ordinary workers
- That narcissistically "dreams" of a world under its hegemony
- That teaches its children to hate the reigning hegemon for standing in the way of achieving this "dream"
- That dismisses the current world order as unjust, and thus thinks itself not only justified, but actually clever and sophisticated, for deceiving its way to dominance by, for example, signing agreements it has no intention of honoring

- That not only has the potential to visit nuclear annihilation on the United States, but also actually publishes maps showing the exact extent of the destruction it could rain down on our country—complete with projected casualties
- That believes, above all, that its manifest destiny is to usher in a new world order, which it calls the World of Great Harmony
- That even imagines, in its hubris, that this new world order will be greeted with joy by the peoples of the world

THE PEOPLE'S REPUBLIC OF CHINA

The PRC is under the control of the same Chinese Communist Party that proved to be Chiang Kai-shek's undoing. But in the decades since driving Chiang from the Mainland it has metastasized from a rag-tag army of rebels to the largest—and arguably the most disciplined—political organization on the planet, with some eighty-nine million members. High-ranking Party members comprise the backbone of the Chinese party-state, and through it control the second largest economy and one of the most powerful military forces the world has ever seen. Core Leader Xi Jinping envisions a Sinocentric world, with China's borders expanding outward, near neighbors reduced to de facto vassals, and countries further afield humbly serving as markets for Chinese products and sources of raw materials. Most of all, it seems, he fantasizes about a day when the current hegemon, the United States of America, will be reduced to impotence.

The role of the hegemon is firmly embedded in China's national dreamwork, intrinsic to its national identity, and profoundly implicated in its sense of national destiny. China's long imperial history as *the* dominant power of East and Southeast Asia has left no doubt in the minds of the Chinese elite that they are the cultural and intellectual superiors of every other people on the planet. They see their country's century-long humiliation at the hands of the West as a temporary aberration and take chauvinistic pride in the conviction that China's Long March back to hegemony is well underway.

The concept of hegemony was, fittingly enough, introduced into modern diplomatic discourse by the Chinese themselves. During Henry Kissinger's secret visit to Beijing in 1971, the Chinese translator's use of this unfamiliar English word sent Kissinger fumbling for his dictionary. There he found definitions of "hegemony" as "a single pole or axis of power," and as "leadership or predominant influence exercised by one state over others."

None of these definitions fully captures the rich and sometimes sinister nuances of the concept of the *ba* in Chinese.

The *ba* is a political order invented by ancient Chinese strategists twenty-eight hundred years ago that is based exclusively on naked power. Under the *ba*, as it evolved over the next six centuries, total control of a state's population and resources was to be concentrated in the hands of the state's hegemon, or *bawang* (literally "hegemon-king"), who would employ this power to establish his hegemony, or *baquan* (literally "hegemon-power"), over all the states in the known world.

What Chinese strategists of old may be said to have invented, then, is an early form of totalitarianism. Not only did the *ba* predate the Western variety of totalitarian rule by almost three thousand years, it was *self-consciously designed to be an instrument of international aggrandizement.* Bureaucratic totalitarianism is often thought to be an invention of the twentieth century, an evil alchemy of nineteenth-century Marxist ideology and twentieth-century Leninist bureaucracy capable of transmuting precious freedoms into base slavery. But the inventor of the iron cage of totalitarianism was not Vladimir Ilyich Lenin—though it is of course his specter that loomed over the peoples of Central and Eastern Europe for so many decades—but the founding emperor of the Qin dynasty, Qin Shihuangdi, and his "Legalist" Machiavelli, Li Si. The goal of the *ba* was to achieve a kind of super-superpower status vis-à-vis neighboring states. In the words of China's ancient strategic genius, Sunzi (sometimes spelled Sun Tzu) in his classic *The Art of War*, "The power of the hegemon is so immense that when his troops invade a large nation, the people of that country scatter."

The twentieth century, which saw two totalitarian states in succession attempt global conquest, has left us all too familiar with the word totalitarianism. Still somewhat exotic is hegemony, which the Chinese introduced to the world, first in theory, and of late in practice. This is the notion that the premier goal of foreign policy should be to establish absolute dominance over one's region and, by slow extension, the world. China's pursuit of hegemony predisposes it to predetermine the outcome of territorial and other disputes by threats, intimidation, blackmail and, if necessary, out-and-out force. Contrast this with the default behavior of democracies, which is to seek peaceful, neighborly relations, and which, in the event that disputes do arise, naturally seek to resolve them by negotiation and treaty.[8]

In the South China Sea both we and the Chinese are acting out our national characters: The United States is consulting with its allies, calling for China to stand down, supporting the decision of the International Court of Arbitration,[9] and suggesting that all parties come to the bargaining table and resolve their competing claims peacefully. China, on the other hand, is behaving like an aggrieved hegemon. Ignoring almost universal condemnation of one of the largest land grabs in history, it is attempting to "overawe its enemies" (Sunzi again). By issuing a barrage of threats and by engaging in a preemptive military buildup, including an island-building campaign, it clearly hopes it will simply cow its smaller adversaries into submission.

Throughout the 1970s and 1980s, the Chinese untiringly accused the Soviet Union of having hegemonic ambitions, that is, of seeking to dominate the entire world. Following the Soviet collapse, they turned their wrath on the United States, ominously and endlessly charging that

America was "seeking hegemony." In fact, all this name-calling was merely a political form of Freudian projection, for China's elite clearly covets the title of hegemon for itself.

In the old—and enduring—Chinese view of the world, chaos and disorder can only be avoided by organizing vassal and tributary states around a single dominant axis of power. And if there is to be a hegemon, Chinese history and culture combine to say, then it should be China. In their obsession with hegemony the Chinese people have their own doctrine of manifest destiny.

For more than two thousand years, the Chinese considered themselves the geographical and geopolitical center of the world.[10] From their earliest incarnation as an empire, they spoke of China as *Zhong Guo*, "The Middle Kingdom," or, even more revealingly, as *Tian Xia*, "Everything under Heaven." They believed their emperor to be the only legitimate political authority and regarded themselves as the highest expression of civilized humanity. This Sinocentric—even narcissistic—worldview survived even foreign invasion and occupation by Xiongnu, Mongols, Jurchens, and Manchus; the Chinese were invariably able to co-opt and assimilate their poorly organized and culturally inferior conquerors within a generation or two.

And far from being a self-serving myth or shallow chauvinism, China's idea of national greatness is firmly rooted in reality. For most of its long history, the Chinese empire was indeed a collection of superlatives. It had the greatest land area, the largest population, the most productive economy, the most powerful army, and the most advanced technology of any power on earth. It took particular pride in having the highest culture as well, and often justified its expansion on the grounds of a *mission civilisatrice*. In the end, China's sway over East Asia was limited only by its own ambitions, not by the counterforce of hostile and competing powers. Chinese explorers did not venture far afield, and when they did they returned and invariably testified that the world beyond China's borders was so technologically and culturally inferior as to be almost beneath notice.[11] Admiral Zheng He's naval expeditions to India and beyond in the early 1500s, for example, convinced the Ming court that the outside world had nothing to offer the Kingdom at the Center of the Earth.

Power of all kinds—economic, military, and cultural—was concentrated in the hands of the emperor, and radiated out from His Radiant Highness, as the occupant of the Dragon Throne was styled. As the distance from the capital increased, the reflected light of His Radiant Highness necessarily diminished, and the locals, whatever their manners and diction, were considered increasingly uncouth. Chinese from the outer provinces were assumed to be inferior in every way to the culturally superior cosmopolitans of the capital. As for the various barbarian tribes who populated the border regions, they were regarded as little better than wild beasts, to which they were often compared.

Under aggressive emperors, the Middle Kingdom quickly grew to the geographical limit—in the days when communications were limited to the speed of a galloping horse—of what could be governed from a single center. With the possible exception of the Roman Empire at its height, the realms of the major Chinese dynasties dwarfed all contemporaneous empires in other parts of the world in population and geographic extent.

By the mid–Qing dynasty (1644–1911), China held sway over a vast territory stretching from today's Russian Far East, westward across southern Siberia to Lake Balkhash and into contemporary Kazakhstan, then southeastward along the Himalayas to the Indian Ocean, and eastward across Laos and northern Vietnam. Vassal and tributary states, which further extended the reach of the imperial court, included Korea, Tibet, Nepal, Burma, Thailand, and parts of Indochina.

Imperial China behaved as a suzerain toward these subordinate states, exacting tribute, imposing unequal conditions, and demanding fealty from their rulers. Those who refused to kowtow to Beijing were regarded as hostile and dealt with accordingly. The Celestial Empire had neighbors only in a geographic sense. Even today, as Ross Munro has observed, China still seems to classify her "neighbors" into one of two categories: tributary states that acknowledge her hegemony, or potential enemies.[12] Present-day Beijing does not desire equality in external affairs, but deference, for it governs not a nation-state—although that is its modern-day pose—but an all-encompassing civilization. It is, as Lucian Pye has remarked, "a civilization pretending to be a nation."[13]

That is not the only pretense that the Chinese have engaged in during their long history. While insisting on the theoretical superiority of their empire over the surrounding "barbarian" kingdoms, various emperors were more than willing to compromise when hostile armies appeared on their borders. Over the centuries, major concessions were made to settle disputes with Tibet and the Turkic Khanate in the west and to placate the restless Khitan and Jurchen states in the north. Most of these concessions go unnoted in the official histories, however, since they contradict the myth of Chinese superiority.[14]

Deluded by their own myths, the Chinese on several occasions severely underestimated the strength of an enemy or provoked one into attacking. This happened, for example, with the Koreans in the seventh century, and again at the turn of the fifteenth century with the Muslim conqueror Tamerlane. According to the official records of the Ming dynasty, Tamerlane had sent a letter of submission, along with a tribute of two hundred horses, to the Chinese court. The Ming Emperor Hongwu evidently believed this fabricated account, for in 1395 he dispatched a "return embassy" to thank Tamerlane for his submission.[15] But it turned out that Tamerlane, one of history's most brutal butchers, had done no such thing. On the contrary, he was furious to find out that Emperor Hongwu considered him a vassal. He locked up the Chinese ambassador and vowed to avenge the insult with a military attack. He did not get around to making good on his vow until 1405, when he set out from Samarkand for Beijing at the head of a two-hundred-thousand-strong army. Fortunately for the Ming dynasty, he died en route.

An even more striking case of self-delusion had occurred a century earlier. Following the Mongol conquest of China, the Chinese historians responsible for compiling the official history of the preceding dynasty took seventy years, or most of the Yuan dynasty (A.D. 1271–1368), to complete their work. It was as if these Confucian scholars could not bring themselves to record how mighty China, with its superior civilization and people, could possibly have been conquered by a roving band of horse lords.[16] When the Chinese reclaimed their empire and established the Ming dynasty, court historians engaged in a conspiracy of silence about the dynasty that had preceded it. The whole Mongol conquest and century of rule went down the memory hole, since there was no way to reconcile that shameful history with their glorious self-image. As Christopher Ford notes, "What could not be explained within the conceptual framework of Sinic supremacy had to be simply ignored or denied."[17]

The Chinese mandarinate, selected on the basis of competitive examinations which tested their knowledge of the Confucian classics, embodied this sense of cultural superiority. If its members condescended to their own people, they regarded foreigners—those outside the magic circle of Chinese civilization—as scarcely human. There was no more polarizing distinction in the Chinese worldview than that between the Sinified (Chinese or *hua*) and the un-Sinified (Barbarians or *yi*). As we have seen, the un-Sinified—those barbarians who had not (yet) adopted Chinese habits of speech, dress, custom, and thought—were often likened to animals.

The *Shanhai Jing* ("Classic of Mountains and Seas"), written at the time of Christ but still quoted as late as the Qing dynasty, describes a western people with human faces but the bodies of snakes, and a southern people as having human bodies and faces, but birdlike wings and beaks.[18] The Ming Emperor Jiaqing was equally unflattering of non-Chinese peoples on the southern border: "The *yi* and *di*, like birds and beasts, are without human morality."[19] The barbarians to the north fared no better in the view of Emperor Taizhong's seventh century advisors: "The Hsiung-nu [Xiongnu or Huns] with their human faces and animal hearts are not of our kind.... [T]heir nature is such that they have no sense of gratitude or righteousness."[20] The Japanese, only partly Sinified, were called "dwarf barbarians" (*woren*). Westerners, when they came, were portrayed in similarly demeaning terms. At first, like most other "barbarians," they were compared to animals. Later, as their military and technological prowess became evident, they were promoted to the status of demons.

When I was first in China, in 1979, villagers would sometimes utter the malediction *gwailo* (Cantonese for "devil man") as I approached. When this was reported to the local Communist Party Secretary, he excused their utterances, ironically enough, on the grounds that "their cultural level is quite low." But such views had actually originated among Chinese whose "cultural level" was quite high—the mandarinate and even the emperors themselves—who of course set the tone for the entire civilization.

Unstated racism remains pervasive among the Chinese elite today. Its members are generally "cultured" enough to avoid comparing people from other races or cultures to animals or beasts in mixed company— that is to say, when foreigners are present—but their true attitude comes through clearly in private conversations and some literary works. During the Tibetan unrest of 2008 the head of the Chinese Communist Party in Tibet called the Dalai Lama a "wolf with a human face and the heart of a beast." Another example comes from the popular 1997 *The Spirit of the Fourth Generation*, whose authors refer to the Japanese as "economic animals", the "eastern heroes" of the "Western materialism" that is inferior to "Eastern harmony."[21]

"Racism is particularly difficult to reform," explains Chinese historian Yang Lien-sheng in reference to his own culture, "if the habit was formed in...the early historical period of a society."[22]

RELATIONS WITH THE BARBARIANS

The first Westerners to reach China by sea were the Portuguese, who by 1557 had established a permanent settlement at Macao. The Spaniards, the Dutch, and the British followed, drawn by the prospect of trade with this huge and prosperous empire. But the Imperial Chinese government, first under the Ming dynasty (1368–1644), then under the Qing, permitted only limited commercial relations with these seafaring traders. Canton, the capital of Guangdong province, was designated as China's sole entrepôt for the western trade, and even there trading was limited to a clearly defined season.

These inconvenient, even degrading arrangements were repeatedly protested by the Western nations, whose emissaries vainly called for free trade and diplomatic representation in Beijing. But they received short shrift. The volume of Chinese trade with the West was insignificant to the vast Chinese empire, while direct government-to-government relations were simply out of the question. The early Qing emperors and their courts were affronted by the notion that they should deal with the "barbarians from the Western Oceans" on a basis of equality. Instead, as an emblem of their disdain, they gave a mere provincial official, the viceroy of Guangdong and Guangxi, responsibility for political and commercial relations with these pushy Westerners. The first emissary of Great Britain to China, Lord MaCartney, arrived in that country in 1792 with no illusions. A Russian friend familiar with Chinese ways had informed him that, for the Chinese, Chinese superiority in all things was axiomatic. The Chinese were civilized and everyone else was a barbarian.[23]

As long as the Qing Empire stayed strong, there matters remained. But by the end of the eighteenth century, the dynasty was clearly in decline, and over the succeeding decades the government became increasingly inefficient, weak, and corrupt. The power of the Western world, on the other hand, was on the rise, fueled by industrialization and scientific advances. The one-time reality of Chinese superiority had become a myth, a self-deluding fiction that led the Qing court to critically under-estimate growing British, and Western, strength.

That fiction was perpetuated by sycophantic officials and court "histories" that included fanciful tales of imaginary tribute. One such tale—similar to the one that had enraged Tamerlane centuries before—asserted that King George III had presented tribute to the Jiaqing emperor in 1804, thus making Great Britain a tributary state of the Qing Empire. The event was pure invention, made plausible in the eyes of the emperor and his officials only by their unshakeable conviction of Chinese supe-riority...and barbarian inferiority.[24]

It was not until thirty-five years later, when the "humble tributaries" from Great Britain astonished the Qing court by sending most of the imperial Chinese fleet to the bottom of the ocean, that Confucian offi-cialdom began to realize the magnitude of its error. The First Opium War (1839–1842), as it is generally known, was humiliating enough, but it was soon followed by a Second Opium War (1856–1860), which shook the empire to its core. The so-called "unequal treaties" that followed reduced China to a semi-colony of the Western powers. Western troops garrisoned China's "treaty ports"—essentially, European colonies—and Western gunboats roamed its rivers. Only the Open Door Policy of the United States, which opposed the creation of exclusive economic zones by the other great powers, saved China from total dismemberment—another historical fact that has been written out of contemporary Chinese history textbooks.

Other humiliations followed. In 1895 Japan defeated China, wresting away control of Korea and gaining control of the Liaoning Peninsula. Meiji-era Japan, busily borrowing from the West, was on the ascent. China, resisting Western ideas and innovations, was failing. Li Hongzhang, a major figure at the Qing court and the leader of the "self-strengthening" movement, was sent to the Japanese seaport of Shimonoseki to negotiate a peace treaty. Count Ito, representing the victorious Japanese government, criticized China as arrogant, deceitful, and uncooperative towards the "family of nations." "Why does not China observe the rules of all other nations?" Ito pressed Li. The question is as timely today as it was in the late nineteenth century.

———

Li Hongzhang could well have replied that it would cost him his position—if not his head—to propose that the Kingdom at the Center of the Earth be downgraded to a mere "nation" and his Radiant Holiness, the Emperor, be reduced to a mere king. Instead he simply observed that it was "a very difficult matter in our country for the Servant [that is, Li] to propose a change to the Sovereign [that is, the Emperor]."

"The Imperial Wisdom," Ito said in response, must surely "recognize the necessity for such a reform."

"Every change will certainly take time," riposted Li.

Li Hongzhang, for his part, attempted to play the race card: "It is quite time the Yellow race should prepare against the White."

But Ito deflected the suggestion of race-based anti-Western alliance. "I think it would be wise," he responded, "to make your young men well acquainted with things European."

China proved unwilling to take advice from a people they had long regarded as inferiors and privately still called "dwarf barbarians." "Japanese success at a time of mounting internal difficulties in China," wrote S. C. M. Paine, "instead of being seen as a way out of China's turmoil, became another 'loss of face' for the Chinese."[25]

Non-Chinese have difficulty appreciating the depth of China's grievances against the West and Japan resulting from these experiences. It was not merely that Western gunboats had twice defeated China in the Opium Wars; China had been defeated before, although never perhaps by organized drug runners. Nor was the bitterness caused simply by the dethronement of Confucian high culture by the West—not only in neighboring states like Japan, Korea, and Vietnam but within China itself—although this comes closer to the heart of the matter.

The underlying problem was this: China had dominated (in every sense—culturally, economically, militarily) its known world almost since the beginning of its recorded history. More than what is today called a superpower, it had been *the* hegemon for century after century, dynasty after dynasty, for over two thousand years. Then, within the span of a few decades, it was cast down from this pinnacle of greatness by the Western powers and Japan and brought low, divided into spheres of influence, and partially carved up into colonies.[26]

The greatest defeat suffered by China was not the loss of sovereignty in treaty ports like Shanghai, however, or even the loss of huge swaths of territory to Russia and Japan. China's borders had expanded and contracted before. But the ideological underpinnings of the country—the deeply inbred notion that the Middle Kingdom was inherently superior to its conquerors—had always held. Now that certainty was shattered by the arrival of the West in force. Now, though, the Western countries were not only technologically more advanced and thus in possession of superior arms, they were clearly ahead of China in terms of their economic development, their institutions of governance, and even their very ethics. For the first time in their long history the Chinese had encountered a civilization which was arguably superior to their own on multiple levels.

To that crushing blow was added another: the stunning revelation that the world was a far larger place, and China a far smaller one, than the Chinese mandarinate had long believed. The maps brought by the Western traders literally turned the cloistered world of the Chinese elite upside down. They made clear at a glance that not only did China and its vassals not comprise *Tianxia*, or "All under Heaven," they did not even comprise the tenth of it. The Western maps revealed the existence of oceans, island chains, and even a new world that had been previously unknown to Chinese mapmakers. Most disorienting of all, these new maps revealed that the empire which styled itself "the Center of the Earth" was not centrally located at all. Instead, it was offset far to the east, relegated to the same peripheral status to which it had itself always consigned barbarians and tributary states. It was a Galileo-like moment for the Chinese, as they realized that their empire was not the fixed and immovable center of human affairs after all, but only a mere satellite of an even more powerful constellation of powers.

All of this cut the very heart out of the Chinese national dreamscape. The Confucian moral order was based on a deeply held belief that the Chinese polity was universal. The god-like Chinese emperor was a father to all men, Chinese and barbarian alike. The Chinese empire he ruled was "the head of a family of nations, presiding with patriarchal wisdom over the junior members around her."[27] Even if all lands and all peoples did not yet acknowledge Chinese hegemony, the mandarinate confidently believed that someday they would. Indeed, they must. This was, after all, the Middle Kingdom's manifest destiny.

As the world expanded, China shrank, and it became ever more difficult to maintain a Sinocentric worldview. Confucian civilization all too obviously failed to encompass the new, larger world that China now found itself at the mercy of. And the prospect of one day Sinifying such powerful peoples or absorbing such large swaths of territory seemed remote indeed. Mighty China had been demoted to a relatively minor player in the global scheme of things, and the emperor reduced to a mere regional satrap. Even the very name of their once-great empire, the Kingdom at the Center of the Earth, seemed now to be an ethnocentric affectation, if not a kind of self-mockery.

Still, the imperial court went to great lengths to maintain the pretense of Chinese superiority, even as the evidence mounted that, in reality, China was markedly inferior in key respects. The constant diplomatic wrangling between the European powers and the Qing court was a kind of Kabuki theater masking the underlying ideological contest between

Sinic universalism and Western-style national sovereignty. The Europeans, aggressively led by Britain, demanded that they be accepted as equals. But this was something that the Qing dynasty could not concede without betraying the Confucian moral order that had for so long informed and animated it.

It was only in 1860, after the Qing forces had suffered another disastrous defeat in the Second Opium War, and with the entire lower Yangtze region in the hands of the Taiping rebels, that the imperial court bowed to European demands. The British, the French, and the Russians were all granted permission to establish permanent embassies in the capital of Beijing. The emperor could no longer hold himself aloof from the rest of the world, but had to grant audiences to the foreign ambassadors, in effect admitting that they represented empires equal to his own. Now even the pretense—never mind the reality—of Chinese suzerainty over "all under heaven" had been torn away.

And so it went for the next ninety years, as the empire gave way to warlordism, and entire provinces fell under foreign control. Tibet and Western Turkestan went their own way, while Korea and Manchuria were colonized by Japan, which later invaded and occupied China's eastern provinces. Never before in Chinese history had that country's claimed preeminence—central to the self-image of the Chinese—been so at variance with the reality on the ground. Never before had so many Chinese been so humiliated at the hands of so many foreign powers. Even minor European powers such as Portugal and Holland—a fraction of the size and population of even a single one of China's many provinces—were able to wrest concessions from the helpless giant.

When Mao Zedong announced the establishment of the People's Republic of China, it was with the words "China has stood up." No longer would a prostrate China be bullied by the West. So strong was Mao's sense of grievance that, despite his desperate need for Soviet economic assistance, he rejected Khrushchev's bid for Soviet naval bases in China. When the Soviet leader petulantly objected that America's allies allowed the U.S. Navy basing privileges, Mao still refused to budge. Foreign naval vessels would never be stationed in Chinese waters again, he declared. That degrading experience belonged to China's treaty port past.

Both the history of China's imperial—and revolutionary—glory and the painful details of her long night of national humiliation are taught in China's public schools and, more important, in her military academies. The result is an excruciating sensitivity to slights, real and imagined. When Secretary of State Warren Christopher visited China in 1994, Chinese officials were personally offended that he had brought his dog. Why? Because it brought back memories of a sign that had purportedly hung at the entrance to a park in Shanghai's foreign concession a *century* ago which read, "No dogs or Chinese allowed."

China's fall from greatness is still a subliminal matter of shame for all living Chinese. This "loss of face" cannot be assuaged merely by allowing China to take its place among "the family of nations." The rectification of China's historical grievances requires not merely diplomatic equality—Beijing enjoys this already—but de facto geostrategic dominance. The lowering of the Union Jack in Hong Kong in 1997 was a start, redeeming China's painful humiliation at the hands of the British in the Opium Wars. But only one thing will completely lift the burden of shame: for the Celestial Empire to resume its rightful place as the natural center of the world.

USING AMERICAN POWER
TO DEFEAT AMERICAN HEGEMONY

It was not only on the issue of naval bases that the Chinese Communist Party elites resisted their overbearing Soviet "older brothers." Despite their ideological kinship with the Soviet Union, they feared that they would be permanently dominated within this sibling relationship. The alliance was to all outward appearances as close as "elder brother–younger brother," in the Chinese phrase, but China was increasingly resentful of Russian claims of superiority for the Soviet model. With the Sino-Soviet split, the old images of Russia as "the Hungry Land"—*Eguo* in Chinese—were revived, and the traditional contempt of the Chinese for the barbarians of the north was once again openly expressed.

China's challenge to Soviet hegemony led it to seek an alliance of convenience with the United States, an ideological foe that it viewed—and continues to view—as a power in decline. This pseudo-alliance, never formalized, lasted from the early seventies to the late eighties, when it suddenly received three deadly blows. The first and most serious was the sudden implosion of the Soviet Union, which robbed the pseudo-allies of a common foe and knocked the principal strategic prop out from under the U.S.-China relationship. The second was the Tiananmen Square demonstrations for democracy, which highlighted for China's leaders the dangers of exposing Chinese youth to the appeal of American democratic ideals and ended in a deadly debacle. The third was America's virtually bloodless victory in the 1991 Gulf War, which underlined the unmatched global reach of the U.S. military, as well as its technological superiority over other countries.

Just as China would not accept—indeed, was moved by its own sense of greatness to challenge—Soviet hegemony, so it has refused to accept the United States as the world's leading power. Since the early nineties, China has become ever less coy about its intentions. The state-controlled press has grown increasingly strident in denouncing the United States, calling America everything from a "dangerous enemy" and a "superpower bully," to a "hegemon on par with Nazi Germany."[28] More to the point, America is now the enemy of choice in war games conducted by the People's Liberation Army (PLA). In the spring of 2000, after threatening to use force against Taiwan to "unify" it with the mainland, the official newspaper of the PLA also warned that it was ready to use its long-range missiles against the United States if the United States came to the island's aid.

The one thing for which China continued to value America's role in Asia until the early nineties was as a regional stabilizer. America's postwar military presence in Japan was not unwelcome, for in the Chinese view it served to keep Japan militarily weak. For decades Beijing feared that a U.S. withdrawal would precipitate Japan's rearmament and eventual re-emergence as a major military power. Since the mid-nineties, however, with the Japanese economy in a deep recession and its own power on the mainland of Asia growing rapidly, China has become increasingly confident of its ability to dominate the region and has ratcheted up its criticism of the U.S. presence accordingly.

The Chinese so relentlessly accuse the United States of "seeking hegemony," and phrase their accusations in such condemnatory terms, that many analysts have concluded that the word "hegemony" is strictly pejorative in Chinese usage. Nothing could be further from the truth. In the view of Chinese strategists, the existence of a hegemon is in fact a natural, even a desirable state of affairs. Following the Spring and Autumn period (772–481 B.C.), when the institution of hegemon first developed, it gradually produced stability, order, and equilibrium in the Middle Kingdom, as neighboring states were gradually absorbed into a single entity. It is the division of the strategic landscape into states large and small that is undesirable, for it leads to instability and chaos. The lesson China draws from its long history is that periods of division are times of disorder and chaos, whereas periods of unity are times of stability and order. In other words, the world needs a hegemon.

That China has an extraordinary fear of chaos and penchant for unity is widely understood. What is less well appreciated is that China projects its own five-thousand-year history onto the wider contemporary world. To put it another way, for Chinese strategists, balance-of-power politics is inherently unbalanced. And racial pride, an overweening conviction of cultural superiority, and a long history of regional dominance all tell the Chinese that the role of hegemon properly belongs to China and its rulers.

Thus the current debate on American China policy—over whether we should "engage" China or attempt, in conjunction with our allies in the region, to "contain" it—misses the essential point. From the Chinese perspective, the United States is already "containing" China by its very presence in Asia, by maintaining a hundred thousand troops in the region, by our network of bases, by our alliances with Japan and the Republic of Korea, by our commitments to the Philippines and Taiwan, by our growing closeness to Vietnam and Malaysia. The much vaunted U.S. "pivot to Asia"—which to date has been more rhetoric than reality—only confirms to the Chinese their fear of envelopment.

That the United States did not seek its preeminent position, but in many respects had its international role thrust upon it following World War II and reinforced by its sudden victory in the Cold War, makes the situation that much more intolerable for the senior leadership of the Chinese Communist Party, which is so anxious to restore China's lost glory. That Providence smiles upon America may be an old story for Americans, but it is one that is difficult for Chinese to appreciate. So is the American ideal of leadership. For example, the resistance of General Washington to those who would make him king renders his character opaque to most Chinese. Surely, they conclude, he must have been plotting for the office all along. After all, for thousands of years those eager to ascend to the Dragon Throne have followed the wisdom of the ancient strategist Sunzi: "When seeking power, make it appear that you are not doing so."

Read between the lines of Chinese criticism of America's leading role in the world, and you find the envy and enmity that come from balked ambition. The *People's Daily*, the official organ of the Chinese Communist Party, says that "The U.S. strategic aim is to seek hegemony in the whole world and it cannot tolerate the appearance of any big power on the European and Asian continents that will constitute a threat to its leading position."[29] Can anyone doubt that the "big power" that has "appeared" on the "Asian continent" referred to here is China itself, moving to overtake America's "leading position"?

The belief in the inevitability of Chinese hegemony, held at a deeper level than mere strategy, motivates China to oppose and undermine the current *Pax Americana*. Zbigniew Brzezinski, who as national security advisor to President Carter played a key role in the 1979 establishment of U.S.-PRC diplomatic relations, believes that "The task of Chinese policy—in keeping with Sunzi's ancient strategic wisdom—is to use American power to peacefully defeat American hegemony."[30]

Sunzi also said that all strategy is based on deception, and the Chinese are customarily oblique in defining their ultimate aims. One exception is the series of white papers entitled *China's National Defense* that the Chinese government produced in response to American urgings toward greater strategic "transparency." Those who expressed pleasure over the promulgation of these documents, happy that the Chinese government was finally complying with our request to be more candid about its ambitions, should read them carefully. Both China's opposition to U.S. dominance and the global scope of its own ambitions come through loud and clear.

In the opening paragraph of the 1998 white paper, China stakes its claim to the next millennium: "Mankind is about to enter the 21st century of its history. It is the aspiration of the Chinese government and people to lead a peaceful, stable and prosperous world into the new century."[31]

In a subsequent section of the white paper entitled "The International Security Situation," the Chinese government goes on to list "factors of instability both globally and regionally" that it regards as threats to its future:

1. "Hegemonism and power politics remain the main source of threats to world peace and stability;

2. "Cold War mentality and its influence still have a certain currency, and the enlargement of military blocs and the strengthening of military alliances have added factors of instability to international security;
3. "some countries, relying on their military advantages, pose military threat to other countries, even resorting to armed intervention;
4. "the old, unfair, and irrational international economic order still damages the interests of developing countries;
5. "local conflicts caused by ethnic, religious, territorial, natural resources and other factors arise now and then, and questions left over by history among countries remain unsolved;
6. "terrorism, arms proliferation, smuggling and trafficking in narcotics, environmental pollution, waves of refugees, and other transnational issues also pose new threats to international security."[32]

Though couched cryptically, the first "factor of instability" is a stinging criticism of the *Pax Americana*. Translated into plain English, it means that the present U.S. political, economic, and military preeminence ("hegemony"), combined with Washington's willingness to exercise it ("power politics"), is a threat to China's national security ("world peace and stability").[33]

The second factor is a veiled reference to the enlargement of NATO and the strengthening of U.S.-Japan defense ties, both of which have alarmed China. In April 1997, China joined Russia in denouncing as (what else?) "hegemonism" the expansion of NATO to include Poland, Hungary, and the Czech Republic, which it called "impermissible." NATO has continued to expand in the years since, with Bulgaria, Estonia, Latvia, Lithuania, Romania, Slovakia, and Slovenia joining in 2004 and Albania and Croatia in 2009.[34] China has not been pleased with this development, which it claims has "worsened the division in Europe" and caused "the current Ukraine crisis." China's real concern, however, is that "some people want to replay this strategy in Asia," that is, by creating an Asian-Pacific counterpart to NATO.

China objected even more vociferously to the redefinition, in early 1996, of the scope of U.S.-Japanese military cooperation from the narrower "Far East" to a wider "Asia-Pacific." The juxtaposition of these two concerns suggests that China sees the strengthened U.S.-Japan Security Treaty not only as an immediate threat but also, as Brzezinski has suggested, as "a point of departure for an American-dominated Asian system of security aimed at containing China (in which Japan would be a vital linchpin much as Germany was in NATO during the Cold War)."[35] The agreement was widely perceived in Beijing as implicitly bringing Taiwan under the protective umbrella of the U.S.-Japan Security Treaty, so the white paper goes on to assail the incorporation, "directly or indirectly," of "the Taiwan Straits into the security and cooperation sphere of any country or any military alliance as an infringement upon and interference in China's sovereignty."[36]

The "military threats" and "armed intervention" referred to in the third factor mean the 1996 missile crisis in the Taiwan Strait, when Washington warned Beijing of "grave consequences" if it continued to bracket the island with missiles and dispatched two carrier groups to guard Taiwan.

The fourth factor reflects continued Chinese unhappiness with the U.S.-dominated economic order and its institutions, such as the International Monetary Fund (IMF), the World Bank, and the World Trade Organization, the last of which China was long unable to join because of its restrictive trading practices. Stigmatizing the existing economic order as "old, unfair, and irrational" at a time when many Asian economies were in free fall, resentful of the tight-money policies of the IMF, and fearful of defaulting on World Bank loans helped to raise China's stature in the region. Such criticisms may be part of an on-again, off-again effort to position China as the advocate of the Third World, and the beginning of an effort to establish a *renminbi* bloc.

The bottom line of this white paper is quite clear. From China's point of view, *all* of its major security concerns arise from the present American dominance on the world stage. Believing that a continuation of the U.S.-dominated international order is not in its national interest, Beijing makes clear that its concerns are not just regional but global, and implies that its goal, in the words of Deng Xiaoping, "is to build up a new international political and economic order."

Skipping ahead fifteen years, we see that the 2013 defense white paper continues to paint the United States as an adversary, complaining that "some country has strengthened its Asia-Pacific military alliances...and frequently makes the situation there tenser."[37] At the same time, Beijing recognizes, in a backhanded sort of way, that America's allies are increasingly ready to defend their own interests, with or without U.S. assistance. Japan is attacked for "making trouble over the issue of the Diaoyu Islands [the Senkakus]," which of course was not an "issue" at all until China made it one by inventing a territorial claim. In the same vein, the paper describes "'Taiwan independence' separatist forces" as the biggest threat to "cross-Straits relations," a phrase that China apparently uses as a synonym for "reunification."[38]

In addition to its complaints about the behavior of the United States, which have become a staple of such white papers, there is a new and disturbing tone of belligerence. Reflecting China's growing confidence in its expanding military capabilities, the 2013 white paper emphasizes that the country will protect its "core interests" of "sovereignty" and "security" at all costs. The white paper quotes Mao's defensive doctrine—"We will not attack unless we are attacked; but we will surely counter-attack if attacked"—but reinterprets it to justify taking the offensive. The new generation of China's leaders apparently wants the world to understand not only that the PRC will defend itself if attacked, but that it also reserves the right to unilaterally incorporate new territories and seas into its sovereign territory and then "defend" these as well. How else is the world to understand China's current combativeness? Even as Beijing is making new territorial claims in the East and South China Seas, it is warning those impacted by such claims that China will "resolutely take all measures necessary to safeguard its national sovereignty and territorial integrity."[39]

It is important to understand that *this is not a defensive doctrine at all but an offensive one.* China is asserting its right not only to make new territorial claims but to defend them with military force on the grounds that it is defending its territorial integrity. It is an approach that seems calculated to cow its neighbors into acquiescence by ruling out negotiated settlements—and implicitly threatening military action—at the outset. As Timothy Heath notes, "This approach shrewdly allows China to quietly consolidate its claims in a manner that minimizes alarm, while throwing the onus on its neighboring powers to risk dramatic action to halt Chinese encroachments, knowing full well that China will exploit any misstep to consolidate its gains even further."[40] China is, in effect, reserving the right to react to any action with military force on the grounds that it is merely "defending its sovereign territory," even as it makes new territorial claims.

Some of the early architects of our China policy, such as Zbigniew Brzezinski, continued to cherish the hope that China was merely seeking an equal partnership with the United States long after its increasingly bellicose rhetoric and actions made that view untenable. Brzezinski maintained until his death in 2017 that China's "central objective" is "to dilute American regional power to the point that a diminished America will come to need a regionally dominant China as its ally and eventually even a globally powerful China as its partner,"[41] a position that seems hopelessly naïve. While he was absolutely correct in asserting that China's near-term geostrategic goal was to "to dilute American regional power," his suggestion that China's ultimate geostrategic end is a global U.S.-China condominium underestimated China's historic mission. China's ultimate ambition is not to ally itself with the reigning hegemon, but to succeed it. It is certainly true, as Brzezinski often noted, that America "Simply by being what it is and where it is...becomes China's unintentional adversary."[42] But whether America wishes it or no, China's drive for hegemony leaves it determined to dethrone its principal adversary in the world.

Our growing difficulties with China are not merely a matter of the U.S. Seventh Fleet being in the wrong place at the wrong time. Many in the Chinese elite believe that the U.S. is deliberately frustrating their country's rise to greatness. From their perspective, America is consciously attempting to force the "peaceful evolution" of China into a democratic state. We challenge China's human rights record at every turn, continually threaten economic sanctions, and have set up a surrogate radio broadcasting service, Radio Free Asia, to encourage insurrection. We passed the Taiwan Relations Act and sell arms to that "renegade province." We followed with the Hong Kong Relations Act, and our congressmen fete Martin Lee and other leaders of the democratic forces in Hong Kong when they visit our shores. Such moves inflame China's already deep sense of grievance against the West, and especially against the one country it sees as the cultural heir and imperial successor to the early great powers.

As every Chinese schoolchild knows, only a century ago the imperial capital of the Great Qing dynasty was sacked by "Western barbarians." No wonder that for some Chinese, the verb "to Westernize" carries the same implications that "to vandalize" does in the West—justifying revenge against these past incursions. Lieutenant General Mi Zhenyu, formerly vice-commandant of the Chinese Academy of Military Sciences, was speaking for the leadership of his country when he remarked, "[As for the United States,] for a relatively long time it will be absolutely necessary that we quietly nurse our sense of vengeance.... We must conceal our abilities and bide our time."[43] Of course, these admonitions are not original with General Mi. They come from the original architect of China's military modernization, Deng Xiaoping himself.

From Beijing's perspective, the continued U.S. military presence in Asia is an unhappy accident and anachronism, the tail end of a century and a half of Western domination over a region that properly belongs within its own sphere of influence. If most PRC insiders want to re-establish the hegemony that China enjoyed over vast parts of Asia for nearly two thousand years, some, inspired by Xi Jinping's "China Dream," want to go even further. They are resentful that China has lost its traditional place as the "Kingdom at the Center of the Earth," and are determined to recover it.

Previously muted, China's impatience to rid Asia of Americans increasingly comes through loud and clear. One telling incident occurred in February 1995, when a U.S. carrier task force was ordered to steam up the coast of North Korea into the northern reaches of the Yellow Sea as a warning to Pyongyang to abandon its nuclear weapons program. This show of American naval might so close to its own shores greatly angered Beijing, which ordered a submarine to sortie from the Qingdao naval base and attempt to close on the task force. Detected as soon as it entered the ocean, the sub was first shadowed and then harassed until it retreated to its homeport. Furious Chinese officials issued a threat: if the U.S. Navy sailed north of the Shandong Peninsula again, the PLA Navy would be given orders to open fire. The Yellow Sea is, it should be noted, like the South China Sea, international waters.

Over time, China has become increasingly likely to challenge U.S. planes and ships in international airspace and waters. The PLA's down-ing of the U.S. electronic surveillance aircraft off Hainan Island is well known. But less serious incidents continue to occur, although they often go unreported. In September 2002, for example, the U.S. Navy oceano-graphic ship USS *Bowditch* was harassed in the Yellow Sea by PLA Navy vessels, another illustration of how Beijing's increasingly expansive claims to territory and belligerent action can lead to conflict.

China's resentment is fueled by wild fantasies about American omnipotence and malice, which are not only given credence by, but actually emanate from, the PRC military and political elite. General Li Jijun, one of China's most distinguished military authors, claims that the United States engineered both the collapse of the Soviet Union and the Iraqi invasion of Kuwait by "strategic deceptions." Most of the Chinese leadership apparently believes that the United States deliberately bombed the PRC embassy in Belgrade to humiliate China, and that the United States is working covertly to "dismember" China, beginning with Tibet and Xinjiang.[44]

All this suggests a PRC that has, in combination, the historical grievances of the Weimar Republic, the paranoid nationalism of a revolutionary Islamic state, and the expansionist ambitions of the Soviet Union at the height of its power. As China grows more powerful and attempts to rectify those grievances and act out those ambitions, it will cast an ever-lengthening shadow over Asia and the world.

It is often said that America is too democratic at home to be autocratic abroad. Not so China, whose autocratic rulers face few domestic limits on the use of their power abroad. As the general secretary of the Chinese Communist Party, the head of state, and the chairman of the powerful Central Military Commission, President Xi Jinping can order his troops into action without a declaration of war by the National People's Congress. He can mobilize the economy to produce weapons of war without the need to convince a skeptical legislature that the expenditures are necessary. And he can command popular passions by orchestrating domestic propaganda campaigns through the Party and the state-owned media.

Few Americans have yet grasped either the depth of China's historic grievances against the West or its vengeful envy of the United States in particular, or the breadth of its resurgent imperial ambitions. China is not just an emerging superpower with a grudge, though that would be worrisome enough. It is the hegemon, waiting to reclaim its rightful position as the center of the world.

2

HEGEMON: THE INVENTION OF THE TOTALITARIAN STATE

*"Just as there are not two suns in the sky,
so there cannot be two emperors on earth."*
—CONFUCIUS[1]

*"After these campaigns, the state of Chu was no longer a
threat to the state of Qin; it was only a matter of time before
Qin made the Grand Unification of All Under Heaven."*
—SIMA GUANG, *The Zizhi Tongjian*
(Comprehensive Mirror in Aid of Governance)[2]

A Chinese emperor—the Oriental despot *par excellence*—wielded far more power than any Western monarch, however absolute. There is nothing resembling a Magna Carta to be found anywhere in the long stretch of Chinese history, much less the equivalent of an Athenian Assembly or a Roman Forum. Neither was there a religious authority comparable to the Roman Catholic pontiff who could impose moral sanctions on wayward emperors. In China, political authority moved unchecked in the opposite direction, as the early despotism of the Shang and Zhou kings was perfected into the totalitarianism of the Qin, Han, and later dynasties.

Concentrating power in the hands of the sovereign was not undertaken as an end in itself. Rather, it, like the totalitarianism of our own day, was designed to accomplish a larger purpose. Communist parties wield power in order to crush class opposition, wage internal and external warfare, and lead the proletariat to communism; Chinese emperors wielded power to quell chaos and disorder on earth by establishing hegemony. Only in this way could what was euphemistically called the Great Unity—*the leveling of all resistance to the rule of the hegemon*—be achieved.

China's early innovations in statecraft—totalitarianism and hegemony—are less well known than its discovery of gunpowder or its cultivation of silkworms, but they may ultimately prove to have the greater impact on the world.

China's absolutist traditions go back to the very founding of the Chinese state.[3] The Shang dynasty (c. 1766–1027 B.C.), the earliest for which we have both archaeological and documentary evidence, was a highly developed state with a tax collection system, a penal code noted for its severity, and—perhaps not unrelated—a standing army. Occupying part of present-day North China, it was ruled by an autocrat who, when addressing his subjects, pointedly styled himself as "I the single one man."[4] No one else mattered.

The Shang dynasty was succeeded by the Zhou dynasty (c. 1027–249 B.C.), which carried on its autocratic traditions. The authority of the King of Zhou over his land and people was absolute, as is suggested by a famous passage from the *Book of Odes*: "All land under heaven belongs to the King, and all people on the shores are subjects of the King"[5] The appellation "Son of Heaven," which has a faintly blasphemous ring to Western ears, was a Zhou invention, and amounted to a god-like claim of universal jurisdiction over all the earth.

The prerogatives of the Zhou kings, though vast, did not lead initially to the complete centralization of power, but rather its dispersal to Chinese feudal lords. To govern the vast expanse of territory under their control, which comprised most of North China, the early Zhou kings enfeoffed kinsmen, bestowing on them limited sovereignty over portions of their domain, along with hereditary titles such as *gong* (duke), *hou* (marquis), *bo* (earl), *zi* (viscount), and *nan* (baron). The aristocracy thus created was initially an extended family, with the king heading the main branch of the family tree, while his uncles, brothers, and cousins headed secondary branches. With its decentralized administration—there were 172 feudal domains at the beginning of the Zhou—this Chinese feudalism bore more than a passing resemblance to that found centuries later in Western Europe. The loyalty of Chinese vassals to their king was guaranteed by kinship rather than sacred oath, however, and regulated by the patriarchal kinship law (*zong fa*) which reserved certain powers to the clan patriarch, who was of course also the king.

With the passage of time and generations, the ties that bound the vassals to their king began to fray. Fifth cousins were obviously less loyal to their sovereign than his immediate brothers or even first cousins would have been. Local lords began to regard their fiefs as independent kingdoms. By the end of the eighth century B.C. the Zhou king was no longer able to command the allegiance of the majority of his vassals, nor to maintain order within what had been his domain. From being *primus sine paribus* he had become merely *primus inter pares*. The King of Zhou's defeat at the hands of the Duke of Zheng in 707 B.C. further reduced him, this time to mere equality with his former vassals.

This removal of central authority at the outset of the Spring and Autumn period (772–481 B.C.) led to a chaotic war of all against all. According to the *Spring and Autumn Annals* (*Chunqiu Zuozhuan*), within a span of two and a half centuries some 483 wars were fought among the scores of feudal states then in existence.

Early in this period it appeared that the large and populous state of Chu, which occupied the middle reaches of the Yangtze River, would quickly emerge victorious. Fear of Chu aggressiveness led the smaller states on the North China plain to turn to the state of Qi, located in modern-day Shandong province, for protection. With a sound economy, a strong military, and an able ruler, Qi was the most respected power in the north. The ruler of Qi, Duke Huan (r. 685–643 B.C), responded to the appeals of his neighbors by convening a series of conferences beginning in 681 to discuss a common defense against Chu. A mutual defense league was set up, and within three years it had grown to include all the central and eastern feudal states. In 678, Duke Huan was officially appointed "hegemon," or *ba,* of the league, charged with preserving the peace and defending the honor of the King of Zhou. He did so ably, protecting member states from raids by Rong and Yi tribesmen, and keeping Chu at bay throughout his rule. Thus was the hegemon born as the head of a kind of early League of Nations that member states could appeal to for help when threatened. But it soon failed.

Duke Huan's early success as hegemon had much to do with a series of political "reforms" initiated by his prime minister, Guan Zhong. With the support of the duke, Guan Zhong organized the population along military lines, imposed state regulation on the marketplace, established a state monopoly on coinage, and put the production of salt and iron under state control. Qi's increasingly strong and well-equipped army and its stable and flourishing economy were a direct result of Guan Zhong's reforms, all of which were designed to enhance the authority of the ruler, diminish the influence of clan leaders and the business class, and generally strengthen the power of the state over society.

Duke Huan was the first hegemon, and Guan Zhong was one of the first "Legalists," as the school of statecraft dedicated to exalting the ruler and maximizing his power came to be called.[6] According to Guan Zhong's precepts, as recorded in the *Guan Zi* ("The Book of Master Guan"), the ruler is to be a law unto himself: "The sovereign is the creator of law. The officials are the followers of the law, and the people are the subjects of the law." Master Guan also insisted that the ruler possessed absolute authority over his subjects, and that, to ensure the success of his rule, he must be willing to exercise that authority by promoting and enriching those who obeyed and physically eliminating those who strayed: "The wise sovereign holds six powers: to grant life and to kill; to enrich and to impoverish; to promote and to demote" (*Guan Zi*, ch. 45). One's very life depended upon the sufferance of the sovereign. There were no inalienable rights, and no space for individual liberty to flourish.

The institution of the hegemon languished after Duke Huan's death, but the revolution in government that he and Guan Zhong had launched continued to spread to other states. Larger and more powerful states, such as Qi, Jin, and Chu, became known as hegemonic powers (*baquan*) and, undertaking political "reforms" of their own, began to regulate their populations more closely and maintain standing armies. Smaller and weaker states were conquered and annexed. Only twenty-two states survived to the end of the Spring and Autumn period, the rest having been absorbed by more powerful neighbors.[7] Behind the treaties, alliances, and armistices of the time lurked a single, overarching goal: conquest.

This struggle for survival intensified during the aptly named Warring States period that followed. The key to survival lay in organization and aggressiveness, in building large standing armies, in mastering the thirty-six stratagems of deceit and deception, and in using these to conquer as much territory and as many subjects as possible. The strong states originally numbered twelve, but as one state after another fell victim to conquest, this number was reduced to seven. This process, as had long been obvious, could have only one end: the creation of a single state ruled by an omnipotent ruler holding all power under heaven. It was a zero-sum game that would be played with unremitting vengeance over the course of the next two and a half centuries.

The rulers of the Seven Powers, who now styled themselves "kings," deliberately set about to cynically and selfishly concentrate as much power in their hands as possible, putting their individual countries on a virtually full-time war footing. In this they were assisted by Legalist counselors, whose governing slogan—still in use today—was to "enrich the state and strengthen the military" (*fuguo qiangbing*). While the chief Legalists reflected deeply on the nature of power and its employment, as a class the Legalists more closely resembled the *consiglieri* of Mafia chieftains, each plotting and conniving to advance the power of his boss against the other bosses. The *Zeitgeist* of the late Zhou dynasty is best expressed by the greatest Legalist of all, a Chinese Machiavelli by the name of Han Fei. "Today the competition depends on having the greatest power," Han Fei reportedly said. "He who has great power will be paid tribute by others, he who has less power will pay tribute to others; therefore the wise ruler cultivates power."[8]

Han Fei and other Legalists were offensive realists on steroids, dedicated to the proposition that "he who has the most power wins." In pursuit of power, they helped to design and implement the series of political "reforms" that were enhancing the authority of the monarch, building and maintaining strong armies, increasing agricultural production, building up an appointed bureaucracy to replace an unreliable hereditary aristocracy, increasing state revenues, improving the state's ability to regulate commerce, intimidating the people into subjection, and crushing any and all dissent. The "totalitarian regulation of society in the service of the state" is how Sinologist Charles Hucker has described the Legalist program.[9]

The essence of Legalist doctrines was the supremacy of the ruler: "The ruler occupies the position of power; [he] dominates the people and commands the wealth of the state."[10] Power could only be concentrated in the hands of the ruler by weakening the nobility and further subjugating commoners, so this is what the Legalist program consciously and with great rigor set out to do.[11]

To strengthen the state at the expense of the nobility, the Legalists advised their sovereigns that they should no longer share power with a class of hereditary feudal lords. Within the court, aristocratic officials serving in inherited posts found themselves replaced by appointed bureaucrats, often ordinary gentry-scholars or non-natives, whom the ruler could discharge, or even execute, at will.[12] In the countryside, feudal lords were displaced by appointed magistrates who served at the pleasure of the ruler. The lords' inherited fiefs were redrawn into administrative units called counties (*xian*). By appointing officials who were mere extensions of themselves, Chinese rulers crushed the nobility and gathered yet more power into their hands.

To strengthen the ruler's hand over the people, the Legalists recommended such policies as:

- accumulation of people as an indispensable component of power: "Therefore the ruler of men desires to have more people for his own use.... The ruler loves the people because they are useful."[13]
- suppression of all voluntary associations: "The early kings always made certain that the interests of their subjects diverged. Thus under perfect governance, spouses and friends, however close to one another, can neither refuse to report another's crimes, nor cover up for them."[14]
- establishment of informer networks: "The wise ruler forces the whole world to hear and to watch for him.... No one in the world can hide from him or scheme against him."[15]
- use of punishment instead of reward: "A well-governed state...employs nine punishments to one reward; whereas a weak state employs nine rewards to one punishment."[16]
- harsh punishment for violations according to set laws: "If crimes are punished by execution, then the law wins over the people and the army is strong."[17]
- mutual surveillance and collective punishment: "The people were commanded to be organized into groups of fives and tens. They must be under mutual surveillance and punished for crimes committed by other members of their group. Those who failed to inform against a crime were to be cut in half at the waist."[18]

The cynical, even immoral, advice of these Chinese Machiavellis grates on Western ears, but it found ready listeners among the dwindling ranks of Chinese kings. By the closing century of the Warring States period, it was clear that all but one of them would be destroyed. Which of them could resist the additional power promised by the Legalists, not just for its own sake, but in order to strike at the others? Who among them did not want to become the hegemon—a term that now no longer described the head of a defensive alliance but rather a murderous tyrant determined to rule over the known world?

Most of these kings embarked upon the Legalist "reforms," carrying out within their territories what Professor Zhengyuan Fu calls a "revolution from above." The Chinese people seem to have put up little resistance to this regimentation, perhaps because five centuries of incessant warfare had left them prostrate, or perhaps because they saw security in the imposition of a rigid Legalist order. This formative period of Chinese history left deep scars on the Chinese mind, which ever after has been prone to irrational fears of "chaos" and "disorder," and all too complaisant vis-à-vis the state and its demands.

As the Legalist reforms took hold, a cynical absolutism became entrenched in state after state. But it was the kingdom of Qin in the west, under the direction of the great Legalist Shang Yang, that took the most drastic measures to eliminate feudalism, centralize political power, and militarize society. The result was the transformation of the Qin state from a backward dukedom to the leading—and most brutal—power in North China.

A sense of the carnage of that era can be gained from the great Chinese historian, Sima Guang, who wrote:

> During the 34th year of King Zhao of Qin (273 B.C.), General Bai Qi attacked the allied forces of the states of Zhao and Wei at the city of Huayang. Mang Mao, the Wei general, fled the field, while the three generals from Han, Zhao

and Wei were captured. Some 130,000 soldiers lost their heads. This was followed by a battle with the forces of General Jia Yan of the state of Zhao, when some 20,000 Zhao soldiers were driven into the river and drowned. During the 43rd year of King Zhao (264 B.C.), General Bai Qi attacked the Han city of Jingcheng, annexing five cities and decapitating some 50,000 heads. During the 45th year of King Zhao (262 B.C.), the state of Qin attacked the state of Zhao at Changping. A ruse led to the surrender of the Zhao army, and the entire force of some 400,000 men was buried alive.

Sima Guang recorded these bloody wars in a section he entitled "The Road to Grand Unification," as if no price was too high to pay to bring All under Heaven under one rule. In the event, the struggle for hegemony did not have much longer to run. The Qin monarch annexed the territory of the last other Zhou king in 256 B.C. and then absorbed the last remaining states during a ten-year campaign beginning in 231 B.C. It was through the ensuing Qin dynasty that the absolutism embodied in the Legalist reforms became encoded into the Chinese political genome, to be practiced down to the present day.

THE QIN DYNASTY MODEL

Prior to the Warring States period, Chinese peasants could go about their daily lives largely unmolested by the government except for taxes and occasional stints of corvée labor. However despotic the ruler who sat on the local Dragon Throne, however much he terrorized his courtiers at his capital and his kinsmen in neighboring fiefs, off in the villages a kind of grassroots autonomy flourished. Peasants summed up their freedom from overbearing government in a folk saying: "Heaven is high and the emperor is far away."

Even before his final triumph over his fellow kings, the first Qin emperor had lessened the distance between himself and his subjects by means of Legalist reforms. Now he sought to eliminate it altogether. During an age when the reach of even the most ambitious rulers almost always exceeded their grasp, the emperor of the Qin sought to make the entire population of China, at the time some forty million people, directly accountable to him. And, acting through an enormous cadre of bureaucrats, a complex network of laws, and a highly elaborated ideology, he very largely succeeded. In so doing, the Qin emperor became the archetype of a political monster that has become all too common in our modern age. More than two millennia before George Orwell coined the term, ancient China endured the world's first Big Brother.

Qin Shihuang is a household name throughout the Orient, yet few in the West outside of a handful of Asian experts, have heard of this ancestor of all Oriental despots. Blessed with vigorous health and assisted by the ruthless Legalist Li Si, he threw all his energies into the quest for power. In 231 B.C., as we have seen, he launched the series of campaigns that within ten years would bring much of what constitutes modern China into his domain, creating one of the largest empires the world had known up to that time. For the next twelve years, until his death in 210 B.C., he ruled that empire with an iron hand.

It was not so much his personality as his policies, crafted in conjunction with Li Si, that so stunningly anticipated the bureaucratic totalitarian empires of our own century. To begin with, a special cadre of commissars was established to keep watch over officialdom. At the provincial level, for example, there was a civil governor, a military commander, and a political commissar. The duties of the commissar—precisely like those of their latter-day counterparts in the People's Republic of China today—were to spy on the governor and military commander and ensure that they did not deviate from the official line or criticize government policy. All civil and military officials were centrally appointed and salaried, and they served at the pleasure of the emperor.

The emperor's Legalist credo was that "a wise prince doesn't ask his subjects to behave well—he uses methods that prevent them from behaving badly." Every area of life was regulated. The people were not permitted to bear arms, and all weapons were confiscated and sent to the capital. Aristocratic families were uprooted from their estates and moved *en masse* to the capital where they could be better kept under control. Trade, regarded as "parasitical activity," was made illegal. Wandering minstrels were banned, replaced by state-sanctioned troupes of singers and musicians whose very repertoires had to be approved by the Ministry of the Interior.

As laws proliferated, the bureaucracies charged with enforcing them fattened. Fierce punishments calculated to squelch any murmur of resistance were meted out to violators. For major capital crimes, not only the offender but his entire family were annihilated. Those convicted of lesser crimes were sent by the millions to labor on government projects in a forerunner of the twentieth-century gulag. For the construction of the Emperor Qin Shihuang's palace, for example, more than seven hundred thousand laborers were conscripted; a similar number were drafted for the construction of his tomb.[19] Hundreds of thousands more labored to build some four thousand miles of imperial highways, as many as were built by the Roman Empire. Countless others dug canals and widened waterways to allow water transport for the twelve hundred miles from the Yangtze to Guangzhou. Others were sent north to strengthen the walls that earlier Chinese states had built.[20]

Yet the lesson of the Warring States period was that safety lies not behind defensive walls, but in a policy of aggressive expansion. Qin Shihuang had risen to power by practicing just such a policy, and he continued it. The Qin emperor launched a series of wars to subjugate neighboring peoples and expand the borders of the nation. Armies were sent campaigning southward against the Yue people, the ancestors of the present-day Vietnamese, whose coastal state then stretched up to modern-day Guangdong. The campaign was long and difficult because the Yue adopted guerrilla tactics, avoiding pitched battles in favor of raids on outlying Qin towns and garrisons. Still, much of southeastern China was brought within the Qin domain, with Qin outposts stretching down to the Hanoi area of today's Vietnam. Armies were sent northward into Inner Mongolia as well, in an effort to drive back the Xiongnu confederation, although the mobility of these nomadic herdsmen made them difficult to subdue permanently.

To concentrate the state power needed to carry out these hegemonic thrusts, the world's first cult of personality was invented. Clever ministers attributed god-like powers to the Qin emperor, and official bards spread stories of his fabulous accomplishments throughout the length and breadth of the empire. One minister had giant footprints four feet long and two feet wide carved in the rock of a sacred mountain and let it be known that these had been made by the august emperor's shoes. At the summit of another sacred mountain, another minister placed a set of chess pieces as tall as a man. The emperor, he avowed, had ascended the mountain and played chess with the gods. Everywhere, steles were raised with deeply carved inscriptions lauding the emperor and the accomplishments of his rule: "All men under the sun work with one heart. Morals have been standardized. Neighbors keep watch on one another, relatives inform on relatives, and thieves lie low!" Few among his fearful subjects dared disobey the Qin emperor's edicts.

Still, despite the harshness of his laws and the strength of his personality cult, occasional acts of sedition did occur. The only way to achieve perfect control over his subjects, Li Si informed Emperor Qin, was to eradicate thought itself:

> Your Majesty...has firmly established for yourself a position of sole supremacy.... And yet these independent schools [Confucianists and others], joining with each other, criticize the codes of laws and instructions. Hearing of the

promulgation of a decree, they criticize it, each from the standpoint of his own school. At home they disapprove of it in their hearts; going out they criticize it in the thoroughfare. They seek a reputation by discrediting their sovereign; they appear superior by expressing contrary views, and they lead the lowly multitude in the spreading of slander. If such license is not prohibited, the sovereign power will decline above and partisan factions will form below. It would be well to prohibit this. Your servant suggests that all books in the imperial archives, save the memoirs of Qin, be burned.

Qin Shihuang agreed, and issued an imperial edict:

Anyone owning classical books or treatises on philosophy must hand them in within thirty days. After thirty days anyone found in possession of such writings will be branded on the cheek and sent to work as a laborer on the northern wall or some other government project. The only exceptions are books on medicine, drugs, astrology, and agronomy.

Private schools will be forbidden. Those who wish to study law will do so under government officials.

Anyone indulging in political or philosophical discussion will be put to death, and his body exposed in public.

Scholars who use examples from antiquity to criticize the present, or who praise early dynasties in order to throw doubt on the policies of our own, most enlightened sovereign, will be executed, they and their families!

Government officials who turn a blind eye to the abovementioned crimes will be deemed guilty by virtue of the principle of collective responsibility, and will incur the same punishment as that inflicted for the offense itself.[21]

The consequences of the edict were swift and devastating. Pyres of burning books lit up the cities and towns as China's ancient literature was reduced to ashes. For possessing forbidden texts, three million men had their faces branded with the stamp of infamy and were deported to the Great Wall. Numerous scholars committed suicide in protest, while others hanged or drowned themselves out of fear.

It is for his punishment of 463 famous Confucian scholars that the Qin emperor is most notorious. These were individuals that the emperor personally tried and found guilty of conspiracy, sabotage and lese-majesty. In the supreme atrocity of a long record of brutality, he sentenced them to the five tortures: beating, amputation of the nose, branding of the cheek, amputation of the feet and castration. Only after being tortured and unmanned were they then they were buried up to their necks in the earth and their heads crushed by chariot wheels.[22]

As far as ordinary people were concerned, they were treated *by* the state as a disposable resource *of* the state. The terra cotta soldiers discovered near China's ancient capital of Changan may have survived far longer than the bones of those construction workers buried alive to hide the location of the tomb from grave robbers, but it is those old bones of real victims—not the terra cotta soldiers—that best express the early history of China's superordination of state over society.[23]

The ruthlessness of the Qin state led to widespread and smoldering resentment, which flared up into open rebellion upon the emperor's death. The insurrection began when a few hundred peasant conscripts were delayed by inclement weather from reporting in to the authorities at the appointed time and place. Knowing the harsh punishment that would inevitably reward such tardiness—they were already dead men at that point—they decided to become rebels. Armed only with wooden sticks, they began a guerrilla war against the government. Within three years, the whole imposing edifice of the Qin state collapsed into ruin.

Although the Qin dynasty did not survive the death of its founder, the Legalist concept of "revolution from above" had transformed China forever. Warring states had been welded together into an empire. The aristocracy had been replaced by a bureaucracy. Power had been centralized into the hands of a Son of Heaven. The autocratic political system that the Qin emperor and his Legalist advisor had designed—with its absolute monarch, centralized bureaucracy, state domination over society, law as a penal tool of the ruler, mutual surveillance and informer network, persecution of dissidents, and political practices of coercion and intimidation—entered China's cultural DNA and continued to replicate itself down through the centuries and the dynasties. It is little surprise that China remains a centralized, autocratic, bureaucratic government—and an empire in waiting—even today.

"CONFUCIAN ON THE OUTSIDE, LEGALIST ON THE INSIDE"

The fall of the Qin dynasty exposed both the strengths and the weaknesses of the Legalist program. On the positive side of the ledger, Legalism had proven admirably suited to the ambitions of ruthless rulers. Acting on the Legalists' frank, brutal, and cynical advice, China's first emperor had created the world's first totalitarian state. But in arguing that the ruler's authority should rest on naked force alone and that the chief instrument of effective government is raw terror, the Legalists had misjudged human nature. While it is possible to terrorize a people into submission over the short term, the continuation of such a policy over time risks not only sullen resistance but open rebellion. Human beings respond far more readily to commands issuing from an authority they recognize as legitimate than from one they merely fear. The Legalists had been so busy telling the people they *must* obey their rulers that they had never gotten around to telling them why they *should*.

The emperors of the succeeding dynasty, the Han, were determined to avoid making the same mistake. Their dynasty would only survive, they realized, if they balanced Legalist intimidation with Confucian indoctrination. Had not Confucius taught that one of a ruler's most important responsibilities was to educate his subjects in virtue through exhortation, persuasion, and, above all, moral example? "If a ruler himself is upright, all will go well without command. If the ruler himself is not upright, even when he gives commands, he will not be obeyed."[24] And: "He who exercises government by means of his virtue may be compared to the North Star, which keeps its place and all stars turn towards it."[25]

The chief Confucian value that rulers were to exemplify and teach their people was *ren*, which has been translated into English variously as benevolence, humaneness, virtue, compassion, tolerance, forbearance, and goodness. Confucius himself defined *ren* as "love of mankind";[26] "humility, tolerance, good faith, diligence and kindness";[27] and as the precept "do not do unto others what you do not want others to do unto you."[28]

Although their worldviews may seem far apart, the Confucians and the Legalists were not really in disagreement on the structure of authority. Both saw the world as properly consisting of a single unified state (*tian xia*) under the centralized political authority of a single all-powerful sovereign. As Confucius himself said, "Just as there are not two suns in the sky, so there cannot be two emperors on earth." Both saw the people in a posture of absolute submission toward this emperor. The difference was that while the Legalists knocked heads together, the Confucians inculcated respect for authority, so that the people would knock their heads against the ground—kowtow, as the Chinese say—of their own accord.

Confucianism was so well suited to the task of persuading the people to become compliant subjects that in 136 B.C. the Emperor Han Wudi declared it to be the official ideology of the empire. Not that he or his successors were themselves true believers in this new state religion. Far from it. Even though the occupants of the imperial throne thereafter made a great show of celebrating Confucianism and its rites in public, they were "Confucianist on the outside, Legalist on the inside" (*wairu neifa*). For cynical and sophisticated Legalist rulers, Confucianism was merely a secret force to police the mind far more thoroughly than cadres of informers ever could. Or as Ross Terrill has elegantly put it, "Legalism was the iron scaffolding of the Chinese empire; Confucianism was its silken costume."[29]

This duality was not always a tightly guarded secret. Emperor Han Xuandi (r. 73–49 B.C.), for instance, was open about his family's continued appreciation of Legalism as well as its disdain for the impracticalities of Confucianism: "The Han family dynasty has its own institution. It is a blending of the Way of the Hegemon [Legalism] with that of the Sage-King [Confucianism]. How can we rely solely on the teaching of benevolence and apply the political rules of the Zhou dynasty? The vulgar Confucians do not understand the expediencies of changing times. They like to praise the ancients and criticize the present. They confuse the people concerning what is nominal and what is real, and they do not know what to abide by. How can they be entrusted with responsibility?"[30]

The official ideology of Imperial China was not "Confucian" so much as a clever amalgam of Legalist principles and Confucian rhetoric.

This was accomplished by rewriting the ancient Confucian texts— *The Analects of Confucius*, *The Great Learning*, *The Doctrine of the Mean*, and *The Works of Mencius*—over the course of the Han dynasty to make them better serve the cause of imperial autocracy.[31] As a result, Confucius was made to express Legalist and Daoist beliefs entirely foreign to his thinking. This inveterate defender of the Golden Age of Chinese antiquity was said to have condemned it in the manner of a Legalist: "If a man living in the present age returns to the ways of antiquity, disaster will certainly befall him."[32] Confucius was made to utter the very un-Confucian idea that the ruler, not antiquity, is the only sure guide to proper behavior: "No one but the Son of Heaven may order the ceremonies, establish standards, and determine the written characters."[33]

Most uncharacteristically of all, this product of the "hundred schools of thought" of the Warring States period, who taught his disciples by means of open discussion and debate, is strangely made to argue that the search for the Truth—the Confucian Dao or Way—means the suppression of dissent: "When the Way prevails, the common people do not discuss public affairs."[34]

In this way, the stolen prestige of China's great sage and of the (newly reconstructed) Confucian classics were cynically used to legitimate Legalist rule and practice. Few emperors made more than a show of following the benevolent Way preached by Confucius, although they all justified their policies as being "for the good of the people." As Professor Zhengyuan Fu writes, "the Confucian text provided ready-made and convincing propaganda for ideological legitimization of authority no matter what kind of person the ruler might be, rationalization of policy no matter what consequences it would result in, and justification of political practice no matter how repressive it really was."[35] Confucian paternalism had become little more than a pleasant mask worn by the emperors to hide the Legalist totalitarianism that lay at the heart of Chinese despotism.[36] Even China's Communist emperors—Mao Zedong, Deng Ziaoping, Jiang Zemin, Hu Jintao, and now Xi Jinping—have made a great show of ruling with paternal solicitousness. But not only do they keep the sword close at hand, they are quick to use it on their enemies.

Some would compare China's Legalist traditions, so manifest in present-day Beijing, to Machiavelli's *The Prince*. But any invocation of Machiavelli is not only anachronistic—the Chinese Legalists anticipated Machiavelli by some two millennia—it is so culturally inapt as to be completely misleading. The Legalists succeeded, through their influence on the first emperor of the Qin dynasty, in completely crushing their Confucian opposition. The "end-justifies-the-means" views Machiavelli espoused in *The Prince* were never able to dominate Western statecraft to the same extent.

Machiavelli's failure to dominate Western political thinking is largely attributable to one thing: the general ameliorating influence of Christianity on Western monarchs combined with the enormous moral authority vested in the office of the papacy. Nothing like the Humiliation of Canossa—when the Holy Roman Emperor Henry IV walked on foot across the Alps to Canossa Castle in Tuscany, Italy, in January 1077 to beg Pope Gregory VII to lift his excommunication—ever happened in Chinese history. Nor could it have. It is difficult to imagine any Chinese emperor, at any point in Chinese history, publicly asking forgiveness from any religious figure, be he Taoist, Buddhist, or Confucian. It is even more impossible to imagine that any occupant of the Dragon Throne would ever, like Henry IV, further humiliate himself by kneeling in the midst of a raging blizzard for three days and three nights before a castle begging an audience with that religious authority. The emperor, as the divine "Son of Heaven" and the highest religious authority in the land, would have had to kowtow to himself. And any religious figure who suggested otherwise would probably have had no head left to kowtow with.

EMPIRE WITHOUT BOUNDARIES

If the internal policy of the once and future Chinese hegemonic power is oppression and thought control (albeit masquerading as virtue), then what is its policy toward the wider world? What countries or territory does the hegemon desire to incorporate into its domain? What countries must submit as vassals, accepting the hegemon's dictates? And what countries, if any, is the hegemon content to leave completely outside the Chinese imperium? What, in short, is the hegemon's grand strategy?

Western security analysts have long sought the answers to these questions in Chinese history. They have immersed themselves in ancient strategic texts and sifted through centuries of imperial pronouncements. They could have saved themselves the trouble. For as Michael D. Swaine and Ashley J. Tellis, have noted, "China's grand strategy has never been explicitly presented in any comprehensive manner by its rulers."[37]

There are sound reasons why no Chinese dynasty, including the present one, ever produced a blueprint for its territorial ambitions. Deeply embedded in the Chinese political genome is the firm conviction that the present international system is just as anarchic as the Warring States period of ancient China. China's leaders see modern states as constantly maneuvering to gain power and territory at the expense of competitors just as during that centuries-long war of all against all. They believe that China's distant past is, in effect, the world's prologue: the future will see all states but one extinguished—or at least reduced to tributary status— by the superpower that emerges triumphant from the chaos of the present age. Xi Jinping's "China Dream," which we will discuss at greater length in chapter six, is to be that hegemon.

In the view of the PRC leadership, the choice is a stark one: either hegemony or annihilation. China must either continuously expand its power to achieve hegemony or, like the failed states crushed and absorbed by the Qin, it will face ultimate defeat and eventual annihilation. This means that Beijing will never be satisfied with a given level of power short of global hegemony even if, as some suggest, it is allowed to recover Taiwan or even dominate the Asian-Pacific. As we have seen, the Chinese political elite are offensive realists—to use John Mearsheimer's phrase— and they have been offensive realists for over two thousand years, driven by a longstanding and completely rational desire to achieve hegemony over their known world.[38] Regardless of what compromises and concessions are offered by America and its allies, China will continue its drive for hegemony, remain suspicious of American intentions, and stay firm in its understanding that, in a world of uncertainty, only hegemony offers security. Han Fei's warning continues to echo in Chinese ears: "He who has the most power wins."

This hegemonic aspiration, as it might be called, is one reason why the jurisdiction of Chinese emperors was, theoretically at least, infinite.

The historical record is generally clear on what provinces and border regions each Chinese emperor did in fact rule, and what kingdoms and tribes farther afield did in fact sent tribute, but there are no lists of the territories he and his advisors thought he *should* rule. And there is certainly no list of territories that were regarded as forever beyond the hegemon's reach. It would have been heresy to contemplate such a limitation on the hegemon's universal sway, and treason to actually publish it. To have explicitly ruled that certain territories and peoples constituted "China" would have implied that other territories and other peoples were forever outside the imperial purview. The Chinese cosmology simply did not permit such a division. That was the reason that no imperial history was ever printed, and no imperial edict was ever issued, that *clearly defined the theoretical extent of the hegemon's imperium*. The hegemon, in theory at least, exercised universal sway.

From the very beginning, the universality of imperial rule was regarded by Chinese hegemons as self-evident. "The virtuous power of the Han has no borders," grandly declared historians of the Han dynasty.[39] An edict of the Tang dynasty went even further, asserting that "The height of the emperor is as great as that of Heaven, his width is as huge as the Earth. His radiance matches that of the Moon and the Sun, his honesty and faithfulness is equal to that of the four seasons."[40] There was no escape from the radiance of the hegemon anywhere on earth, according to another Tang dynasty document: "Any creature, so long as they exist in the world, must receive the emperor's nurture."[41]

The emperors themselves possessed a lofty sense of infinite jurisdiction and frequently testified to their own hegemonic omnipotence. Indeed, the emperor's sense of entitlement as the hegemon is so breathtakingly broad it is often indistinguishable from megalomania. So we find the Emperor Taizong of the Song dynasty (960–1279) calmly asserting that his divine aura "has worked a transforming influence on China and Barbarians, our favors have even spread to animals and plants."[42]

The aura cast by the hegemon elevated the people of his chosen capital, as well as the province of which it was a part, above the rest of China. Their dialect, bearing, and customs inevitably came to define what it meant to be Chinese. Away from the capital, accents grew thicker, customs stranger, and the people less recognizably Chinese. Even today, the residents of Beijing automatically assume that visitors from the outer provinces are culturally inferior. Since the sway of the hegemon is theoretically infinite, however, it doesn't matter if his nominal subjects are indistinguishable from barbarians, cannot read, write or speak Chinese, and don't acknowledge him as their proper ruler. They are still his subjects.

Western analysts, trained to think of China as just one nation-state among many, are ever hopeful that China's elite will give up their pretensions, or abandon their drive for hegemony. Surely China's peaceful integration with the rest of the world's nation-states is inevitable, they think. It is just a matter of time before the Chinese elites' inflated idea of their country's own centrality in the scheme of things shrinks to a more manageable size. I am inclined to reject this conclusion, based as it is on the mere ethnocentric imposition of a Western worldview on the Chinese mind.

The truth is that it was never necessary for China to develop a highly elaborated grand strategy of conquest and dominion, for the simple reason that the strategy of the hegemon is self-evident to any Great Han chauvinist. As the imperial mandarinate down through history instinctively understood, the Manifest Destiny of the Chinese hegemon is *to rule the world*. This is still the unstated goal of the Communist mandarinate today, as it rationally and relentlessly seeks hegemony as the only sure guarantee of security.

This Chinese hegemony observed borders when it was constrained to do so, of course, but its natural tendency was to expand its reign of virtue. The unstated grand strategy of the hegemon was one of continuous aggression against neighboring states, absorbing them when he could and accepting tribute when his reach had exceeded his grasp. This is why, for example, traditional Chinese maps show no trace of meridians. Foreign locations are not arranged topographically, that is, in relation to their actual place in the physical world. Rather, they are arranged topologically based on their degree of submission to the emperor. The well-known "All-Under-Heaven Complete Map of the Everlasting Unified Qing Empire," published in 1806, has been aptly described as a cartographic expression of the Qing tribute system. The map is scaled not in terms of distance but rather by the degree to which a country has kowtowed to, or been subjugated by, the Dragon Throne.

The hegemon's unchanging ambition was that all the world would one day come to enjoy his beneficent rule. Hegemony is like a crystal that, in the proper medium, continues to replicate its existing structure indefinitely. Other states, by their very existence, challenge this principle by limiting its jurisdiction. Perfect hegemony would have no external expression at all, because it would have brought all neighboring states and peoples under its rigid, crystalline structure of control.

Many students of Chinese history argue that Chinese rulers generally ruled by moral suasion rather than physical coercion. They read into the stratagems of Sunzi, China's ancient military genius, a preference for subtle diplomatic maneuvers rather than the direct application of force to defeat an enemy. John King Fairbank, the long-time doyen of American China studies, was a leading voice among those who maintained that the Chinese historically and culturally "disesteem violence."[43] I once gave a talk at the CIA on China's hegemonic ambitions, only to be politely chided by one of the senior China analysts present—a former student of Fairbank's as it turned out—who insisted, following his late professor, that the civilization that he had spent his entire life studying was innately pacifistic. He was so mesmerized by the silken costume of Confucianism that he was completely oblivious to the iron framework of Legalism that had first created and then, over the centuries, supported and maintained the Chinese imperium.

Anyone who looks closely at the historical record, though, will have no trouble seeing in stark relief the specter haunting Asia. It is the iron fist of Legalism, raised high and striking down the domestic and foreign enemies of the reigning hegemon with astonishing frequency. According to Chinese military sources, China fought an incredible three thousand, seven hundred ninety (3,790!) wars from the beginning of the Zhou dynasty in 1100 B.C. to the end of the Qing dynasty in 1911. This total includes civil wars fought within China proper, as well as conflicts with peoples on the periphery, and averages out to *1.26 wars per year.* Even China's most "defensive" dynasty, the inward-looking Ming, fought an average of 1.12 wars per year throughout its existence—and this counts only the wars fought against barbarians.[44]

China's thousands of wars were neither small-scale police actions nor bloodless dramas resolved by ruse and stratagem. The emperor fielded armies of a hundred thousand men on average—the armies of feudal Europe were a fraction of this size—and million-man armies were not uncommon. Sunzi's stratagems notwithstanding, battles were pitched and bloody affairs costing far more casualties, it has been estimated, than did comparable conflicts in Europe.[45] All this is to say that, though Europe endured a Hundred Years' War, Chinese hegemons may be said to have been engaged in almost constant warfare for three thousand years.

Sunzi's stratagems came into play only after the larger strategic question—whether or not to go to war at all—had been answered by the emperor in the affirmative. *The Art of War* is a tactical manual for generals, not a diplomatic primer for effete mandarins. Sunzi sets out ways to vanquish one's opponent on (and off) the field of battle while minimizing one's own casualties, which is a quite different thing from advocating the avoidance of conflict at all costs.

All in all, a study of Chinese military history does not reveal a polity committed to Confucian pacifism, but rather one bent upon Legalist domination. Far from "disesteeming violence," as Fairbank had it, the imperial court was all too ready to unleash its armies against the lesser peoples on China's periphery, or use them to put down peasant revolts within its borders. It is no exaggeration to say that the use of force is endemic to China. Neither is there any real mystery about why this should be so: it is, as we have seen, built into the hegemonic project as a rational response to a world of insecurity.

The first goal of the aspiring hegemon in Chinese history was the unification of the 1.5 million square miles of the Chinese heartland— roughly the eastern half of present-day China that is known as "China Proper."[46] But the desire for hegemony that drove the hegemon to these early conquests was not sated when these boundaries were reached. Armed with the manpower and resources provided by the conquest of China proper, the ambitious hegemon customarily went on to incorporate another one to two million square miles into his imperial realm. East Turkestan, Tibet, Korea, Mongolia, Vietnam, and Manchuria were frequent targets of Chinese aggression. The outer limits of the territory under the hegemon's control was dictated not by the satiation of his hegemonic appetites (which, as we have seen, were essentially insatiable), but by the relatively primitive means of transportation and communication he was forced to rely upon and the higher costs of administering outlying regions, which were generally poorer and more sparsely populated. Beyond this point, the hegemonic imperative found expression not in conquest but in compelling outlying territories to acknowledge the hegemon by becoming vassal or tributary states. The Chinese hegemon almost always sought to rule his known world. And he almost always succeeded.

At times of dynastic expansion, China dominated, in one form or another, much more territory than it controls today. Its greatest expansion took place under the Mongol or Yuan dynasty (A.D. 1279–1368), when its empire stretched from the Bering Sea all the way to the gates of Warsaw. At its most robust, the Mongol Empire dominated an area remarkably similar in scope to the Sino-Soviet bloc from a single center.

But even during less tumescent periods the regnant Chinese dynasty remained the world's leading power until the industrialization of the West.

The greatest empire of the ancient world in the West was governed from Rome. It reached its maximum territorial extent in A.D. 211, when it exercised control over the entire shoreline of the Mediterranean Sea, most of the Black Sea, and England. It had a polyglot population of some sixty million souls[47] and a standing army of perhaps three hundred fifty thousand men. In addition to the Praetorian Guard, thirty legions of ten thousand men each were deployed abroad, garrisoning the frontier provinces and border states.[48]

Yet far to the east, a greater empire had already been in existence for over four hundred years. The collapse of the Qin dynasty was immediately succeeded by the rise of the Han. Dating from 202 B.C., the Han Empire was more impressive in scope and organization than the contemporaneous Roman Empire. Its sway extended from Korea eastward across Mongolia to Central Asia, and it included most of contemporary China except Hainan Island and Tibet. It possessed a standing army of over a million men. A census taken in A.D. revealed a population of some sixty million, which presumably continued to expand until the end of the dynasty two centuries later brought turmoil to China.[49]

In a pattern that was to be repeated again and again throughout Chinese history, the unification of China Proper under the Han dynasty brought foreign conquests. During the long and brilliant reign of Han Wudi (140–87 B.C.), Han armies marched to all points of the compass. In the northeast they conquered the Korean peninsula, incorporating Korea into the Chinese empire in 108 B.C. In the south, they brought all of what is now South China under their control and carried their arms as far southward as the Gulf of Tonkin, in present-day Vietnam. Their major effort was directed against the northwest "barbarians," especially the Xiongnu. Alliances against this common foe were made with various Central Asiatic peoples. To coordinate the alliances, an official named

Zhang Qian was sent to the west, traveling as far as Bactria, or modern-day Kyrgyzstan. The power of the Xiongnu was broken and the Han rule was extended into what is now Xinjiang. The remains of fortresses and walls built by the Han to guard their frontier in the far northwest can still be seen today.

The first century A.D. saw further Han conquests in the west. Under General Ban Zhao the Chinese became masters of parts of Central Asia. Their armies reached the shores of the Caspian Sea in A.D. 97, and a Chinese embassy was sent to the Persian Gulf. Partly because of the control by the Han of the caravan routes to Central Asia and partly because of the possession of Tonkin and the south, commerce was maintained with the Roman orient—known to the Chinese as Daqin (Ta-ch'in)—both by land and by sea. Chinese silks were carried to the Mediterranean world, while products from Central Asia and the Hellenistic world were brought to China.

Both Rome and the Han built walls—Hadrian's to protect Roman Britain, and the Han emperors to thwart invaders from the steppes—but neither faced the world in a defensive crouch. As Owen Lattimore has remarked,

> Neither Chinese nor Romans, retreating in the face of aggressive barbarians, dug in on a fortified line to save civilization. On the contrary, Chinese and Romans, each exploiting a geographical environment that had recognizable characteristics, built up the highest civilizations of their times. They expanded to take in all the terrain that could be profitably exploited by the techniques they already had, until they reached a zone—the depths of Mongolia, the depths of Germany—which because of costs of transportation and distances from metropolitan markets could not be further integrated with the urban-rural oikumene. Further expansion would mean diminishing returns—too much military expenditure, too little additional

revenue. That was where they dug in and why they dug in. Their "defense lines" were in fact the limits which they themselves set on their own expansion.

It was China that proved to have the broader limits, and the more staying power. Although Han dynasty China may not have surpassed ancient Rome in population, it exercised a more direct control over that population through a civil service, the first the world had ever known. While Rome ruled through military governors, consuls, and proconsuls, as well as through the heads of vassal states, the Han emperor ruled directly through civil officials he personally appointed. The Chinese empire was a more intricate financial, economic, and security organization than the Roman, not merely because of its greater size, but because of its greater complexity.

The aspiration of elites among the various peoples who lived under the Roman Eagle was to be able to say *Civis Romanus sum,* "I am a Roman citizen"—that is, to be formally admitted into the Roman polity, with all the rights and duties that such inclusion implied. By this means the upper social strata of many peoples along the Mediterranean littoral were partly assimilated into Roman culture, adopting Roman dress and speaking Latin, at least in dealings with the state. Rome's cultural superiority, although not unquestioned, especially by the Greeks in the eastern half of the empire, reinforced its imperial power and gave it a tremendous advantage over the multicultural empires common in other parts of the world, where rule by brute force remained the norm.

In China this process of assimilation went much deeper. The assurance of cultural superiority was not only a matter of arrogance on the part of the Chinese elite, but a perspective often shared by other peoples within China's expanding shadow. The superiority of the Chinese way of life, with its advanced agriculture, its written language, and its highly developed arts, was attractive enough that those who fell under Chinese rule often came to admire their conquerors greatly and actively sought to assimilate. This cultural superiority was underlined by Confucian ritual, which stressed harmony, hierarchy, and discipline, and it was enforced with cruel and calculated ruthlessness by Legalist rulers. Unlike the states absorbed into the Roman Empire, where assimilation occurred mainly at the top, whole peoples conquered by the hegemon quickly redefined themselves as Chinese; adopted Chinese language, dress, and agricultural practices; and disappeared without a trace into the Chinese demographic sea. More than conquered, they were thoroughly Sinicized. Ancient Chinese texts make many references to peoples who long ago ceased to exist as separate ethnic groups, so completely have they been assimilated into Chinese culture.

Civil officials replaced military governors within a generation or two as the identity of the conquered peoples merged with that of the conquerors. China's unity became not merely the artificial construct of military force or the nominal allegiance of elites, as in the Roman Empire, but something rooted in a deeply held and popular desire. It was reinforced by the civil service, professionally trained and competitively recruited, and by rigid Legalist controls on public and private activities.

Cultural homogeneity enabled the Han dynasty to last for some 360 years. Even more important, it enabled China, after a period of division into several states, to re-coalesce into the Sui-Tang dynasty in A.D. 589. The Roman Empire, less culturally cohesive, had split into eastern and western empires in A.D. 412 and continued to wane, with the western empire soon ceasing to exist. China, on the other hand, has gone through successive cycles of unification and fragmentation right up to the present day, with the centripetal forces of language, culture, and brute force overcoming again and again the centrifugal forces of decay and deterioration.

At each dynastic recrudescence, China became once again the largest and most powerful empire on earth. And with each reassertion of unity came foreign conquest. During the early decades of the Sui-Tang dynasty (589–906),[50] border territories that had been lost, such as Korea and Xinjiang, were recaptured. Then Chinese armies struck to the southwest and entered Tibet, eventually crossing the Pamirs into north-west India. At one point even Persia sought and received aid from the Tang against the Moslem Arab wave of invasion. The Song dynasty (960–1279) saw similar exploits in its early years.

The period of China's greatest imperial expansion came during the Yuan or Mongol dynasty (1260–1368), when the empire included all Asia north of the Himalayas except Japan, and reached to the heart of Europe. From his capital of Khanbaliq, near the site of modern-day Beijing, Kublai Khan ruled not only over China but also over most of his father's Mongol Empire, with its western frontiers in Mesopotamia and Europe. Armies were sent into Champa, Annan, and Burma, and armadas against Java and Japan. The expeditions to the south ended in a somewhat inglorious retreat, the attempt on Java was unsuccessful, and the armada against Japan was destroyed by a typhoon. Still, for a time much of the Eurasian land mass was ruled from a Chinese capital. It may be argued that it was the tactical mobility of the Mongol horse archers that created the largest empire the world had ever known, but it is equally true that its center of gravity was China, which provided its strength, its stability and, increasingly over time, its sense of purpose. Not for the last time, barbarians from the north provided the military means to achieve in China and beyond the paramount end of power: hegemony.

Of course, modern-day Chinese no longer regard Genghis Khan and his heir Kublai Khan as foreign invaders but have proudly adopted them as legitimate emperors of their own country. In part this is because the Mongols, at least those living in the Inner Mongolia Autonomous Region of China, have long since been Sinicized and, as we shall see in chapter five, declared to be co-equal descendants of the Yellow Emperor.[51] But the chief reason they have been transformed into Chinese icons is because they were so stunningly successful at expanding China's borders. The Mongol Empire does not loom as large in the mind of contemporary Chinese as the more recent Qing dynasty does, but it is still proudly remembered as a time when *China*, fulfilling its destiny, ruled over a good portion of the world.

The Ming dynasty (1368–1644), which followed, is often described as inward-looking, but its early history recapitulates that of its predecessors. Its founder, Hongwu, managed to oust the Mongols and keep China from fragmenting. An outgrowth of this continued unity was conquest. Hongwu and his successors sent expeditions to the south and southeast as far as Java and Ceylon. One of the princes of Ceylon was brought captive to China, and for years tribute came from the island. Under a succeeding monarch, an expedition was sent by sea as far as the Persian Gulf. Korea was invaded under the Ming emperors, Annan [northern Vietnam] for a time became subject to China, and frequent wars with the Mongols kept those ancient enemies beyond the wall. As we have already noted, the "inward-looking" Ming fought no fewer than 308 wars in its two and three-quarter centuries of existence.[52]

China's neighbors did not share the smug assumption of the Ming hegemons that, because they had once been under Chinese imperial rule, they were forever fated to share China's destiny. Vietnam in particular, which had been independent *for four centuries* beginning in A.D. 939, disdained the role of humble tributary. The early Ming Emperor Yongle first hurled an Imperial Denunciation at the Vietnamese king and then, when this failed to cow him, an army. Yet even as his soldiers laid waste to the Vietnamese countryside, the emperor continued to posture as the benevolent Confucian father of the Vietnamese people, declaring, "The people of Annan are all my little children." The invasion, he explained, was necessary because the Vietnamese king "has oppressed the people of the country and the people hate him to the marrow of their bones. The spirits of Heaven and Earth are unable to tolerate this." Exuding Confucian virtue, the emperor told his troops that they were on an errand of mercy, "proceeding there [to Vietnam] to relieve [the people] of their suffering. Do not delay." The reality, of course, was that Chinese armies were proceeding to Vietnam to inflict pain on a nation and a people for refusing to acknowledge Chinese superiority and submit to Chinese rule. It was necessary to destroy Vietnam, it might be said, to save the hegemon's face.[53]

The Qing Empire, like its predecessors, was held together by an exquisitely organized mandarinate, whose members were selected by competitive examinations and represented the best and brightest of the Chinese elite. The Qing rulers instituted the same rigid Legalist controls over society as previous dynasties. Scholar-officials could not meet in groups of more than ten without official approval, books were subject to rigorous censorship, newspapers were unknown, school curricula were controlled, and independent voluntary associations were strongly discouraged, if not absolutely forbidden. "No private undertaking nor any aspect of public life could escape official regulation," observes French Sinologist Etienne Balazs.[54] Civil society—that part of the social system that is not under the control of the state—was largely unknown and ideological unity was strictly enforced.

Under the able leadership of Kangxi (1662–1722) and Qianlong (1736–1796), a prosperous China went on the march. Qing armies conquered Manchuria and Mongolia. Under Kangxi they added Tibet and Formosa to their possessions. Under Qianlong, Ili and Turkestan came under Chinese rule. Qianlong's legions penetrated Burma, Nepal and Annam. Korea paid tribute.

It is important to note that the Tibetans and the Mongols, who then ruled Xinjiang as well as Mongolia, were not disarmed by their admiration for Confucian principles, nor did they submit in awestruck deference to China's cultural superiority. Instead they were, in each case, subdued in brutal campaigns of conquest. When the Zunghar Mongols in 1756 rebelled against Qianlong's rule, the hegemon ordered his commanders to "show no mercy," take the Zunghar women "as booty," and "massacre" the men. Neither could they save themselves by surrendering. Young men who surrendered were to be executed, while the elderly, children, and women "would be spared and kept as slaves."[55] It was a brutal campaign of extermination—a genocide, in modern terminology—and it was totally unconstrained by Confucian niceties. It was, in other words, raw Legalism in action.

The Qing dynasty circa 1800 was an impressive assertion of hegemony. The imperial center directly ruled a vast territory stretching from the Russian Far East across southern Siberia to Lake Balkash, southward across Kazakhstan, and eastward along the Himalayas, Laos, and Vietnam. Through vassal and tributary states it controlled Burma, Nepal, Indochina, Thailand, and Korea. More than three hundred million people lived within the Celestial Empire, while tens of millions more resided in surrounding tributary states. The economy was the world's largest and the military, although beginning to fall behind the West in technological innovations, was still impressive in numbers.

One of the lessons of this glorious history, a lesson deeply etched in the minds of Chinese students today, is that each of China's empires—the Han, the Sui-Tang, the Song, the Yuan, the Ming, and the Qing—had no contemporary peer. No other power of comparable might existed in the world. Few of China's neighbors proved capable of resisting her determined expansion. The reigning Chinese hegemon projected power almost at will over his periphery, constrained at times by hostile powers but more commonly only by his own whims.

For over two thousand years the Middle Kingdom was the center of the universe, a huge, self-satisfied continent of people whose elite, wealthy, and cultured, had only disdain for the barbarians living on their periphery. Smugly convinced of their country's cultural and military superiority, China's leaders wanted little from the rest of the world except its deference.

In 1792, King George III thought to entice China into a trading relationship by sending emissaries bearing gifts of British manufactured goods. Whatever modest goodwill this gesture may have won was dissipated when the British refused to kowtow to the emperor. His imperial majesty, deeply offended by this lack of due deference, sent them packing.

The edict of their expulsion reveals the invincible self-confidence, verging on arrogance, that would remain embedded in China's cultural marrow in the centuries ahead: "We, by the Grace of Heaven, Emperor, instruct the King of England to take note of our charge: The Celestial Empire, ruling all within the four seas...does not value rare and precious things...nor do we have the slightest need of your country's manufactures.... Hence we...have commanded your tribute envoys to return safely home. You, O King, should simply act in conformity with our wishes by strengthening your loyalty and swearing perpetual obedience."

But by the time Emperor Qianlong so haughtily dismissed the English envoys the empire was already fraying at the edges. Within a few decades it would be defeated by Great Britain in the Opium War of 1839–1842, and "treaty ports" (read: colonies) would be carved out of its coast. For China this was more than just a military defeat; it was a profound cultural humiliation. The deeply ingrained sense of superiority, inculcated over millennia of dominating its near neighbors, stood revealed as hollow pride. The demeaning political realities of the past hundred years have only deepened the insult.

3

THE **HEGEMON AWAKENS** FROM ITS **SLUMBERS**

"The Chinese people have stood up....
Let the domestic and foreign reactionaries tremble before us!"
—CHAIRMAN MAO ZEDONG[1]

Mao Zedong announced the founding of the People's Republic of China in words of wounded national pride, in a speech that drips with a desire for vengeance against those who had brought the Middle Kingdom low:

> The Chinese have always been a great, courageous and industrious nation; it is only in modern times that they have fallen behind. And that was due entirely to oppression and exploitation by foreign imperialism and domestic reactionary governments. For over a century our forefathers never stopped waging unyielding struggles against domestic and foreign oppressors.... Our forefathers enjoined us to carry out their unfulfilled will.... Ours will no longer be a nation subject to

insult and humiliation. We have stood up.... The era in which the Chinese people were regarded as uncivilized is now ended. We shall emerge in the world as a nation with an advanced culture.

Our national defense will be consolidated and no imperialists will ever again be allowed to invade our land. Our people's armed forces must be maintained and developed with the heroic and steeled People's Liberation Army as the foundation. We will have not only a powerful army but also a powerful air force and a powerful navy.... Let the domestic and foreign reactionaries tremble before us![2]

Mao's revolution breathed new life into the old hegemonic power which, awakened from its slumber, would soon set out upon the same well-traveled road it had traversed so many times before. In the eyes of China's Communist elite, a cabal of Western and Western-oriented countries—Great Britain, France, Germany, Russia, Japan, and America—had treacherously combined to attack the old Chinese empire, loosening China's grip on hundreds of thousands of square miles of territory and a dozen tributary states in the process. It was time to recover it.

Mao harbored special rancor for the United States, fulminating in a bitterly sarcastic speech called "'Friendship' or Aggression" in late 1949,

The history of the aggression against China by U.S. imperialism, from 1840 when it helped the British in the Opium War to the time it was thrown out of China by the Chinese people, should be written into a concise textbook for the education of Chinese youth. The United States was one of the first countries to force China to cede extraterritoriality.... All the "friendship" shown to China by U.S. imperialism over the past 109 years, and especially the great act of "friendship" in helping Chiang

Kai-shek slaughter several million Chinese the last few years—all this had one [purported] purpose…first, to maintain the Open Door, second, to respect the administrative and territorial integrity of China and, third, to oppose any foreign domination of China. Today, the only doors still open to [U.S. Secretary of State] Acheson and his like are in small strips of land, such as Canton and Taiwan.[3]

As we shall see in the next chapter, it was not long before the "concise textbook" that Mao called for in this speech appeared in print. For the next two decades that potted history was widely used to indoctrinate Chinese youth in the many "crimes" that America had supposedly committed against China. Although this anti-American screed was taken off the market in the eighties and nineties, it has now—tellingly—been republished in China.

FIRST EMPEROR OF THE MAO DYNASTY

Mao Zedong was better versed in Chinese history than in Marxist dialectics; he saw himself more as the founding emperor of a new dynasty than the ruler of a Communist state. His most famous poem, "White Snow," reveals not only his imperial ambitions but also his boundless narcissism. Mao begins by exalting the beauty and majesty of the north China landscape in winter and ends by exalting himself—and denigrating the founding emperors of previous Chinese dynasties. Written at a time when the Long March had reduced the Chairman's ragtag Red Army to fewer than eight thousand men (but not published until many years later), the poem stands as an extraordinary exercise in egotism and self-aggrandizement:

How beautiful these mountains and rivers,
enticing countless heroes to war and strife.

Too bad that Emperors Qin Shihuang and Han Wudi lacked
culture
and that Emperors Tang Taizong and Song Taizu lacked
romance.
Genghis Khan was the pride of his time,
though he was only good at shooting eagles with his bow.
They all belong to a time gone by,
Only today is a True Hero present.[4]

The "True Hero" was proposing himself, more or less accurately as it worked out, as the superior in both ability and ruthlessness to other dynastic founders. If Mao was offended by comparisons that many made between himself and Emperor Qin Shihuang, arguably the most hated figure in Chinese history, it was only because he saw himself as Emperor Qin's superior in cunning and cruelty. At the Second Plenum of the Eighth Party Congress in May 1958, Mao scoffed, "Emperor Qin Shihuang was not that outstanding. He only buried alive 460 Confucian scholars. We buried 460 *thousand* Confucian scholars. [Some] have accused us of being Emperor Qin Shihuang. This is not true. We are a hundred times worse than Emperor Qin. To the charge of being like Emperor Qin, of being a dictator, we plead guilty. But you have not said nearly enough, for often we have to go further."[5]

In another of his poems, Mao contrasted his admiration for Emperor Qin Shihuang and the Legalist order to his utter disdain for Confucius:

Please don't slander Emperor Qin Shihuang, Sir
For the burning of the books should be thought through
again.
Our ancestral dragon, though dead, lives on in spirit,
While Confucius, though renowned, was really rubbish.
The Qin order has survived from *age to age*.... [Emphasis
added.]

Mao's disdain for Confucianism was rooted less in his Marxism-Leninism than in his Legalism. Like the Legalist Emperor Han Xuandi, Mao despised the old Confucian orthodoxy for its impracticalities, for its moral niceties, for its preachiness about virtue and benevolence. Even more, he despised it because its tottering remains stood in the way of building a strong state that would dominate not just the Chinese people but neighboring peoples as well. Mao's respect and admiration were reserved for the "ancestral dragon," the Emperor Qin Shihuang of the Qin dynasty, who just happened to be one of the greatest tyrants in the long history of the human race.

Growing up at the turn of the twentieth century, Mao had steeped himself in Chinese historical classics, absorbing the frank and brutal Legalist advice they offered to would-be hegemons.[6] "Know the future in the mirror of the past," as the Chinese say, *Jian wang zhi lai*. Mao cast his eye over China's long history and decided that it was the brutal Emperor Qin Shihuang that he would seek to emulate, and the hegemonic "Qin order" that he would seek to recreate. Never mind that more than twenty-two centuries had passed since his "ancestral dragon" had walked the earth. Mao, too, would forge a new dynasty by naked force. He, too, would rule China with an iron fist, resurrecting the totalitarian institutions earlier employed by his merciless hero.

To successfully establish the "Qin order" in the modern age, however, Mao needed two things. He needed to reconfigure Legalism for modern times. And he needed a replacement for Confucianism, a new "silken costume", as it were, that would soften the harshness of his governance in the eyes of the people.

With the victory of the Communist revolution in Russia, Mao and the rest of China's revolutionaries found an unlikely vehicle for their authoritarian ambitions: an imported Marxist ideology that was every bit as statist and elitist as traditional Chinese political culture, while at the same time claiming to be even more "modern" and "progressive" than its chief ideological opponent, liberal democracy.

Democracy, after all, is the hegemon's bête noire. It disperses power among elected representatives instead of concentrating it in the hands of the ruler. It weakens the state instead of strengthening it. And, worst of all, it empowers the people instead of subjugating them. The principle of the self-determination of peoples is a particular threat to an ambitious hegemon because it justifies efforts by numerically dominant minorities living in border regions such as Tibet and Xinjiang to go their own way.

Marxism-Leninism, on the other hand, while formally acknowledging civil rights and the equality of man, was an enabler for the hegemon. It defended the monopoly of power by an educated elite and defined a relationship between state and society that was very much in keeping with China's autocratic tradition. It was a much more effective tool of indoctrination than Confucianism, and its pseudoscientific terminology provided a stronger defense for autocratic rule. As a bonus, it even commanded a respectful audience in the very heart of Western society.

Communism was, in fact, an allegory for hegemony. It provided a road map showing how the revolution that had come to China was predestined to spread to neighboring countries. Meanwhile, China was justified in keeping a tight grip on border regions, since it would only be a matter of time until a common proletarian identity melded China's diverse ethnic nationalities into one Sinic whole. For Chinese intellectuals who admired Western scientific advances but were repelled by the radical individualism underlying Western values and fearful of China's survival as a nation if democratic rule were adopted, "scientific" Marxism-Leninism offered a comfortable compromise. Thousands of them were drawn into the Chinese Communist Party by the promise that, while Western science would be used to strengthen China, in the meantime the authoritarian Party structure would ensure that China did not fall asunder. The Chinese empire in which they took so much pride would remain intact, while chaos—the fracturing and disintegrating of the Chinese polity—would be avoided at all costs.

So even as Mao was importing Marxism-Leninism from the West, he was adapting it to China's unique totalitarian heritage. The Leninist party structure was a natural fit with pre-existing Chinese imperial practices at both the ideological and the organizational levels. Transitioning from the absolute authority of the emperor to the absolute authority of the CCP and its leaders required only a minor mental adjustment.

This fact is not lost on contemporary China scholars such as the National University of Singapore's Zheng Yongnian. They agree that the Chinese Communist Party, despite its *superficial* resemblance to the former Communist Party of the Soviet Union, is an entirely different species of political animal. Zheng himself calls this new-old system "an organizational emperor," emphasizing that the current structure is an outgrowth of imperial practices. "In many respects," Zheng says, "[the CCP] wields its power in a way similar to Chinese emperors of the past.... For example, like an emperor in dynastic China who regarded himself and also was regarded by society as the only legitimate ruler (an individual), the CCP has also perceived itself and is perceived by others as the only ruling party (as an organization) in the country."[7]

While Zheng's phrase "organizational emperor" is an apt description of the collective leadership that preceded the consolidation of power by Mao Zedong, during the final decades of his life the Great Helmsman clearly wielded his authority in a more imperial manner. It is not literary license that has led countless writers to describe Mao as an emperor.[8] The appearance of collective leadership that followed Mao's death was largely an artifact of Deng Xiaoping's apparent reluctance to dominate the public stage in the same way that he dominated private decision-making. And, as we will see in chapter six, following Xi Jinping's elevation to the position of Party leader, he has moved rapidly to concentrate power into his own hands. Xi's formal title may still be General Secretary of the Chinese Communist Party, but Big Daddy Xi, as he is known, is for all practical purposes already a Red Emperor in the Maoist mold.

As far as the highly bureaucratized nature of Party rule is concerned, what is this but a natural elaboration of a complex set of imperial offices that, under the control of the nine-tiered mandarinate, had been in existence in China for centuries? From an organizational point of view, all the Leninist party system did was enable the imperium to be concentrated even more effectively in the hands of the Politburo than the traditional structures previously relied upon by the emperors. So the new power structures were instantly recognizable, and largely acceptable, to patriotic intellectuals eager see the hegemon awaken from its century-long slumber.

For the illiterate or semiliterate villagers who became the foot soldiers of Mao's armies, the principles of liberal democracy were unknown and the abstractions of Marxist-Leninist ideology a mystery. But resonance with dynastic China's Confucian beliefs and imperial traditions helped to make communism and its leader acceptable. Marxist dialectics militated for change, just as did yin-yang theory and the *I Ching (Book of Change)*. The state remained the grand provider on whom all ultimately relied for their survival. The paternalistic Party as the vanguard of the proletariat was understood as a stand-in for the "father-mother officialdom" of imperial times. And its "chairman" was the omnipotent savior—the Red Emperor—upon whose benevolent rule all of his subjects depended.

Mao's "personality cult" was already flourishing by April 1945, when the new Party constitution declared the "Thought of Mao Zedong" essential to "guide the entire work" of the Party. The Chairman was praised as "not only the greatest revolutionary and statesman in Chinese history but also the greatest theoretician and scientist." Much of this fulsome praise was written by Mao's own hand.[9]

The cult of the Party chairman was seen as a continuation of the cult of the emperor. The Party went to extraordinary lengths to prey upon the superstitions of the people. Mao was endlessly exalted as a larger-than-life figure, a kind of living god who would rescue the people from all manner of suffering and oppression. As soon as the Communists captured a village in the civil war, its buildings would blossom with slogans such as "Mao Zedong is the great savior of the Chinese people."

As for Mao himself, he may have served communism, but only because it served his own purposes so well. If the emperors had been "Confucianist on the outside, Legalist on the inside," then Mao was effectively "Communist on the outside, Legalist on the inside." As cynical and sophisticated as the most ruthless Legalist rulers, he took full advantage of China's millennia-long totalitarian tradition to consolidate his rule. A study of references and quotations in Mao's *Selected Works* is revealing in this regard. Some 24 percent come from Stalin, the most ruthless Soviet leader. But almost as many—22 percent—come from traditional Chinese sources.[10] In his later speeches, references to traditional sources become even more common, while Stalin and his sayings disappeared down the memory hole. Mao Zedong had become what he had long admired: the founder of a new dynasty, an emperor of the Legalist school, and the latest in a long line of hegemons.[11]

As the Chairman of the Chinese Communist Party, Mao controlled an organization that even Qin Shihuang would have admired for its rigid discipline, its highly elaborated organizational structure, and its designs on the total control of society. A Communist party, Mao instinctively understood from the beginning, is a "war party."[12] War is its element, protracted conflict its means, and the seizure of power its ultimate end. It is so admirably suited to these martial purposes that it is, in effect, a force multiplier. By organizing his initially tiny base areas—first in Jinggangshan and later in Yan'an—along military lines, Mao was able to punch well above his weight, vanquish his intra-party enemies, and eventually conquer the entire country.

Wei Jingsheng, one of China's long incarcerated and now exiled dissidents, notes that, even today the CCP is organized and run as if it and the country it controls were at war.[13] And, in one way or another, it is. China's military-industrial complex, which operates under the rubric of civil-military integration (CMI), is second to none.[14] The CCP wars on its own population through political campaigns such as the one-child, now two-child, policy and the persecution of the Falungong. And China is at war with the world (whether the world knows it or not) through its territorial claims in the South China sea and elsewhere, through its use of destabilizing proxies such as North Korea, and even more directly through its theft of technology, its currency manipulations, and its highly sophisticated and incessant cyberattacks.

THE LEGALIST RESTORATION

With the establishment of the People's Republic of China on October 1, 1949, both the Chinese people and the world were told that the future had come to China. Viewed from a long-term historical perspective, however, it looked suspiciously like a case of *back to the future*.[15] The ideological justifications used to legitimate Communist rule differed in many particulars, to be sure, from those of its Confucian predecessors. The central political myth of imperial China was that the emperor held his place by divine sanction and led by moral example, and that as long as he maintained Confucian standards of public virtue he would continue to enjoy this "Mandate of Heaven." The central myth of the People's Republic of China, at least for decades after its founding, was identical to that of other Communist states, namely, that the Chinese Communist Party ("the Vanguard of the Proletariat") and its leaders were temporarily exercising dictatorial power on behalf of the "masses" for their own good and in anticipation of the eventual "withering away" of the state.

But if the wineskin was new, its contents remained the bitter gall of vintage Legalism. The CCP takeover reversed the brief efflorescence of civil society in China in the first decades of the twentieth century, restoring the traditional Chinese pattern of state-society relations in which society is almost totally subservient to the state. Legalism was reborn in China, although it was veiled in Communist terminology and gave formal deference to a theory of civil rights that the emperors would have scorned. Communist to all outward appearances, the new Chinese state was Legalist in essence, continuing the autocratic tradition of the imperial Chinese state by:

- imposing an official ideology (Marxism-Leninism-Maoism) with interesting functional parallels to Chinese imperial orthodoxy (Legalism-Confucianism);
- concentrating political power in the hands of a tiny minority, often of one, with power deriving ultimately from control of the military and wielded without appreciable institutional constraints;
- treating the penal code and the legal system as tools of governance wielded by the ruler, who acts above legal constraints;
- dominating most, and at times all, aspects of domestic commercial and economic life;
- controlling all forms of social organization outside the nuclear family, which itself is severely restricted;
- engaging in political practices familiar from dynastic times, such as censorship, large-scale persecutions, purges of the bureaucracy, court intrigues, and elite factional conflicts;
- regarding the people as its property, as subjects rather than citizens.

The nascent civil society that had grown up during the republican era was eradicated. Those formerly in leadership positions were "re-educated" or simply executed. The organizations they had formerly headed were either co-opted or destroyed. Newspapers and magazines were brought under state control or closed down entirely. Private and Christian schools were taken over by the state. Voluntary associations were disbanded or amalgamated into Party-led front groups. By the end of the five-year period following 1949, few vestiges of China's once-flourishing civil society still survived. Chinese society had come to resemble that of an archetypal Communist state—or equally, that of a Chinese imperial dynasty.[16]

As an emperor of the Legalist school—that is to say, the hegemon—Mao believed that the Mandate of Heaven gave him license to dominate, well, *everything*. He was obsessed by the idea that he could become the leader of a truly global revolutionary movement, and that China's greatness would be manifested through him as he reshaped the world in China's image. Using Communist internationalism as an ideological cover, China would return to the center of the world by supporting the Third World and "liberating" all humanity.[17] First and foremost, of course, there was the matter of firmly subjugating the Chinese people. The incessant political campaigns of the PRC's early years came about because of Mao's determination to emulate China's "ancestral dragon" and eliminate, utterly and without mercy, all possible opposition to his absolute rule within China.

At the same time, China's traditional dominions cried out to be returned to the embrace of the Middle Kingdom. What kind of hegemon would Mao be if he did not recapture lost territories, recover straying vassals, and force one-time tributary states to again follow China's lead? Military action—engaging the Japanese invaders, defeating the Nationalists, and capturing the cities—had delivered China into his hands. Now military action would restore the empire. For these reasons Mao intervened in Korea in the early years of his rule, invaded Tibet, bombarded Quemoy, continued to bluster over Taiwan, attacked India over Tibetan border questions, confronted the Soviet Union, and sent troops and massive amounts of war material to Vietnam.

Mao may also be said to have invented "mapfare"—the use of contrived maps to establish territorial claims to outlying territories. Under his direction, maps were drawn up showing China's borders extending far to the north, south, and west of the area that the PLA actually controlled. Any territory that had been touched by China, however briefly, was regarded as rightfully Beijing's. Father Seamus O'Reilly, a Columban missionary who was one of the last foreign Catholic priests to leave China in 1953, recalls seeing, in the office of the local Communist officials who interrogated him, a map of the PRC that included *all* of Southeast Asia— Vietnam, Laos, Cambodia, Burma, Thailand, and Singapore—within China's borders.[18]

But such maps were initially marked for internal distribution only. For Mao, although willing to undertake limited military actions to restore China's imperium piece-by-piece, was uncharacteristically coy about his overall hegemonic aims. There were powerful forces arrayed along his borders, and he did not want to face them all at once. The United States occupied Japan and South Korea, and had bases in the Philippines and Thailand. The British were in Hong Kong and Malaysia. Even his erstwhile ally, the Soviet Union, was occupying huge swaths of Chinese territory in Manchuria, Inner Mongolia, and Xinjiang. Thus, even as his troops were engaged in Korea or Tibet, Mao continually sought to reassure the world, in the policy equivalent of a Freudian slip, "We will never seek hegemony."

"When hemmed in, resort to stratagems," advised Sunzi. The diplomatic establishment of the PRC, headed by the charming and crafty Premier Zhou Enlai, developed not just one stratagem, but three. The first was for China to play the role of a loyal member of the Soviet-dominated Communist bloc. The second was to take an anti-colonial posture as a member—indeed the leading member—of the Third World, a posture used to great effect with India, for example. The third stratagem, which proved increasingly useful as time went on, involved posing as a responsible member of the post-Westphalian international system, a respecter of international agreements and international borders, as merely one nation-state among many. Each of these postures seemed to reflect a certain truth about the PRC. But each of them was based on a deception.

Mao's adopted ideology demanded that lip service be paid to international Communist unity, but the relationship of China's "revolutionary, statesman, theoretician and scientist" with Stalin was complicated from the beginning. Mao was grateful for Stalin's aid but suspicious that the Soviet leader was trying to keep China disunited and weak, and more often than not he rejected his advice. In 1936 Mao ousted the "28 Bolsheviks" that Stalin's Comintern had foisted upon the CCP, thus reducing Moscow's influence over his guerilla movement. In 1945 he rejected out of hand Stalin's staggering suggestion that he disband his army and join Chiang Kai-shek's government, advice he later ridiculed.[19]

The USSR's late entry into the war against Japan had allowed Soviet troops to occupy parts of Inner Mongolia, Manchuria, and Xinjiang. Mao could do little about this insult to China's sovereignty until the CCP had emerged victorious in the civil war, at which point he journeyed to the Soviet Union for two months of hard negotiations with Stalin. The terms of the Treaty of Friendship, Alliance, and Mutual Assistance that Mao and Stalin signed on February 12, 1950, gave Moscow a degree of economic and political leverage within China all too reminiscent of the old colonial days. For example, Mao had told Edgar Snow in the late 1930s that Mongolia would "automatically" be part of the new China, but now he was forced to concede the existence of a separate "People's Republic of Mongolia."[20]

By 1958 Mao was publicly expressing unhappiness over the way these negotiations had gone: "In 1950 I argued with Stalin in Moscow for two months. On the questions of the Treaty of Mutual Assistance, the Chinese Eastern Railway, the joint-stock companies and the border we adopted two attitudes: one was to argue when the other side made proposals we did not agree with, and the other was to accept their proposal if they absolutely insisted. This was out of consideration for the interests of socialism."[21]

Despite his unhappiness at Russian "colonialism," Mao had accomplished his principal goals, which were the removal of all Soviet forces from Chinese soil, the return of the China Eastern Railway and Dalian (Port Arthur), and the avoidance of any additional territorial concessions. Mao's determination to recover China's lost grandeur did not include kowtowing to one of the imperialistic powers that had humiliated it, even if it happened to be a member of the same ideological camp. For the Chinese, Soviet ascendance meant domination by a people that, rightly or wrongly, they regarded as culturally inferior. "The hungry land," as they called Russia, was not going to devour any additional Chinese territory.[22]

On January 12, 1950, Secretary of State Dean Acheson gave a speech at the National Press Club, the main thrust of which was that China, if left alone by the West, would soon break with the Soviet Union. The Soviet "absorption" of Outer and Inner Mongolia, Xinjiang, and Manchuria, he vigorously asserted, was "the most important fact in the relations of any foreign power with Asia." America must avoid conflict with China so as not to "deflect from the Russians to ourselves the righteous anger and the wrath and the hatred of the Chinese people which must develop."[23]

Ironically, Acheson's speech is not remembered for its prescience on the issue of a Sino-Soviet split but for its contribution to the outbreak of hostilities on the Korean peninsula. Having been assured that Stalin had not targeted South Korea for aggression, Acheson famously failed to include it within the U.S. defense perimeter in Asia as he defined it. Seizing upon this omission, North Korean Communist dictator Kim Il-Sung soon thereafter convinced Stalin to allow him a "limited offensive." On June 25 of that same year, the entire North Korean army poured across the border and fell upon the almost defenseless south.

This was Mao's first opportunity to reassert China's traditional prerogatives over one-time vassal states, and he did not hesitate. With the world's attention fixed on the Korean peninsula, he sent elements of the People's Liberation Army to take control of Tibet. On October 21, 1950, the Dalai Lama was forced to sign an agreement acknowledging

Chinese sovereignty. Tibet became a protectorate of China, although it would continue to control its own domestic affairs for a time, albeit under ever-increasing Chinese scrutiny and supervision.

Over on the Korean peninsula, the war had quickly turned against Kim Il-Sung. By late November 1950, American forces under the command of General Douglas MacArthur were approaching the Yalu River, which separates Korea from China. With his half-kingdom fast disappearing, Kim appealed to China for succor—exactly what tributary states were expected to do when threatened by outside powers.

Mao promptly responded with a grand imperial gesture, throwing a huge "volunteer" army into the fray. He was not reacting to a threat but seizing an opportunity, namely, reestablishing Chinese suzerainty over a once and future tributary state.[24] Recklessly inviting casualties, the Chinese army advanced by overwhelming the beleaguered Americans in wave after wave of attacks, eventually forcing them to retreat south of the 38th parallel. After intense fighting, the front was consolidated near the 38th parallel in October, and Kim Il-Sung's half-kingdom was restored.

Mao later summed up the Korean War in a 1958 speech to his generals as "a big war in which we defeated America and obtained valuable experience."[25] If Korea is regarded strictly as a military contest, Mao's comment may seem mere conceit. After all, the PLA lost at least a quarter of a million men (as opposed to some thirty-four thousand American casualties), gained no territory over the original North-South partition, and settled for a negotiated armistice. But viewed as a bid by the hegemon to recover a tributary state, Mao's intervention was an impressive first step. He had fought the United States to a standstill, establishing China as a military power to be reckoned with. He had impressed the Soviets, who had been unwilling to commit ground forces to the fray. Even more important, he had brought at least the northern half of the Korean peninsula back into its traditional relationship of dependency on China (and away from its dependency on the Soviet Union). The second step toward the restoration of Chinese hegemony over Asia had been taken.

THE SINO-SOVIET SPLIT

Although Mao was never comfortable with the Soviet domination of the Sino-Soviet relationship, he was for many years careful to avoid open criticism of the Russians. But Khrushchev's "secret speech" discrediting Stalin, delivered to the CPSU Twentieth Congress in February 1956, marked a turning point. Whatever compunction Mao may have felt about criticizing the Soviet leadership, at least in private, vanished. Talking to the Politburo in 1956, Mao warned, "We must not blindly follow the Soviet Union.... Every fart has some kind of smell, and we cannot say that all Soviet farts smell sweet." He was irritated at his countrymen's propensity to worship all things Soviet. He complained at one point that he "couldn't have eggs or chicken soup for three years because an article appeared in the Soviet Union which said that one shouldn't eat them.... It didn't matter whether the article was current or not, the Chinese listened all the same and respectfully obeyed." He mocked Chinese artists who, when painting pictures of him and Stalin, "always made me a little bit shorter, thus blindly knuckling under to the moral pressure exerted by the Soviet Union at that time."[26] He remained conciliatory in public, however, largely because he was hoping to get his hands on Soviet nuclear weapons.

Mao's eagerness to acquire nuclear weapons, so as to confirm China's newly achieved great-power status, knew no bounds. It was an essential part of his "prepare for war" campaign, which was the basis of all his economic programs.[27] Although he had earlier rejected a Soviet offer to set up its own nuclear-armed bases on Chinese soil as an affront to Chinese sovereignty, Mao managed to convince Stalin's successor to aid China's nuclear weapons program. When Khrushchev initially declined, Mao resorted to bombing and strafing the Nationalist-held islands of Quemoy (Jinmen) and Matsu (Mazu), provoking a confrontation with America that carried serious risks for the Soviet Union.[28] As Mao had hoped, the fear of nuclear war with the United States scared Khrushchev into providing China with the technological assistance Mao's engineers needed to make the bomb. A nuclear technology transfer agreement to this end was signed in 1957. Under this agreement, Khrushchev later recalled, the Chinese received "almost everything they asked for. We kept no secrets from them. Our nuclear experts co-operated with their engineers and designers who were busy building a bomb."[29]

The Soviets were about to hand over a prototype bomb when Mao's continued saber rattling over Taiwan gave them second thoughts. As Mao prepared to invade Quemoy and Matsu in September 1958, Khrushchev advised caution. Mao was deeply offended, in part because he no longer respected Soviet military advice.[30] When Khrushchev pointedly reminded him that America possessed nuclear weapons, Mao airily dismissed the possibility of mass casualties. "So what if we lose 300 million people," the Great Helmsman told a stunned Khrushchev. "Our women will make it up in a generation." He had made the same point the year before in only slightly less dramatic fashion. In his famous speech "American Imperialism Is a Paper Tiger" given at the World Communist Representative Meeting in Moscow in November 1957, Mao had said, "I'm not afraid of nuclear war. There are 2.7 billion people in the world; it doesn't matter if some are killed. China has a population of 600 million; even if half of them are killed, there are still 300 million people left. I'm not afraid of anyone."[31]

In June 1959 Khrushchev, convinced he was dealing with a madman, or at least a pathological narcissist, unilaterally abrogated the agreement that was to have provided China with an atomic weapon.[32] Mao was furious. He privately denounced Soviet meddling in Chinese affairs, telling members of the Military Affairs Commission in September, "It is absolutely impermissible to go behind the back of our fatherland to collude with a foreign country."[33] The Soviets were "revisionists," China was soon telling the world, and as such constituted a greater threat to the world than American "imperialism." Going its own way, China was now less a part of an international revolutionary movement than the reawakening hegemon slowly regaining control over its known world.[34]

With the onset of the Cultural Revolution (1966–1976), the war of words escalated, and armed clashes broke out at several points along China's four-thousand-mile border with the Soviet Union. Mao dispatched additional troops to the border and on March 2, 1969, on the Chairman's orders, a battalion-sized PLA force ambushed Soviet patrols on the Wusuli River. The Soviets promptly retaliated, and during the next two years there were repeated skirmishes at many points along the frontier.

The Ninth Party Congress, held April 1–24 that same year, took an openly hegemonic tone. The only published speech was that of Lin Biao, then Chairman Mao's heir apparent, who repeated Mao's formula that a third world war would promote revolution and dig the graves of both revisionism and imperialism. "We must be ready for a conventional war and also for an atomic war," Lin said. "Both the Soviet Union and the United States are paper tigers." The present border between the Soviet Union and China could be made the basis of negotiation, he avowed, but Moscow would first have to admit that the historical border treaties were "unequal treaties."[35]

The Soviets threatened nuclear attacks on the Chinese heartland and deployed forty-four heavily armed mobile assault divisions along the border. Though the crisis passed with no territory changing hands, the message was clear: the existing border was ultimately dependent on Soviet strength, not Chinese acquiescence.

STRANGLING TIBET

After PLA troops entered Tibet in 1950, the government of the Dalai Lama was gradually isolated. Members of the international community who questioned Chinese actions were haughtily informed that the Tibetan question was a purely internal affair. The Himalayan plateau had been an integral part of China for centuries, Beijing's story went, having been brought under China's sway as early as the seventh century, when the Tang Emperor Li Shimin sent his daughter Princess Wencheng as a bride to the great Tibetan King Songtsen Gampo. The princess bestowed culture on the uncouth Tibetans, bringing them and their land forever into the debt and the orbit of China's superior civilization.

In fact, the emperor sent his favorite daughter, famed for her beauty and talents, as a peace offering to Songtsen Gampo because he had a healthy respect for the military prowess of his Himalayan neighbors, not because he intended to civilize them. Had the Tibetan king been seeking a closer association with Chinese culture, the tribute would have flowed the other way.

The Chinese Communists, having promised to respect Tibet's autonomy, instead gradually suffocated its political and religious institutions over the course of the 1950s. Half of what had traditionally been considered Tibetan territory was carved up and handed over to other provinces where Chinese were in the majority. The process of Sinicization was accelerated during the chaotic days of the Great Leap Forward (1958–1962), when Mao's cadres carried class warfare into the Land of the Snows, sacking monasteries and killing monks. When the Tibetans rose up in protest in 1959, Beijing, claiming that the Tibetan local government had "instigated a rebellion," used brute force to consolidate total control.[36]

On March 25, 1959, after heavy fighting, Chinese Communist troops occupied Lhasa. The Dalai Lama fled the capital. Beijing announced that its army had "swiftly put down the rebellion in Lhasa and was mopping up the rebels in some other places in Tibet." The Tibetan government under the Dalai Lama was formally dissolved, replaced by a puppet regime headed by the twenty-one-year-old Panchen Lama. For the first time since the thirteenth century, the Tibetans did not control their own country.[37]

To justify their intervention, the Chinese Communists invented a mythological Tibet where the masses were enslaved by a slothful priestly class. The propaganda machine churned out horror stories of a dark and brutal theocracy of bonded labor, vast monastic fiefs, indolent monks, and immoral abbots. As late as 1998 the Chinese Communist Party, in the person of Party Secretary Jiang Zemin, was still patting itself on the back for ending monkish "slavery" in Tibet.[38]

In order to bring the partly nomadic Tibetan population under control, the Chinese herded them into the commune system, a new form of serfdom far worse than anything in Tibet's past. As in China proper, the commune system proved to be an economic and ecological disaster of the first magnitude. Chinese agricultural officials ordered the Tibetans to raise wheat rather than the barley they preferred, and the resulting crop failures on the high Himalayan plain, with its short growing season, left the Tibetans malnourished and starving.

Meanwhile, the monasteries and nunneries were emptied and the monks and nuns put to work in the communes. The seventy-thousand-character Petition of the Panchen Lama, written in 1962, states that 97 percent of Tibet's two thousand monasteries were destroyed, presumably by the People's Liberation Army, following the 1959 uprising. A few years later, the Cultural Revolution completed this destructive work. All of China suffered from the depredations of Chairman Mao's Red Guards, but Tibet, outside the Chinese cultural sphere, was a special target. Thanks to Beijing's propaganda, the young Red Guard zealots saw Tibet as the very embodiment of a corrupt and exploitative feudal tradition, and they set about with picks, shovels and even their bare hands destroying every religious edifice and artifact they could find. By the time their rampage ended, Tibet's few remaining stupas and lamaseries were in ruins.

WAR WITH INDIA

Prime Minister Jawaharlal Nehru of India insisted on recognizing China's "rights" in Tibet despite the pleas of the Tibetans, along with many Indians, that he weigh in against this new form of Chinese hegemony. His appeasement of the "New China" came back to haunt him in 1959 when the Chinese, having disposed of the Dalai Lama and his followers, began building military roads right up to the existing Indian-Tibetan border, and then, in early September, crossed over into India.

China's aggression took Nehru completely by surprise, which is perhaps less a consequence of his naiveté than of Zhou Enlai's sophisticated sales pitch about the two countries being fellow victims of the Western imperial powers. The Chinese premier had first visited the Indian prime minister in New Delhi in April 1954, stopping over on his way back to China from the signing the Geneva peace accord on Indochina. Zhou played the stratagem to the hilt, portraying the PRC as a country with impeccable anti-colonialist, anti-imperialist credentials, a country that was a natural member of the Third World club. Nehru bought it.

The Indian prime minister, to be sure, had been favorably disposed toward the People's Republic of China from the beginning. India had been the first "capitalist" country to recognize China (in April 1950), the leading non-Communist proponent for admitting the PRC into the United Nations, and the principal intermediary between Beijing and Washington during the Korean War.

The result of Zhou's 1954 visit was a joint communiqué based on China's "Five Principles of Peaceful Coexistence." Nehru breathlessly announced that relations between India and China would henceforth be governed by "mutual respect for territorial sovereignty, mutual non-aggression, mutual non-intervention in internal affairs, equality and mutual benefit, and peaceful coexistence." These high-sounding principles were reaffirmed at the April 1955 Conference of Asian Countries in New Delhi, and again at the Conference of Asian and African Countries in Bandung, Indonesia.[39] By that point, Nehru had assumed the role of Zhou's patron, eager to advance Zhou's cause by smoothing over China's past support for destabilizing guerilla movements throughout the region. For his part, Zhou spoke of the "Bandung Spirit," a new policy of peacefully wooing nonaligned nations in the region according to the Five Principles. Mesmerized by the Five Principles and the Bandung

Spirit, Nehru could not bring himself to see that India and China had fundamentally divergent interests. He didn't understand that having a shared border with the hegemon, which always sees "borders" as merely temporary accommodations to existing geopolitical realities, was a risky business.

The Indian delegation at the UN was arguing passionately on behalf of Communist China's admission to the General Assembly on the very day that PLA forces began pouring across the border into India. As Nehru pondered Chinese perfidy, PLA troops continued their march southward, seizing two important mountain passes that guard approaches to Sikkim and India.

On September 4 an obviously nonplussed Nehru announced that the Chinese Communists had accused India of "aggression" and demanded that India evacuate "Chinese territory." At first he called the dispute "rather absurd" and indicated that he would be willing to make some minor adjustments to the border. But Nehru soon realized that the Chinese claim was "much more serious" than he had originally thought and "quite impossible for India ever to accept." He declared that India had "undertaken the defense of Sikkim and Bhutan, and anything that happens on their borders is the same as if it happened on the borders of India."

Nehru allowed two years of border skirmishes before responding to the pleas of his generals for leave to stop the slow-moving Chinese steamroller. In the event, the ill-planned Indian counterattack proved a disaster, and the Chinese advance picked up speed. As tens of thousands of square miles of disputed territory passed into Chinese control, Nehru panicked and requested help from the Soviet Union and America. Moscow condemned the Chinese advance, and the Seventh Fleet steamed up the Bay of Bengal. The Chinese, having gotten what they wanted, offered a cease-fire. An overwrought Nehru, who had begun to have nightmares about Chinese troops on the Ganges, was only too glad to accept.

EXPANSION BY GUERRILLA WARFARE

The PRC had initially supported Maoist-style Communist parties in Malaysia, Indonesia, Japan, Burma, India, and Thailand. The Malaysian Communist Party launched an armed rebellion, which the PRC supported until it became clear that the guerrillas were losing to a brilliant British counterinsurgency campaign. At the Bandung Conference, a conciliatory Zhou Enlai declared that those Chinese who adopted another nationality should be good citizens of the countries they joined. But this pious statement did not completely allay suspicions that China was encouraging indigenous Communist movements among the citizens of other Southeast Asian countries.

After the invasion of India, Beijing once more began manifesting a new militancy toward countries in Southeast Asia. The Bandung Spirit was a thing of the past. Instead, Communist China began to act in accordance with an ancient Chinese strategem known as *yuan chiao chin kung*, meaning "to appease distant countries while attacking those nearby."[40] Faraway Canada, Italy, Belgium, Chile, and Mexico were courted for diplomatic recognition while neighboring countries such as Burma, Indonesia, Thailand, India, and Laos were attacked in word, and sometimes in deed.

Laos, one of three Indochina states covered by Southeast Asia Treaty Organization (SEATO) protection, was a specific target. Although small in size and population, the country was important because of its strategic location between China, North Vietnam, and the non-Communist states of Burma, Thailand, Cambodia, and South Vietnam. It also had had a tributary relationship with China going back to the year 1400. In the late fifties, China began supplying the Pathet Lao Communist guerrilla group with ever increasing amounts of military aid. The United States countered with its own expanded program of military and economic assistance. The conflict intensified in 1959 as North Vietnam, with Chinese encouragement, sent military units across the border to reinforce the Pathet Lao. On September 4, Laos appealed to the UN to dispatch an emergency force to counter aggression by North Vietnam. The United States responded by warning both the Soviet Union and Communist China that it would help counter any new danger to peace in the region. The Soviets responded positively and with the support of the United States a peace treaty was signed between the Pathet Lao and Prince Sihanouk's government in 1962. Mao, having none of it, encouraged the North Vietnamese military to support the Pathet Lao. By 1964 several thousand more North Vietnamese troops were battling in Laos, and the peace treaty was a dead letter. China responded by stepping up its aid to the Pathet Lao, who eventually won control of the country, bringing Lao back into China's orbit.

Mao's goal in Southeast Asia was clear: to re-establish the tributary states that had existed during the height of Chinese imperial rule. This time, however, he would use the guise of communist "liberation" to enforce Chinese influence in the region. In reality, it was more of the same system that existed before—establish the Middle Kingdom as the hegemon of the region.[41]

When America began sending military assistance to South Vietnam in the early sixties, China responded by coming to the aid of its tributary. China not only positioned large numbers of forces on the North Vietnamese border as a deterrent to a U.S.-led thrust into the north, it also deployed forces in country. One study has reported that between 1965 and 1972 over 320,000 PLA troops served in Vietnam, peaking at 170,000 troops in 1967. They served largely in antiaircraft and engineering capacities, seeking to bring down U.S. aircraft and repair the damage caused by the U.S. bombing of transportation nodes.[42] In addition to men, copious amounts of materiel also flowed into North Vietnam. China supplied an estimated 270,000 guns, 5,400 artillery pieces, 200 million rounds of ammunition, 900,000 artillery shells, over 700 tons of TNT, 200,000 military uniforms, and 4 million meters of cloth to Hanoi over the course of the conflict.[43]

In Indonesia, the local Communist Party, responding in part to encouragement and aid from Beijing, launched a coup against General Sukarno's increasingly restive generals in 1962. This particular gambit backfired on Beijing. The result was a bloody purge of suspected Communists, which quickly developed anti-Chinese overtones. As many as a million lives were lost, many of them ethnic Chinese. The food distribution system and other large sectors of the economy that had been run by this mercantile minority consequently collapsed. Centuries after assaults upon Java and Sumatra by imperial Chinese forces, the Indonesian archipelago had once again eluded China's grasp.

TAIWAN

Mao's principal obsession throughout the '50s was the recovery of Taiwan. No sooner was the Korean armistice in place than the hegemon ordered the PLA to begin preparing for final battle of the Chinese civil war: the invasion of Taiwan. There was only one problem: the PLA invading force would have to cross the ninety-mile-wide Taiwan Strait, which was patrolled by the carriers and cruisers of the U.S. Seventh Fleet. Moreover, the Nationalist army was growing more formidable as a U.S. Military Assistance Advisory Group helped to train and equip its expanding ranks.

On August 14, 1954, China's state-owned press issued a blistering denunciation of the "American imperialists" for their continued "occupation of Taiwan." The island would be "liberated," Beijing blustered, and by force if necessary.[44] Battle-hardened Communist divisions were moved to staging areas along the Fujian coast and MIGs appeared over the Taiwan Straits.

Chiang Kai-shek did not back down. He put the Nationalist army on alert and strengthened his garrisons on the offshore island groups his forces still controlled. Neither did the PRC's bellicosity unnerve President Eisenhower. When the question of Communist China's war preparations came up at a press conference on August 17, he replied that he had recently reaffirmed standing orders to the U.S. Seventh Fleet to defend Taiwan against any attack. "Any invasion of Formosa," the former general remarked, referring to the island by its Portuguese name, "would have to run over the Seventh Fleet."[45]

Deterred from launching a full-scale attack on Taiwan, the Communists shifted their attention to the offshore islands. Chief among these were the Dazhens, located midway between Shanghai and Keelung; the Mazus, ten miles off the port of Fuzhou and opposite the northern end of Taiwan; and the Jinmens (Quemoys), two miles off the port of Xiamen (Amoy). These islands had helped the Republic of China and the United States to maintain a fairly effective blockade of the South China coast, and had also served as intelligence-gathering posts and commando bases. Both Chiang and Mao regarded these islands as stepping stones. Mao was as eager to capture the offshore islands preparatory to an invasion of Taiwan as Chiang was to employ them as staging areas for what he imagined would be the eventual recapture of the mainland.[46]

On September 3, the Chinese Communists began an intense artillery bombardment of Jinmen and Little Jinmen. The Nationalist air force responded by bombing Communist artillery positions on the mainland. Fearing that an invasion was imminent, the Nationalist government requested U.S. aid. Eisenhower, however, preferred to wait until an actual assault materialized and it could be seen whether the landing was limited in scope or preliminary to one on Taiwan. His position—defend Taiwan but not the offshore islands—was shortly to be written into the Mutual Defense Treaty of December 2, 1954.[47]

Taking Eisenhower's wait-and-see attitude as a signal that the Americans would not intervene, the Chinese Communists assaulted the northernmost island in the Dazhen chain, a place called I-Jiang Shan, on January 20, 1955. The garrison force of 720 soldiers died to the last man defending the tiny island. Convinced that the two remaining Dazhen islands were indefensible, Eisenhower pressured Chiang Kai-shek to abandon the chain, offering the U.S. Seventh Fleet to cover the evacuation of the 20,000 civilians and 11,000 Nationalist soldiers stationed there. Chiang reluctantly gave way, withdrawing the last of his forces on February 6, 1955.

At the same time, Eisenhower warned the Chinese Communists that the United States would resist an attack on the remaining offshore islands, with nuclear weapons if necessary. To further clarify the American position, Eisenhower asked Congress on January 25 to pass a resolution authorizing him "to assure the security of Formosa and the Pescadores" and, if need be, other "closely related localities" which he did not identify. This resolution, which passed on February 26, convincingly demonstrated to Beijing that the American president and Congress were united in their intention to resist further attacks on Nationalist-held territory. It emphatically underlined the importance of the Sino-American Mutual Defense Treaty, which had been ratified by the Senate just a few weeks before. Not only was Taiwan an indispensable link in the chain of U.S. mutual security agreements ringing Communist China, but the defensive perimeter of the treaty itself was in effect extended to the offshore islands.[48] The use of force had given the Communists nothing except an insignificant chain of islands. Faced with a virtual promise of heavy U.S. retaliation in the event of any further attacks, Mao shifted course. It was a textbook example of how the strategy of "escalation dominance" could be effectively utilized.[49] The shelling of Jinmen and Mazu came to an abrupt halt, as did the feverish preparations for an assault on the islands. The ever-genial Zhou Enlai arrived at the Bandung Conference, held in Indonesia in April 1955, bearing an olive branch: the PRC was willing to sit down with the United States at the negotiating table to discuss ways to ease cross-strait tension.[50]

By the end of May, an informal ceasefire held on the Taiwan Strait. Talks between the United States and the PRC began in Geneva and dragged on for months. Washington repeatedly pressed for a joint renunciation of the use of force in the Taiwan area. Beijing balked at this, favoring instead a toothless pronouncement on world peace, and this only in exchange for ministerial-level talks. Seventy-three sessions were held in all, but the impasse went on. No formal armistice was ever reached, nor did Beijing agree—then or ever—to renounce the use of force.[51]

Instead, traditional Chinese truculence reasserted itself. The Chinese Communists continued building up their military establishment opposite Taiwan and constructed a number of new airfields. In the face of this militancy, the United States in 1957 deployed Matador surface-to-surface missiles, capable of carrying nuclear weapons, to Taiwan. Construction began on a major air base near Taichung, in central Taiwan, with a runway long enough to accommodate B-52 strategic bombers. The ROC fortified the offshore islands and reinforced the garrisons stationed there.

When the Soviet Union launched *Sputnik*, the first space satellite, in 1957, Mao saw it as proof that the Communist bloc had surged ahead of the United States, and he was eager to press its newly won strategic advantage. Following a meeting with Nikita Khrushchev in Beijing, he suddenly unleashed a fierce bombardment on Jinmen on August 23, 1958. Tens of thousands of artillery rounds rained down on the island while Communist jets launched strafing attacks. Offshore, torpedo boats attacked Nationalist convoy and transport ships. On August 29, Radio Beijing announced that an amphibious landing on Jinmen was imminent. The 100,000-man Nationalist garrison on the island was on alert as PRC torpedo boats continued swarming about the island and gunners concentrated their fire on Jinmen's landing beach and airstrip, rendering them unusable. But the threat of invasion had been a feint: the real intent had been to impose a blockade. It was only a matter of time before the garrison force, deprived of reinforcements and supplies from Taiwan, would be starved out.

Eisenhower, realizing that the PRC's ultimate objective remained the capture of Taiwan itself, publicly warned the regime not to attempt an invasion of the offshore islands. "Let us suppose that the Chinese

Communists conquer Quemoy," he remarked in a radio address. "Would that be the end of the story?...They frankly say that their present military effort is part of a program to conquer Formosa.... [T]his plan would liquidate all of the free world positions in the Western Pacific."[52] To demonstrate its commitment to the defense of Taiwan, the United States immediately shipped a host of modern weapons to the island. Further underlining U.S. resolve, Nationalist Chinese and American Marines, on September 8, staged a large-scale amphibious landing on southern Taiwan.

Meanwhile, the blockade of Jinmen had continued for two weeks, until on September 7 a convoy of Nationalist supply ships, escorted by warships of the U.S. Seventh Fleet and the ROC Navy, steamed directly for the beleaguered island. The U.S. naval squadron escorted the supply ships to a point three nautical miles from Jinmen, then stood off while they continued on to land and unload their cargo. The commander of the U.S. squadron had permission to return fire if fired upon, but the Communist guns were silent. Mao had blinked.[53]

Still, Beijing's bizarre behavior persisted. An "even-day" ceasefire was announced on October 25 and gradually became a regular part of island life. On even days, convoys could arrive without being challenged; on odd days, the attacks continued, but with diminishing intensity. The Taiwan press condemned this as a cruel game. Eisenhower called it a Gilbert and Sullivan war.

Eventually the Taiwan Strait crisis passed. The Eisenhower-Dulles policy of facing down Communist aggression wherever it might occur, along with the resolve of the Nationalist government, had prevailed. At the same time, the failure of the Great Leap Forward and the ensuing famine, along with unrest in Tibet, may have turned the attention of the Communists to their growing domestic problems for a while.[54] Although the artillery bombardments would continue sporadically for decades afterward, the Chinese Communists have never again challenged the government of the Republic of China on Taiwan over the offshore islands.[55]

BLOODY BORDERS

Because of its peace-loving rhetoric, the People's Republic of China has largely avoided the reputation for bellicosity that it deserves for its history of aggression against peoples on its periphery. In the first few decades of its existence, the PRC intervened in Korea, assaulted and absorbed Tibet, supported guerilla movements throughout Southeast Asia, attacked India, fomented an insurrection in Indonesia, provoked border clashes with the Soviet Union, and instigated repeated crises vis-à-vis Taiwan. The latest incarnation of Chinese hegemony was behaving very much according to type.

When an opportunity arose to send out China's legions, Mao and his successors generally did not hesitate—especially if the crises involved a former tributary state, which is to say almost all of the countries with which China has a common border. Although the PRC is not as well known for its militarism as the Islamic states, it has far more often resorted to violence in settling international disputes. Up to 1987, China had employed violence in fully 76.9 percent of its international crises. The comparable figure for the Muslim states was 53.5 percent. China's propensity for violence is even more striking when compared with the Soviet Union (28.5 percent), the United States (17.9 percent) and the United Kingdom (11.5 percent). China, in scholar Samuel Huntington's phrase, has "bloody borders."[56]

The last two decades of the twentieth century were not as conflict-ridden as the earlier three decades of the PRC's existence, as Deng Xiaoping followed his own advice and "bided his time", concentrating on China's economic development. Nevertheless, the world saw China use force against India, Vietnam, and the Philippines during this period. And while contemporary Chinese thinkers continue to explain that China's exceptional civilization will make the PRC a peaceful and harmonious superpower, when they are probed for details it turns out that in their view even extreme violence qualifies as "peaceful" in the service of the new world order that China is so eager to establish.[57] China's history is replete with examples of how nations and peoples that were not eager to join the Sinocentric world have been "harmonized" and "pacified" until they did.

All in the name of the Great Harmony, of course.

4

THE DIMINUTIVE HEGEMON: DENG XIAOPING

"A 'new cold war,' Deng Xiaoping reportedly asserted in 1991, is under way between China and America."
—SAMUEL P. HUNTINGTON[1]

On his own terms, Mao Zedong was a failure as hegemon. Eager to restore China's lost grandeur, recover its still-alienated territories, and once again dominate the vast marches of Asia, the founder of the People's Republic of China cannot be said to have succeeded on any of those fronts. His failures were spectacular, to be sure, but they were failures nonetheless. The socialization of industry, the collectivization of agriculture, the Great Leap Forward and the Cultural Revolution, to name just a few of his incessant political campaigns, failed to lift China into the first rank of nations, or to fuel its expansion.

Mao died without achieving his goal of reconquering all of Greater China. The same Marxist-Leninist ideology and Communist organizational prowess which propelled him to victory in the Chinese Civil War paradoxically denied him the economic clout and military means necessary to rebuild the Chinese imperium. He recovered Manchuria from the Japanese and Inner Mongolia and Xinjiang from the Soviets, wrested Tibet from the Tibetans and half of Korea from the Americans, but beyond this his hegemonic ambitions were frustrated. Large parts of what Mao considered to be Chinese territory, including Taiwan, the South China Sea, Mongolia, the Russian Far East and Central Asia, remained outside of his control. As Mao complained to Henry Kissinger in 1973, "[I]n history the Soviet Union has carved out one and a half million square kilometers from China."[2]

Asia was dominated by two powers: the "socialist imperialist" Soviet Union, which held sway over the landmass to the north and west, and the "capitalist imperialist" United States and its allies, which ruled the oceans and territories to the east and south. At the time of Mao's death in 1976, China had unresolved irredentist claims in every direction of the compass: to the north and west in the Soviet Union, to the south in Pakistan, India, Nepal, Bhutan, and Sikkim, to the southeast in Myanmar (Burma), Thailand, Vietnam, Malaysia, Indonesia, Brunei, and the Philippines, and to the east in Taiwan and Japan. Mao's failure to act on these claims reflected a lack of means, not a lack of will. If China had possessed a blue water navy and a modern air force in the fifties, Mao would have tried to take Taiwan by force. If China had enjoyed the same advantage over the Soviet Union that, say, the United States enjoys over Canada, there is no doubt that Mao would have abrogated the 1860 Sino-Russian Treaty of Beijing, under the terms of which the Qing government had ceded the territory that is now known as the Russian Far East to Russia.

Mao's primal mistake, if it could be called that, was in choosing as the instrument of China's national aggrandizement an economic policy totally inadequate to the task of rebuilding a hegemon that could compete with twentieth-century capitalism. True, communism was the perfect vehicle for achieving half of the essential Legalist program of "enriching the state and strengthening the military" (*fu guo qiang bing*). But while it could "strengthen the military" up to a point, it could not "enrich the state." Communism enabled Mao to recruit and effectively deploy a huge standing army and police force, and to concentrate all *existing* economic resources in the hands of the state. Communism brought the Chinese heartland under his control. But the strength of Maoism, like that of its imperial predecessors, lay in reducing the people to obedience rather than in producing an abundance of goods. Communism was simply incapable of generating new wealth and technology at the rate that capitalism did; this made it difficult for a Communist nation to equip its army, however vast, with weapons sophisticated enough to challenge its capitalist adversaries.

By the end of his life, Mao was increasingly frustrated by the economic setbacks of his years in power. He chose to blame them on what he called his "lack of training in economics." But China's economic difficulties were not such that enrolling Chairman Mao in a macroeconomics course—save one taught by Milton Friedman—would have helped. And Mao surely would have had Milton Friedman shot for questioning Legalism's presupposition: that power politics deserves primacy over private economic transactions.

DENG XIAOPING AND THE "FOUR MODERNIZATIONS"

Given the remarkable economic progress that China has made in the four decades since Mao's death, it sometimes seems to foreigners that Mao's successors have completely repudiated the ideas of the Communist Party founder. Nothing could be further from the truth. That Mao's rule was mostly good (70 percent) and only partly bad (30 percent), remains Party dogma. While it is true that Maoist economics has long since been abandoned in favor of a kind of marketized Marxism, on many other issues China's political elite continues to hold opinions identical to the late chairman's. On such questions as the recovery of Taiwan or China's proper place in the world, for instance, there is no daylight between the views of Mao Zedong and his successors, first Deng Xiaoping, then Jiang Zemin, Hu Jintao, and now Xi Jinping.[3] Chairman Mao's giant portrait continues to grace Tiananmen Gate, and his memory is still revered by many. Fully 85 percent of the Chinese people still say that Mao's merits outweigh his faults, which makes him by far the most popular of history's mass murderers.[4]

Deng Xiaoping had joined the Communist Party around the same time as Mao, in the early 1920s, and for the same reasons: both believed that this newly founded organization and its governing ideology could return to China the dignity and unity it had lost to the invading imperialist powers. The tiny, taciturn general was a study in contrasts with the large, voluble Mao. He cared nothing for the trappings of office, wrote no poetry, and had no imperial pretensions, being content to wield authority from his "lowly" post as vice-premier. Yet he possessed the same steely conviction of Chinese superiority over neighboring peoples, near and distant. And he shared the view that only the complete recovery of China's lost possessions would fully vindicate China's humiliation at the hands of perceived inferiors.

If Deng and Mao agreed about end of hegemony, they clashed about the means that China would have to use to achieve it. During the fifties, when Mao sought to streamline China's socialist economy by eradicating "selfishness," his principal means were forced collectivization and endless moral exhortations. Deng, on the other hand, accepted self-interest as a fact of life. After the disastrous Great Leap Forward, he and Liu Shaoqi, the head of state, sought to stimulate productivity by offering tiny garden plots to peasants and small bonuses to workers. Deng saw these practices as helping peasants stave off starvation. Mao saw them as corrupting the "New Socialist Man" he was trying to create. And so, at the beginning of the Great Proletarian Cultural Revolution that he orchestrated in 1966, Mao ordered Deng and Liu arrested.

Deng's sudden, devastating fall from grace—a "fall of a thousand feet" as the Chinese say—could easily have been fatal. So it proved to be for Liu Shaoqi, who was tortured to death by his Red Guard captors for continuing to insist on his innocence after Mao had declared his guilt. Deng, on the other hand, readily admitted that he had made mistakes, but maintained that his "intentions" had been correct.[5] By this he meant that he had always been loyal to the Great Helmsman and to his goal of building a New China, modern and strong. He had erred in opposing Maoist means only because he had been so intent on achieving Mao's larger goals. Deng's distinction between means and ends probably saved his life, but it was more than a clever ploy. On the essential Legalist program of "enriching the state and strengthening the military," there was no daylight between Deng and Mao.

Following his rehabilitation in 1973, Deng developed with then-Premier Zhou Enlai a new campaign to modernize and strengthen China that became known as the "Four Modernizations." Zhou had first broached the idea in a 1964 speech, advocating the "comprehensive modernization of agriculture, industry, national defense, and science and technology by the end of the century." Now in early 1975 he returned to this theme, proposing in his "Report on the Work of the Government" to the National People's Congress that China undertake to modernize in these four key areas.

The Four Modernizations were, in a sense, merely a restatement of the Legalist program. Modernizing "agriculture" and "industry" enriched the state, modernizing the "national defense" strengthened the military, while modernizing "science and technology" benefited both. As a set of goals, the Four Modernizations were unobjectionable to Chairman Mao and enjoyed the enthusiastic support of the vast majority of the Chinese political elite, who were eager to see China return to its storied preeminence. As the discussion shifted to methods, however, the same differences that had long divided Deng and the Maoist radicals reemerged, this time more sharply than ever.

Deng, by now first vice-premier, began pushing for the use of material incentives, for more academic specialization, and for the import of foreign technology. The radicals, who considered such policies anathema, began maligning Deng as the "bourgeois within the communist party" and claiming that he was bent upon a restoration of capitalism in China. The last straw for the radicals came when Deng and his allies drafted a series of documents on modernization, industrialization, and the development of science and technology. In 1976 they retaliated by stripping him of all his posts and once again sending him into internal exile.[6]

Mao's death later that year saved Deng for a second time. The Maoist radicals, bereft of their champion, were arrested, stigmatized as the Gang of Four, and imprisoned. Deng returned in triumph to the capital. The Chinese people, their economy threadbare and their morale exhausted by the disastrous years of the Cultural Revolution, welcomed him with open arms, pleased by the prospect he offered of an end to brutal political campaigns and the promise of a better material life. But the Chinese elite, Deng included, had fundamentally different aspirations. Beijing's phrasemakers called the Four Modernizations program "The New Long March," and looked forward with confidence (and prescience as well) to the year 2000, when China would have arrived at a state of relative modernity and become a military and economic power the world would have to reckon with.

A Legalist program to strengthen China and allow it to resume regional hegemony had carried the day. Under Deng's guiding hand, the egalitarian ethos of Maoism was abandoned in favor of market incentives, while state planning entered into an uneasy coexistence with the organized chaos of the free market. The agricultural communes were dissolved in favor of family farms, and privately owned businesses sprang up all over the country. China opened up to the West, which proved more than willing to enter into joint ventures with Chinese firms, transfer the technology needed to set up new production lines, and buy container loads of the cheap goods that underpaid Chinese workers churned out. Deng, who had a knack for aphorisms, urged his skittish compatriots to go into business for themselves by saying, "It doesn't matter if the cat is white or black; if it catches mice, it's a good cat."

This greater economic openness was never an end in itself—though it was seen as such by many foreign observers and some Chinese—but merely the means to an end: a wealthy and powerful Chinese state. Deng gambled that temporarily weakening the state by relaxing its stranglehold over the economy would strengthen it over the long run through economic growth—a wager that he arguably won, since the Chinese economy has been expanding at a double-digit clip for most of the past thirty-five years.

Deng is well known for saying, "To get rich is glorious." He might well have added, *sotto voce*, "To strengthen the state is divine." Though it no longer plans the economy down to the last ounce of steel, the Chinese state effectively controls vastly more resources today than it did in 1979. If Deng's Four Modernizations were really the Legalist goal in another guise, his much-vaunted openness to the West was merely a ploy to enlist foreigners to provide the means to achieve these hegemonic ends. Both were highly successful.

THE "FOUR ABSOLUTES"

Although he was portrayed in the West as a "pragmatic reformer," Deng was actually a born Legalist—a life-long member of the Chinese Communist Party who was just as firmly committed to the continuation of the Communist dynasty founded by Mao as Mao himself. So it was that, in addition to his Four Modernizations, Deng also let it be known that there were Four Absolutes: (1) the dictatorship of the proletariat, (2) the leadership of the Communist Party, (3) Marxism-Leninism–Mao Zedong Thought, and (4) the socialist road. Deng was saying that the Chinese people should not imagine that the economic reforms on which he had embarked would lead to political liberalization. The Chinese

Communist party-state would continue to maintain its monopoly on political power, impose an official ideology, and firmly control its subjects, much as China's ancient Legalists had taught.

Deng Xiaoping's commitment to the Four Absolutes was tested at Tiananmen Square some eleven years later. For seven weeks in the spring of 1989, the Chinese people put on a spectacular show of defiance against the regime and its aging leader. By the end of May, a million or more people were surging through the streets of Beijing in protest of corruption, bureaucracy, and dictatorship. Deng did not waver. One might have thought that the experience of the Cultural Revolution would have softened this one-time "Capitalist Roader." Not only had he been imprisoned and tortured by Red Guards, but his family members had as well: his son Deng Pufang had been thrown out of a three-story window by his captors, broken his back in the fall, and been paralyzed from the waist down as a result. Deng spent the rest of his days nursing his wheelchair-bound son, but even this was not enough to turn him against the idea that the Party should rule with an iron fist. He answered the peaceful, nonviolent Tiananmen protests with deadly force, telling his generals to put an end to the demonstrations even if this meant, as he put it, "spilling a little blood." On the night of June 4, as the West watched in horror, the People's Liberation Army opened fire on unarmed demonstrators with automatic weapons and rolled over them with tanks and armored personnel carriers. By morning the dictatorship of the proletariat was once again firmly in control.

For the Deng-led leadership, the killing of thousands of demonstrators was no accidental mishap. The ruling elite got exactly what it wanted from the cold-blooded killing: the renewed submission of the Chinese people to its rule and the perpetuation of its monopoly on power. When Secretary of State James A. Baker III, meeting with then-Premier Li Peng, characterized Tiananmen as a "tragedy," Li would have none of it. "The actions in Tiananmen Square were a good thing," he retorted. "We do not regard them as a tragedy."[7]

The paradox of Deng Xiaoping still puzzles many in the West. How could the chief architect of China's market reforms also be the master butcher of Tiananmen? To resolve this riddle they imagine that Deng was afflicted with a kind of schizophrenia that made him part pragmatic liberal and part orthodox socialist revolutionary. They attribute the twists and turns of the reform process, with its alternating phases of liberal relaxation and conservative retrenchment, to Deng's supposed ambivalence as he was driven first by one set of impulses, then by another.[8]

But Deng did not suffer from the political equivalent of bipolar disorder. It is just that debates over economic policy are conducted with the Communist Party leadership in a fundamentally different fashion from debates over politics. The economic debate revolves about the *means* for achieving power; the political debate is over the *ends* that power is devoted to achieving. One can be "pragmatic," even "liberal" when discussing economic policy while remaining "orthodox" and "conservative" when discussing politics. The economic debate is relatively open to participation and tolerant of diverging views; the political debate is closed to all but the top leaders, and it is a dangerous game even for them.

Disagreeing with the leadership on, say, the privatization of state-owned enterprises is not a career-ending move; an official can always argue, as Deng had with his Red Guard captors during the Cultural Revolution, that his intentions are good—essentially, that his proposed policies will "enrich the state and strengthen the military." Disagreeing with the leadership on when to enforce the Four Absolutes or to assert Chinese hegemony, however, can be politically fatal. So it was for two of Deng's chosen successors, Hu Yaobang and Zhao Ziyang, both of whom he cashiered for such political incorrectness before settling upon a third, Jiang Zemin. Jiang survived in power because he demonstrated a Deng-like grasp of the threat posed by political reform as opposed to the economic variety. Zhao, who did not, spent the last decades of his life under house arrest.[9]

Zhao Ziyang was the Chairman of the Chinese Communist Party in 1989 when the student protesters occupied Tiananmen Square. He sympathized with their complaints and urged his fellow Politburo members to enter into a dialogue with them. He was overruled by Deng, who came out of semi-retirement to demand a declaration of martial law, which he got on May 20. When Zhao refused to be a party to this decision, he was sidelined and placed under house arrest. Charged with "supporting turmoil and splitting the Party," Zhao was officially dismissed from his position as chairman five weeks later, at the Fourth Plenum of the 13th Central Committee. In the meantime, Deng had ordered in the army, which began butchering the peaceful protesters in the streets. As for Zhao, he spent the remainder of his life under guard at his modest home near Beijing, passing away in 2005.

Unbeknownst to his captors, however, he left behind an autobiography. Entitled *Prisoner of the State: The Secret Journal of Premier Zhao Ziyang,* it was published in 2009 and became an overnight sensation.[10] In its 306 pages Deng appears as a kind of Mafia don: the Godfather in a Mao jacket. Other leaders jockey for access to him. They use his words to attack one another. Above all, they dare not contradict him lest they suffer Zhao's fate. From the outside looking in, Zhao was able to see clearly that the PRC was being ruled by "a tightly-knit interest group...in which the political elite, the economic elite, and the intellectual elite are fused. This power elite blocks China's further reform and steers the nation's policies toward service of itself."[11]

In Zhao's book this Communist royalty—the two dozen or so Communist leaders at the very top of the party-state—appear oddly out of touch with the commoners they rule. This is perhaps not surprising given that, as Kerry Brown has noted, these mandarins "move about society in a sort of well-guarded corridor, their visits to inspect places minutely choreographed."[12]

Zhao's years under house arrest brought him in contact with ordinary people and gave him much time for reading and reflection. The former chairman of the Chinese Communist Party eventually came to praise Western parliamentary democracy, stating "it is the only way China can solve its problems of corruption and a growing gap between the rich and poor."[13] Zhao did not mean that he envisaged an immediate end to one-party rule, however. Rather he argued—much as Sun Yat-sen, the founder of the Nationalist Party, had argued a century before—that a long period of political tutelage was necessary. This meant that, even if democracy was the best form of government for China, it still required that the Chinese Communist Party maintain its leading position "for a very long time."

The rise and fall of Zhao Ziyang should serve as a cautionary tale to those who imagine that a "democratic reformer" will one day emerge from China's political system. Such a scenario seems extremely unlikely. After all, the upper echelons of the party-state are the domain of aspiring hegemons, not a hotbed of secret reformers. Even modest steps in the direction of a more open political system would be met with fierce resistance from the entrenched party-state elite. Zhao was sidelined not for proposing devolving power to elected assemblies, but for merely suggesting that dialogue, rather than brute force, was the way to handle the Tiananmen demonstrators. Zhao did not reach his later, more heretical views about the merits of parliamentary democracy until he had been ostracized and effectively imprisoned for a decade or more.

Zhao's democratic views do not seem to have had have a wider impact. Upon his death China's top leaders formed an "Emergency Response Leadership Small Group" and declared "a period of extreme sensitivity." The People's Armed Police were put on special alert, and the Ministry of Railways was ordered to screen travelers heading for

Beijing.[14] They did not want China's democracy activists to seize upon the occasion of Zhao's death to launch another round of demonstrations. In the event, none occurred.

THE DRAGON SWALLOWS A PEARL

Hong Kong and Taiwan were at the top of Deng's hit list. He was a bulldog during the 1982 negotiations with Prime Minister Margaret Thatcher over the future of the British Crown Colony of Hong Kong, known as the "Pearl of the Orient." Thatcher originally insisted on the continuing validity of the treaties under which the Qing dynasty had permanently ceded Kowloon and Hong Kong to the British crown and sought to renegotiate the lease on the New Territories, set to expire on June 30, 1997. Deng insisted that the British were only in Hong Kong on Chinese sufferance, and that China could and would resume sovereignty over the entire colony whenever it so chose. In a September 30 press release the New China News Agency said that "the unequal treaties" were "illegal, and therefore null and void." The Communist Chinese government would not shirk its "sacred mission" to recover Hong Kong and thus right the wrong done by British imperialism against China a century before.[15]

In the end, it was the Iron Lady who caved. Once she accepted the Chinese position that the British were in Hong Kong illegally, only the details of the transfer of power remained to be negotiated.

Deng, who up to this point had been opaque about the character of the coming Communist Chinese rule in Hong Kong, dropped a series of bombshells on June 22, 1984. Dashing hopes of a "three-legged stool," he declared that Hong Kong would have no separate voice in the negotiations. The interests of the ethnic Chinese residents of Hong Kong would be represented by the Communist Chinese government, not by the British or the people's own representatives. Then he revealed that the People's Liberation Army would be stationed in Hong Kong after 1997. When reminded by Hong Kong reporters of earlier promises that the PLA would be kept out of Hong Kong, he barked "bullshit" and dared them to "now go and print it."[16] On June 30, 1997, when Hong Kong reverted to Chinese rule, the People's Liberation Army did indeed march in.

Deng wanted to assert political control over his prize, but he also respected the economic power that Hong Kong would lend to his modernization efforts. To preserve Hong Kong's "capitalist system and lifestyle," he originated the idea of "one country, two systems." Hong Kong's successful reunification under this formula, he reasoned, might ultimately also entice Taiwan back into China's grip. Yet he placed clear limits on Hong Kong's "second system." Deng reserved to the "Chinese People's Government" the right to appoint Hong Kong's chief executive and senior officials, and later he vetoed efforts (admittedly feeble) by British governors to move in the direction of self-rule.

Beijing-appointed governors have gradually assumed more and more control over a city once known for its laissez-faire ways. Hong Kong's freewheeling press has been tamed in subtle ways. While there is still theoretically freedom of the press in Hong Kong, the major dailies are now owned by tycoons friendly to Beijing, and journalists critical of CCP rule have been threatened, intimidated, and fired. The Hong Kong Journalists Association (HKJA) reported in July 2014 that the preceding year had been the "darkest for press freedom" in several decades.[17]

Direct elections for the governor of Hong Kong were slated to begin in 2017, according to a timetable laid down by the last British Governor, Chris Patton, and agreed to by Beijing. Surprising no one, the Chinese party-state reneged on its promise. On August 31, 2014, the National People's Congress declared that Hong Kong's "Chief Executive shall be a person who loves the country" and that the people of Hong Kong would only be allowed to vote for candidates pre-approved by Beijing.[18] The hegemon, in other words, was not about to let the Pearl of the Orient enjoy democratic self-governance, regardless of past promises or the wishes of the people of Hong Kong.

A "White Paper" published by the Chinese State Council in 2014 goes even further, implicitly calling into question the "one country, two systems" formula. It stresses that "the high degree of autonomy" promised in the 1997 Accord has strict limits, and that Beijing will be the ultimate arbiter of where those limits lie.[19] The "power to run local affairs" granted to Hong Kong exists, it says, only insofar "as authorized by the central leadership." The White Paper even calls into question the continuation of the rule of law—a central promise of the Accord was that the colony's existing legal system was to be left in place—by suggesting that the courts in Hong Kong must "take into account the needs of China" in their decisions.

The people of Hong Kong have little recourse against this betrayal of their democratic aspirations, other than to hold largely futile protests. And for the most part, the world has been intimidated by the hegemon into averting its eyes from their fate. But despite its iron-fisted control of the situation, the Chinese party-state is still subject to fits of irrational paranoia over the mere possibility that the democratic disease might undermine its absolute authority. What else is one to make of the Chinese official who stridently warned "external force[s]" not to use Hong Kong "as a bridgehead to subvert and infiltrate the mainland"?[20] The suggestion would be risible, if the reality of the mainland's "infiltration and subversion" of Hong Kong were not so painfully evident.

Deng originally thought to use the "one country, two systems" formula to entice Taiwan back into the embrace of the motherland as well, but the Taiwanese weren't buying. In the years since, seeing the freedoms of Hong Kong gradually eroded away under that same formula, their skepticism has only deepened. Although the formula remains the official policy of the PRC vis-à-vis Taiwan, even Beijing has stopped trying to promote it.

While the gradual eclipse of freedom in Hong Kong has not gone unobserved in Taiwan, I am afraid that the rest of the world has missed its larger significance: *the hegemon simply does not feel bound by the normal rules that govern international relations*. If China can repudiate the treaties by which Hong Kong and Kowloon were ceded in perpetuity to Great Britain on the grounds that they were signed when China was relatively weak and the treaties were therefore "unequal," then it can repudiate any international agreement at any time on the same grounds. And in fact it is backing away from its agreement of only twenty years ago with Great Britain to allow the direct election of Hong Kong leaders. As China grows stronger, we may expect that it will come to regard all the international agreements that it signed in years' past—when it was relatively weaker—to be "unequal" in precisely this sense, and summarily declare them null and void.

There was a time in Chinese history when breaking one's word was considered to be dishonorable. At the beginning of the Warring States period, for instance, the nobility still practiced honor in battle. Duke Xiang of the State of Song (died 637 B.C.), for example, is remembered for not taking the forces of Chu by surprise as he came upon them crossing a river. Instead, he ordered his army to wait until Chu had formed up into ranks. He is feted by Confucian scholars for this gentlemanly behavior, even though he was defeated and grievously wounded in the battle that followed. Later Legalists, including the present rulers of China, have had no use for such niceties. Mao Zedong himself once acerbically remarked, "We are not Duke Xiang of Song and have no use for his idiotic virtue and morality."[21]

WAR WITH VIETNAM

Deng willingly accepted the Chinese imperial "burden" of overseeing the "less-cultured" peoples living on China's periphery. When, for instance, tens of thousands of ethnic Chinese fled Vietnam for their ancestral land in the late seventies, tales of their brutal persecution by the Vietnamese regime were widely circulated in China by the state-run media, angering officials and ordinary folk alike. Following Vietnam's invasion of Cambodia, a Chinese ally, in the autumn of 1978, Deng convened a meeting of the Military Affairs Commission (MAC) to discuss this new insult. He proposed that the pro-Soviet Vietnamese leadership be taught a lesson, and the members of the MAC wholeheartedly concurred. Deng telegraphed his intentions during his post-normalization goodwill visit to the United States in late January 1979.

And no sooner had he returned to Beijing than a Chinese expeditionary force numbering 330,000 men poured across the border. The Chinese—who with their typical euphemistic flair termed their invasion a "self-defensive counterattack"—expected to inflict a quick, decisive defeat on the Vietnamese army. Instead, the PLA was bloodied by 150,000 well-armed and battle-tested Vietnamese defenders. By the time Deng declared victory and moved to withdraw, 26,000 PLA soldiers had been killed and another 37,000 had been wounded.[22]

The Chinese leadership was privately unhappy with the way the campaign had been prosecuted. Vietnam "was only hurt a little" in its war with China, Politburo member Chen Yun complained. "We didn't break their fingers, but merely hurt them. In some respects, we actually helped them." MAC vice-chairman Nie Rongzhen was said to have called the tactics employed against Vietnam "unsatisfactory."[23]

Still, the PRC had reason enough to declare victory. The invading force had driven far enough into Vietnam to capture four county seats. Even more important, after the conflict Hanoi seemed to ease its persecution of its Chinese minority, and the stream of refugees fleeing northward died down to a trickle. And if Vietnam had not been taught a lesson, China's other neighbors had. Two lessons, actually. The first was that if you seriously mistreated your Chinese minority, the PRC would intervene, perhaps militarily. The second was that if you attacked a Chinese tributary state, there was a good chance that China would attack you in turn.

PLAYING THE AMERICA CARD

Deng knew that China's border clashes with the Soviet Union, in combination with a perception that the Soviets were winning the Cold War against the Americans, had led Zhou Enlai to attempt to redress the growing imbalance of power. With Mao's blessing, Zhou had thrown China's weight to the perceived weaker side, the United States. That China and the United States lacked common values and institutions and, in the years before the U.S.-China trade assumed significant dimensions, common economic interests did not matter. As Henry Kissinger remarked, with Zhou, "Only one principle was inviolate. No nation would be permitted to be preeminent."[24]

But Kissinger was imposing his own Eurocentric worldview on Zhou Enlai's motives. What Kissinger took as Zhou's long-term commitment to European-style balance of power politics was actually only a temporary expedient for China's premier. Kissinger should have written, *With Zhou, only the Sinocentric principle was inviolate. No other nation would be permitted to be preeminent until China itself was able to reassume its rightful role as hegemon.*" Kissinger, though, was blind to the desire for hegemony that animated Zhou and the rest of the Communist elite—and still animates them down to the present day.

China was drawn into a *rapprochement* with the United States solely out of fear of growing Soviet might, a fear that Kissinger rather clumsily did everything in his power to exaggerate. But as the years passed with no further border clashes between Chinese and Soviet troops, Deng became increasingly suspicious of Kissinger's overwrought claims about the Soviet military threat to China and uncertain about the notion that the world's geopolitical center was actually shifting in the direction of the USSR. We don't pay much attention to the Soviet threat, he told Kissinger when the latter visited China in November 1974. He went on to say that "the Soviet military strength in the East is not just directed against China. It is also directed against Japan and your Seventh Fleet, your air and naval forces." Deng's increasing and ever more bluntly expressed reluctance to go along with the idea that the Soviets posed a clear and present danger to China so irritated Kissinger that he began privately referring to Deng as "a nasty little man."[25]

Deng also had begun to look askance at U.S. involvement in crises around the world. "The U.S. is always in the forefront," he complained to Kissinger during this same visit, pointing to Cyprus and the Middle East as examples. He went on to draw a parallel between U.S. intervention in these crises "and the Indochina issue and the Korean issue too." Kissinger attempted to bring the conversation back to the Soviet threat, suggesting to Deng that in "firing cannons [at the United States]" he "should not hit [his] own fortifications." "They haven't," Deng replied tersely, in effect dismissing any suggestion of a common defense against the USSR.[26]

The following autumn, when Kissinger was next in China, Deng went even further. "We have always believed that we should rely on our independent strength to deal with the Soviet Union," he told Kissinger. "…China fears nothing under heaven or on earth. China will not ask favors from anyone…. We rely on millet plus rifles to deal with all problems internationally and locally, including the problems in the East."[27]

An irritated Kissinger reported to President Ford that U.S.-China relations had taken a turn for the worse because of the Chinese leadership's "insolent behavior and self-righteous lack of responsiveness."[28] But Kissinger's expectation of a Sino-American entente, which had led him to make preemptive concessions on Taiwan and other issues, was overblown from the beginning.[29] It seems unlikely that Deng and the Chinese leadership, mindful of past conflicts with America and anticipating a future of Chinese hegemony, had ever intended anything more than a temporary accommodation. Even Deng's Four Modernizations policy, which unlocked China's voracious appetite for foreign trade, technology, and capital and began in the late seventies to generate common economic interests, did not move the two countries any closer to political compatibility.

In fact, just the opposite seemed to occur. By the 1980s, increasingly confident in China's growing economic strength, Deng was truculently informing every foreign visitor he saw, whether from Communist or capitalist countries, that no one was entitled to tell China what to do.[30] Without specifying, he left no doubt that he was talking about the United States.

As the military build-up under President Reagan eclipsed the might of the former Soviet Union, Deng began actively working to improve relations between China and the USSR. It was largely on Deng's initiative that Gorbachev visited Beijing in May 1989.

"A NEW COLD WAR WITH THE UNITED STATES"

When the Soviet Union collapsed, Americans reacted with euphoria, and expected China to do the same. But the steely-eyed heirs to a two-thousand-year tradition of hegemony took a far less sanguine view of the new world situation. To the surprise and consternation of many China hands, Deng Xiaoping not only dissolved his country's *de facto* alliance with the United States, but went even further, declaring in September 1991 that "a new Cold War" between China and the sole remaining superpower would now ensue.

Some China watchers viewed Deng's hostile utterance as nothing more than a fit of verbal pique over American criticism of the Tiananmen massacre; a blip, as one put it to me, on the rhetorical radar screen. But the ensuing years have proven it to be revelatory of a far more deep-seated antagonism.

The Chinese leadership is apparently prone to wild fears of American omnipotence and a deep-seated desire to replace us as the presumed hegemon. That we have a more modest view of our role in the world—a mere superpower being something less than an all-powerful hegemon— is discounted in Chinese calculations. Had we understood this, we would have anticipated that Deng and his colleagues would immediately begin opposing American primacy once it became evident that we had won the "old Cold War" *No nation will be permitted to be preeminent*, one can almost hear China's one-time Paramount Leader saying to his colleagues, *unless of course that nation is China.*[31]

Notwithstanding Deng's private attacks on the United States, in public he was largely content to make nice to the world's only superpower. This was in part because he was distracted by internal unrest, in part because China was too weak—militarily and economically—to risk an open clash with the United States. Deng spent his energies keeping the Tibetans, the Uyghurs, and the Chinese people themselves in check. He did essay the recovery of Hong Kong, and he ordered the chastening of Vietnam, but it should be noted that neither of these efforts brought him into direct conflict with the United States. Deng was content to follow his own advice and "bide his time and hide his capabilities." The same would not prove true of his successor, Jiang Zemin.

The hegemon was about to show its claws.

5

HEGEMONY UNDER JIANG ZEMIN, GENERAL SECRETARY OF THE CHINESE COMMUNIST PARTY, 1989-2002

"We must prepare well for a military struggle"
against the "neo-imperialists."
—JIANG ZEMIN[1]

Deng was hard on his anointed successors, chiefly because he saw them as being too soft on democracy and demonstrators. He axed Hu Yaobang in 1986 after a spate of demonstrations wracked Shanghai and other cities. And as we have seen Zhao Ziyang fell from grace in 1989 as the Tiananmen demonstrations paralyzed the city of Beijing. His next choice, Jiang Zemin, had a more authoritarian bent. Jiang seconded Deng's decision to declare martial law at the time of Tiananmen, agreeing with the Paramount Leader that it was necessary to "spill a little blood" to quell the uprising. For six years thereafter he stood quietly, patiently in Deng's shadow, awaiting his chance. He echoed Deng's speeches, undertook no new policy initiatives, and avoided making mistakes.

Finally, in mid-1995, Deng was struck down by illness. At long last, Jiang was free to act without fear of removal. His remaining colleagues, men like Zhu Rongji, Li Ruihuan, Li Peng, and former National People's Congress chairman Qiao Shi, were roughly his equals in age and seniority. They were in no position to seriously contest his leadership. Instead, like hegemons throughout history, it was Jiang who went on the offensive, working frantically to consolidate his power. He deftly forced Qiao Shi into an early retirement and assumed the post of Chairman of the Central Military Commission—and thus control over the PLA's guns. He appointed people who were personally loyal to him—they came to be called the "Shanghai faction"—to key positions in the military, party and government, men like Guo Boxiong and Xu Caihou, both of whom later became vice chairmen of the Central Military Commission.

Throughout the nineties, thee economic reforms Deng had initiated continued to produce double-digit economic growth, and the sector of the economy outside of direct state control grew ever larger. Internet use spread rapidly, Marxist-Leninist-Maoist thought was moribund, and there was little talk of the Four Absolutes in the state-controlled press. Yet the more China changed, the more it remained the same.

If Deng had governed China from the shadows, Jiang wanted to leave no doubt who occupied the Dragon Throne. He mimicked the Maoist imperial style and, like the Great Helmsman, had a penchant for mass movements and propaganda campaigns. The media must be controlled by "trustworthy Marxists who are loyal to the party," he frequently remarked, which meant that it should at all times show deference to the party central authorities "with Comrade Zemin at its core."[2] Jiang Zemin encouraged a cult of personality, becoming a fixture on the nightly news broadcasts, one night patting the backs of soldiers guarding Tibet, the next night handing out gifts to poor peasants in Sichuan. He frequently traveled abroad and was given to grandstanding. On a trip to

Mexico, he went swimming in the ocean off Cancun, despite the fact that the beach was closed to swimmers because of rough seas. Supported by two hefty bodyguards, he spent only enough time in the water to be photographed. A stunt all too reminiscent of Mao's highly publicized 1966 dip in the Yangtze River, it made many Chinese cringe.[3]

Jiang's growing cult of personality came complete with a padded resume. Despite an unremarkable performance as Minister of Electronics in the early 1980s, he was now said to have laid the foundations for China's hi-tech industries during this time, and to have begun work on Star Wars strategies.[4] He maneuvered to have Deng Xiaoping Thought enshrined in the party constitution, largely to bolster his own legitimacy as Deng's heir, but at the same time moved away from Deng's open-throttle economic reform, which the Jiang coterie quietly blamed for causing hyperinflation, corruption, and a growing gap between China's haves and have-nots. Jiang's solution was to emphasize "Spiritual Civilization"—a pretentious hodge-podge of Maoism, Marxism, and traditional Chinese values—and the egalitarian goal of lifting all Chinese out of poverty by the year 2000. He instructed Chinese cadres to "self-consciously resist the decadence [of Western thoughts] and counter peaceful evolution [towards democracy]."[5] Like all Chinese supremos, he imagined, or at least wanted others to believe, that his pronouncements constituted a major advance in political philosophy, and so grandly dubbed them "Jiang Zemin Theory." In fact, the goals of the Spiritual Civilization campaign followed a pattern familiar from late-Imperial China onward, stressing the superiority of Chinese culture, broadly defined, while advocating that only selected Western scientific and industrial "techniques" be adopted.[6]

For all the differences in style and substance between Jiang and Deng, the two men shared a determination to realize the Legalist dream of a "prosperous country and strong military." If anything, Jiang was even more convinced than Deng that these could be attained without taking the "Western" road of democratization and respect for human rights. Instead of encouraging free and open debate, which is the soul of science, he was more interested in improving the "technological quality" of the Chinese race. Jiang often quoted Deng's 1986 remark that "Our national power will be augmented immensely through reform, modern science and technology, and putting emphasis on politics." He highlighted a Dengist codicil that singles out "science and technology" as the "primary productive force."[7]

Jiang did not hesitate to use the Chinese party-state's vast coercive power. He had cut his teeth on Tiananmen and had little compunction about using deadly force to meet even modest challenges to his power. He personally ordered the vicious persecution of the Falungong, the Buddhist sect whose leaders made the mistake of holding a peaceful demonstration outside of Zhongnanhai on April 25, 1999. Hundreds of thousands of Falungong "practitioners," as they call themselves, were arrested over the ensuing years, and the number of those who died in police custody as a result of torture, mistreatment, *and the harvesting of their organs,* is said to be in the thousands.

Crackdowns on dissent precede any visit by major foreign dignitaries, and President Bill Clinton's 1998 visit to China was no exception. But this time the crackdown did not end with Clinton's departure, but intensified as the years passed. Jiang's justification for the continuing crackdown, articulated in a December 1998 speech, was the need to maintain "social stability," a frequently used euphemism for the government's iron-fisted control of society. Sounding a lot like Mao, Jiang said, "Whenever any element that undermines stability raises its head, it must be resolutely cut off."

Those in charge of Jiang's *yanda* ("strike-hard") anti-crime campaign apparently took his admonitions seriously. Party documents reveal that more than sixty thousand alleged criminals were executed in the four-year period from 1998 to 2001, a staggering figure which, as Andrew Nathan and Bruce Gilley have noted, was "far higher...than even the highest Western estimates."[8] Included in this number are

Chinese Christians, Tibetan Buddhists, Turkish Muslims, and political dissidents of all stripes, groups that were targeted on the express orders of Jiang's security chief, Luo Gan.

Because of Deng's reforms, which continued under Jiang, by the end of the millennium China had transformed itself from an isolated, largely agrarian state into an economic giant and a major military power. Despite twenty years of quasi-capitalist reform, however, the "people's proletarian dictatorship" remained unchanged. (Not that very many people, even within the ranks of the Party, subscribed any longer to the Communist myth that the state is temporarily exercising power temporarily on behalf of the masses and will ultimately "wither away," or that the Party is the "vanguard of the proletariat.") So what was to be done about the new class of "capitalists" that the reform had created in this supposedly "classless" society? How did this new economic elite—neither workers, nor peasants nor, certainly, communists—fit into the equation?

The answer Jiang Zemin offered to this question was nothing short of communist heresy. In 2000, Jiang gave a series of speeches announcing a controversial dogma he called the "Three Represents." The Party, claimed Jiang, has consistently represented three factors: (1) "the development of China's advanced productive forces," (2) "the development of China's advanced culture," and (3) "the fundamental interests of the overwhelming majority of the Chinese people," in that order. It sounded a lot like the Soviet concept of the "state of the whole people," which the Chinese Communist Party had attacked as "revisionism" at the time of the Sino-Soviet split.

But Jiang went even further. In a speech on the Party's eightieth anniversary on July 1, 2001, he told the assembled CCP elite that they should begin actively recruiting "outstanding elements" of society, including *entrepreneurs and other members of the new economic elite,* into the Party's ranks.[9] The speech sent a shock wave through the ranks of old-line cadres. Here was the secretary-general of the Chinese Communist Party proclaiming that that the "greedy capitalists" they had once despised and persecuted—and even now merely tolerated as a source of side income—could become Party members in good standing. To them, it seemed as if Jiang was formally rejecting a fundamental principle of communism by sharing power with the "black classes": intellectuals and capitalists.

To quell the rising chorus of dissent, Jiang maintained that the "Three Represents" had *always* been Party policy, and that the induction of economic and intellectual elites was a necessary adaptation of classic Marxism-Leninism-Maoism to modern Chinese realities. In fact, this was a down-the-memory-hole moment, since the "Three Represents" changed everything. The CCP had never been the broad-based party of the Chinese "masses" that it claimed to be, of course, but a kind of new mandarinate, interested first and foremost in protecting its own prerogatives. Now, thanks to Jiang, it would become a kind of exclusive club that catered not only to China's political elites but to its *nouveau riche* and tech-savvy intellectuals as well. Jiang might as well have formally renounced communism in favor of, say, a new identity as "national socialists" (or Nazis for short)—since that was what the Party would now come to resemble.

While the official ideology of communism was in headlong retreat, this did not constitute a fundamental threat to the current array of power holders. Because communism was always just an updated version of Chinese autocracy, its pending death (if it is not already dead) will leave these autocratic traditions intact. The traditional pattern of state-society relations will probably continue, even if the legitimating ideology, sagging under the weight of years, is getting a face-lift—or an entirely new face.

JIANG SEEKS TO ASSERT REGIONAL HEGEMONY

Looking abroad, Jiang was very vocal about what might be termed the America threat, warning his Politburo colleagues in August 1995 that "Western hostile forces have not for a moment abandoned their plot to Westernize and 'divide' our country." There was more at work here than merely irritation over Radio Free Asia broadcasts and the continued separation of Taiwan.[10] In Jiang's comments were echoes of the kind of conspiratorial paranoia that leads not only to aggressive rhetoric but also to aggressive actions. Jiang believed that there were enemies prowling about, and he repeatedly cautioned the Chinese people not to "forget the lesson of history, that a weak country would be susceptible to bullying and drubbing."[11]

A strong China, on the other hand, will not hesitate to "bully" its near neighbors, as Jiang demonstrated on a visit to Hong Kong in October 2000. Tung Chee-hwa had just been installed for a second term as Hong Kong's chief executive, and a local journalist pointedly asked Jiang if Beijing had issued an "imperial order" for his reappointment. The question brought Jiang up out of his chair. Jabbing his finger at the journalist, he first issued a threat: "If your reports are not accurate enough, you will have to be held responsible." Then he fulminated that he had given no imperial order, that the Hong Kong media was "good for nothing," and that it "should not criticize me." In fact, as the journalist—and nearly everyone else in Hong Kong—knew, Jiang had backed Tung for a second term, making his "re-election" a foregone conclusion. Jiang ended his tirade by angrily shouting, "Hong Kong belongs to the government of the People's Republic of China!" thus unmistakably confirming his view of Hong Kong as an imperial possession, and of Tung Chee-hwa as a mere provincial official."[12] Jiang behaved, as Ross Terrill notes, like "an emperor addressing the lesser folk from the fringes."[13] Or, one might say, like a hegemon.

Like Mao and Deng before him, Jiang remained fundamentally hostile to the "imperialist-dominated" world and believed that armed conflict—sooner or later—was inevitable. "We must prepare well for a military struggle" against the "neo-imperialists," Jiang said in 1997.[14] The plots of the "neo-imperialists" to "split up" and "westernize" China could only be stopped by a modern and robust PLA. He was seconded by the high command, including General Chi Haotian, whom Jiang later made the vice chairman of the Central Military Commission and the highest ranking military officer in China. General Chi is known for such bellicose utterances as this one, made in December 1991: "Viewed from the changes in the world situation and hegemonic strategy of the United States to create monopolarity, war is inevitable."

Jiang's commitment to hegemony came through in multiple ways: as we shall see in more detail below, on his watch the PLA bracketed Taiwan with missiles, constructed a military base on the disputed Mischief Reef in the South China Sea, announced that the PLA Navy intended to dominate the sea lanes out to the "first island chain" (which includes Taiwan) altered the PLA Air Force's defensive posture to one of attack readiness, and developed a new nuclear-capable missile, the DF-31, able to reach the Western United States.[15] The former electronics engineer was a strong advocate of "modern, electronic, three-dimensional warfare," and presided over double-digit increases in the PLA's budget.

Given the military buildup and warlike rhetoric that marked Jiang's tenure, outside observers were surprised in early 1999 when it was reported in Hong Kong that fifty retired PLA generals had signed a "strong protest" against President Jiang Zemin's "weak" policies toward the United States, Japan, and Taiwan. Whatever else such a protest signified, it did *not* mean that Jiang was a "closet democrat," a "liberal reformer," or even a "moderate." (Despite the fuzzy logic reckoning that because the generals are "conservatives," the target of their protest must be a "liberal.") Nor did it mean that the leadership was at odds over fundamental questions such as China's long-term strategic goals. Jiang and his generals were of one mind that Taiwan should be recovered, Japan neutralized, and the United States driven from Asia. But the generals were impatient to act immediately, while Jiang wanted to wait until China was stronger.[16] One of the key strategic lessons drawn from China's Warring States period is that one must not strike at the reigning hegemon too soon.

This was a lesson that Jiang had learned the hard way during what is called the Third Taiwan Strait Crisis in 1995, which he himself had provoked by ordering missiles fired into Taiwan's offshore waters. He was furious that ROC President Lee Teng-hui, whom the PRC's state-run media had denounced as a "traitor" and a "splittist," had been allowed by Clinton to visit the United States.[17] It was clear by then that Taiwan would under no circumstances accept the same formula for reunification that had been imposed on Hong Kong. So Jiang decided it was time to take off the kid gloves. Acting in China's now familiar role as the Bully of Asia, the Chinese leader ordered his generals to fire several DF-15 missiles in the general vicinity of Taiwan, which they did in late July.[18] The DF-15 is a short-range, road-mobile, solid propellant, nuclear-capable, ballistic missile. Jiang justified his actions by echoing Mao's war-is-peace rhetoric of a quarter century before. "If we abandon the threat of force against Taiwan," Jiang told the *Asahi Shimbun* in August 1995, "then it is not possible that peaceful unification will be achieved."

On the eve of Taiwan's presidential elections in March 1996, China again went ballistic, bracketing Taiwan with DF-15 missiles that splashed down north and south of the island. The PLA went on to rehearse an invasion of the island in the neighboring province of Fujian, using amphibious-assault landings, troop-transport drills, helicopter sorties, and artillery firings. The reckless brinksmanship of the Chinese initially unnerved the Clinton administration, though Clinton eventually dispatched two carrier battle groups to Taiwan's offshore waters and sent a warning to Beijing. The people of Taiwan, however, refused to be intimidated, going to the polls on March 23 and electing Lee Teng-hui as president by a larger than expected margin.

Jiang stood down at this show of resolve, and many years would go by before he again directly challenged the United States. He seems also to have recognized—even if his generals did not—that aggressive rhetoric and saber rattling only expose one's impotence if one does not have the will and the means to back them up. He would "hide his capabilities and bide his time," as Deng had advised.

So Jiang accelerated the PRC's military buildup, and purchased from Russia several classes of weapons designed to counter U.S. Navy carrier battle groups. When Chinese Premier Li Peng visited Moscow in mid-December 1996, he contracted for the delivery of two Sovremenny-class destroyers from Russia armed with anti-ship cruise missiles. Subsequent orders for modern attack submarines (Kilo Class) and warplanes (76 Su-30MKK and 24 Su-30MK2) followed. Also, in August 1996 a Ministry of Foreign Affairs official with responsibility for arms-control issues reportedly threatened to use nuclear weapons against Taiwan if the island declared independence. China's "no first use" pledge not to use nuclear weapons did "not apply" to Taiwan, the official said.[19]

China was also extending its reach into the South China Sea, although in these early years it preferred to advance by stealth rather than by armed confrontation. For example, in 1994 it occupied Mischief Reef, which is less than a hundred miles from Palawan, the Philippines, on the pretext that it was merely building a shelter for its fishermen. In the years since, the Reef, known in the Philippines as Panganiban Reef, has been expanded into a modern PLAN naval station.

Jiang also made changes in the PLA's strategic doctrine, expanding the operational area of the PLA Navy. The Navy was told in 1997 that it "should focus on raising its offshore comprehensive combat capabilities within the first island chain, should increase nuclear and conventional deterrence and counter-attack capabilities, and should gradually develop combat capabilities for distant ocean defense."[20] The "first island chain" includes the East China Sea and the South China Sea—and Taiwan. The PLA Air Force followed suit in 1999, moving from a doctrine which emphasized defense to one in which offensive operations, especially in the maritime and aerospace theaters, have primacy. That was also the year that a new nuclear-capable missile, the DF-31, able to reach the

Western United States, was successfully tested, although the first one was not actually deployed until 2006.

The second tier of leaders was no less hegemony-minded than Jiang. Take former Premier Zhu Rongji, Jiang's second-in-command from 1998 to 2003. Here we have another Chinese leader who, at least initially, was widely regarded in the West as a "moderate." Responsible for China's economy, Zhu pushed for further economic reforms, for China's membership in the World Trade Organization, and for downsizing inefficient state-owned enterprises. Yet Zhu was no less of a hardliner than Jiang—or the hardline PLA generals, for that matter—when it came to China's place in the world. When Zhu received standing ovations from military audiences it was for emphasizing China's growing strength, not for advocating closer ties to the United States. Nor was he any less of a xenophobe than his fellow Politburo members. "The Chinese are the smartest people," Zhu has been quoted as saying, "with the highest level of intelligence."[21]

JIANG'S REIGN CONTINUES UNDER "PUPPET" HU JINTAO

When Jiang Zemin handed off his role as General Secretary of the Chinese Communist Party to Hu Jintao in 2002, it was lauded as a peaceful transfer of power to the next generation of Chinese leaders and a sign that the succession problems that have plagued the Chinese Communist Party from the beginning were on the way to being resolved. In fact, it was no such thing. It was peaceful enough, to be sure, but it was not a transfer of power, nor did it institutionalize succession in any meaningful way.

Not only did Jiang remain the chairman of the Chinese Military Commission for the next two years, but the members of his so-called Shanghai clique would continue to occupy hundreds of key positions in the Party, military, and government for the next ten. Just as Deng had remained in effective control of the Chinese party-state until his death, so would Jiang Zemin remain the final arbiter of Chinese affairs for a decade after resigning his last formal office.

There was not much that a hamstrung Hu could do about this, even after Jiang resigned from the Central Military Commission in 2004. Jiang had formally stepped down from his last remaining official post, to be sure, but he had left in place two vice chairmen, Guo Boxiong and Xu Caihou, who were both personally loyal to him. Through them and other senior officers whose careers he had promoted, he retained effective control of the military.[22]

As far as the outside world was concerned, President Hu Jintao was firmly seated upon the Dragon Throne, dictating events and directing China's affairs. Inside elite circles, however, another voice dominated. Like the Empress Dowager Cixi who ruled China from her curtained seat behind the throne during the minority of the Emperor Tongzhi (1861–1872), so too did Jiang "rule from behind the yellow curtain."

The popular caricature of Hu Jintao as a dull functionary is unfair. It is less a reflection of his personality than a tribute to his studied pose— a kind of protective coloration that he was forced to adopt by his anomalous position. Hu surely understood better than anyone that, in comparison with his exalted title, his real rank in the CCP hierarchy was considerably further down the list. It would have been politically dangerous for Hu to begin behaving as the hegemon. Had he grown too obstreperous the actual hegemon, Jiang Zemin, might well have had him removed, just as Deng had orchestrated the removal of two of his own chosen successors. As there cannot be two suns in the sky, so there cannot be two hegemons.

Things might have turned out differently if Hu Jintao had been Jiang's own protégé, rather than Deng's. But Hu had lost his principal patron with Deng's death in 1995. Neither was he a "princeling"—the son of one of the founding fathers of the PRC—and so he did not have access to a network of family friends and allies among the top leadership. He was, as it were, totally on his own. That he had even survived the next seven years as Jiang's heir apparent is no small accomplishment given the brutally Byzantine nature of Chinese politics.

Hu served out his ten-year term as general secretary of the CCP in Jiang's shadow, apparently unable to dislodge key members of Jiang's Shanghai clique from power, or to end the rampant corruption that they were accustomed to practice. He was apparently content to continue to play the role that he had perfected during his decade as Jiang's understudy, that of a quiet and unassuming Dmitry Medvedev to Jiang Zemin's boisterous Vladimir Putin.

This is not to say that China's domestic or foreign policies would have been noticeably different if Hu *had* cleaned house or exercised real power, merely that the Communist elite continued to resemble a collection of Mafia dons, each controlling his own "territory," each promoting his own Mafiosi, and each striving to be *capo di tutti capi,* or boss of all bosses. No democrats need apply.

In Hu's case, despite his kindly appearance, there is no evidence that he had any sympathy for parliamentary democracy, student dissidents, or democratic reform. On the contrary, he seems to have been Zhao Ziyang's polar opposite. He had won the patronage of China's "Paramount Leader" precisely because of his ruthless January 1989 crackdown on unrest in Tibet in early 1989. His "bold and resolute" handling of the situation, during which, according to government figures, more than sixty pro-independence "splittists" were killed by police and PAP officers, was applauded by Deng and the other senior leaders.[23] In fact, Hu's crackdown in Tibet, which we will discuss in detail below, may well have been the model for the CCP's even more ruthless crackdown on the pro-democracy demonstrators occupying Tiananmen Square a few months later.

Hu and Jiang undoubtedly saw eye to eye on the necessity to use the Chinese state's vast coercive power. He and the other so-called "fourth generation" leaders had not only cooperated wholeheartedly in Jiang's brutal assault on the Falungong from the beginning, but also, after moving into the top leadership positions themselves, had actually intensified the campaign. While this was probably in part a matter of impressing the semi-retired "senior leaders" with their diligence, there is little doubt that Hu shared the Communist mandarinate's distain for and distrust of dissidents of any stripe.

According to the Chinese Academy of Governance, the number of protests in China doubled between 2006 and 2010, reaching a total of some hundred and eighty thousand reported "mass incidents" in the final year. These generally involved disputes with workers over unpaid wages or disputes with farmers over land seizures. The offending factory or development, if it was not wholly owned by local officials, had generally bought them off. This meant that the officials could be counted on mobilize the security forces to disperse demonstrators upset by these usurpations. Like Andrew Carnegie's Pinkertons gunning down American workers demonstrating at Homestead Mill in 1892, the Chinese police today frequently resort to deadly force when challenged. In one protest over land ownership in Guangdong province in 2005, for example, around twenty protesters were reportedly shot dead by the security forces. But what was an isolated atrocity committed by a private security force in America over a century ago is being repeated in today's China over and over again, in acts of violence carried out against Chinese citizens by the government's massive army of uniformed security forces.

There is no evidence in Hu's writings or actions that indicate that he found anything very objectionable in this iron-fisted Legalist approach. He and Premier Wen Jiabao, who took office in 2003, spoke loftily of using "scientific" means to develop the economy. But they put equal if not greater emphasis on indefinitely extending the mandate of the existing party-state. The "scientific socialism" that they spoke of was nothing new either, merely an updated version of that old oxymoron, "scientific Marxism." Throughout his tenure Hu remained painfully aware of the continued popular resistance to CCP rule, but his reaction was not to conciliate the government's critics but to crush them. He cemented the continued loyalty of the military and security services to the Party by lavishing money and attention on them.

If there was one incident in which Hu Jintao revealed himself to be an aspiring hegemon, it was in his response to the Jasmine Revolution in Tunisia. The revolutions in Tunisia and Egypt in 2011 sparked hope in the hearts of Chinese democracy and human rights activists.[24] They saw how online connectivity enabled people to overcome fear, rapidly organize, and bloodlessly—or nearly so—bring down a tyrannical regime within a few weeks. But when they attempted to emulate this model they found that the Chinese government had preempted key elements of their plan and was able to strangle their peaceful revolution in its cradle.

Tunisia, which had languished in the grip of the dictator Zinc El Abidine Ben Ali for twenty-three years, was especially instructive in illustrating for Chinese dissidents how modern means of communications could enable the mobilization of tens of thousands of people. The Jasmine Revolutionaries spread the word on social media, took to the streets, overcame fear through sheer numbers, avoided a Tiananmen-style massacre, and succeeded in overthrowing the regime and driving Ali into exile in just eighteen days.

It is not surprising that the activists in China sought to follow this same formula. Sometime in mid-February 2011—the exact date depends upon what news source you rely upon—the first call for a Jasmine Revolution for China appeared. On Saturday, February 19, the organizers released a very specific plan for the following day. The plan named thirteen gathering places, directing participants to appear at 2:00 p.m. on Sunday, February 20, at thirteen different locations in as many Chinese cities. It even outlined specific slogans for them to shout, to wit, *"We want food, we want work, we want housing, we want fairness, we want justice, start political reform, end one-party dictatorship, bring in freedom of the press, long live freedom, long live democracy."*

The regime responded quickly—so quickly, in fact, that it is clear in retrospect that contingency plans for just such an event had long been in place, dating back to at least the 2008 Olympics, and probably first devised in their most rudimentary form in the aftermath of the Tiananmen Massacre itself.

Even before the first calls for a Jasmine Revolution for China were voiced, Chinese President Hu Jintao, as the commander-in-chief of the PLA and the general secretary of the Chinese Communist Party, had issued a directive to the military to be prepared for contingencies. The directive, issued on February 10, specifically instructed Party cells within the military to study a document entitled *Regulation Governing the Works of the Party Committees in the Military,* the ostensible purpose of which is to strengthen the Party's control over the military. According to an explanatory note, "Each one of the 33 articles in the regulation centers on ensuring the absolute control of the party over the military."

In urging the military to study the regulation at that time, Hu was anticipating that the unrest in the Arab world might potentially spread to China. If circumstances required him to send in the military to put down demonstrations, he wanted his commanders ready to follow orders—whatever those might be. Was Hu concerned that some military commanders might refuse to carry out orders to fire on unarmed demonstrators, as they had initially in Beijing twenty-two years before? Was Hu concerned that the military might shift their allegiance in the event of a conflict and prove to be, as happened in Tunisia and Egypt, the most potent weapon of the opposition in overthrowing the current regime? Probably both. The document pointedly reminds the military that all its members owe their allegiance first and foremost to the Party, and then to socialism, then to the state and finally to the people. If the Party finds itself in a major confrontation with the people, the military is to support the Party at all costs, even to the point of shedding blood.

On February 19—the same day that the dissidents issued their detailed plan for peaceful demonstrations in the thirteen major Chinese cities—Hu Jintao held a meeting of top officials to combat the perceived threat of unrest. According to the official New China News Agency, the meeting included not only all nine members of the CCP's powerful Polit-buro Standing Committee but also provincial heads, ministry chiefs, and senior military officials.

Such a high-level meeting could not have been organized overnight, suggesting again the preemptive nature of the Chinese government's response to the upheavals in the Arab world and its determination to prevent this contagion from spreading to China. Hu referred to "new changes in domestic and foreign situations" and to the need for senior CCP cadres to adopt a unified response from the outset. The divisions in the top leadership that had for a time prevented the CCP from respond-ing forcefully to the Tiananmen demonstrations were to be avoided.

In his surprisingly blunt address, Hu stressed that the Chinese Com-munist Party (CCP) had to strengthen its "management of society" to stay in power. In a major departure from standard Maoist rhetoric, Hu defined the "management of society" to be "managing the people as well as serv-ing them." The Party had long insisted that it existed to "serve the people." No longer. In Hu's formulation the people were viewed not as a clientele to be served but as a problem to be "managed." The purpose of this soci-etal management, Hu went on, was to "maximize harmonious factors and minimize non-harmonious ones." Those who adhered to the Party line were to be encouraged, in other words, while those who departed from it were to be silenced.

Hu went on to outline specific ways in which the "management of society" could be strengthened. Heightened control over cyberspace, to include better monitoring and control over Internet-transmitted informa-tion and improved guidance of public opinion over the Internet, was a priority. He also called for the establishment of a national database of migrant workers and of "specific groups of people" (communist parlance for political dissidents, religious leaders, and other dangerous groups) so that they could be better "managed."

The following day—the very day, in fact, slated for the demonstrations—the Politburo member in charge of national public security weighed in.

Echoing Hu Jintao, Zhou Yongkang called on the Party not just to serve the people, but to manage the people as well, and announced specific ways in which this "management" would be carried out. First, a national database containing information on everyone in the country, with a special focus on Hu's "specific groups of people," would be set up. Second, with strong leadership from the Party, cyberspace was to be brought under strict government control, with strict enforcement of anti-sedition laws. Third, foreign nongovernmental organizations in China will be subjected to a "dual system of supervision"—which could only mean that they will be subjected to heightened scrutiny by several different Chinese government agencies. Fourth, an early warning system will be put in place to alert the authorities to social grievances, so as to allow them to defuse problems before they deteriorated into outright social unrest.

None of this was really new; it was rather a strengthening and elaboration of what had gone before. The Ministry of State Security already had extensive files on Chinese who had questioned this or that government policy. The Chinese government's monitoring and control of the Internet had been growing for years. Foreign organizations had always been viewed with suspicion, and Chinese citizens had always been monitored by Party-run social monitoring networks.

Take social-monitoring networks, for example. From the beginning of the People's Republic of China, the state has kept an eye on the masses by means of regular police patrols on the streets, mutual monitoring by peers in the workplace, and surveillance by neighborhood committees.

By the time of the 2008 Olympic Games, this three-tiered system had morphed into what China's public security minister, Meng Jianzhu, called a five-tiered social-monitoring network, which included camera surveillance in public areas, Internet surveillance, regular police patrols on the streets, mutual monitoring by peers in the workplace, and monitoring by neighborhood committees. This was not, as has sometimes been reported, an *ad hoc* system created in 2008 to ensure security during the Olympic Games and the subsequent Shanghai Expo, but an ever more technologically sophisticated elaboration of what has been a constant feature of life in the PRC from the beginning. Those who argue that China's economic reforms would lead to political liberalization need to take note.

As these policy pronouncements were being made in anticipation of the attempt to import the Jasmine Revolution to China, the Chinese authorities were already preemptively moving to suppress dissent by arresting human rights lawyers, confining university students to their campuses, banning the use of certain keywords ("democracy," "freedom") on mobile phone messages, and deploying an overwhelming police presence on the streets. The China Support Network reported that some dissidents were taken away to "black" or illegal jails, while others were placed under house arrest. According to the Hong Kong Information Center for Human Rights and Democracy, over one hundred people were detained in this way. Other dissidents were warned against attending any of the demonstrations, and questioned about their possible role in organizing them.

Internet filters were set up to block the word "jasmine." Also blocked, in Beijing at least, was the sending of multi-recipient text messages. The thirteen announced protest sites were all cordoned off by hundreds of plainclothes and uniformed police. On the day of the planned demonstrations, small crowds gathered in Beijing and Shanghai but were quickly overwhelmed and dispersed by the police. In the other cities the massive police presence seemed the only response to the Internet calls for protests.

Some foreign observers have called these moves on the part of the regime an "overreaction" to events. This is a misreading of what actually happened. The government wasn't *reacting* to events at all; it was *anticipating* them. The actions described above were all taken in advance of any major public demonstrations, and are properly characterized as a kind of preemptive suppression. The speed and thoroughness of the Chinese government's action suggests years of planning and preparation for just such a potential mass uprising, and the determination of those in power to squelch all dissent using all the manifold tools of "social management" at its disposal.

This interpretation is also supported by the speed at which the Chinese government went on the offensive, attacking websites overseas that carried information about or in any way encouraged a Chinese-style Jasmine Revolution. Online calls for a "Jasmine revolution" in China apparently first appeared at the website Boxun.com. A few days later, Boxun announced that it would no longer carry Jasmine-related information because of actions taken by the Chinese government against their server, and threats made against their staff and their families. In response, a federation of eight dissident websites announced in early March that they would carry such material. These websites in turn all experienced cyber-attacks emanating from Beijing. By March 11, three of the eight sites had been completely shut down by such cyber-attacks. The other pro-Jasmine web sites continued to experience denial-of-service attacks for the next several weeks.

It is clear that the government's response to the call for a Chinese "Jasmine revolution" in February 2011 was a continuation of an ongoing campaign to suppress all expressions of civil society, including religious and ethnic affiliations, that could conceivably—at least in the minds of conspiratorially minded senior Communist Party officials—pose a threat to the power, wealth and privileges that they enjoyed. Hu Jintao and the other neo–Red Guards who dominated the upper reaches of the Party and government, because of their Maoist "education" in deadly power politics during their formative years, turned out to be much more likely to brutally confront dissent than to compromise with it. Mao Zedong would have been proud. Jiang Zemin probably was.

TIBET AND XINJIANG REPRESSED

While the Jiang-Hu regime was vigilant in repressing dissent among the ethnic Han majority in China, it was nothing short of vicious in stamping out any hint of separatist sentiment among the ethnic minorities living in the empire's border regions. Largely out of the view of the outside world, protests in Tibet and Xinjiang continued—and were nearly always been met with deadly force.

There has always been tension between the Chinese party-state and the Tibetans and the Uyghurs, of course, ever since their lands were reabsorbed into the expanding Chinese empire after the establishment of the PRC. But economic development—and government policy—have intensified this conflict by bringing hundreds of thousands of Han Chinese into both regions. Beijing encourages the internal migration of Han Chinese into these areas, luring them there with attractive bonuses and favorable living conditions. And, not surprisingly, with this flood of outsiders has come rising rates of ethnic conflict.

As Chinese immigration into Tibet increased with the opening of a direct rail connection to Lhasa in 2006, so did the anger of the Tibetans, who see themselves in danger of becoming a minority in their own country. The Tibetan government in exile estimates that half to two-thirds of the population of the Tibetan capital is now Han Chinese, with the Tibetans increasingly ghettoized in the older, poorer sections of the city.

In 2008 their resentment boiled over. Anti-Chinese riots broke out not only in Lhasa but in numerous cities, towns, and monasteries throughout the historic Tibetan heartland. The party-state responded in typical fashion, not by offering to negotiate with the Tibetans but by brute force. A monk bravely carrying a Tibetan flag in a demonstration was shot in the head. Hundreds of other monks, along with ordinary Tibetans, were killed. In the aftermath of the demonstrations, Beijing installed a permanent police presence *inside* of the major monasteries. Stringent internal travel restrictions were put in place, placing Lhasa off limits for most Tibetans. Finally, anyone even suspected of being a dissident was subject to summary arrest and detention.

Today, the once bucolic capital of Tibet resembles an armed camp. The streets are crawling with uniformed and plainclothes security personnel. Every street corner is under security camera surveillance. Having a picture of the Dalai Lama in one's home or on one's person is a criminal offence.

The severity of the ongoing crackdown, observes Tibet scholar Warren W. Smith, suggests that China is now determined to crush Tibetan nationalism for all time. It certainly goes well beyond the level required to maintain social order. Many Tibetans no longer believe, if they ever did, in the possibility of real autonomy under China, or that China will allow more than a few remnants of Tibetan culture to survive. The hopelessness that the Tibetans feel about living in what is, in effect, an occupied country manifests itself in self-immolations. Well over a hundred Tibetan nuns and monks have burned themselves alive in recent years in a desperate attempt to raise international awareness of the plight of their ancient country and religion.[25]

There is surprisingly little sympathy for either Tibet or Tibetans among the Han Chinese. Most do not understand that Tibet is the homeland of a high and ancient civilization with its own written language, extensive literature, and unique religious culture, nor that for centuries it had a functioning government administering a defined territory. Ignoring a thousand years of history, most Chinese deny that Tibet ever enjoyed an existence as a separate nation. They even dismiss the notion that the Tibetans constitute a separate people, asserting that they are really just one more offshoot of the Yellow Emperor's seed, albeit more backward and superstitious than most.

Tibet is instead seen as an integral part of China, and if this is questioned many Chinese will react angrily. I held a post-Tiananmen human rights conference in early 1992 to which I invited several dozen well-known Chinese dissidents. All of them openly opposed the Chinese Communist Party and were strong advocates of freedom of speech, open and free elections, and respect for human rights. But I had also invited to this gathering a representative of the Dalai Lama, who in her speech called for *exactly these same principles* to be applied to Tibet. The reaction of the Chinese dissidents to her call for democracy in Tibet was nothing short of astonishing. Up jumped the assembled dissidents, shouting out that she was a traitor, a reactionary element, and that Tibet has always been a part of China. Shaken by the sudden transformation of my mild-mannered, democracy-loving friends into screaming national narcissists, I had to intervene to restore order.

Not only do nearly all Chinese assert that Tibet is an integral part of China, they view it as an essentially empty frontier territory that is—as it should be—wide open for Han settlement and resource exploitation. Such sentiments are nothing new. Chairman Mao perfectly expressed the hegemon's view of Tibet back in the early 1950s, when he said that Tibet should fulfill China's need for resources while China would fulfill Tibet's need for people. At the end of the day Mao's approach would, leave Tibet bereft of both resources and Tibetans.

When asked about the plight of Tibetans, most Chinese simply regurgitate government propaganda about how well Chinese minorities are treated. Parallels will be drawn between U.S. affirmative action programs and the special programs that the Chinese party-state has supposedly created to help the Tibetans and other minorities. For the Tibetans to complain even though they actually enjoy *more* rights and privileges than ordinary Han Chinese, just shows how "privileged" and "spoiled" they really are. (Most of the special programs being referred to in fact involve putting minority children in special boarding schools where they are taught in Chinese and discouraged from speaking their native language. Since the goal of these schools is to Sinicize their young charges as quickly and as thoroughly as possible, they resemble nothing so much as a kind of cultural "Lebensborn" program.) Han Chinese also insist that Tibetans, Manchus, and other minorities enjoy other privileges, such as exemption from the one-child policy. In this they are repeating an assertion by their government that is simply untrue. Manchus and Tibetans whom I have personally interviewed testify that they are subject to the same Planned Birth regulations as the Han Chinese.[26]

Mao's view of the utility of Xinjiang—or Eastern Turkistan, as its Turkish Uyghur inhabitants refer to it—were undoubtedly similar to his vision for Tibel. The Chinese claim that Xinjiang has belonged to the hegemon since ancient times. They point to the Han dynasty armies that, in an effort to secure the profitable Silk Road, drove the Xiongnu out of the region in 60 B.C. and set up a series of forts in what the Han then called the Xiyu, or "Western Region." For most of the succeeding two thousand years, however, this region was under the control of various Turkish khanates, not China. This is why when the Manchu dynasty conquered it in 1759 they gave it a new name, Xinjiang. Xinjiang literally means "new frontier," a name that does not suggest a restoration of Chinese rule as much as the assertion of a new claim. Be that as it may, the Chinese hegemon operates under a different and more expansive principle: once it controls a territory—however briefly its armies stay, or however lightly it actually governs—it owns it for all time.

Mao reasserted Chinese control over Xinjiang in 1949, after a Chinese plane carrying Uyghur leaders to Beijing for negotiations on local sovereignty mysteriously crashed. In the decades since, Han migrants have flooded into the region. The Uyghurs, who number around ten million, are now a minority in many parts of their traditional homeland. Like the Tibetans, the Uyghurs resent the fact that the economic benefits of development disproportionately accrue to the newcomers.

The hegemon has long used state-sanctioned mass migration to pacify newly conquered regions. But the Sinification that is happening in Xinjiang today is not just a matter of bringing in trainloads of Han Chinese, but of actively discouraging the Uyghurs from using their language or practicing their religion. The Uyghur language is marginalized in the schools and the workplace and Uyghur religious traditions are disrespected. During the holy month of Ramadan officials put pressure on teachers, students, and civil servants not to observe the ritual sunrise-to-sunset fast. Exit visas for pilgrimages to Mecca are only grudgingly granted. Veils are discouraged, mosques are under surveillance, and sweeping restrictions on congregating for religious purposes are in place.

As in Tibet, the heavy-handed actions of the Beijing regime have fueled discontent in Xinjiang, sparking a major uprising in 2009 and almost continuous unrest in the years since. Random attacks on civilians have become more common, with the violence spreading well beyond Xinjiang. There was an attempted suicide attack on Tiananmen Square in October 2013. Then in March 2014 there was a horrific attack at the Kunming railway station in which knife-wielding attackers hacked at least twenty-nine people to death. The worst violence occurred on July 28, 2014 when, according to official accounts, nearly one hundred people were killed, most of them Uyghurs.[27] Uyghur exiles say that the body count was far higher. The Chinese state calls this "terrorism," while Uyghur leaders say that it is a reaction to the extreme repression that their people are enduring and their discontent at Chinese rule. However such attacks are characterized, their most likely result is to stiffen the resolve of the Chinese party-state to crush all opposition. Indeed, this has been the standard reaction of the hegemon over the centuries when faced with resistance.

In recent years the Chinese party-state has turned up its alchemist's crucible to a white heat and is busily transmuting Uyghurs, Tibetans, and other minorities into Chinese as quickly as possible. In Xinjiang, Party authorities have banned most Muslim baby names on the grounds that they have religious significance, a move roughly equivalent to Washington forbidding Americans to name their sons after the twelve apostles.[28] The Chinese government has even begun embedding cadres in Muslim Uyghur homes during Ramadan to make sure that they neither fast nor pray during Islam's holy month.[29]

The vast majority of Han Chinese fully support these and other Draconian measures implemented by the Chinese party-state in response to the recent unrest. They already find themselves a little resentful of minorities anyway because of the "special privileges" that their government tells them that these peoples supposedly enjoy. (Most Han Chinese swallow that propaganda whole.) The prevailing opinion is that China's non-Han minorities should abandon their barbarian ways, learn Chinese, and be humbly grateful for the opportunity to become a part of the greatest civilization the world has ever known.

If you want to see what Tibet and Xinjiang will look like in a half century or so, look at modern-day Inner Mongolia or Manchuria, where the historical sequence of conquest, in-migration, and assimilation is almost complete. Mongolia, for example, was incorporated into the Qing dynasty's empire in the seventeenth century. After the collapse of the dynasty in 1911, Outer Mongolia gained its independence, retaining it in subsequent decades thanks in no small part to the machinations of the Soviet Union. Inner Mongolia, on the other hand, remained a part of China. Massive Han Chinese in-migration has over time reduced the Mongol population to a fraction of the whole. Government statistics claim that Mongols constitute 16 percent of the total, but even that may be an exaggeration. Whatever the actual percentage, it is unquestionable that ethnic Mongols have been reduced to a tiny minority in their own homeland, and that many are now culturally indistinguishable from the Han.[30]

The Manchus are even further gone. I travelled to a so-called Manchu Autonomous County in northern Hubei on one of my recent trips to China. This is a county that was ostensibly created in a Manchu-majority area by the Chinese party-state and so that the Manchus there would be free to run their own affairs. The Manchus I interviewed confirmed their Manchu heritage to me in perfect Mandarin, since neither they nor I could speak their now-dead native language. Manchu names, customs, and religious practices were likewise long dead. "We are no different from our Chinese neighbors now," one told me. "We have been mixed together for a long, long time."

No wonder the Tibetans and Uyghurs who, unlike the Mongols, lack a separate homeland to which to retreat, are nervous about their future.

TOUGH AT HOME, EVEN TOUGHER ABROAD

Despite his mild-mannered appearance, Hu Jintao turned out to be just as paranoid about U.S. intentions and xenophobic towards the rest of the world as any of the Chinese leaders who had preceded him. As early as 1999, when he was still only China's vice president and a member of the Standing Committee of the Politburo, Hu was chosen to appear on state television to denounce the NATO bombing of the Chinese Embassy in Belgrade. Sounding very much like the Red Guard schooled in anti-foreign Maoist dogma that he once was, he declared that "hostile forces in the U.S. will never give up their attempt to subjugate China."[31]

The senior leadership in Beijing, along with many ordinary Chinese, saw the inadvertent bombing of the Chinese Embassy as a deliberate attack—and a prime example of the malignant "neo-hegemony" over the rest of the world that the United States was seeking to establish. NATO's apology, which pointed out that the building had simply been mistakenly targeted, was rejected out of hand. It did not comport with China's view of the world. That view continued to be very much on display in Chinese Defense White Papers, which continued to warn that "certain big powers" were still pursuing "neo-interventionism," "neo-gunboat diplomacy" and "neo-economic colonialism" in ways that threatened "world peace and security."[32]

Each of those appellations could be accurately applied to China. What else could an objective observer conclude from China's incessant cyber-attacks, its growing arsenal of offensive weapons, its worsening human rights record, and its increasingly assertive territorial claims? China was clearly a real and growing threat to regional, and even global, stability. Beijing's assurances that it would *never seek hegemony* were, in the view of its near neighbors, merely a rhetorical smokescreen thrown up by the Bully of Asia to disguise its efforts to accomplish precisely that.[33]

From the perspective of China's leaders, concern over China's behavior was unwarranted and overblown. All China was doing was

reasserting its traditional prerogatives in Asia. China's neighbors—
South Korea, Japan, the Philippines, Vietnam, Singapore, Australia,
and so forth—should accept the fact, as one Chinese diplomat patron-
izingly remarked, that China is a "big country" and that they are
"small countries."[34]

Instead, the "small countries" of Asia turned to the United States for
protection, strengthening alliances, carrying out joint exercises and, in
places like Australia and the Philippines, granting new basing rights to
U.S. forces. It was in part in response to pleas from democratic allies in
the region such as Japan and India that President Bush in 2005 began
what came to be called the "pivot to Asia," redeploying additional naval
assets to Asia, along with 60 percent of America's submarine force.

Hu Jintao himself complained openly about the marginally increased
U.S. presence along China's periphery, reading into this natural response
to his country's warlike rhetoric and actions a plot "to keep China
down." Each new deployment or alliance continued to be interpreted as
further evidence of the existence of a strategy by the "neo-imperialists"
to contain China and hinder its rise to superpower status. Were China's
leaders blind to the fact that it is their own aggressive actions that are
provoking neighboring countries into increasing their military budgets
and seeking allies?

In the always solipsistic view of China's leaders, the former tributary
states around China's periphery should be quietly submitting to the
hegemon, not daring to increase their military budgets. They should just
relax and allow China to reclaim its birthright as the "center of the
earth," not turn to the United States and Japan for succor. The only possible reason that China's neighbors were behaving in such an untributary
fashion, they conclude, was that they must have been either bribed or
coerced into an anti-China containment plot by the omnipotent superpower.

Throughout President Hu Jintao's tenure, the Chinese party-state
saw containment everywhere. At no time did it admit that its own

aggressive actions may have been responsible. Instead, Chinese leaders continued to prattle on about never seeking hegemony. To ward off the growing perception of a "China Threat," President Hu insisted on China's *heping jueqi*, or peaceful rise. Or, as Premier Wen Jiabao sought to assure a global audience in 2004, "China's emergence will not come at the cost of any other country, will not stand in the way of any other country, nor pose a threat to any other country."[35]

Given China's recent history of aggression and its unwillingness to submit its territorial claims to international arbitration, most of its neighbors now dismiss such rhetoric as mere propaganda. As Sunzi might have said, "When pursuing hegemony, make it appear as if you are not doing so."

6

MOVE OVER, GREAT HELMSMAN, "BIG DADDY" XI IS HERE

"The Soviet Party fell apart because no one had the balls to keep it together."

—XI JINPING, *speaking to senior leaders in 2012*[1]

Elected general secretary of the Chinese Communist Party on November 15, 2012, Xi Jinping moved with startling swiftness to consolidate power. He purged Jiang Zemin's highest-ranking supporters under the guise of an anti-corruption campaign and drove his predecessor, Hu Jintao, into obscurity. He seized control of the Central Military Commission, arresting its two senior members, and placed his own long-time supporters from the Fujian Military District in charge.

If this were all Xi had done, he could be compared to Deng Xiaoping, who had the hapless Hua Guofeng removed as CCP Chairman, or Jiang Zemin, who insisted that his Politburo contemporaries retire so as to clear the field for his unfettered rule. But Xi seems to be harkening back to an earlier model of leadership. He has bent the PLA to his will by demanding personal pledges of loyalty from the generals, something that hasn't been seen in Chinese politics since the time of Chairman Mao. His personality cult already makes Jiang's pale by comparison—he is known as Big Daddy Xi to his adoring public—and several books of his speeches and sayings have already been published *a la Mao*. He has even reinstituted such Maoist practices as "self-criticism" sessions, and his quotations are blossoming on village walls.[2]

The world should take notice, since Xi Jinping is not only mimicking Mao Zedong at home, but obviously shares Mao's expansive view of China's leading role abroad. China's increasingly bellicose behavior is clearly not a result of a general or two going rogue, which would be worrisome enough, but of the entire PLA military establishment reflecting the hegemonic ambitions of its new commander-in-chief, Xi Jinping.

What has emerged from the boiling cauldron of the Communist Party's factional politics, in other words, is a creature familiar to students of Chinese history. A new Chinese hegemon—the latest in a long line of such despots—has arisen. As we will see, Xi is self-consciously modeling himself on the "first emperor" of the PRC dynasty, Mao Zedong, even wearing an unfashionable Mao suit to increase the likeness. But like all Chinese hegemons, he ultimately harkens back to China's "ancestral dragon," the brutal Qin Shihuang who first unified the Middle Kingdom. And Qin Shihuang, as we have seen, was no George Washington.

This was not supposed to happen. After the excesses of the late Chairman Mao, whose bloody career not only cost the lives of tens of millions of ordinary Chinese but, more important to the ruling class, brought about the deaths of many members of the Red aristocracy, the survivors were determined to prevent a reprise. Led by Deng Xiaoping, they attempted to forestall the rise of another capricious tyrant like Mao by dispersing power among those at the very top of the political pyramid. They declared that the responsibility for making decisions would no longer be in the hands of one man but would henceforth be shared among the nine members of the Standing Committee of the Politburo. They attempted to put further checks on the concentration of power by imposing ten-year limits on the tenure of the president and premier and by insisting that no one over the age of sixty-seven be considered for membership on the Standing Committee. They let it be known that their successors would practice collective leadership.

Outside observers applauded. Francis Fukuyama, for example, declared that "China's authoritarian system is distinct because it follows rules regarding term limits and succession." He went on to say, "Tunisia's Ben Ali, Egypt's Mubarak, or Libya's Qaddhafi, not to speak of authoritarian African leaders like Robert Mugabe or Meles Zenawi, would be much more fondly remembered by their people had they stepped down after their first ten years in office and arranged for an orderly transfer of power."[3]

But in reality these purely administrative rules agreed to by a handful of octogenerians, however good they sounded in theory, changed nothing in practice. Both Deng Xiaoping and Jiang Zemin violated the spirit of the rules by remaining in effective control of the party, government, and military—the three centers of power in China—long after they had left formal office. Deng overruled the Standing Committee in 1989, a fateful intervention that led to the Tiananmen Massacre. Jiang, as we have noted, went on to violate the letter of the rules as well, by remaining as the Chairman of the Central Military Commission (CMC) for nearly two years after "resigning" as president in 2003. Even after stepping down from the CMC, he ran the Commission through proxies for the remaining eight years of Hu Jintao's tenure.

But in his relatively short time in power, Xi Jinping has gone even further. He has not merely violated the rules put in place by his predecessors— rules that were designed to forestall the rise of another hegemon—he has changed the rules themselves. He has reduced the number of seats on the Standing Committee of the Politburo, the party's top decision-making body, from nine to seven. At the same time, Xi has added a new layer of authority at the very top in the form of new committees in charge of everything from government reform and finance to the overhaul of the armed forces and cyber-security—committees which he himself heads. For example, he created "The Central Committee's Leading Small Group for Comprehensive Deepening of Reform" and put himself in charge. Behind its clumsy sounding title lies another Xi Jinping power grab: the "Reform Group" gives the Communist Party General Secretary effective control over China's government, which would usually be the domain of Premier Li Keqiang.[4]

Xi has also restructured the Central Military Commission, redrawn the military districts, and appointed new commanders to the newly created positions. Like Mao, he is determined to create a PLA whose loyalties are not to state or party, but to Big Daddy Xi himself.[5] Xi has even taken over the domestic security portfolio—the State Security Commission—once held by the widely feared but now-imprisoned Zhou Yongkang. In making these changes, Xi has not only reduced the number of his near peers, but he has also positioned himself, through his command of the military and the security forces, to be able to threaten those who remain—a should they resist his leadership—with arrest and prosecution. The police, the secret police, and the courts all report to him.

Gary Locke, the former American Ambassador to China, notes that Xi is "at the center of everything."[6] China's new hegemon was not content to reign supreme as president of the People's Republic of China, general secretary of the Chinese Communist Party, and chairman of the Central Military Commission. He also appointed himself to head important Party committees on foreign policy, Taiwan, and the economy. Still not satisfied with his grasp on power, he created new bodies overseeing everything from the Internet and national security to government restructuring and military reform and put himself in charge. An American president has two titles—president and commander-in-chief—Xi Jinping has ten.

So quickly has Xi concentrated authority into his own hands that it now seems increasingly likely that the rule limiting his time in office to ten years will eventually go by the wayside as well. Why should he step down in five or six years' time, assuming he remains in good health? In

2022 he will only be sixty-nine years old. Moreover, in the interim he will have not only packed the Politburo with members of his faction but also elevated himself to a demigod in the eyes of the Chinese public, who will with one voice urge him to stay on. Or so they—and we—will be told by the state-run media that he controls.

The purge of sitting Politburo member Sun Zhengcai is another indication that Big Daddy Xi does not intend to go quietly into that good night once his second five-year term ends. Sun, who had earlier been picked by Jiang Zemin and Hu Jintao to one day succeed Xi, was serving as the party secretary for the city of Chongqing when he suddenly vanished on July 15, 2017.[7] Ten days later his political obituary appeared on the front page of the *People's Daily* in the form of an editorial (by an unknown "commentator") accusing Sun of a "serious violation of discipline."[8] Formal charges of corruption will invariably follow, but Sun's real crime—if you can call it that—is obviously that he was the heir apparent to a dictator who brooks no heir.

I predict that Xi will either retain his current positions, or else formally resign but continue to wield power through loyal surrogates—Chinese Dmitry Medvedevs, we might call them. One way or another the current Chinese supremo, who was born in 1953, is a good bet to continue to singlehandedly dominate party, military, and state in China for several decades to come.

This outcome would not come as a surprise to anyone who is familiar with the Chinese political system in both its ancient and modern versions. For over two millennia China has been run by a highly sophisticated and highly centralized bureaucracy, whose *raison d'etre* was always to help the hegemon manage China's millions. If the American political ideal is "government of the people, by the people, for the people," then the Chinese political ideal is "government of the people, by the bureaucracy, for the hegemon." The *Tao* of the mandarinate, one might say, is to serve as an enabler of the hegemon, who can't effectively rule China's vast population without such a cadre of intermediaries. Or to adapt a Jeffersonian metaphor, if the people are the horse, then the bureaucracy is the saddle and reins, ready for the booted and spurred hegemon to ride.

Although the purpose of the Chinese mandarinate from the beginning was to deliver power into the hands of the emperor, in imperial China there was still a creative tension between the two. This came about because the emperor and the mandarinate were selected in different ways, and from different classes. The emperor was drawn from the aristocracy, and inherited his throne. The officials who filled the ranks of the bureaucracy, on the other hand, were recruited by merit in national examinations, especially during the Tang (A.D. 618–907) and later dynasties. While this is far from constituting a separation of powers, it did set up a kind of competition of interests between the inherited wealth and power of the aristocracy, on the one hand, and the best and the brightest scions that China's landed gentry could produce, on the other. Each of these two groups served as a check upon the other, and upon the emperor himself, enabling Chinese dynasties to survive good emperors and bad. When the Wanli Emperor of the Ming dynasty became addicted to opium during the last years of his reign,[9] refusing to attend meetings or to sign official documents, the dynasty did not collapse for lack of leadership. Instead, the senior mandarins did their best to carry on the governance of China while the emperor passed a languid decade in a drug-induced stupor.

The last imperial examinations were held in 1905, six years before the fall of the Qing dynasty. With its demise died this useful tension between aristocracy and mandarinate. When the Chinese Communist Party arrived on the scene, it recruited members not by objectively administered standardized tests but rather by subjectively evaluating an applicant's class background and ideological purity. At least this was the theory. In practice the end of the imperial exams meant that politically well-connected Chinese were free to revert to their particularistic ways and promote their own. Recruitment became an exercise in *guanxi,* the ancient Chinese practice of building one's network of personal relationships. Communist Party leaders may have been virulently anti-Confucian, but they nevertheless relied upon the Sage's "five relationships" in building up their own coterie of Party followers. Leaders recruited talented followers, fathers recruited sons and nephews, husbands recruited wives and in-laws, older brothers recruited younger brothers and cousins, and friends recruited friends, classmates, and fellow townsmen.

The end result was an organization—the Chinese Communist Party—whose formal structure of governance masks a myriad of clan-like factions in which the real power resides. This enormous maze of shifting interrelationships and alliances is sometimes called "byzantine," but this does not begin to do justice to its scale or complexity. There is simply no Western equivalent, historical or modern, to the machinations of Chinese power politics within the now nearly ninety-million-member CCP.

In traditional times, being born into an aristocratic family conferred no advantage in the imperial examinations. Today, being born into the "red aristocracy"—as a son or daughter of a provincial or national leader—means automatic party membership, a path to high office, and the chance, however remote, to become *the* hegemon. This state of affairs was precisely what the imperial examination system was set up to avoid—and largely did avoid—for a thousand years.

Once it took power, the Chinese Communist Party systematically eliminated competing centers of political power and societal influence. The early years of the People's Republic saw a series of political campaigns designed to eliminate groups—landlords, entrepreneurs, intellectuals—that Mao imagined might oppose his "dictatorship of the proletariat." The sole remaining route available to the politically ambitious to achieve upward mobility was Party membership. Even today, despite China's economic progress, both hegemon and bureaucracy are drawn from the ranks of the same Leninist party. In this sense, the Chinese Communist Party is truly an "organizational emperor," since its ranks provide both the personnel to staff the military and civilian bureau-cracy, and the very person of the modern-day emperor.

More than six decades after the founding of the PRC, we are now witnessing the culmination of this predictable process. Power in China today is no longer wielded by the best and the brightest, but by the well-born and the well-connected. To Americans perpetually enraptured by the idea of progress it may come as a surprise, but *power in China today is probably less rationally allocated by talent, and more heavily concentrated by blood, than it was in imperial times.*

"Princelings," as they are called, not only dominate the upper echelons of the Party but also, with the ascension of Xi Jinping to be the general secretary of the CCP, provide the very person of the hegemon himself.[10] The end result of this inbreeding—no other word is appropriate here—is to both make tyranny at home and hegemonic behavior abroad, increasingly likely by concentrating power in the hands of the few.

Princelings rely primarily on their family's factional ties to amass wealth and advance to leadership positions in the party, military, and government. By brokering their connections into lucrative—if shady—investment deals, by peddling their influence as silent partners in some of China's biggest enterprises, and by serving as backroom "fixers" when legal, labor, or other problems arise, many have become fabulously wealthy over the course of the past few decades. A *New York Times* investigation revealed that the family of former premier Wen Jiabao, by trading on his name and connections, had managed to accumulate a fortune worth more than $2.7 *billion* during his ten years in office.[11]

Of the seven current members of the Standing Committee of the Politburo, five can be considered members of the "princeling party." [12] This means that they owe their positions in no small part to having been sired by influential parents from the founding generation of Communist revolutionaries.

- Yu Zhengsheng, the chairman of the Chinese People's Politicial Consultative Conference, is the son of a revolutionary leader named Yu Qiwei. Yu (also known at Huang Jing) was party secretary and mayor of Tianjin in the early 1950s. He was also the ex-husband of Chairman Mao's third wife, the notorious Jiang Qing.

- Wang Qishan, who serves as the secretary of the Central Commission for Discipline Inspection, is the son of a mere professor, but he married well. He is the son-in-law of Yao Yilin, a former Politburo Standing Committee member and vice premier, and so may be considered a member of the princeling party by marriage.

- Zhang Dejiang, the chairman of the National People's Congress Standing Committee, is a princeling. He is the son of Zhang Zhiyi, a PLA major general, who served as acting commander of the Artillery Force in the Jinan Military Region.[13] Zhang's wife, Xin Shusen is also politically well-connected, being a member of the Chinese People's Political Consultative Conference.

- Premier Li Keqiang's father was the head of Fengyang County, Anhui Province. The elder Li enlisted his son into the ranks of the Communist Party in 1976 at the age of twenty-one and put him in charge of a production brigade. As the son of a mid-level official, Li is not exactly a princeling, but he is far from being the son of an ordinary Chinese worker or peasant either.[14]

- The other two Standing Committee members, Zhang Gaoli and Liu Yunshan, are not princelings, but rather owe their positions to their once-powerful patrons, Jiang Zemin and Hu Jintao.

- And then there is Xi Jinping himself, who is a princeling among princelings. He is the son of Xi Zhongxun, a former Politburo member and vice premier who was one of the architects of China's Special Economic Zones in the early 1980s. Xi the Elder was an early follower of Chairman Mao and a veteran of the Long March, which means that Xi the Younger springs from a Red bloodline matched by few of his contemporaries.

HEGEMON RISING

One measure of Xi Jinping's meteoric rise is the speed at which his predecessors have been eclipsed from public view. Observers were surprised when neither Hu Jintao nor Jiang Zemin was present at the opening ceremony of the 12th National People's Congress session that commenced on March 8, 2015. The former President of China, Hu Jintao, now ranks a lowly number twenty-seven on the CCP protocol list, a humiliation that must have cut all the more deeply because the state-run media insisted that it took place at his own request. Jiang Zemin, at number twenty-six, is only one rung higher. When Jiang tried to put himself back in the public eye by making a pilgrimage to Hainan province's Eastern Mountain in January 2015, news of his visit was quickly quashed on the Internet, presumably on Xi's orders. As the Chinese say, "Just as there is only one sun, there can only be one hegemon."

But the most compelling evidence of Jiang and Hu's increasing political impotence is that senior associates of both have been investigated for corruption (read: purged). This, more than anything else, makes it clear to their respective factions—and to everyone else in China, for that matter—that their one-time patrons no longer have the power to protect them. Hu was unable to shield his closest ally, Ling Jihua, from the consequences of his son's misdeeds. To be sure, Ling's son had embarrassed the Party elite by crashing his $500,000 Ferrari (!) in downtown Beijing in 2012, killing himself and seriously injuring his two female passengers, who happened not to be wearing any clothes.

Despite these salacious details, in years past Ling Jihua would at most have been demoted. The new hegemon, however, in a show of political strength, decided to make an example of him. In December 2014 Ling was placed under formal investigation by Xi ally and fellow Politburo member Wang Qishan, who heads the CCP's anti-corruption agency.[15] He was cashiered from all his government positions in the following weeks.

As for Jiang Zemin, he called for an end to the anti-corruption drive in early 2014 when he apparently began to fear that his own sons would be targeted. But the purge continues,[16] and his eldest son, Jiang Mianheng, was subsequently dismissed from his government positions in early 2015—the usual prelude to formal prosecution—and rumors continue to abound about the corrupt business dealings of Jiang's younger son, Jiang Miankang. Jiang may be able to stay Xi's hand while he lives, but his death may remove this final obstacle. Xi's "anticorruption drive" has already led to the downfall of Zhou Yongkang, the highest-ranking official to be purged since the days of Mao.

On his way to the top, Xi also eliminated another princeling, the charismatic Bo Xilai, from contention. Bo was the party chief of the southwestern provincial-level city of Chongqing. He was hugely popular In China for his well-publicized assault against corruption and possessed the common touch as well, all of which may have led Xi to view him as a rival, and perhaps a role model. Bo is now serving life in prison for— what else?—corruption and abuse of power. A quarter of a million other officials have been rounded up as well and are either in jail awaiting trial or have already been sentenced to long prison terms. Local and provincial officials are so terrified by the thought of public disgrace and long imprisonment that the mere arrival of party investigators has prompted some to commit suicide.

Officials at the Ministry of Foreign Affairs bristle at the suggestion that President Xi could be engaged in anything so vulgar and distasteful as a purge of his political enemies. Students of one-party dictatorships are skeptical, however, that what is being publicly billed as an anti-corruption campaign actually is an anti-corruption campaign, rather than, say, the contrived sacking of officials who are suspected of disloyalty to the new hegemon. What makes it hard to distinguish one from the other is that virtually every Communist party official of any stature is vulnerable to charges of corruption, given the widespread bribery, fraud, and sheer criminality that characterize official (mis)conduct in China. Observers also note that Xi's protégés from Fujian province, where he recently served as Party secretary, have not only been spared from prosecution, they have been promoted, or, as the Chinese say, "they have ridden a helicopter" right to the very top. In any case, everyone who is anyone in China is lying low in the face of this display of raw political power. Sales of luxury cars such Mercedes Benz, Ferraris, and Lamborghinis have plummeted, as have purchases of luxury goods that are favored as bribes.

Since becoming military chief and general secretary of the Chinese Communist Party in November 2012 and president in March 2013, Xi has made it clear that the country is no longer ruled by committee, but by a man. At 180 centimeters, or just under 5' 11", Xi is the tallest leader since Mao—a giant by the standards of this height-obsessed nation. The comparison with Mao is apt in other ways as well. In his own way, Xi is just as flamboyant as Mao, who used to appear in Tiananmen Square before hundreds of thousands of cheering admirers and take well-photographed swims in the Yangtze River. Xi, influenced by Western politicians, has a more personal touch, and is not above playing to the public gallery. But while he wears a Western suit on foreign trips, he often reverts to a Mao suit or a general's uniform while in country—sartorial symbolism that is not lost on the Chinese.[17] His movements, like Mao's, remain a closely guarded secret. He doesn't hold press conferences and he doesn't explain himself—ever—to the lesser beings that he rules.

Big Daddy Xi is ramping up his personality cult in ways not seen since the heyday of the Great Helmsman. The first volume of Xi's collected speeches, *The Governance of China* was published in 2014, with more planned. The cover of this volume bears an uncanny, and surely not accidental, resemblance to the cover of Mao's collected works. Small concessions to modernity have been made—Xi's picture is in color while Mao's stern visage was gold embossed on red—but the resemblance would not be lost on any living Chinese, much in the same way that a black-bound Bible would be instantly recognizable by any Christian believer. Xi's book is even published by the same press in Beijing that published Mao's.

Within five months of the publication of *The Governance of China* on October 1, 2014, seventeen *million* copies had reportedly been sold (or, more likely, handed out to Party members with orders to read it before the next meeting of their Party cell.) Not every Chinese has a copy yet, but at the current rate at which the state-owned Foreign Languages Press is churning out copies, they will by the time Xi's ten-year term is up. Several books of quotations from his speeches and essays have also been published and are flying off the bookshelves.

Xi Jinping has published another book as well, this one containing 274 quotes from speeches he has given since 2012. The book, published in 2014, is actually called *Excerpts of Xi Jinping's Remarks on Overall Deepening Reforms*. But its pedigree—it is edited by the Party Literature Office and published by the Central Party Literature Publishing House—puts it very much in line with the famous "Little Red Book" of *Quotations from Chairman Mao Zedong*. Then there is the *Excerpts of Xi Jinping's Remarks on the Strict Maintenance of Party Discipline*, which came out in January 2016. Why publish what were originally highly classified internal speeches to senior Party leaders? Obviously, Xi wants to let rank and file Party members—and everyone else for that matter— see that he has successfully crushed his political enemies (whom he disparages as "inflated with a political will to power"(!) and that he has consolidated his control over the Party as "the core of the Party leadership," which is to say China's new hegemon.[18]

For those Chinese who don't read books, the state media have plastered scores of Xi's past speeches across the pages of the newspapers and magazines it controls. Dating back in some cases ten or fifteen years to when Xi was in Zhejiang and Shanghai, most of these deal with what he likes to call "the art of leadership" (*lingxiuxue*). Some phrases seem to echo Mao Zedong Thought, as when Xi talks about the indomitable human spirit and the need to persevere in the face of adversity: "There is no mountain that is too tall for mankind, no road that is too long for our feet," or "Open up a road if you are blocked by mountains; build a bridge if you come across a river."

Mao often wrote and spoke about leadership to his cadres, but did so in general terms. When Xi speaks of leadership, he is at pains to make it clear that it is he, Xi Jinping, who is in the driver's seat. "The leader's quality and ability is the key" to the success of the Party and the state, he has said on more than one occasion, leaving little doubt that he is referring to himself. "The top cadre must set a good example for—and vigorously push forward—the task of implementing the spirit of the zhongyang [Party center].... Whether the train can travel fast depends on the lead locomotive." Since Xi himself is the "lead locomotive," all of this sounds more than a little self-serving.

At times, Xi and his underlings seem determined to convince every last one of China's 1.3 billion people that he, and he alone, has mastered the art of leadership sufficiently to govern them. Summing up Xi's views on *lingxiuxue*, a *People's Daily* commentary averred, "We must have one goal; one chain of command and one coordinating authority; one decision and strategy; one [heavy] dosage of firmness and devotion; and one way of thinking." Among the qualities that a leading cadre should possess, according to Xi, are "firm faith and strategic resoluteness." This resoluteness is required because a leading cadre's willingness to tackle difficult tasks is intimately linked to "the Chinese Communist Party's determination to remain [China's only] ruling party." There is no doubt that Xi believes that he is the "leading cadre" in question, the one China has been waiting for, who will keep the CCP in power for decades to come.

Although presumably not everyone in China believes that Big Daddy is a paragon of flawless leadership, his benignly smiling visage can be seen everywhere. He is a fixture on the front pages of Party newspapers—his picture appears there twice as often as Hu Jintao's did during *his* first years in office.[19] Xi beams out of the souvenir plates that people buy on visits to the capital. His face even adorns the red-tasseled good luck charms that people hang from the rear-view mirrors of their cars, as if Xi were the new patron saint of road safety. For old China hands, however, the clearest sign that Xi aspires to be China's next hegemon comes from a creepy echo of ancestor worship. Visitors to the homes of ordinary Chinese report seeing huge posters of Big Daddy looking loftily down from the main walls of living rooms, occupying the exact space once given over to equally large posters of Chairman Mao—the same sacred space where the family's ancestors were once venerated.

To be sure, Chinese hegemons have always cultivated a larger-than-life image. This practice goes back at least to Qin Shihuang, who instructed that propaganda troupes should be organized to travel about the countryside singing his praises in every hamlet, village, and town they passed through. As Chairman Mao's personality cult blossomed during the Cultural Revolution, the propaganda troupes of his day grew to include every Chinese in the country, who were ordered to wave their Little Red Books in the air and perform songs and dances in the Great Helmsman's honor. I once saw a former Red Guard turn crimson with embarrassment as she performed—at my request—what might be called the "Mao Shuffle" while warbling "The East Is Red," which opens with the line "China has produced a Mao Zedong."

Under Xi's rule, the Chinese people are not waving *The Quotations of President Xi* in the air or dancing in the streets. At least not yet. But the level of public adulation, stoked by the state media, is in the rise. And people *are* singing Big Daddy's praises, so far voluntarily. Songs and poems about Big Daddy Xi can be heard on the radio, seen on television, and downloaded from the Chinese Intranet. Such songs have no trouble getting through the Great Firewall that China's cyber-censors have erected, and indeed are actively promoted by the state's propaganda apparatus.

One song that has gone viral is called "China has produced a Big Daddy Xi." As every living Chinese knows, this is a riff on "The East Is Red," but with "Big Daddy Xi" taking the place of "Mao Zedong." The complete lyrics go like this:

> China has produced a Big Daddy Xi,
> No tiger is too big for him to fight.
> He fears neither heaven nor earth,
> Dreamers all look to him!
> China also has a Mama Peng,
> Gift her flowers beautiful and fresh.
> Protect her, and bless her,
> Rise up family, rise up country, rise up Chinese empire![20]

Other songs similarly fete him as a loving as a loving father to his people ("Big Daddy"), as the scourge of the corrupt and powerful (the "Big Tigers"), and the leader who will realize the "strong China dream" of China "Dreamers," namely, world domination. What I have translated as "Chinese empire" is actually the phrase *tian xia*, which as we have seen refers to "all under heaven," a not-so-veiled reference to China's once and future hegemony.

One popular song—I am not making this up—even advises young Chinese women in the marriage market to set their sights on someone like Big Daddy Xi. "If you want to marry, marry someone like Xi Dada," goes the song's refrain, describing him as "a man full of heroism with an unyielding spirit."

Another recent creation is entitled "How Should I Address You?" As the camera follows Big Daddy on a visit to a remote village, the chorus sings of the love affair between the Chinese people—"old hundred names"—and their dear leader: "We are in your heart, and you are in our heart. You love the people, and we 'old hundred names'—so deeply, deeply—love you, love you, love you." The song may remind you of the theme song of a television show for very small children sung by a purple dinosaur named Barney. The only thing missing is the final line, "We're a happy family," but it is surely implied. The effort to elevate Big Daddy Xi by infantilizing those he rules goes on apace.[21]

It is impossible to exaggerate how ridiculous such sappy ditties sound to Western ears. No one in China is laughing though, at least openly, out of a caution that is born of equal parts of self-preservation and—one must say—authentic hero-worship. The tendency of the true hegemon to exalt himself above those he rules is only matched by the tendency of many Chinese to abase themselves before such magnificence.

The prominent role that Mama Peng is playing in all of this exuberant mythologizing of Big Daddy is surprising. In the Chinese patriarchal political context, women are either vilified, if they are politically powerful—or ignored, if they are not. China has only had one female "emperor," Wu Zetian of the Tang dynasty, in its entire three-thousand-year history, and the chroniclers of Chinese history have not been kind to her rule. More recently—and even more hated—is Mao's wife Jiang Qing, who tried to seize power in the last years of the Chairman's life, only to be arrested three weeks after his. Her nickname—the "white-boned demon"—is borrowed from one of the most evil characters of Chinese fiction, a shape-shifting demoness in *Journey to the West* who hungers to eat human flesh.

Mama Peng, for her part, has thus far shown no political ambitions. As an accomplished singer, she is a celebrity in her own right. Her presence helps to humanize Xi, with her feminine charm and beauty helping to offset the impression made by his own rather blocky, fleshy visage and increasingly dictatorial pronouncements.[22] Anything that suggests that Xi is less than a loving husband to his wife is covered up in the state-run press. When Vladimir Putin placed a shawl on Mama Peng's shoulders as they were seated next to each other at the 2014 APEC conference—Xi and Obama were nearby talking business—China's censors did their best to ensure that no one in China came to know about Putin's gallant gesture, because it would imply that Big Daddy was neglecting his wife.[23] Party censors have even gone after Winnie the Pooh, banning images of the beloved children's book character on Chinese social media platforms. Pooh's crime? Memes comparing the pot-bellied bear to the portly Big Daddy have appeared on the Internet.[24]

Much of this may seem petty but, truth be told, Big Daddy Xi's burgeoning cult of personality is no trivial or laughing matter. It suggests that, like the Chairman Mao before him, Xi is increasingly unrestrained by other senior leaders, who would normally frown on such self-promotion by one of their number—*if they were not afraid to do so*. None of them has forgotten what happened to Mao's longtime comrade-in-arms, General Peng Dehuai, back in the 1950s when the general began to oppose Mao's efforts to glorify himself as "The Great Helmsman" and "The Great Savior of the Chinese People." Among other things, General Peng, as Minister of Defense and a member of the Politburo, refused to allow "The East Is Red" to be taught to PLA soldiers, condemned the practice of hanging portraits of Mao in public places, and orchestrated the deletion of a phrase praising "The thought of Mao Zedong" from a draft PRC Constitution. In retaliation for this—and for his criticisms of the Great Leap Forward—Mao had him purged in 1959. Peng was arrested again by Mao's minions when the Cultural Revolution began and died in prison some years later.[25]

Big Daddy Xi could easily damp down the Party's propaganda machine if he chose to do so. Instead, he and his faction consciously encourage this outpouring of cultish crapola. Why else would news of his travels and speeches now dominate the pages of the *People's Daily* to a degree not seen since the heyday of Chairman Mao? And why else would he undertake a political pilgrimage to Mao's revolutionary base in Yan'an just before the 2015 Chinese New Year's celebrations, a time when Chinese customarily visit their ancestral homes, if not to invite comparisons between himself and the Great Helmsman? It is true that Xi spent much of the Cultural Revolution confined to a village not far from Yan'an, but in the hard-nosed world of Chinese politics nostalgia is not what motivates such excursions.

Big Daddy's leadership style has struck a chord with the Chinese people, who have seemingly embraced their new hegemon with open arms. Although Chinese opinion polls showing Xi's soaring popularity are worthless, since those who hold contrary views would be careful to keep their opinions to themselves, it is telling that a neighboring strong-man is held in extraordinarily high esteem. Russian President Vladimir Putin consistently receives a better than 90 percent approval rating from the Chinese—this according to annual surveys carried out since 2008 by *InTouch Today*, produced by China's Shenzhen-based mass media giant Tencent.[26] The fact that Putin is widely praised in the state-run media undoubtedly boosts his numbers.[27]

This is probably no accident. Xi Jinping's propaganda machine may be deliberately promoting Putin's tough-guy image because, in doing so, they implicitly promote their bosses' own. Chinese researcher Guo Jinyue actually admits that the Chinese people have a certain "psychological need" for a powerful leader that Putin's "brave and energetic character" satisfies.[28] Xi Jinping's brand of authoritarianism satisfies the same deep-seated need.

Indeed, even some of the great monsters of the twentieth century are viewed favorably by the Chinese people—and not just Chairman Mao himself, whose mausoleum dominating Tiananmen Square still draws long lines of people. Stalin, who was Mao's teacher in so many ways, continues to be revered to the present day, his reputation defended by battalions of party-state censors. And then there is the bête noir of all bête noirs, Adolf Hitler, who isn't remembered by the Chinese for the Holocaust, but rather for achieving "social stability with a very high human cost." "In general, the [Chinese] refer to him as very *lihai*, very hardcore, someone who is strong, powerful," comments Rabbi Nussin

Rodin, a Chabad representative in Beijing. "You can be strong and powerful and good, and strong and powerful and bad. It's weird. I don't know what to say."

What I would say is this: the respect paid by many Chinese to tyrants helps to ensure that they will be ruled by one.

————

Big Daddy Xi's repeated invocation of Maoist phrases and practices suggest he knows *exactly* what he is doing in channeling the late Chairman. For instance, he has called for everyone to study the "mass line," a phrase which retired Party official Bao Tong compared to "a magical obedience spell" which is cast by Party leaders whenever they want to warn the Chinese people that they "won't be allowed to take part in elections or express their opinions [about political matters]."[29] Invented by Mao (not Marx) to purge cadres who did not bow to his wishes, the "mass line" was first used by the chairman as a political weapon in the Yan'an days, the central period of the Chinese Communist revolution from 1936 to 1948 following the Long March.

But most older Chinese will instinctively associate it with the Cultural Revolution, when the demand for Maoist groupthink reached hysterical proportions, leaving hundreds of thousands of those who were suspected of harboring heretical thoughts dead.[30]

Xi not only echoes Mao's policies, he does so in a style that leaves no doubt that he is consciously modeling himself on the Great Helmsman. When he decided to rein in artistic expression, for example, he held a "Beijing Forum on Art and Literature" in 2014. It was a twenty-first century reprise of Mao's 1942 "Yan'an Forum on Literature and Art," and it was convened for *exactly the same purpose*. Mao used his original "forum" to instruct those doing "cultural" work in the Communist base areas that *their* literature and art would henceforth serve politics and advance the cause of socialism—or else. The message delivered by Xi to his "forum" attendees was virtually identical, namely, that *their* art should serve the Party's—which is to say his own—political goals. Lest anyone miss the connection between the two Forums, exactly seventy-two members of China's cultural elite were invited to the gathering, one for each year that had passed since the original Yan'an Forum seventy-two years ago. In this and other ways, China's state media went to great lengths to link the two "Forums," and thus to link the past and present hegemons.[31]

The general secretary of the Chinese Communist Party—somewhat incongruously in light of what was to follow—began by telling the assembled six dozen cultural doyens about his great love of art and literature. Then, still smiling, he proceeded to instruct them—just as Mao had instructed his captive audience decades before—that their art and literature should "serve the masses." Xi told them that they should strive to ensure that their art should "embody socialist core values in a lively and vivid way," that it should "uphold Chinese spirit" and "rally Chinese strength." He insisted that Chinese writers and artists should create literature and art that would instill patriotism in the young and help achieve the China Dream of a strong China. He also, as we will see in more detail below, encouraged the assembled artists to show distain for all things American in their works.

Xi's new diktat marks a huge step backwards in terms of freedom of expression. For it was only a little over three decades before that Deng Xiaoping and the rest of the CCP leadership had decided that Mao's doctrine that "literature and art are subordinate to politics" was an "incorrect formulation."[32] This 1982 decision, which, after the horrors of the Cultural Revolution, was greeted by writers and artists as a kind of emancipation proclamation, has now been effectively rescinded. In making his brand of "China Dream" politics the ultimate arbiter of all things artistic, Xi has rejected Deng's reforms and returned to Mao's hardline approach.

Xi's actions have matched his words. He has ramped up the detention of dissidents of all stripes and launched an Internet crackdown.[33] He has rounded up of dozens of activists, from human rights attorneys to those representing peasants whose hand has been misappropriated. Even those calling for officials to be more open about their wealth—an action that would seem to fit in well with the theme of Xi's own anti-corruption campaign—are being targeted.

One of the first to be arrested in Xi's crackdown was billionaire Chinese-American businessman Charles Xue, who was detained in Beijing in August 2013 on the charge of soliciting a prostitute. Xue was held in jail without bail for eight months, branded a "moral degenerate" and before his release was forced to make not one but two public confessions on state television for broadcast throughout China. Xue's televised confessions was reminiscent of Stalin's show trials—and, even more chillingly of the "struggle sessions" of the Cultural Revolution. In a "struggle session," a regular feature of life in the harshest period of Chairman Mao's rule, the chosen victim was publicly humiliated, beaten, and forced to confess to crimes he had not committed.[34]

There is little doubt that Xue's *real* crime—in the eyes of Xi Jinping and his censors—was criticizing the failures of the party-state on his social media account on Weibo. After all, he was one of the biggest of the "big V's"—as "verified" (publicly identified) Chinese bloggers are called—and under the penname of Xue Manzi had some twelve million followers. Hegemons have long put fear into their critics by using a tactic known in China as "killing the chicken to warn the monkeys." In this case, Charles Xue was the sacrificial "chicken"—a high-profile victim who was publicly pilloried in order to intimidate the other chattering Internet "monkeys" into silence.[35]

Another high-profile scapegoat was the eighty-one-year-old dissident writer Tie Liu, who was arrested on vague charges of "causing trouble," apparently because he had criticized propaganda chief Liu Yunshan in an online article.[36] China's leadership in general, and Big Daddy Xi in particular, are more and more frequently resorting to coercion and detention to silence critics. Not only businesspeople and activists but also the lawyers who try to defend them have been taken away by the internal security forces. Many people have simply disappeared for months at a time into so-called "black" (illegal) jails before facing trial.

Despite the growing climate of intimidation under Big Daddy Xi's rule, many reform-minded Chinese dismiss comparisons with Mao, arguing that no Chinese leader in his right mind would want to revive the excesses of the Great Leap Forward or the Cultural Revolution. But that is a fundamental misreading of what Xi is attempting to do. Mao launched the Cultural Revolution—a virtual civil war—to regain political power he had lost following the disastrous Great Leap Forward.[37] Xi doesn't intend to lose power in the first place, least of all by reckless experimentation with a successful economic policy that has produced over three decades of double-digit economic growth. Rather, he intends to emulate the Mao of the early fifties, when the Great Helmsmen was firmly in control of China's destiny.

Big Daddy simply doesn't need to launch a second Chinese Cultural Revolution. He sits unchallenged at the very top of China's power pyramid. Xi controls not only the Party (as general secretary), but also the government (as president), and the PLA (as chairman of the Central Military Commission). The collective leadership practiced by the PRC since the death of Chairman Mao is largely a thing of the past. Xi has already won the struggle for power within the Party, controls the military and the government, and is now casting himself as a political demigod to unify the larger mass of the Chinese people behind him.

There is little open discussion in China of the dangers of reverting to such Maoist practices. Bao Tong, a senior party official who was purged after opposing the massacre of unarmed students at Tiananmen Square in 1989, has mildly suggested that Xi risked alienating supporters within the Party by stifling debate and dissent. High-profile academic Hu Xingdou, who teaches at the Beijing institute of Technology, offered an even more cautious appraisal. Said Hu, "It's understandable that Xi is eager to establish his authoritative status, a role China is much in need of now. But such authority should be established by legal means, rather than through dictatorship." Of course ordinary citizens know better than to criticize their senior leaders, given that even relatively innocuous comments can lead to a visit from the police. What hints of criticism do manage to emerge through the cracks in the Internet concrete are drowned out by the chorus of affirming voices.

Chinese dissidents outside the Great Chinese Firewall and beyond the reach of Xi's public security forces have been less restrained in their criticism. Xiao Qiang, who monitors the Chinese media for the *China Digital Times*, said that Xi's demand that artists and writers serve the masses rather than their own creative impulses "made Xi Jinping look like an idiot." Xiao resides in the United States and so is safely beyond the reach of the public security forces. One suspects he will not be visiting China any time soon.

Those who praise the new leadership and endorse its policies, on the other hand, are feted within China. Celebrated author Mo Yan, who won the Nobel Prize for his graphic depictions of rural life, is so closely tied to the regime that he has virtually become the public face of the new censorship. In June 2012 he agreed to lead a state-sponsored project to get famous authors to hand-copy Mao Zedong's 1942 "Talks at the Yan'an Forum on Literature and Art." These infamous "Talks," in which Mao ordered "cultural workers" to use their craft to serve the revolution—or else—were widely reviled by writers following Mao's death. Officially repudiated by the Party in 1982, under Xi they are once again being held up for adulation. Some Chinese writers courageously refused to join the project. Mo Yan, however, not only agreed to take a leading role but also defended the "Talks" as a "historical necessity." During the Chinese civil war, he said, they had "played a positive role."

Although intended to deceive the people, a cult of personality can come to deceive the leader himself, convincing him that he is something more than mortal. The same sycophantic subordinates who helped to create the god-like aura that now surrounds the object of the cult begin to irrationally defer to it, and he himself becomes first immune to criticism, and then—on those rare occasions when his subordinates dare to offer it, which happen less and less frequently over time—angered by it. Presumably Nikita Khrushchev did not know that Chairman Mao had, as we shall see in the next chapter, talked privately with his inner circle about setting up an "Earth Control Committee," but he nonetheless concluded that the Great Helmsman was mad with power. And this was even before the Cultural Revolution, with its wild excesses of public adulation, drove Mao into full-blown megalomania. The ancient Greek proverb, as old as China itself, is applicable here: "Those whom the gods would destroy, they first make mad."

Big Daddy Xi seems to be getting drunk on his own wine. Not content to be a triumvirate of Party, military, and government unto himself, he has also appointed himself chairman of the "Leading Small Groups" in the Party that control important policy sectors. What but an exaggerated regard for his own abilities could have led him to install himself as the head not only of the "Groups" that are responsible for the military, domestic security, and cyberspace, but also of those for foreign policy, economic policy, and finance?

But those who say that Xi's power grab is a sign of weakness and insecurity are practicing psychoanalysis without a license. China's leader is following a well-worn path to total domination.

Perhaps Xi's traumatic family history should have given him a searing lesson in the risks of cultish obedience to a supreme leader. We know that his father, Xi Zhongxun, was driven from power in 1962 after Chairman Mao accused him of seeking to subvert the Party. And we also know that, once the Cultural Revolution erupted in 1966, the Red Guards took matters even further. Acting on Mao's explicit orders, they arrested and tortured Xi's father, long regarded as a "revolutionary hero," for having crossed the Chairman.

Outsiders may imagine that these experiences forged Xi Jinping's character into something resembling Mao's opposite. But the lesson he learned as a boy of thirteen from watching his father publicly humiliated clearly had nothing to do with the dangers of dictators and personality cults. Rather, it had to do with how to avoid coming out on the losing side of a power struggle. Xi's father was purged because he went up against the reigning hegemon, Mao Zedong…and lost. During the chaos of the Cultural Revolution this failure could easily have proven fatal not only to him but to his entire family, as it had proven to be for countless others during China's long history.

"He who succeeds becomes the emperor; he who fails becomes a bandit," goes an ancient Chinese aphorism. And it is Xi's aspiration— one he would have imbibed with his mother's milk—to become hegemon. In setting out to become the Mao Zedong of the twenty-first century, Xi Jinping did not model himself on his father, but on his father's nemesis. The Great Helmsman won the Dragon Throne by concentrating as much power in his hands as possible, by dealing decisively with his political enemies, and by building a personality cult second to none. To all appearances these are lessons that Big Daddy Xi has learned very well. He has firmly grasped the reins of power, he has jailed his enemies and sidelined his competitors, and his name is on everyone's lips. If China has hegemonic ambitions, it is because it is now being once again led by a hegemon.[38]

The world should take notice, since Xi obviously shares Mao's expansive view of China's dominant role abroad. China's increasingly bellicose behavior in the South China Sea and elsewhere is not a result of a PLA general or two going rogue, which would be worrisome enough, but of the entire PLA military establishment reflecting the bounding ambitions of the new hegemon. And as we will see in later chapters, the arrogance of power that seems to have Big Daddy Xi increasingly in its grip is already having consequences for China's neighbors.

What does the increasing concentration of power in Xi Jinping's hands mean for the United States and the rest of the world? First of all, it means that our own hope that China will, by embracing elements of the free market, peacefully evolve into a nation that respects human rights and individual liberty is bootless. The Middle Kingdom is moving in the other direction, arresting dissidents, passing new laws restricting freedom of speech and association, in short, turning backwards towards the same kind of imperial system of governance that it has imposed on its people for over two thousand years.

This means that it is now almost impossible to imagine circumstances under which China will simply integrate itself into the existing U.S.-dominated, world order. Whatever concessions the United States makes to China's growing power, Xi Jinping has far grander ambitions on the global stage than playing second fiddle to America. There is simply no way that the United States can meet China halfway, since Xi's "China Dream" is not a U.S.-China condominium, but the encirclement of the globe with Chinese power.

Surveys indicate that the vast majority of Chinese share Xi's "China Dream" of a world in which China is *the* preeminent power. But, in the end, it is Xi's views that matter most. For the new Chinese emperor, who is only sixty-four years old, is a good bet to continue to rule China with an iron fist for a couple of decades to come.

7

GREAT HAN CHAUVINISM: THE NEW RELIGION OF A NATION OF NARCISSISTS?

"A century of humiliating defeats and of falling behind did little to erase China's underlying arrogance and self-centeredness. All it did, really, was to flip the self-obsession to the other extreme, the extreme of self-abasement. Then, when China did begin to grow strong again, the self-centeredness flipped back towards narcissism and arrogance, only now it had more steam."

–LIU XIAOBO, *China's leading political dissident, killed by the Chinese party-state in 2017*[1]

Liu Xiaobo, China's most famous dissident, died a prisoner of the Chinese party-state in 2017, after languishing in a Manchurian prison for eight years.[2] Liu had spent decades calling for respect for human rights and far-reaching political reform, efforts that in 2010 won him the Nobel Peace Prize. In awarding him the prize, the Nobel Committee noted "his long and non-violent struggle for fundamental human rights in China."[3] Liu was only the third person in history to receive the Nobel Peace Prize while in jail, and only the second to be denied the right to have a representative accept the Prize on his behalf. The first, it is worth recalling, was Carl von Ossietzky, a German pacifist jailed by Hitler in 1933 for repeatedly warning of the dangers of militarism and Nazism. Ossietzky, too, died in jail.

Liu had committed the ultimate counter-revolutionary act, courageously calling for an end of one-party dictatorship. But it was not solely for this crime that he was charged with "inciting subversion of state power" in 2009 and sentenced to a prison term of eleven years. Liu's problems with Chinese political culture, and the party-state's problems with him, went much, much deeper.

Professor Liu was a polymath—he was literary critic, prolific writer, poet, and human rights activist all rolled into one—but he was also the most incisive social critic that China had produced since Lu Xun. And he was roundly hated by the regime not only for questioning its authority but also for criticizing its increasingly frantic efforts to legitimize its rule in the eyes of the Chinese people through hyper-nationalistic appeals. In his essays—collected by Perry Link in *No Enemies, No Hatred*—Liu scorned the "bellicose nationalism" preached by the Chinese party-state and exposed the underlying national narcissism of the Chinese mind that it played upon. It was for this that he was repeatedly attacked, jailed, and, ultimately, murdered.

Liu tirelessly promoted constitutional government, respect for human rights, and other democratic reforms for decades, but his critique went much deeper than this. In an essay entitled "Bellicose and Thuggish: The Roots of Chinese 'Patriotism' at the Dawn of the Twenty-First Century," he argued that the Chinese party-state has consciously (and self-servingly) channeled the collective narcissism of the Chinese people into a kind of hyper-nationalist insanity. This xenophobic, jingoistic patriotism, he believed, had led to a general loss of reason among the population, obliterated universal values of human rights, and rendered the Chinese blind to the faults of their leaders.[4]

He also believed that the Party's Orwellian control over society—and the ceaseless stoking of Great Han Chauvinism by the state-run media, by party-state mouthpieces masquerading as intellectuals, and by other members of the political elite—has meant the death of critical thought. A Great Wall against the truth had been erected in the minds of the Chinese. The result was that most of China's population was by now so uncritically accepting of the Party's propaganda that they mistook the illusions spun by a dictatorial regime intent upon its own aggrandizement for actual reality.

Since Liu Xiaobo's travesty of a "trial" was held in secret, we cannot know how he answered the charge of "inciting subversion of state power," but I suspect that he just continued his lifelong practice of speaking truth to power. And the truth necessarily threatens, undermines, and, yes, subverts, a regime built on lies. It is not surprising that the Chinese party-state imprisoned him for pulling back the curtain and exposing its machinations. Later, by denying him medical care when he became ill, that same regime effectively sentenced him to death. This form of execution is so common in China today that it even has a name: "murder without spilling blood."[5]

It is not hard to see why the Chinese Communist Party views itself as under threat. With the ideological rationale for one-party rule ebbing away and its foundation in raw force increasingly exposed to public scrutiny, the Party has been frantically searching for alternative sources of legitimacy for a quarter century now. Relentlessly pushing economic development and reducing overt government interference in the economic lives of the populace has bought the Party a certain grudging acceptance from the people. But stoking the fires of a narcissistic nationalism, the party-state has discovered, is much more effective at winning the hearts and minds of the Chinese people. If patriotism is the last refuge of the scoundrel, for Party leaders it is more akin to a first resort. Whenever the Japanese prime minister visits the Yasukuni Shrine to memorialize

Japanese war dead, or an American carrier task force transits the vast reaches of the South China Sea, or an American president questions the One China policy, the Party's propaganda machine goes into spasms of patriotic indignation. And while it wasn't so long ago that China's past was violently rejected by Chairman Mao Zedong, now the Chinese are constantly reminded that they are the "descendants of the dragon," heirs to the greatest civilization on earth, and a people set apart by their superior abilities. Forgotten now is the Great Proletarian Cultural Revolution, which sought to erase every last wisp of Confucian thought and feudal attitudes from the Chinese mind. A half century ago violent Red Guards dragged the desiccated corpses of the Ming Emperor Wanli and his empresses out of the tomb where they had lain for three and a half centuries, publicly—and *very* posthumously—"denounced" them, and then set their remains on fire. How things have changed. Today the Party itself circulates fables about the lost glories of the Yellow Emperor of five millennia past and encourages narcissistic fantasies about the intellectual gifts of the "Yellow Race."

Some aspects of what might be called Great Han Chauvinism are merely silly, as when the government churns out propaganda reports claiming that China was first in everything from the use of knives and forks (which later gave way to chopsticks) to the game of golf, the use of toilet paper, and the cultivation of tulips. But the party-state has much more serious purposes in mind as well, chiefly its own survival. The point of encouraging patriotism, in the words of the "Policy Outline for Implementing Patriotic Education," is "the invigoration of the spirit of the nation, the enhancement of national cohesion, the establishment of national self-respect and pride, as well as the strengthening and development of the broadest possible patriotic national front." What this means in practical terms, to quote Sinologist Geremie Barme, is "the rearticulation of national-racial icons like the Yellow Emperor and the 'Chinese race,' *Zhonghua minzu*, to define ultra-Chinese sensibilities, as well as debates about the shape of a future Chinese commonwealth." The Party is the self-proclaimed rallying point of the new "patriotic national front," and hopes thereby to make itself indispensable in the eyes of its citizens.[6]

If the Chinese party-state is bent on hijacking the minds of the Chinese people, it is worth asking why these minds are so easily "jacked." Liu Xiaobo aside, Chinese intellectuals have always been prone to fall prey to a narcissistic nationalism: a deeply held conviction that their nation, culture, and race is superior to all others. This disposition of mind makes them easy prey for the chauvinistic fantasies that the Party is promoting, which in turn produce a suppliant, even sycophantic attitude toward the state. Many Chinese seem to give in all too readily to the notion of "my state, right or wrong, but still my state"—according to which any political action can be justified by a cultural-historical-racial appeal to unity.

"BELLICOSE NATIONALISM"

Writing in vivid prose, Liu described with pinpoint accuracy the "bellicose nationalism" that China now exhibits at every turn and the national psyche that undergirds and sustains it. He saw Chinese nationalism as based on an unstable witch's brew of deep-seated arrogance and conceit mixed with on-again, off-again spasms of inferiority, which are themselves back-handed psychological expressions of the same underlying narcissism.[7] As Liu explained,

> When a people like ours, who struggle with feelings of inferiority, have to face the facts of inadequate national strength, or of less than full respect from others, one way we try to feel better is to grab onto any piece of historical material that can make us proud. It is even all right to exaggerate a success wildly, so long as it contributes to an image of "number one" for the group. If it is hard to deny that we are inferior to others materially, we can claim, as Mao did, that we are superior

spiritually. If we are not as good as others now, we can build the myth that we are bound to be the most powerful nation someday, because we certainly were in the past.[8]

Liu saw the "China-as-Center Mentality" as a product of China's extreme self-absorption, based less on objective reality than on blind self-confidence, empty boasts, and pent-up hatred.[9] These insights— which, again, won him a long prison term—help to explain China's craving for international respect no less than its often undiplomatic— even warlike—rhetoric when it feels itself slighted.

China's extraordinary sensitivity to slights is an outgrowth of the view that the world is divided between civilization (China) and barbarism (everything else). It is bad enough to be insulted by one's equals, but to be insulted by one's perceived inferiors is simply intolerable. And in the view of the committed Great Han chauvinist every other nation, culture, race, and ethnicity is—or soon will be—inferior to China. China's excesses of both pride and humiliation, says China scholar William Callahan, are a direct outgrowth of this classical civilization-barbarism distinction.[10] Both national pride and national humiliation work to integrate the party-state's propaganda policy with grassroots popular feelings to produce, in Callahan's words, a "national aesthetic that unites elite and mass views of identity and security."[11]

Arguing along the same lines as Liu, Callahan describes a Chinese national psyche that has, at its root, both a "superiority complex" and an "inferiority complex."[12] The superiority complex comes from their millennia of dominating their near neighbors, while the inferiority complex is a result of the devastating effect that the clash with Western civilization has had on their collective psyche. Mao Haijian, a professor of Chinese history at East China Normal University, agrees, explaining further that his compatriots' tendency to boast about their culture is actually an attempt to disguise their deep-seated feelings of inferiority.[13]

If you visit the Ming Tombs north of Beijing, where thirteen emperors of the Ming dynasty (1368–1644) are buried, you will see an illustration of the kind of mythologizing that Liu is referring to. Along the four-mile long "Spirit Way" (*Shendao*) that leads into the necropolis there is a map that supposedly outlines the geographical extent of China under the Ming. The problem with the map is that it depicts an empire far larger than the one the Ming emperors actually ruled. Huge swaths of territory to the north, west, and south that were never controlled by the Ming emperors are shown as being under their direct sway. Why lie about the size of Ming China? Is it a case of Chinese officials exaggerating history to gratify their own pride? Is it a mirror of their ever more expansive geopolitical ambitions? Or is it, perhaps most troubling of all, a hint of coming "historical claims." Beijing has, after all, developed the practice of redrawing ancient maps and reinterpreting musty texts in order to justify new territorial claims into an art form.

These tendencies explain why, whenever China's exaggerated self-image comes under threat, members of the Chinese elite shift very quickly from extreme self-abasement to extreme self-aggrandizement, while at the same time they are abandoning positive, optimistic interpretations of China's relations with other nations in favor of negative, pessimistic ones about impending conflict and even war.[14] Although Liu, writing from his privileged position inside of Chinese culture, was more explicit than Callahan, they both describe a national character that, at its core, is highly narcissistic. Indeed, Liu viewed the Chinese leadership's obsession with overtaking the West and replacing the United States as the hegemon—as opposed to, say, simply improving the living conditions of ordinary Chinese—as an expression of "pathological narcissism."[15]

It is worth emphasizing that just because China's elites are well served by the grandiose view of China's place in the world that they propagate to the masses, *this does not mean that they don't believe it themselves*. For the most part, they are no less in thrall to national narcissism than the schoolchildren that they miseducate, or their forebears in dynasties past, for that matter. Many Chinese analysts are now employing, as a model both for domestic politics and international affairs, the same "Sinic civilization versus barbarism distinction" (*huay-izhibian*) used in imperial times.[16] Moreover, virtually all of China's top thinkers see the end of history arriving in a stark "China wins, barbarians lose" scenario. This belief colors everything from industrial policy to trade deals and creates sharply differing expectations. American trade negotiators, operating under a "win-win" paradigm, see their role as negotiating equitable deals that are advantageous to both sides. Chinese negotiators nod sagely in apparent agreement, only by "win-win" they mean something entirely different: that China wins twice. The first "win" comes in the terms of the trade deal, which they humbly insist should favor China "as a less-developed country." The second "win" for China comes when it arrogantly goes on to cheat on those same terms. This is so well understood in China that the phrase "win-win" has become a national joke, while we remain clueless.

By all accounts Xi Jinping and other fifth-generation leaders sincerely believe that it is their manifest destiny to usher in a Sinocentric global order. Not surprisingly, this belief periodically leads them to overreach— to claim, for example, nearly all of the South China Sea as sovereign Chinese territory. Even if it wasn't part of China since "ancient times" (as Beijing now claims), in the minds of China's leaders it deserves to be. That's why Chinese passports now include a nine-dash line outlining that body of water as part of China's sovereign territory.[17] A self-centered, self-absorbed hegemon has no natural boundaries—and no national borders.

Liu Xiaobo wasn't the first leading Chinese intellectual to identify narcissism as a key trait of the Chinese cultural genome. In the early twentieth century Lu Xun, one of the greatest writers in Chinese history, wrote about the narcissism and cultural myopia that characterized late Qing and early Republican China. In the iconoclastic "True Story of Ah Q," he railed against the national character with its superiority complex and its obsession with "face," its servility before authority, and its cruelty towards the weak.[18] As the story unfolds, Ah Q meets with a series of crushing defeats and public humiliations. But convinced of his own superiority and self-worth, he manages to deceive himself into believing that these defeats are actually "spiritual victories" (*jingshenshengli*). Lu Xun's cautionary tale remains a window on China's boundless craving for respect and admiration, deserved or not.

Another Chinese intellectual who took up the same theme was the social critic Bo Yang, who was born in China but followed the defeated Nationalist army to Taiwan in 1949. In his book *The Ugly Chinaman*, published in 1986, Bo described the Chinese as constantly oscillating between two extremes: fits of unbridled arrogance about Chinese racial and cultural superiority alternating with stark feelings of inferiority before the West and Westerners.[19] Both extremes lead to irrational behavior, of course.

SURVIVAL OF THE FITTEST . . . RACE

Social Darwinism—the idea that the survival of the fittest applies not just to plants and animals but to human races and cultures—entered China through translations of T. H. Huxley's *Evolution and Ethics* and Herbert Spencer's *Study of Sociology* by the Chinese scholar Yan Fu. But Yan was not content merely to introduce Huxley's and Spencer's thoughts to his Chinese audience. Instead, he added his own interpretation, applying the concept of the struggle for existence to the ongoing struggle of the Chinese culture and people to survive against the incursions of the Western barbarians and their culture.

Yan, following Spencer, summarized Darwin's views thus—"Peoples and living things struggle for survival. At first, species struggle with species; then as [people] gradually progress, there is a struggle between one social group and another. The weak invariably become the prey of the strong, the stupid invariably become subservient to the clever"—and explained that Spencer's sociology was "not merely analytical and descriptive, but prescriptive as well."[20]

There was probably not a Chinese intellectual alive at the time—as the Qing dynasty was tottering towards collapse—who could read Yan's book without fearing that the Chinese were the "weak" who were doomed to become the "prey of the strong" Westerners. Thus Yan's work had an enormous impact among Chinese scholars who were obsessing about precisely the same question that he was: whether their culture, and perhaps even their race, was ultimately facing absorption or even extinction. Many among the narcissistic elite who had imagined that their empire represented the pinnacle of civilization simply went into denial like Ah Q in Lu Xun's tale. Others, convinced of their surpassing cleverness and determined to be predator instead of prey, set out to co-opt Western science, overcome China's backwardness, and outcompete and subjugate the West.

Social Darwinism is generally discredited in the West, in part because of the racist atrocities of the Third Reich, in part because Western societies are increasingly multicultural and multiracial. But the expression of such views is not only still acceptable in China, it constitutes a surprisingly large part—perhaps the largest part—of the ongoing public discourse about China's place in the world. "All Chinese intellectuals, including myself, are social Darwinists," says Mao Haojian. "We are all sensitive to Western superiority, and boast about the Chinese race because in our hearts we feel inferior. We realize this is irrational, dangerous, even wrong, but still we feel it."[21]

Such feelings wreak havoc not merely in the minds of China's intellectuals, but on the world stage as well. As Callahan notes, "The guiding idea of Social Darwinism's struggle between race nations helps to explain why, even in the 21st century, citizen intellectuals [in China] still see international politics as a life-or-death issue, where the Chinese race continues to risk extinction."[22] This explains why Chinese negotiators are often so intransigent in their demands, almost regardless of the objective importance of the issue at hand. It is hard to reach agreement with negotiators who believe—almost below the level of conscious thought—that *any* concession is a potentially life-or-death issue that may compromise their country's very survival.

The ranks of China's social Darwinists extend up to the very top. Among those who share a burning concern about "losing the country and extinguishing the race" must be numbered President Xi Jinping himself. While he was governor of Fujian province, Xi edited a book entitled *Science and Patriotism*, in which he asserted that "Today, Yan Fu's scientific and patriotic thought is still not out of date."[23] Xi's goals of the "great revival of the Chinese nation" and the "China Dream" must be viewed through a social Darwinist lens, as a struggle not just for national (and racial) survival, but for national (and racial) dominance.

Chinese intellectuals and leaders deny that the Chinese harbor racial prejudice. One-time Party Secretary Zhao Ziyang even went so far as to declare that racial discrimination is common "everywhere in the world— except China." Both official documents and public intellectuals echo this sentiment, characterizing racial discrimination as a Western problem from which China is gloriously free.

The reality is that China's identity and politics has long been infused with the concept of a hierarchy of races—and still are today. Yan Fu and other leading reformers of the late nineteenth century abandoned the Confucian classics in search of another ideology that could, in Frank Dikotter's words, "bind all the emperor's subjects together into a modern, powerful nation capable of resisting foreign encroachments. They were delighted to discover the Western notion of 'race,' and they happily adopted the new evolutionary theories from England to present the world as a battlefield in which different breeds struggled for survival, as 'yellows' competed with 'whites' over inferior 'browns', 'blacks' and 'reds.'"[24]

The cohesiveness of the Chinese empire had long been grounded in a common Confucian culture, but this had failed spectacularly to meet the threat posed by the Western powers—and even by "little" Japan, which had humiliated mighty China in the 1894–1895 Sino-Japanese War. A new source of national unity was desperately needed. The late nineteenth-century reformers located this in the supposed "common bloodline" of all Han Chinese, which they proceeded to trace back to the legendary Yellow Emperor (*Huangdi*). Thus was the "Cult of the Yellow Emperor," which had first been prominent during the late Warring States and early Han dynasty, reborn. The reformers declared that this mythical figure, who was said to have reigned over parts of North China from 2698 to 2598 B.C., was the "First Ancestor" of all living Han Chinese. This meant that all people of Chinese descent, regardless of where in China (or the world) they lived, were all brothers—or at least distant cousins. Given the strength of clan sentiment in traditional China, where many people lived in same-surname villages and could trace their ancestry back many hundreds of years, the idea that they were all members of the same huge lineage was one that seized the imagination. The Yellow Emperor thus became a potent symbol of racial unity for the Han Chinese against their "foreign" Manchu rulers as they sought to overthrow the tottering Qing dynasty. As Chinese historian Sun Lung-kee acknowledges, "The claims that the five-thousand-year-old Chinese civilization was inaugurated by Huangdi and that Chinese people are the descendants of Huangdi are products of the twentieth century."[25]

With the fall of the Qing, competing warlords divided up China into province-sized chunks, while outlying regions such as Tibet, Mongolia, and Western Turkestan (Xinjiang) went their own way. Nationalist politicians, eager to glue the pieces of the fragmenting empire back together, decided it was time to extend the reach of the Yellow Emperor's genome. They now declared that he had been not only the "First Ancestor" of the Han Chinese, but the direct progenitor of *all* of the major ethnicities—the *zhonghua minzu*—that lived within the borders of Greater China. The Mongols, Manchus, Hui Muslims, and even the Tibetans all owed their earthly existence to the founder of the Chinese state, or so it was conveniently claimed. It was a blatantly racist appeal to groups with clearly distinct national identities and ancestral origins—one deliberately calculated to convince them to submit once again to Chinese rule and submerge themselves in the Chinese crucible.

The cult of the Yellow Emperor was resurrected again by the Chinese party-state in the 1980s, and for the same reason: to bolster national identity in the face of the centrifugal forces—Westernization, modernization, the decline of communist ideology, the rapid spread of Christianity—that threatened to weaken it. The mausoleum of the Yellow Emperor, located in Shaanxi province, has been carefully restored in the years since, and in 1993 a huge Xuanyuan Temple complex where regular sacrifices are offered was added. The chief official celebration of Yellow Emperor's cult is held each year on or about April 5, the date on which traditional-minded Chinese customarily go to worship their ancestors, spruce up their tombs, and offer food and paper money to their spirits. In recent years, various senior leaders have taken part in rites on that day that pay homage to the mythical ancestor of the Chinese race.

It is a bizarre thing to watch a member of the Central Committee of the Chinese Communist Party engage in what can only be called ancestor worship. After all, the Chinese Communist Party, which remains officially atheistic, railed for decades against precisely these kinds of "feudal superstitions." The Party's new-found respect for China's First Ancestor has little to do with religion, however, any more than the Confucian rites practiced by thoroughly secular mandarins in dynasties past had anything to do with the supernatural. Both are intended to forge and reinforce loyalties to the hegemonic state and to the reigning hegemon.

The renewed traditionalism of the Chinese party-state is thus comparable to the classicism that was promoted by fascist Italy and Nazi Germany. That is to say, it is not being promoted as an end in itself, but merely as a means of reinforcing, through cultural and racist appeals, the Chinese people's devotion to the party-state. This came through loud and clear in the speech of Governor Lou Qinjian of Shaanxi province, who was the chief celebrant at the 2013 memorial ceremony. Invoking the Yellow Emperor and quoting Big Daddy Xi, Governor Lou proclaimed that "All Chinese around the world, be they from the mainland, Hong Kong, Macao, Taiwan, or abroad, share a common ancestor and a common dream. The rejuvenation of the Chinese nation is on the horizon."[26]

Such explicitly racial appeals—intended, as always, to stoke nationalistic fervor—are troubling in themselves. They also point to a widely held belief of the Chinese people in a hierarchy of races, which is itself necessarily racist. In this hierarchy, the Chinese people think of themselves—the Yellow race, they proudly say—as occupying the top rung. They award the next rung on the ladder to the White race, which in their view is almost (but not quite) equal to the Yellow race in intelligence, but which falls far short in cunning. The Red and Brown races are further down the ladder, while the Black race languishes at the very bottom. An American exchange student recalled to me his shock when he discovered that his Chinese tutor, an educated man, believed that all Indians were "dirty" and "unsophisticated." "But in the eyes of my Chinese friends," he recalled to me, "nothing compared to how 'dirty' all black people were. Sounding like denizens of the antebellum South, they all said that they would never date a black." A Shanghai company even ran a television commercial for a detergent called Qiaobi which depicted a dirty and bandaged black man making advances towards a beautiful Chinese girl. The girl responded by thrusting him into a washing machine loaded with the detergent. The man emerged "cleaned up" into a handsome Chinese.[27] Foreigners who complained about the jaw-dropping racism of the advertisement were scolded by the state-owned *Global Times* for being "too sensitive."[28]

In other countries such prejudices are largely the province of the poor and illiterate. Not in China, where the party-state encourages the Chinese people to believe that they are culturally and genetically superior to every other "race" on the planet. While anthropology outside of China emphasizes the common origins of homo sapiens, mainstream thought within China has moved in the opposite direction. Studies have been published purporting to show that the Chinese evolved separately from the rest of humanity and are biologically distinct.[29] In the words of the hugely popular song, "Descendants of the Dragon" (which has been heavily promoted by Beijing), the Chinese are the "black-eyed, black-haired, yellow-skinned descendants of the dragon." The state is also trying to construct a unique and pure "Chinese school of archaeology" by generously subsidizing research projects and digs throughout China. The goal of this "archaeology with Chinese characteristics," as one might call it, is the promotion of the idea that the Middle Kingdom, since time immemorial, has been a "homeland for the Yellow race" and a uniquely exceptional country.[30]

EXCEPTIONAL COUNTRY, EXCEPTIONAL RACE

The ironclad belief of China's leaders that their nation and their people are superior to all other nations and peoples is central to the self-image of the hegemon. But keeping faith in the race has not always been easy, especially during the last two centuries of decline and decay. The collective shame associated with China's technological and material inferiority led to extreme self-abasement before Westerners, especially on the part of the Chinese elite. But what may have appeared to foreigners as a supine acceptance of the new world order was actually something very different. It may seem strange that China's leaders react to humiliation by almost reveling in it. But there is a sound political reason why China celebrates its defeats like other countries celebrate their victories. Each new generation of Chinese must be forced to experience anew how it feels to be humiliated at the hands of hostile barbarians. Chinese history is written as a morality play designed to make the hearts of impressionable young Chinese burn with resentment against the outside world. Today, foreigners are still portrayed in state-approved textbooks as a purely negative force: invaders, capitalists, imperialists, barbarians, and devils who are "pirates" when at sea, and "bandits" when on land.[31]

Even during the darkest of times, however, China's leaders never stopped searching for ways that the hegemon could prove its exceptionalism. The Nationalists, although they looked to the United States for a model of governance, were nonetheless disinclined to blame modern China's backwardness on its own culture and traditions. Instead, they heavily promoted the positive contributions made by the "unique" Chinese culture through a vaguely defined theory of a "national essence" (*guocui*).[32] For the rest, in typical Chinese fashion, they looked outward to see where the fault lay. If the hegemon had fallen behind, there was, to their way of thinking, only one possible explanation: it had been brought low by a coalition of extraordinarily malevolent and aggressive barbarians—this time not from the northern plains or the Western deserts but from beyond the seas.

After the success of the Communist revolution, it was not long before Chairman Mao, in his role as hegemon, sought to extend the reach of Chinese authority well beyond China's borders. China posed as the leader of the non-aligned nations in the 1950s, while in the mid-sixties it emerged as the chief sponsor of and cheerleader for national liberation movements. Despite its continued poverty and technological backwardness, China was still driven by its own pretensions to imagine itself to be the vanguard of world progressivism. Chairman Mao himself not only subscribed to but propagated a Sinocentric view of foreign affairs that bore little resemblance to the contemporary reality. In 1956, he announced to his inner circle, "We must control the Earth. In the future we will set up an Earth Control Committee, and make a uniform plan for the Earth."[33] There was something more than mere personal hubris at work in the expression of such grand schemes at a time when the PRC's economy was far smaller than Argentina's—and only a tiny fraction the size of America's.

Chairman Mao's view that the version of Marxism-Leninism-Maoism he practiced was a uniquely appropriate model for the global Communist revolution is, of course, another expression of his national and personal narcissism. He was correct in seeing that the peasant rebellion that he had organized and led was a more suitable model for other peasant uprisings than the urban-based worker revolution of the Bolsheviks in Russia. But the Maoist ideology and organization—Mao Zedong Thought and the People's Republic of China—were scarcely applicable outside of China's borders. A hegemon in the Chinese mold could successfully essay the kind of mind control that Mao Zedong Thought required of the Chinese, but it was far beyond the reach of ordinary rebel leaders in other countries and completely foreign to their followers. The PRC could not serve as a model for other countries. It was a uniquely Chinese recrudescence of a rigidly hierarchical, controlling, and corrupt bureaucracy of the kind that simply did not exist—and still does not exist today—in most less-developed countries.

All this was lost on Mao, who as the reigning hegemon saw himself and his country as a paragon of righteous revolutionary conduct. Campaigns such as the Great Leap Forward and the Cultural Revolution had their origins in Mao's effort to achieve a purer, more exalted form of communism worthy of China's greatness. Even the isolationism of the Cultural Revolution had at its core the notion of Chinese centrality. Christopher Ford explains this apparent contradiction:

> Reassertion of China's prerogatives as *a* nation was not just consistent with world revolution but, in fact, essential to it: Mao's Middle Kingdom would be the catalyst for, the vanguard of, and the civilizational core for a post-revolutionary global order in which All under Heaven would, as of old, turn in awestruck submissiveness toward the Celestial Empire.
>
> Given this understanding, there is, thus, no paradox in finding the Cultural Revolution, for example, to have been both "internationalist and nationalist." Nor, despite its inward-looking focus and disgust for conventional forms of

international engagement and propriety, was cultural revolutionary China really "isolationist." As seen through Maoist eyes, the proper ideological purification and moral reconstruction of Chinese society was the necessary starting point for China's supreme engagement with the outside world: the revolutionary transformation of world order.[34]

Mao seems to have expected to catalyze a transformation of the international environment in large part by the mere force of China's example. This proved to be yet another narcissistic conceit. Like previous efforts over the previous century to assert China's exceptionalism and superiority, this, too, came to naught.

Lately the Chinese party-state has been insisting that the world is entering a "new era" in which the exceptional country that it rules will resume its rightful place as the center of the earth. What is different now is that China has the economic heft to begin to make good on its ambitions, *if* it can translate its economic success into hard and—especially—soft power. This may prove difficult. Geoff Dyer points out that soft power is not something "that can be solved by bureaucrats—by throwing money at it."[35] It emerges, rather, from the character of the country as a whole. Here the United States, "the first universal nation" as Ben Wattenberg has called it, has a huge and perhaps insurmountable advantage in its openness, its liberty, and its sheer inventiveness.

The very different character of the PRC was cast millennia ago, in the fires of the Warring States period. The historical antecedents of the Chinese Communist Party can, despite its apparently post-Enlightenment pedigree, be traced back to the very founding of the Chinese civilization, when Chinese emperors flaunted the silken costume of Confucianism but ruled with the iron fist of Legalism. Similarly, the Communist Party engages in the public pretense that it practices something called "Socialism with Chinese characteristics," but the manner of its heavy-handed, dictatorial rule would be instantly familiar to officials of dynasties past. A more accurate description of China's current system of government would be "Chinese bureaucratic totalitarianism with some socialistic characteristics." The National People's Congress may bear a passing resemblance to a deliberative body, but everyone in China knows that the real power resides in the Communist Party leadership and, above all, in the person of the Party's General Secretary himself.

This is not the first time that China has appropriated Western advances without changing the essence of their own political culture. Indeed, the slogan of the reformers of the late Qing era—"Chinese learning for the essence, Western learning for utility"—specifically eschewed fundamental change. Throughout its long history, Chinese officialdom has never been averse to incorporating military and technological advances from the outside world. Mongol horses, for example, were incorporated into the imperial army in order to defeat the barbarians. At the same time, Chinese officials were absolutely opposed to making fundamental changes to their culture, including to their political culture, which they regarded as superior in every way. China's system of governance is a uniquely Chinese development, totally unsuitable for the governance of other cultures and peoples. The system of government invented by the Founding Fathers of the United States, on the other hand, has been successfully adopted by dozens of peoples around the globe, peoples with widely differing histories and cultures. The ultimate testament to its universality is that it has even been adopted by the Chinese living on Taiwan.

There is little doubt that the United States and China are now engaged in a great power–style competition. The difference is that the United States is entering the lists in the company of dozens of long-time allies from around the world. The Chinese party-state, on the other hand, will undertake this long twilight struggle largely alone, allied with a few like-minded dictatorships to be sure, but isolated from most other countries and peoples by its racist and xenophobic nationalism.

THE YELLOW MAN'S BURDEN

The popular manifestation of that xenophobia is predictably unpleasant to behold and even more bitter to experience. Embedded in Chinese popular novels is a geo-racial politics that can only be called "Yellow supremacism." One comes across passages stressing that the Chinese race is the "most outstanding race" that is "even better than the white race." Many in China—sounding for all the world like Oriental Rudyard Kiplings—now speak of the "Yellow Man's burden." Like the British Empire of old, they see their resurgent nation as having a global mission: to pacify and Sinicize the world, mostly by saving it from America. The self-abasement of yesteryear has given way to a cultural and racial triumphalism. Whites were once admired for their technological prowess and economic success. Not anymore. They have now joined the other races—Browns, Reds, and Blacks—on the roster of deplorables who are inferior to the Descendants of the Dragon.

Among the specific traits that Han Chinese routinely point to as evidence of their unique genetic endowment of high intelligence is their superior cunning (*jiaohua* in Chinese) as compared to the non-Han world. They disparage their chief rivals, the Americans, for being especially naive and simple (*danchun*), describing us as being almost like children who can be easily deceived and manipulated. This is certainly the view of Politiburo member and Xi henchman Wang Qishan.[36] In May 2011, while in Washington as head of the economic side of the annual China-U.S. strategic and economic dialogue, Vice-Premier Wang remarked, "It is not easy to really know China because China is an ancient civilization...the American people, they're very naive and simple."[37] This is not an unusually arrogant statement for a Chinese official. Even barely literate village officials routinely claim that China and the Chinese are simply *too sophisticated* to be understood by non-Chinese.

But despite what Vice-Premier Wang may believe, this is a clash of cultures not reducible to Chinese sophistication versus American simple-mindedness. Those who believe that deceiving others for national (or personal) gain is no vice will hardly be impressed by those who believe that telling the truth is a virtue. Neither will those coming from the Judeo-Christian tradition—who have been taught to let their "yes" mean yes and their "no" mean no—think much of those who belittle truth-tellers for lacking cunning. Still, Chinese officials understand perfectly well what many of their U.S. counterparts do not, namely, that the two countries are already engaged in a cold war. And they remember the words of Sunzi, their ancient and equally duplicitous forebear, that *all warfare is deception.*

Having lived in the Chinese world for a decade, I have personally witnessed many obnoxious manifestations of Han chauvinism on the part of ordinary Chinese towards foreigners. It is most evident in the casual, unthinking racism that many Chinese display towards those at the bottom of their racial hierarchy: Black Africans. I have seen a gaggle of Chinese children raise their fingers to their noses at the sight of a Black African, in the traditional Chinese gesture that means "You stink!" I have heard Chinese ask African men if they (like monkeys) still live in trees. I have heard Chinese men shouting epithets like "whore" (and worse) towards a Chinese girl in Hong Kong who was dating an American Black. This on a public street, in broad daylight, within the hearing of many passersby. Even today, in the south of China, the dark-skinned, regardless of their country of origin, are colloquially referred to as "black devils" (heigui). African-American friends who have lived in China more recently report that little has changed. Several African Americans I knew were fed up with the casual racism in China, which exceeded anything they had experienced in other parts of the world, and was far, far worse than anything they had heard or seen in their own country. One recounted that merely stepping into an elevator seemed to cause panic among the Chinese there, who pulled back in alarm and cradled their children in protective embraces.

Chinese racism against Whites is usually more subtle, reflecting their higher perceived status. But jokes can still be heard on Chinese TV and radio likening foreigners to uncultured monkeys.[38] A friend of mine who spent several years in China spoke of how the doctors would chuckle at him during his annual physical because he was so "hairy." He only belatedly realized that the doctors were laughing in large part because of his perceived similarity to a monkey. I have experienced discrimination as well. Being called a "foreign devil" in public is an experience that one is not likely to forget. Having a Chinese scholar reject an invitation to tea because of his stated aversion to socializing with a non-Chinese makes a lasting impression—and not a favorable one.

As more Chinese have more contact with the outside world, one would expect these attitudes to erode away over time. Change would come naturally, albeit slowly. We are, after all, talking about the largest mass of ethnically homogeneous people on the planet, most of whom will have no personal contact with anyone from the outside world over the course of their lifetimes. In *Chinese Whispers*, Ben Chu suggests that small, tentative changes in Chinese attitudes are in fact occurring, although he undercuts his own thesis by recounting numerous examples of casual xenophobia and racism that he has personally observed. Still, it is hard to disagree with his view that Chinese culture is neither monolithic nor unchanging. At the same time, the party-state is consciously and continually trying to instill a sense of cultural superiority among the population, not to mention stir up anti-foreign feelings. In the dog-eat-dog world of Yan Fu's Social Darwinism, less "developed" and less "civilized" cultures will always be looked down upon. Just ask the Japanese.

NARCISSISTIC TO A FAULT

What can one say about a civilization, a culture, and a race whose members believe that they are superior to any other civilization, culture, or race that has ever walked on the planet? This transcends mere ethnocentrism, the natural tendency of every human group to judge others by the standards and customs of their own culture. This is ethnocentrism on steroids, not only making Sinic civilization the measure of all things, but exalting it—and its practitioners—beyond all reason.

In the West, the hideous face of pathological national narcissism was exposed in the Nazis. It was their pretensions to national and racial superiority that Isaiah Berlin was referring to in his essay "Kant as an Unfamiliar Source of Nationalism": "No one, as far as I know, had ever prophesized the rise of modern national narcissism: the self-adoration of peoples, of their conviction of their own immeasurable superiority to others and consequent right to domination over them."[39]

Unbeknownst to Isaiah Berlin, the Descendants of the Dragon had no need to *prophesy* the rise of national narcissism, modern or otherwise. After all, they had already been practicing it for over two thousand years. Just as hegemony was an innovation of the Chinese state so, too, was the narcissistic cult of nationalism—the conscious promotion of the godlike superiority of the Middle Kingdom and its inhabitants over all other nations and peoples. Indeed, China's collective narcissism provided a ready-made justification for hegemony. It created, at least in the minds of the Chinese elite, an almost divine right to rule the lesser peoples of the periphery.

No one would claim that all Chinese are collective narcissists. The very existence of social critics such as Lu Xun and Liu Xiaobo, who criticized precisely this aspect of their own culture, is proof of that. Moreover, there are competing belief systems in China that orient their tens of millions of followers—be they Christians, Buddhists, Muslims, or dissidents of various other stripes—away from aggrandizing their race, culture, and country and towards more modest conceptions of their place in the cosmos. But it is also true that many Chinese, perhaps a majority of the intellectual and political elite and certainly most members of the Chinese Communist Party, manifest an extreme form of collective narcissism that is best described as national narcissism.

China isn't the only country to hold itself in high esteem, of course. Books have been written about the French solipsism, Russian nationalism, and American exceptionalism. But China still stands out in the modern world for its extraordinary self-regard, the fervor with which the party-state promotes such views, and the corresponding blindness and irrationality that this produces among both Party elites and the "broad masses."

National narcissists are, in language we can borrow from Eric Weaver, "obsessed with their own nation, hold a belief in the superiority of their own nation over all other nations, have a narcissistic lack of interest in other nations or national groups [unless] . . . a characterization of these groups can be used to support the view that their own nation is superior."[40] Weaver was writing about Hungary, but his description of national narcissists rings true for China as well.

Studies have confirmed not only that national narcissism, loosely defined as "an inflated view of the imperative and deservedness of one's own nation,"[41] is real, but also that it is a powerful predictor of international attitudes and foreign policy preferences. While national narcissism, as the Hungarian example above suggests, is not unique to China, it seems to exist in a particularly exaggerated form there. According to one study, the Chinese show huge levels of anxiety with regard to international symbolic losses. Americans, on the other hand, generally reported something approaching indifference towards symbolic losses on the international level. The difference was significant.[42]

Weaver says that one sign of a national narcissist is that he will nurture a cult of national heroes. There can be no more telling example of this than China's "Yellow Emperor," who is nothing less than the founding father of the entire Chinese race. Relevant here too are the personality cults that have been cultivated around China's leaders, the most recent of which exalts the heroic wisdom of Big Daddy Xi.

National narcissists also obsess over the achievements of their fellow nationals. Witness here the collective mania about the Chinese medal count during the 2008 Olympics in Beijing, where beating the United States became a national obsession. Or the disappointment that swept China eight years later, when China came in third in the gold medal count in Rio, far behind its archrival. Sounding a lot like Lu Xun's Ah Q, the state-run media tried to portray this crushing disappointment as a spiritual victory, even going so far as to suggest that it was the result of a deliberate decision "to place greater emphasis on human spirit, respect and friendship than simply winning titles."[43] Be that as it may, "titles" continue to loom large in the Chinese mind as evidence of national excellence. Many Chinese intellectuals, for example, take inordinate delight in pointing out that eight members of the "Yellow race" have won Nobel prizes in the sciences. They generally fail to mention that all were U.S. citizens, either by birth or naturalization, when they won their prizes, and that their ground-breaking research was conducted in the United States, not in China—perhaps because these facts call into question whether it was really their ethnicity that was the critical factor, or if it was the freedom of thought and action that they enjoyed in America that led to their success.

Chinese like Liu Xiaobo, who challenge the idea of national superiority or, worse yet, point out national failings, are seen as traitors to the race (not to mention to the People's Republic and, indeed, to Sinic Civilization as a whole) by the national narcissists in charge. The Chinese leadership tends to act with extreme aggression towards those of its own it sees as threatening the groups' collective self-esteem. Liu's eleven-year prison term for the vague crime of "subversion"—and his medical execution—is an example of this kind of overreaction. One might say that Liu's real crime was "subverting" the grandiose image of the PRC that the national narcissists in the leadership are constantly trying to promote among the citizenry. Needless to say, Liu's Nobel Peace Prize is the one Nobel Prize that goes unmentioned in Chinese medal counts, as it is emphatically not a matter of nationalistic pride—even though it was earned in China itself.

Because China's national narcissists have an opinion of themselves that does not comport with reality, they continually encounter threats to their inflated self-image from outside of China and tend to react aggressively, even violently, to real or imagined provocations. One example is the 2010 Senkaku boat collision incident. When the Japanese coast guard discovered a Chinese vessel engaged in illegal fishing near the Senkaku Islands, they ordered it to stop and be boarded. The Chinese captain instead tried to escape, ramming two Japanese coast guard vessels in the process. The delinquent captain and his crew were subsequently arrested, and their vessel was impounded.

These reasonable actions on the part of the Japanese authorities were greeted by outrage in China. The Chinese party-state, which had recently reasserted its own claim to the Senkakus, told the Chinese people that the actions of the Japanese coast guard were a violation of China's sovereign territory. (No one else accepts China's claim, which was only advanced in 1970, but national narcissists are good at ignoring such realities.) Nationwide protests were not only encouraged by the regime, they were organized and led by government and Party officials.

Even though the ship and its crew were released almost immediately, Beijing continued to irrationally escalate. Long-scheduled official meetings at the ministerial level and higher were cancelled. Four Japanese employees of Fujita Corporation were summarily detained on trumped up charges of "filming military targets." Perhaps most seriously, the Chinese party-state embarked upon economic warfare. It halted exports of "rare earths" to Japan, thus threatening the shutdown of that country's advanced electronics industry, for which these elements are a vital input.

Japanese Foreign Minister Seiji Maehara described China's reaction to the continued detention of the captain as "hysterical." He could just as easily have called it "typical." The national narcissists who run the Chinese party-state are known for overreacting in this petulant ways to any threat to their grandiose self-image. The Japanese government released the captain a couple of weeks later. By this time, it just wanted to resolve the incident as quickly as possible and return to business as usual with China.

As this incident suggests, it is difficult to get national narcissists to move on. They are generally unwilling to forgive and forget previous insults or unfairness to their nation or people, since their inflated self-image is so easily wounded. The Treaty of Versailles inflamed the hearts of the German National Socialists against the French for a generation. The "unequal treaties" signed after the First and Second Opium Wars continue (with more than a little help from Beijing's propaganda machine) to enrage young Chinese nearly two centuries later. This grievance mentality was on display vis-à-vis Great Britain when the negotiations over the return of Hong Kong to Chinese sovereignty stalled in 1983. China's state-owned film studios quickly spooled up a patriotic blockbuster called *The Burning of the Summer Palace*, an account of the Anglo-French expeditionary force that had looted and torched the Jesuit-designed palace of the emperor in 1860.

In that film the British are portrayed as a bunch of bloodthirsty brutish oafs who wantonly burned, raped, looted, and killed anything and anyone Chinese who stood in their way. No fewer than a *dozen* scenes played in gruesome succession showing groups of unarmed Chinese prisoners being executed by British firing squads. Then, just to make sure that no one in the audience missed the point that the British were bloodthirsty brutes, the next scene shows the British general arriving at the killing field. Surveying the slaughter, he expresses unhappiness at the slow pace of the executions and, to speed up the killing, orders cannons to be turned on the massed ranks of prisoners. History records no such slaughter, of course, but that wasn't the point, which was to arouse the Chinese masses against the reprobate British, who were stubbornly refusing to hand over their ill-gotten gains in South China, specifically Hong Kong.

In truth, the authorities need not have bothered to inflame public opinion. The surge of Great Han triumphalism that accompanied the anticipated recovery of Hong Kong required very little fanning by the state-owned media. In the popular mind, one more historical wrong was being righted, one more imperialist power was paying down its historical debt.[44] That the people of Hong Kong, where I was living at the time, did not share their enthusiasm and would have preferred to have been given their freedom and independence passed without note in the official press.

When disputes between nations arise, China's national narcissists are likely to interpret ambiguous events, or even accidents, as a threat to their national image or security and react aggressively. Consider the reaction to the accidental bombing of the Chinese embassy in Belgrade in 1999. As we have seen, China's leaders immediately concluded—despite U.S. apologies—that the bombing was a deliberate attack on a Chinese diplomatic outpost. Many ordinary Chinese, predisposed by decades of anti-American propaganda, did so as well. They found it easy to believe that the reigning hegemon, just like the hegemons of the Warring States period, was ruthlessly trying to keep a would-be challenger down.

"THE RELIGION OF CHINA IS CHINA"

National narcissism, in its extreme form, comes over time to resemble a religion. Its adherents exalt their nation, their culture, and themselves collectively to the point where these things take upon an almost sacred aura. Emile Durkheim, the French sociologist, remarked that the tribal gods of primitive peoples were really just the tribes themselves reified into deities. Although China is far from primitive, something along the lines of this kind of homespun deity seems to have evolved in the Middle Kingdom over the centuries. The hegemon—here defined as the countless descendants of the Dragon—seems to have become a god unto itself, with the entire country serving as its temple, and its people serving as both the worshipers and the worshiped.

This observation is not entirely original with me. Reflecting along similar lines, Sinologist Ross Terrill once remarked that, given the absence of a transcendental religion, "the religion of China is China."[45] Something similar was also suggested by Lucien Pye, who explained that, for the Chinese, "The most pervasive underlying Chinese emotion is a profound, unquestioned, generally unshakable identification with historical greatness. Merely to be Chinese is to be part of the greatest phenomenon in history."[46]

The enormous self-esteem of China's national narcissists is enormously fragile. And no wonder. For the past two centuries, the Chinese have been grappling with the crippling fear that their god has failed. Of course they leap to its defense and are quick to interpret the actions of other nations and peoples as signs of disrespect, criticism, or disapproval. How could they not? Is it not their sacred duty as the guardians of the temple precincts to protect it against the barbarians who would profane it? Criticism of China is intolerable, for it violates a sacred commandment: *Thou shalt not take the name of China in vain.* Those who speak against China are blaspheming. Even those foreigners who would propitiate the hegemon are often seen as failing to show proper respect and deference. How can anything that mere barbarians do or say possibly assuage the righteous anger the Chinese hegemon continues to feel for past injustices and mistreatment? Those who are not descended from the Yellow Emperor should simply kneel before the awe-inspiring sight of the hegemon and submit, silently and unconditionally.

Among those who have discovered that deference to China's wishes is a self-defeating proposition is China watcher David Shambaugh. I recall once inviting Professor Shambaugh to speak at a conference on human rights in China that I was organizing. At the time he declined on the grounds that he preferred to avoid criticism of China in order "keep [his] channels to Beijing open." In more recent years he seems to have come to understand that those "channels" run in only one direction, from the lofty heights of Chinese supremacy down to the foreigners who are expected to abase themselves before it. In his latest book, *China Goes Global*, Shambaugh notes that, for Chinese officials and the culture they represent, *criticism equals misunderstanding, and agreement equals understanding.*[47] Dogma is always dictatorial, and the Chinese variety is no exception.

The concrete expression of these quasi-religious sentiments is on display at the Yuan Ming Yuan, the old Summer Palace. Destroyed a century and a half ago by Anglo-French forces, and then again during the Boxer Rebellion, it has been turned into a kind of national shrine. Chinese school children are brought here on "pilgrimage" by the tens of thousands in order to make a kind of secular "way of the cross" through the ruins. They enter at the main gate, where a sign reminds them to "never forget this national humiliation." (This is not only a government propaganda slogan: similar graffiti has been scratched on many of the ruins by visiting superpatriots.)

This Chinese *via dolorosa* continues inside, as the guides take the children to ruined pavilion after ruined pavilion, explaining to them how the barbarians went on a rampage of destruction. They are told that they should all feel shame that that China was crucified in this way and that they should burn with a righteous anger against the foreigners who did it. The final station of the cross, as it were, is the resurrection of China's greatness by the Chinese Communist Party. The students are reassured that China is becoming so "wealthy and powerful" (*fuqiang*) that no other country will ever dare to violate its territory or commit such atrocities ever again. Soon, they are told, China will return to its historical preeminence, rejuvenated (fuxing), and will reign forever as the hegemon.

China could easily rebuild the Summer Palace, restoring it to its lost glory, and there have been calls from within China to do just that. Aside from the reconstruction of some minor pavilions, however, all such suggestions have been brushed off by the ruling authorities, who prefer to keep it in its present desolate state as a propaganda tool. To get a sense of what is going on here, imagine if the burned-out hulk of the first White House still stood by the Potomac, kept as a stark reminder of the War of 1812 and its torching by British Marines. Imagine further that

American children were bused in from all over the mid-Atlantic states by the government to see the ruins and seethe in anger at British perfidy.

There is something profoundly unhealthy about China's relentless pillaging of the past to promote ultranationalism and xenophobia in this way. One Chinese citizen, upset with the government's plans for even a partial restoration of the ruins, made a revealing comparison: "Can't we maintain the present-day ruins of Yuanmingyuan [Summer Palace] just like Israel keeps its Wailing Wall?" The Wailing Wall, of course, is the last remaining structure of the Temple Mount that the Jews built to worship Jehovah. By analogy, the ruins of the Summer Palace become a place where the Chinese go to worship their own past glories and—when all is said and done—themselves.

THE "CATCH-UP MENTALITY" AND "THE CHINESE CENTURY"

Every Chinese leader since the Opium Wars has attempted to realize the Legalist dream of a "wealthy country and a strong military."[48] Each one has sought, in different ways, to reclaim China's preeminence in the world. The adoption of Western learning, the development of a modern economy, and even the Communist revolution itself, were all undertaken for this "higher" purpose. Sinologist C. P. Fitzgerald, writing of the 1919 May Fourth Movement, notes that Chinese intellectuals of the time believed that Western "learning was essential only to save China, not valuable in itself; not necessary for a full and wider understanding of the whole achievement of the human race, but necessary to give back to the Chinese the power to compete on equal terms with the West."[49]

The entire country is currently in the grip of a feverish "catch-up mentality."[50] But everyone understands that the goal is not merely to reach the ranks of the developed nations, or compete on equal terms with the West, or even catch up to the United States. Those are just way stations on China's train to glory. The real goal is to accumulate more wealth and power than any other country and, specifically, more wealth and power than the United States of America. "How soon will we overtake the United States?" is the subject of endless debate in the media, in the classroom, and in coffee shops. Every success, from winning more Olympic Gold medals to buying more cars than the United States, is trumpeted. But this is not just about cars or planes, or even missiles and ships. Every advance is measured against U.S. achievements in the same area for a specific purpose: to see *how much further China has to go to overtake the reigning superpower.* Every advance China makes, whether economically, militarily, or into space, is seen as accelerating the countdown to the day when China will finally be Number One.

It is this sense of historic mission that makes China unique among major modern states, argues Christopher Ford. Since 2002 every PRC official has reportedly taken an oath of office that includes a pledge to "struggle for the prosperity and empowerment of the motherland."[51] The 2002 Defense White Paper issued by Beijing echoes this idea, declaring that "[t]he fundamental basis for the formulation of China's national defense policy" is "unremittingly enhancing the overall national strength." In other words, China's national security strategy—indeed its very national identity—is premised upon becoming the hegemon.

The Chinese believe that past is prologue, and that China will one day soon utterly dominate those countries which once humiliated it. This is why China's national narcissists indulge themselves in futuristic fantasies in which their country enjoys unlimited power and unparalleled influence. In one such fantasy, set in the year 2050, the author Yan Xuetong envisions a world in which China has an economy so large that it dwarfs that of the United States, Europe, and Japan *combined.*[52] He writes that believes that the rise of China will make the world "more civilized." This is a feeling apparently shared by a great many of his compatriots (but likely by very few foreigners).[53]

Popular Chinese culture is replete with novels that similarly predict a glorious future for a China as the wealthiest and most technologically advanced nation on earth. In these Sinophilic fantasies, the authors imagine that other nations are so jealous of China's successes and so envious of her wealth that they often resort to military force. In these fictional worlds, the hegemon is frequently forced to defend itself militarily from the depredations of other countries, but is *never, ever* the aggressor.

Many Chinese believe that America, Japan, and other countries are trying to block China's rise chiefly because they are "jealous."[54] The state-run media lashed out at Barack Obama for "interfering in China's internal affairs" when he met with the Dalai Lama in February 2014, claiming that *the chief reason he did so* was that the United States was resentful of a rising China. If you find it hard to believe that adults can actually think this way, consider the comments of Professor Jin Canrong, the vice dean of the School of International Studies of Renmin University. This distinguished professor, who teaches at one of the PRC's most prestigious universities, told the *People's Daily* that China had racked up international victories "dwarfing" U.S. diplomatic accomplishments in the recent past and that meeting the Dalai Lama was a way for the U.S. to "hold China back by the elbow."[55] That we may have been acting out of a legitimate concern for the plight of the Tibetan people under China's oppressive rule seems not to have occurred to this national narcissist.

THE BEIJING OLYMPICS AND TIBETAN UNREST

The 2008 Olympics can serve as an interesting case study of the behavior the Chinese party-state. Here we saw both China's obsession with its own superiority and its irrational anger towards those who threaten its collective self-esteem on display.

The party-state saw the athletic event as China's grand coming-out party to the world and thus spared no expense. Entire neighborhoods in Beijing were razed—and their residents sent packing—to make way for stadiums worthy of China's greatness. Beijing spent an astounding $42 *billion dollars* preparing to host the games, three times more than any other nation had ever spent. But China was not just another nation: it was the once and future hegemon out to impress the visiting barbarians with the splendor of its courts.

Chinese from all walks of life, from Politburo members down to taxi drivers, were convinced that the West would get to *know* China through the games and would thus inevitably come to *like* China.[56] It is unimaginable to most Chinese that anyone who knows the real China could dislike it, just as it is unimaginable to them that anyone who knows the real China could possibly be afraid of it. One man told of how extremely proud he was to have been chosen as a driver for the games, since these "marked China's emergence as a leading nation."[57]

But, just as China was about to make its dramatic entrance on the world stage, the obstreperous Tibetans once again made their presence known. Several months before the opening ceremony, the Tibetans in Lhasa began demonstrating their distaste for continued Chinese rule. Both sides blamed the other for the resulting violence. China's state media claiming that nineteen Chinese had died at the hands of Tibetan rioters, including one policeman, while the Dalai Lama reported that at least four hundred Tibetans had been killed, and thousands more arrested, by Chinese security forces.

Demonstrations in support of the Tibetan people were held in dozens of cities throughout the United States, Europe, and India. The demonstrators were nonviolent, with the participants asking merely that the Chinese leadership meet with the Dalai Lama and discuss when it might begin keeping its half-century-old promise to grant a measure of local sovereignty to the Tibetan people. Nevertheless, China's national narcissists immediately worked themselves up into a lather over this threat to their inflated self-image. Chinese officials aggressively attacked all critics—especially other Chinese who expressed sympathy for the Tibetans or suggested that China should dialogue with the Dalai Lama. These were pilloried as traitors to the race. Opinion on the Internet actually ran in favor of *intensifying* the crackdown on Tibetans as punishment for the disloyalty that these fellow descendants of the Yellow Emperor were displaying towards the Middle Kingdom. The usual scapegoats made their appearance as well. There was the "wolf in sheep's clothing", which is how the Dalai Lama is often referred to in the Chinese media. And lurking behind him were the ominously vague but ever-present "hostile western forces."

As the Olympic Torch, in an impressive display of Beijing's authoritarian organizational skills, made its way around the world, it was greeted in many cities by hostile demonstrators instead of the cheering crowds that China had expected. The torch relay was disrupted in London and Paris, and had to be restricted in the cities of San Francisco, Islamabad, New Delhi, and Jakarta. This was too much for the Chinese party-state, which instructed its embassies and student organizations around the world to "let China's voice be heard" by organizing counter demonstrations.

Chinese overseas student organizations were only too happy to comply, taking to the streets *en masse* in an effort to silence critics by sheer force of numbers. A pro-Beijing rally in Canberra became embroiled in a street fight with pro-Tibet demonstrators, mostly Westerners, whom the Chinese hit with handheld flagpoles. As Professor Callahan cogently put it, "Rather than wondering why Tibetans would protest Beijing's rule, many Han Chinese, at home and abroad, rallied against the 'bias' of Westerners, who they felt had unfairly criticized their homeland. The Tibetan unrest was thus transformed from being a serious domestic issue of racial politics, into an international issue of pride and humiliation that pits China against the West."[58]

This is exactly the sort of hypersensitive behavior that theories of collective narcissism would have predicted, in which China reacts with extreme hostility towards its foreign critics. The Chinese generally view foreign criticism as part of a Western plot to prevent China from resuming its rightful role in the world, and as therefore illegitimate. That's why any and all criticism from abroad, not only concerning Tibet but *on any subject whatsoever*, is routinely denounced as "groundless," or as "an interference in China's internal affairs," or as "hurting the feelings of the Chinese people."

The Chinese in general are rock-solid in their belief that Tibet was a blighted, backward, feudal province filled with ignorant, oppressed, superstitious peasants before the PLA arrived. This is, after all, what they have been taught in the schools, and it is a characterization that is very comforting to the Chinese, since it supports the view that their own nation and culture are superior to all others. They are also convinced that China's rule since 1949 has been a model of tolerance and benevolence and that the Tibetan complaints about Chinese heavy-handedness are completely without merit. Finally, even though they are well aware that the state-run media do not always report events accurately (what Tiananmen Massacre?), they are absolutely certain that they have the fullness of the truth about Tibet, while non-Chinese do not.

All criticism of China's actions in Tibet was met by Chinese officials and ordinary citizens alike with a recital of purportedly irrefutable facts. All Chinese know, or think they know, that Tibetans are vastly better off now than they were under the feudal rule of the Dalai Lama and that each and every advance since that time has been due to the generosity of the Chinese government and people. That the Tibetans might prefer to govern themselves and enact their own laws instead of being governed by a foreign race with a superiority complex is simply inconceivable to them. The same Chinese who will rail for hours about the evil foreigners who colonized China in centuries past, will angrily defend China's right to colonize Tibet in the present day.[59]

If you want to know what the world under Chinese hegemony would look like, visit present-day Lhasa. The Chinese party-state's efforts since the Tibetan uprising of 2008 to eradicate all opposition within Tibet by means of repressive force have been extraordinarily heavy-handed and, to all appearances, effective. The Tibetans have now been reduced to a dhimmi-like status in their own native land. Without irony or embarrassment, the Chinese party-state actually touts its "benevolent rule" over Tibet as an example of the "harmonious world" that China will create once it has reached pre-eminence.

As we have seen, the party-state had hoped that the 2008 Olympics would be a coming-out party for China, a chance to showcase China's growing economic clout and confirm its status as one of the world's leading powers. These goals it arguably achieved. Its ability to concentrate and deploy resources for this huge effort requiring enormous organization and discipline were impressive. The opening ceremony alone, with its thousands of identically dressed, impassively faced little marching martinets, is not easily forgotten.

At the same time, however, the Beijing Olympics taught the world another, more troubling lesson. It revealed the depth and irrationality of contemporary Chinese narcissistic nationalism. One of the most astute observers of the Tibetan and Chinese scenes is Warren W. Smith Jr. of Radio Free Asia. Smith writes:

> When it comes to issues of identity, security and foreign relations, the vast majority of Chinese are at one with their leaders—they are Hegemons.
>
> The reaction of overseas Chinese to what they regarded as insults to their pride and China's reputation during the Olympic torch relay was an ominous and frightening display of the irrationality, intolerance, and threat of Chinese nationalism when it is aroused. The sort of aggrieved nationalistic defensiveness that was on display in the popular Chinese reaction to criticism about Tibet reveals much about China itself.

The overseas Chinese did not regard the issue as being about Tibet at all. All they could see was an intentional insult to China, based on nothing but an anti-China bias, which evoked a finely cultivated sensitivity about their country's victimization in the past. It was ominous to see how intolerant of contrary opinions, how arrogant even in its ignorance, and how threatening and frightening in its aggressiveness Chinese nationalism could be. This display of mindless Chinese nationalism, while claiming the utmost rationality, was a frightening prospect not only for those who hope that China might someday treat Tibetans a bit better, but for any who hope that China might play a non-confrontational, cooperative role in the world.[60]

Two hundred years after the Qing court refused to countenance a visit from Britain's emissary unless he kowtowed to the hegemon, its latest reincarnation, still supremely solipsistic, is once again demanding obeisance. Those who refuse to bend the knee are met with blind, unreasoning anger. Welcome to China's world.

8

THE SUM OF ALL CHINA'S FEARS

*"China's leaders consistently characterize the United States
as a 'hegemon,' connoting a powerful protagonist and
overbearing bully that is China's major competitor."*
—U.S.-CHINA ECONOMIC AND SECURITY REVIEW COMMISSION,
Annual Report, 2002[1]

Xi Jinping is encouraging his people to dream, and to dream big. They are the generation of China "Dreamers," he tells them, who will help the party-state realize the "strong China dream" of world domination. This Chinese national dreamscape is a series of tableaus: past and future. The distant past is a stirring collection of civilizational triumphs over uncultured barbarians. The immediate past is a series of greatly resented humiliations at the hands of technologically advanced but culturally inferior Caucasians. The immediate future is a pleasant fantasy of Sinic vengeance upon the Western powers that brought China low. Looming in the distance is a return to the "Great Harmony" of centuries past, when a resurgent China rules the world to the benefit of all peoples. So goes the fantasy spun by the party-state's propaganda machine.

It was Confucius himself who said that the first task of any government is "to rectify the names." What the Sage meant by this was that it was necessary for the political authority to ensure that everyone from the highest mandarin to the lowest peasant understands his proper place in the political and social hierarchy. Once the people were properly indoctrinated in Confucian teachings and taught their place in the pecking order by Confucian rituals social stability would follow. It was an early form of mind control, which led naturally to development of what the Chinese Communist Party calls, with unabashed candor, *xi nau*, which literally means "washing brain," or brainwashing.

It is important to understand that the CCP, at least from the Yenan period in the 1940s on, has practiced "brainwashing" not merely on outspoken dissidents but on everyone. The point of the "self-criticism" sessions that were a regular feature of life under Chairman Mao—and that have been reinstituted under Xi Jinping—was to bring everyone's thoughts into alignment with the Party's, that is to say, with Mao's—and now Xi's—own. Even today, there is nothing akin to a Western "right of privacy" or "right of conscience" that would prevent the party-state from imprinting its policies wholesale on the minds and bodies of its subjects.

Consider the so-called "one-child policy," under which the state has in effect seized control of every single human reproductive system in the entire country. An exaggeration, you say? Those who think so should reflect on the words of Vice Premier Chen Muhua, who formerly headed China's Family Planning Board. In launching the policy in 1979, Chen declared, "Socialism should make it possible to regulate the reproduction of human beings so that population keeps step with the growth of material production."[2] China's Planned Birth campaign continues to be an integral part of the country's five-year economic plans, including the 13th Five-Year Plan, which runs from 2016 to 2020. The two-child policy, announced in 2015, is nothing more than an effort to ramp up reproduction rates to meet China's need for future workers.

If one's body belongs to the Chinese party-state, then of course one's mind does as well. One can almost hear Deng Xiaoping—or Xi

Jinping—saying *Socialism should make it possible to regulate the production of thought the same way that it regulates the production of goods.* Big Daddy Xi is ratcheting up controls over all kinds of "thought work," and has made it clear that all Chinese media must serve the interests of the ruling Communist Party. China's top Internet regulator recently told the operators of mobile and online news services such as Tencent and Sohu.com that they must immediately shut down all their "current-affairs news" operations. Henceforth web services were to carry *only* state-approved media news, said the Cyberspace Administration of China, which justified the change by saying that such companies had "seriously violated" Internet regulations through their original reporting and caused "huge negative effects." From now on the only news that they will be allowed to report is that provided by government-controlled print or online media.[3]

The *China dream of the past* is easy for the party-state to conjure up in the minds of men, while the *China dream of the future* requires only a small leap of faith. After all, most Chinese view history as cyclical, so that it should be only a matter of time until the wheel turns and China comes out on top again. The stumbling block is the *China dream of the present.* It is all well and good for the Party's promoters of national narcissism to speak of the excellence of the Chinese race and the superiority of Chinese civilization, but all of this self-adulation raises a troubling question: If the Chinese are such a superior race, if they were so dominant in ages past and are destined to dominate again in the future, *why are they not dominant now?* The Chinese Communist Party has a one-word answer to this conundrum: foreigners.

A suspicion of things foreign is reinforced by the party-state at every opportunity. The state-controlled media is constantly reminding the population how Western barbarians have mistreated the Middle Kingdom over the years, from burning the Summer Palace to the ground more than a century ago, to bombing the PRC embassy in Belgrade during the Kosovo air campaign of the nineties, to illegally transiting the South

China Sea (which the party-state absurdly claims has been a Chinese lake since time immemorial). It is the young, above all, that the Party is determined to prejudice against the wider world. For the past quarter century, a xenophobic nationalism has been codified into the education curriculum and force-fed to students from kindergarten to college.

PATRIOTIC EDUCATION:
A PRIMER FOR BUDDING NATIONAL NARCISSISTS

The Great Han Chauvinism (*Dazhonghuazhuyi*)—the potent and peculiarly Chinese form of ultranationalism that relies in equal measure on collective narcissism and xenophobia—that we explored in the last chapter is what the keepers of state orthodoxy have seized on as a substitute for communism. If Eastern European Communists saved themselves following the collapse of the Berlin Wall by becoming "social democrats," then post-Tiananmen Chinese Communists saved their one-party system—China's new Great Wall against democratization—from collapse by becoming Great Han Chauvinists. China's current crop of Legalists has replaced the decaying myth of communism with a robust race-based chauvinism, and the vanguard of the proletariat has reinvented itself as the protector of the Great Han Race, promoter of its superior culture, and protector of its glorious traditions.

The Chinese Communist Party has always portrayed itself as the paramount patriotic force in the nation, but following the Tiananmen debacle it desperately sought to shore up its crumbling mythology by all the institutional means under its control. The comprehensive program of political indoctrination that followed was described by the then-mayor of Beijing, Chen Xitong, as "systems engineering" (*sitong gongcheng*).[4] It was certainly *social* engineering on a grand scale. The entire educational system was mobilized to teach students about China's "history of shame;" every state-run factory in the country required its workers to sit through patriotic indoctrination sessions and the state-controlled media as well as the schools relentlessly promoted Chinese exceptionalism through what is called "state-of-the-nation education" or *guoqing jiaoyu*.

The official Party definition of *guoqing* (literally "national situation") is that "China is a nation that has successfully established a socialist system that over time has proved superior to capitalism but that, nonetheless, requires further political and economic reform.... China has an ancient history that has given birth to numerous positive national traditions and traits. The negative ideological influence of the old society, however, has not been entirely eradicated." Only the Chinese Communist Party, the not-so-subliminal message runs, can provide the strong central government required by China's unique *guoqing* and current national priorities, along with continued economic growth and the means to recover Chinese preeminence in Asia and accomplish the "rectification of historical accounts"—which requires wreaking havoc on the United States and other "imperialist" powers.[5]

These efforts achieved a bureaucratic apogee in September 1994 with the publication of a sweeping Party directive called the "Policy Outline for Implementing Patriotic Education."[6] The directive ordered that "Patriotic education shall run through the whole education process from kindergarten to university...and must penetrate classroom teaching of all related subjects." While PRC history textbooks have always stoked nationalist fervor and xenophobia, these same attitudes were now to be inserted into everything from beginning readers to junior high school social science textbooks to high school political education classes. The resulting kindergarten-through-college curriculum has been custom-designed to breed young national narcissists.

A second-grade reader includes the story of a young cowherd who "led the Japanese devils into an ambush" by the Communist Eighth Route Army during the Second World War, sacrificing her own life in the process. Another primer, "Ten Must-Knows for Elementary School Students," issued to commemorate the fiftieth anniversary of the People's Republic of China, cites "one hundred years of Chinese people opposing foreign aggression" as the raison d'être for the country's founding. An eighth-grade social science textbook begins, "Our motherland in history was once an advanced and great nation...but after the invasions of the European and American capitalist Great Powers, a profound national crisis occurred."

Complex historical events are twisted to fit a simple morality tale of good Chinese patriots versus evil foreign imperialists, especially Americans. Neither the Manchus nor the Nationalists are praised for avoiding outright colonization, only condemned for the insults to China's greatness that occurred on their watches. The Taiping Rebellion, a mid-nineteenth-century uprising with Christian roots that sought to overthrow Manchu rule, is transmogrified into "the largest peasant war in Chinese history," put down by "foreign and Chinese reactionary forces." The Boxer Rebellion, in which a fin-de-siècle secret society brutally killed tens of thousands of Chinese Christians, hundreds of missionaries and their families, and assorted other foreigners, is venerated as "the high point of the struggle to oppose imperialistic aggression."

"History is a maiden, and you can dress her up however you wish," the Chinese say. The Patriotic Education policy is less about accurately depicting past events than about propagating a meta-narrative designed to stir the blood of young Chinese. It goes like this: The Middle Kingdom's centuries of national grandeur were ended by foreign imperialists at whose hands the Chinese people suffered a hundred years of humiliation, but now, under the strong leadership of the Chinese Communist Party, the Chinese are dreaming the "Strong China Dream" of reasserting their traditional place in the world.

Rewriting history is nothing new in China. In imperial times, every dynastic founder was at pains to commission a warts-and-all history of the previous dynasty. By elaborating in excruciating detail how the previous ruling house had lost the Mandate of Heaven, the new ruler bolstered his own claim. But now, fifty years after the founding of the PRC, the potted histories of the present leadership have a slightly different purpose. They are designed not so much to delegitimize the Nationalist regime that preceded the Communists as to implant the idea that China is absolutely unique among nations, that the People's Republic is a natural outgrowth of China's imperial, dynastic past, and that only the Chinese Communist Party can lead a unified China into the future, recovering lost Chinese lands and tributaries by undoing the imperialist powers that occupy them.[7]

What this patriotic education comprises, in broad strokes, is a kind of Chinese *Mein Kampf*. Like Hitler's work, it lays out a grand strategy for world domination. Winston Churchill's summation of *Mein Kampf* has to be altered very little to describe the story the Chinese people are hearing from their government today:

> The Chinese are a great race that for millennia has rightly dominated its known world. But the foreign imperialists humbled us, brutally tearing off and devouring living parts of the Chinese race and nation, even threatening the whole with disunity. But China has now stood up and is fighting back, determined to recover her lost grandeur no less than her lost territories. We must be wary of things foreign, absorbing only those that make us stronger and rejecting those, like Christianity and Western ideas of democracy and human rights, which make us weaker. The first duty of the Chinese state is therefore to nationalize the masses and resist these foreign ideas. Only the Chinese Communist Party has the will and determination to lead the struggle. The new China must gather within its fold all the scattered Chinese elements in Asia. A people that has suffered a century and a half of Western humiliation can be rescued by reviving its self-confidence. To restore the Chinese nation, the PLA must become modernized and invincible. The world is now moving toward a new

millennium, and the Chinese state must see to it that the Chinese race is ready to assume its proper place in the world as the hegemon.[8]

And it is all too easy to imagine Xi Jinping saying, as Hitler did in the conclusion to *Mein Kampf*, "A state which in this age of racial poisoning dedicates itself to the care of its best racial elements must some day become lord of the earth.[9] Just substitute the word hegemon for "lord of the earth"—which, come to think of it, is a pretty good synonym—and you have the gist of Beijing's program.[10]

To achieve this goal it is not enough for the Chinese leadership to merely promote a love of country. Narcissistic hypernationalism of the kind practiced in China demands a foil, an enemy in whom one can see the dark, fearful shadow of the "other." In the case of the Nazis, that was the victorious Allies of World War I—Great Britain, France, Russia, and Italy—who had imposed the Versailles Treaty on a prostrate Germany. In the case of China, it is the United States of America. Of course, some of China's rancor is directed at America's allies, especially Japan, rather than at America itself. But the lion's share is aimed at the country that China's leaders love to hate, the United States.

Just as flint requires steel to strike a spark, so does narcissistic nationalism require an antagonist to light a fire in the minds of men. So it is that the Chinese people are taught that all of China's present-day ills arise from a single source: the United States of America. It is American machinations over the past century and a half that have kept China down. It is America that stands in the way of China's long march to national glory. And, were it not for the continuous opposition of the ruthless reigning hegemon (that's us), the Middle Kingdom would already be center stage in the affairs of men. Such views are not just propaganda fodder for the unwashed masses, they are firmly held by the top leaders as well. "China's leaders consistently characterize the United States as a 'hegemon,'" notes the U.S.-China Economic and

Security Review Commission. "[This] connotes a powerful protagonist and overbearing bully that is China's major competitor."[11]

America lives rent-free in the minds of the Chinese leadership as the sum of all their fears. It is American power that prevents the New China from seizing the "breakaway province" of Taiwan and forcibly returning it to the embrace of the motherland. It is America and its allies that encircle and contain China within a ring of alliances. It is American ideals that inspired the Tiananmen demonstrations for democracy that threatened to topple their rule. And they remain convinced—against all evidence to the contrary—that it was America that engineered the collapse of the Soviet Union in 1991 by means of a strategic deception. "In the parlance of the Warring States period," writes Michael Pillsbury, "[the U.S. is said to have] trapped the Soviet youth and idealists with a "beautiful honey pot" and then used them as "spies to sow discord in the enemy camp."[12] The Chinese leadership was and is determined to avoid being "duped" in the same way by what appears to them to be a dazzling display of American statecraft.

The Tiananmen demonstrations alerted the Politburo that the "beautiful honey pot" of American ideals was "sowing serious discord" within China itself. If there had been any doubt in the minds of Deng Xiaoping and other hardliners about who was responsible for the occupation of Tiananmen Square by tens of thousands of students, the appearance on the Square of a thirty-three-foot-tall statue modeled on the Statue of Liberty erased it. When they saw the Goddess of Democracy, as she was called, they were outraged. "This is China, not America!" they thundered, demanding that the "abomination" be taken down.[13] Deng ordered troops to clear the Square and the surrounding streets, killing hundreds or thousands in the process (the exact death toll is still a matter of debate.) But that was just the beginning. Reflecting on what had happened, the Deng-led government concluded that the Communist party needed to improve its "thought work." So they ordered Voice of America broadcasts jammed, an overarching narrative of foreign invasion and humiliation of China taught to old and young alike and, most important, the history of U.S.-China relations completely rewritten to put America in the worst possible light. Chinese of all ages, but especially the impressionable young, were once again to be taught to regard the country known in Chinese as the "Beautiful Country" with suspicion, if not outright enmity.

HOW THE CHINESE PARTY-STATE TEACHES CHILDREN TO HATE AMERICA

For the past twenty-five years, largely unnoticed by the outside world, anti-American propaganda of the most vicious kind has been taught to Chinese children in an effort to inoculate them against American democratic ideals. The most telling example is the recent reprinting of a 1951 "history textbook" called *A History of the U.S. Aggression in China*. Written by a Party hack by the name of Wang Chun, the book was commissioned by Chairman Mao himself. In his 1949 speech, "'Friendship' or Aggression," Mao directed that "The history of the aggression against China by U.S. imperialism, from 1840 when it helped the British in the Opium War to the time it was thrown out of China by the Chinese people, should be written into a concise textbook for the education of Chinese youth."[14]

In announcing the reprinting of *A History of the U.S. Aggression in China* in 2012, the Chinese Academy of Social Sciences (CASS) ponderously explained, "Although time has progressed, the historical facts contained in this book are still true. They do not change due to the change of the times."[15]

The first villain to be trotted onto the stage of this modern Beijing opera is the hapless John Tyler, the accidental American president whom Mao claims imposed upon China "the first unequal treaty signed as a result of U.S. aggression against China."[16] America had not been a belligerent in the First Opium War (1839–1842), but that didn't relieve Tyler from responsibility for what followed. In the Chinese view, the devious American president had cleverly adopted the Warring States stratagem of "waiting at leisure while the enemy labors." Then, when British seapower had brought the Qing dynasty low, he struck. He demanded that the Emperor sign the Wangxia Treaty, granting to the United States all the concessions that Great Britain had wrung from China. This allowed the United States to join Great Britain in engaging in what one textbook calls "illegal actions to exploit China."[17]

From Mao's perspective, which now animates the history that Chinese students are force-fed, all early American activity in China, from the trade that flowed innocently through the treaty ports to the hospitals, universities and churches started by missionaries was "spiritual aggression." The United States "worked so hard and deliberately at running these undertakings" as part of a secret, long-term plan to manipulate, control, and ultimately assert complete hegemony over China.[18]

The next American leader to earn the wrath of Chinese hawks was that evil genius, Abraham Lincoln. Honest Abe may be fondly remembered in America for preserving the Union and freeing the slaves, but in China he is regarded as just another grasping American imperialist. The "unequal treaty" that he forced upon China after the Second Opium War was a further step in the enslavement of the Chinese people. As Michael Pillsbury writes,

> A professor at Renmin University named Shi Yinhong has argued the Lincoln wanted "China to be dominated, or even exploited, within the international community." According to this version of history, that's why Lincoln sent the diplomat Anson Burlingame across the Pacific to normalize relations between China and the Western world. According to Mei Renyi at the Center for American Studies at Beijing's Foreign Languages University, the Burlingame Treaty of 1868 forced China "to follow Western cultural norms." It broke down

native rituals and China's system of etiquette in favor of Western diplomatic traditions and made possible Lincoln's dream of American control of the Pacific.[19]

Then came the Boxer Rebellion of 1900, when patriotic Chinese rebels rose up against the scheming, arrogant Americans and attempted to cleanse the Middle Kingdom of all foreign devils. The United States, under that China-hating monster William McKinley, retaliated by organizing all of the imperialist powers into an eight-nation expeditionary force, which set about butchering the poorly armed rebels and imperial troops with modern weapons. The American-led force—"killing with a borrowed sword" in the words of another Warring States stratagem—cut a swath of death and destruction across northern China, capturing the capital and burning the Summer Palace. The United States and its allies then "looted a burning house" by demanding heavy reparations (some $67 billion in 2016 dollars) from the Qing court.

The cunning Woodrow Wilson was the next American imperialist intent upon dismembering and dominating China. Wilson pretended to push for the self-determination of peoples at the Versailles peace conference, say the Patriotic Education textbooks, but secretly intended to sell out the Chinese people all along. Breaking his promise to return the captured German colony of Shandong to the Chinese government, he handed it over to Japan instead. Chinese supernationalists, says Pillsbury, see "Wilson's dream of liberty and global military cooperation to secure peace [as] a clever ruse to fool the world into sanctioning America's hegemonic aggression.... Like a duplicitous hegemon from the Warring States period, Wilson was clandestinely subverting a weakened Warring State."

Franklin Delano Roosevelt proved to be a surprisingly adept master of Warring States strategy as well. According to Chinese historians, this American Machiavelli was nearly able to realize the century-long American dream of bringing all of China within America's sway. The sly

Roosevelt first connived at the Japanese invasion of China in the 1930s, and then for the next few years "sat atop the mountain and watched the tigers fight." Professor Tang Qing has written how Roosevelt "caused the Chinese people to pay a greater sacrifice in the War of Resistance," because it was "good for the United States to keep the Chinese fighting the Japanese, make China a base against Japan, [and] promote wartime cooperation between China and the United States, so that the U.S. could someday completely dominate China and the entire world."[20] The United States "watched the fires burning from across the river," husbanding its strength. Then, when its two East Asian rivals had spent themselves in years of constant warfare, the United States, having "obtained a safe passage to conquer," fell upon its nearly helpless victims.[21]

It is hard to see Richard Nixon's opening to China as anything but the great boon to backward China that it proved to be—unless, of course, you are a Chinese conspiracy theorist determined to tar every American president with the blackest motives possible. In Nixon's case, hawkish Chinese historians now allege, he went to China in the hope of goading the Soviets into launching a nuclear war against the People's Republic. After the two Communist countries destroyed each other (while the United States once again "sat atop the mountain and watched the tigers fight"), the United States would reign unchallenged as the sole superpower for generations to come. Chairman Mao beat Nixon at his own game, however—or so the Chinese version of history goes—by sagaciously adopting a strategy from the Three Kingdoms period (A.D. 220–280) of "allying with Wu in the east to oppose Wei in the north." Mao understood that "Wu in the east"—the United States—might prove to be the greater threat to China in the decades to come, but in the meantime it was "Wei in the north"—the Soviet Union—that needed to be checked using the borrowed might of its temporary ally of convenience.[22]

This fabricated history of U.S.-China relations is an insult to every American, living or dead, who ever tried to help China in years past, from the schoolchildren who donated their lunch money "for the starving children of China," to the missionaries who selflessly populated the Chinese landscape with churches, schools, universities, and hospitals. President Tyler did not set out to "exploit China" but simply to make a treaty to regulate trade. He first wrote the Emperor of China a "letter of peace and friendship," saying about his proposed concord: "Let it be just. Let there be no unfair advantage to either side."[23] The treaty that resulted was favorable to China, establishing equitable diplomatic relations, opening Chinese ports to trade while discouraging traffic in opium, and permitting Americans, for the first time, to legally learn Mandarin.

President Lincoln's gift to China was Anson Burlingame, a former Republican congressman and fellow opponent of slavery. The new minister to the Qing Empire, a man of high principle, was determined that China would be treated with "fair diplomatic action," instead of "the old doctrine of violence." And, against all odds, he succeeded. The European powers agreed that they would "give to the [unequal] treaties a fair and Christian construction; that they…never would menace the territorial integrity of China."[24] Qing court officials were so impressed by Burlingame's sincerity and success that, at the end of his term of office, they asked him to head a Chinese diplomatic mission *back* to the United States. The treaty that resulted, named after Burlingame himself, was the first equal treaty between China and a Western power. This is somehow never mentioned in Chinese history books.

The eight-nation expeditionary force organized in response to the Boxer Rebellion was not an invading army but a rescue mission. Thousands of Chinese Christians had sought refuge inside the Legation Quarter and the Beitang Catholic Church when the uprising began, joining the hundreds of foreigners already there. Both were under siege by the rebels, who clearly intended to kill them all.[25] The United States, for its part, not only tried to restrain the other foreign soldiers from raping and pillaging, it later used much of its share of the indemnity money to pay for over a thousand Chinese students to study in the United States in the years that followed.

President Wilson, for his part, went to Versailles determined that Shandong province would be returned to China. He even obtained a promise from the Japanese that their occupation would be temporary, a promise that was later violated.

Roosevelt was not trying to subjugate China, but to save it. As a result he took a series of actions that so antagonized the Japanese militarists that they helped to provoke the attack on Pearl Harbor. Among other things, he encouraged the formation of the Flying Tigers—American volunteer pilots for the Chinese Air Force—which had some of the best kill-ratios of the entire war.[26] Japanese forces were bogged down in China, to be sure, but it was the American island-hopping campaign, the sinking of Japanese naval and merchant fleets and, of course, the atom bomb that finally brought Japan to its knees.

Nixon, rather than encouraging a nuclear holocaust between the Soviet Union and China, actually helped to prevent it. In 1969 the Soviets hinted to the U.S. government that they were preparing to launch a first strike against China's small arsenal of nuclear weapons. Nixon strongly objected, and the Kremlin dropped the idea.

As far as the Tiananmen demonstrations were concerned, they were in no way planned or orchestrated by the United States. Rather, they were a spontaneous expression of the desire of the Chinese, especially the young, for a more open and democratic society.

Presumably not all Chinese historians, especially those trained in the United States, believe these fabrications, but they are all required to parrot them. When Michael Pillsbury asked one Beijing professor why he was teaching his students about the "evil China policies" of Presidents Tyler, Wilson, and Lincoln, the man stammered in embarrassment: "I do not pick the text materials. The entire faculty is Party members and the Central Committee keeps files on us. Deviating from approved teaching materials would end our careers."[27] Pity the poor Chinese historian who has to falsify history as the price of being allowed to teach it.

Such a false and defamatory reading of the history of U.S.-China relations is not simply written into textbooks and curricula, it is carved into some of the hundreds of concrete monuments throughout China that have been built on the orders of the Chinese Communist Party. The 1991 "Patriotic Education Campaign", notes Wang Zheng, "required local governments of all levels to establish "patriotic education bases." Visits to these anti-foreign memorials, he explains, have been mandated by the Ministry of Education and so have become a regular part of the "education in national shame" that every Chinese child is subjected to.[28] The vast majority of the students, unless they go on to study overseas, will have no idea that they are being misled.

The Party-controlled media have seconded this educational curriculum with a drumbeat of propaganda about the Chinese people and their past designed to appeal to Chinese pride, fan the fires of nationalism, and bolster the Party's own flagging image by identifying it with potent nationalistic symbols. For this program they have found a receptive audience. By 1994, only three years into the Patriotic Education Program, workers, farmers, and science students ranked "patriotism" in first place on a list of values, up from fifth place a decade ago. Among young people as a whole "patriotism" had climbed into second place, topped only by "self-respect" in importance.[29]

The antidote to this poisonous propaganda is, of course, the truth, but Chinese students are not exposed to it. Never again, the leaders of the Chinese party-state have determined, will Chinese students occupy the main squares of Chinese cities waving signs with quotations from Washington and Jefferson. Never again will they build a replica of the Statue of Liberty on China's central square. If they want quotations, they can quote Mao and Xi. If they want monuments, they can gaze upon the patriotic monuments that we have constructed and ponder the anti-foreign inscriptions there. In fact, we will mandate that they do so.

If students are easily indoctrinated, one would expect better of China's intellectuals, who should know enough not to thoughtlessly imbibe this witches' brew of falsehoods. After all, the truth about such matters is easily accessible on the Internet, even from behind China's Great Firewall. Sadly, it has proven all too easy for the state to indoctrinate Chinese intellectuals against Western ideals of liberty and human rights. They have always been prone to fall prey to a nationalism that is not only narcissistic, but extremely xenophobic—a deeply held conviction that their nation, culture, and race are superior to all others. As Liu Xiaobo noted, this narcissistic nationalism produces a suppliant, even sycophantic attitude toward the state.

Intellectuals in China seem to give in all too readily to the notion of "my state, right or wrong, but still my state," according to which any action can be justified by a cultural-historical-racial appeal to unity, especially against an outside threat. An example of the current symbiosis between those who rule and those who think is *China: Just Say No!* Written by five young intellectuals of the sort who a generation ago would have been demonstrating in Tiananmen Square, this tract urges the Chinese people to resist the American "conspiracy" to keep China from assuming its rightful place in the world. In his preface to this popular book, author He Peiling writes that

> the direction that China—as the single existing socialist superpower—will take has become the focus of the world's attention. The U.S., because of deep-rooted ideological differences and its intention to dominate the world all by itself, views China's ascendance with considerable anguish and concern. From [the U.S.] perspective, China might well become a rival that can deter the global hegemony of American culture, economy and military power. Therefore, a conspiracy from the "free world" that is aimed at China has begun to take shape.... In sum, the basic policy of the U.S. is the containment of China. The U.S. has already launched a new cold war aimed at China.[30]

Like all books published in the PRC, *China: Just Say No!* could not have appeared in print without an official imprimatur.[31] And the party-state had no reason not to give it, since the book blames all of China's problems on a foreign conspiracy. In recent years, the state-run media has grown ever more strident in its blame of "overseas," "foreign," and "Western" forces (all synonyms for the United States) for China's internal problems—whether the issue at hand is unrest among the native Tibetan population or student demonstrations for democracy in Hong Kong.

As for the top leadership, which authorized the publication of this book and the larger anti-American campaign of which it is a part, what do they believe? Is the anti-American vitriol pouring out of Beijing merely a kind of opiate for the masses, concocted by their political masters to distract them from problems closer to home, or are the masters themselves invested in their own propaganda? They certainly talk as if they have convinced themselves that America wants to encircle China, choke off its trade, strangle its economy, cause internal divisions, and ultimately defeat its rise to preeminence. But is this just rhetoric?

Xi Jinping himself has made no secret of his anti-American views. At his 2014 celebration of the Yenan Forum on the Arts, for example, he specifically praised the blogger Zhou Xiaoping for showing "positive energy."[32] Zhou is best known for his rabidly anti-American screeds, such as his essay entitled "Nine Knockout Blows in America's Cold War Against China." Published in the state-run *Guangming Daily*, it argued that America was carrying out a cyberwar against China, deliberately using the Internet "to poison Chinese civilization and manipulate public opinion." Citing everything from the movie "Superman" to Christianity, Zhou claimed that American culture has "erode[d] the moral foundation and self-confidence of the Chinese people" and that American news reports on China "promote racism…and…a feeling of inferiority." He even compared this "indiscriminate smearing of an entire race" to Hitler's treatment of the Jews.

Zhou is no one-hit wonder. In another online essay, he claimed that the West has "slaughtered and robbed" China and other civilizations since the seventeenth century. Now America was "brainwashing" China using the Internet, he said. [33] This is the everyman's edition of the Patriotic Education Program that not only Xi Jinping but the entire party leadership subscribes to. To judge by their public statements, they are no less in thrall to national narcissism than the schoolchildren that they miseducate, or their forebears in dynasties past, for that matter. They resent American military, economic, and cultural dominance and look forward to the day when they can dominate America instead.

The Beijing regime constantly stokes this narcissistic, xenophobic nationalism with whatever fuel happens to be handy, be it a recent visit of the Japanese prime minister to the Yakusuni Shrine to memorialize Japanese war dead or the transit of an American carrier task force across the vast reaches of the South China Sea.

Following the accidental bombing of the Chinese embassy in Belgrade in 1999, for example, the official propaganda machine turned up the anti-American rhetoric to a white heat. "Evildoers doomed to meet destruction," read one headline in the *People's Daily,* the voice of Party orthodoxy, which went on to compare America's supposed efforts to dominate the world with those of Nazi Germany. The bombing of the embassy was a deliberate attack, the paper charged, a shot across the bow of an increasingly powerful China warning her not to challenge American hegemony. The Chinese people are aware of America's "vicious" intentions, the article concluded, and will work hard to "build up [China's] national strength and beef up its competitiveness."[34]

The vast majority of the Chinese people saw the attack as intentional. They simply refused to believe the attack was a "mistake," and rejected NATO's apology. Instead, they claimed that their embassy had been deliberately targeted for destruction because China was vigorously denouncing "U.S. hegemonism." The *Beijing Youth Daily* reported that a public opinion survey found that *every one* of the 831 people polled believed America had carried out the bombing deliberately. A majority of 56 percent said they thought America was "barbaric and crazy," (that is, that we are crazy barbarians). Thirty-seven percent averred that the U.S. government was "controlled by Nazis."[35]

Nazis, that's us.

9

AS CHINA ADVANCES, AMERICA MUST NOT RETREAT

*"No other nation today poses a greater danger
to American national security than China, a state engaged in
an unprecedented campaign of information warfare...."*
–BILL GERTZ, *iWar: War and Peace in the Information Age*[1]

There are no "safe spaces" in the anarchic world we live in. The militarily weak and technologically backward PLA that Deng Xiaoping commanded to "bide its time and hide its capabilities" has been replaced by a mighty military-industrial complex furiously engaged in a military buildup whose obvious purpose is to challenge the United States for dominance on the land, sea, air, and space. The Chinese party-state commands an economy approaching the size of America's own. When leading Chinese military figures like General Chi Haotian openly express the view that war between the U.S. and China is "inevitable," it would be foolish not to regard this explosive concatenation of capabilities and intentions with some alarm—especially when the Chinese party-state has deliberately added inflammatory territorial claims against countries America is committed by treaty to defend.

Is this just sabre rattling, or is China truly bent on becoming the dominant power on the planet—the hegemon? If it is, we should be able to find ample evidence that it is acting on that intention.

In addition to threats of war and demands for territory, we would expect to find China's drive for dominance expressed in other ways as well. We could reasonably expect, for example, to find China engaged in a massive military buildup. We would also expect the Chinese to be conducting a covert cyberwar against the United States in an effort steal dual-use technology and discover vulnerabilities that could be exploited in the event of open conflict. We could expect to find the PRC aggressively engaged in an undeclared trade war with the United States in order to beggar its more powerful neighbor, as well as a worldwide quest to control critical resources. Finally, we could expect to find China assiduously seeking to build up its "soft power" both in the United States and other countries, in order to extend its influence farther afield by non-kinetic means.

And this is exactly what we *do* find.

THE COMING CLONE WARS

The country's burgeoning defense budget, which is now indisputably the second largest in the world, is testament enough not only to the country's regional ambitions, but to its global ones as well. There are many reports detailing China's ongoing military buildup. According to the Pentagon's 2016 annual report to Congress on Chinese military and security developments, China's total military-related spending in 2015 came to over $180 billion. But these raw numbers do not come close to telling the whole story, given that Beijing can field men and equipment faster and in greater numbers, and at considerably lower cost, than the U.S. presently can.[2] "Quantity," as Joseph Stalin is supposed to have remarked, "has a quality all its own."

Beyond this, there are three factors, often overlooked, that play to China's advantage. The first is China's phenomenally successful cyberespionage efforts, which have enabled it to dramatically shrink America's lead in military technology over the past fifteen years. The PLA no longer needs to reverse-engineer stolen helicopters and drones, it simply downloads the design and technical specifications from whatever U.S. defense contractor's computer network it has managed to penetrate and builds the ship or missile, weapon or radar system following the specifications of these stolen plans.[3]

Cyberespionage, in other words, has enabled China to take latecomer's advantage—in which a rising power can achieve rapid technological innovation and industrial upgrading by imitating, importing, and, in China's case, *outright stealing* existing technologies—to a whole new level. In this way, China has not only dramatically lowered its research and design costs, but is also leapfrogging entire generations of military technology to arrive at something close to the state of the art, whatever particular military art we might be talking about. In the best-case scenario such thievery dramatically shortens our technological lead; in the worst case it eliminates it entirely. China's stolid state-owned enterprises are notably deficient in their ability to research and develop innovative new and militarily useful technology. Cyberespionage means they don't have to. They simply steal ours.

It is no surprise that, as a number of commentators have pointed out, China's latest generation of weapons, from stealth drones all the way up to strike fighters, bears an uncanny resemblance to our own. The United States spends a trillion dollars developing the F-35 Lightning II and then, before it is even fully operational, China steals the plans and makes a cheap and probably reasonably effective knock-off called the Shenyang J-31, which was unveiled in late 2014.[4] In sum, China's ongoing cyberespionage against the United States is providing China with exploitable intelligence on U.S. capabilities and weaknesses as well as state-of-the-art weaponry. If China were to attack us with cloned weapons nearly as potent as our own, things could go very badly for U.S. forces.

The second factor in China's favor is its growing economy, which many predict is on the cusp of surpassing that of the United States. I am somewhat skeptical, since much of China's enormous GDP growth has been funded by soft government credit, and Japanese-style stagflation may already be setting in as a result. Moreover, as America's growth accelerates under President Trump, and our country once again begins to capitalize on its huge advantages over China in income, in natural resources, and in (surprisingly) labor, it may well be decades, rather than years, before China's economy eclipses America's.

But the fact remains that the U.S. hasn't faced an adversary whose economic heft comes close to matching our own in a hundred years. This means that the Reagan tactic of bleeding the Soviet Union dry by forcing it into a disastrous and unsustainable military buildup while denying it access to Western loans and technology will simply not work with China. The Chinese elite have studied the Soviet collapse, and they are determined not to repeat it. The PRC's economy is already too large, its military buildup too well-calibrated, and its cyber-raids on our technology too successful to make John Mearsheimer's proposed "strangulation" a viable strategy.[5] Whatever we do in terms of our relationship with China, including reducing our trade deficit and bolstering our cyber defenses, nothing will forestall that country's ability to build a military-industrial base as large as, or even larger, than, our own—and a military to match.

China's final advantage, when it comes to building up a military second to none, lies in the difference between the political systems of the two countries. America's two political parties have radically different views of their country's role in the world. Republicans generally embrace the U.S. military and, prizing it as a force for peace and stability in the world, seek to strengthen it when they are in office. Democrats, on the other hand, are generally suspicious of the American armed forces, favoring instead a lower international profile and peacekeeping efforts led by the UN. In fact, when in power, Democrats are prone to declare a "peace dividend," and divert as much of the Pentagon's budget to domestic programs as the minority party will allow. In this way, U.S. military capabilities and readiness tends to expand or contract depending upon which party is in control.

By way of contrast, the senior leaders of the ruling Chinese Communist Party are united in their desire to enhance the reach and might of China's military.[6] They hold this view in part as a matter of simple political self-preservation: they all understand that their collective power ultimately rests upon the loyalty of the military. But they also subscribe to this view because they are, to a man, Great Han Chauvinists, committed to building the People's Liberation Army into the most powerful military force the world has ever seen. Xi Jinping's "China Dream" of ultimately achieving the fabled "Grand Harmony" of one world under China is not his alone, but is a vision shared by all members of the Chinese elite.

It is also worth keeping in mind that, unlike American presidents who come and go with constitutionally dictated regularity, Xi Jinping is likely to be in power for decades. Having once served as a personal assistant to the minister of defense, he also has the kind of personal ties to the military that guarantee the continued support of the generals. Nor is this reincarnation of Mao Zedong going to toy with the sort of political reforms that might deflect China's energies into domestic concerns, or allow his political contemporaries to amass the kind of power that would allow them to challenge his policies or even his rule. Instead, he has embarked upon what the Pentagon calls a "long-term, comprehensive modernization of the armed forces...sweeping organizational reforms to overhaul the entire military structure...strengthen the Chinese Communist Party's (CCP) control over the military, enhance the PLA's ability to conduct joint operations, and improve its ability to fight short-duration, high-intensity regional conflicts at greater distances from the Chinese mainland."[7]

In sum, China's security policies are broadly consistent over time and are likely to remain so, while America's oscillate around our four-year election cycle and are equally likely to continue to do so. The resulting great power competition is beginning to resemble nothing so much as the classic race between the tortoise and the hare. And we all know how that turned out.

TRADING PLACES

China is already at war with us in the economic sphere. It consistently flouts the rules and breaks its promises. Its goal is to outstrip the United States, and it is not averse to undermining the existing international economic and political order in order to do so. China's outrageous theft of intellectual property is of a piece with its equally outrageous claim to own the entire South China Sea. Its devastating currency manipulation and illegal dumping violate both the letter and the spirit of the World Trade Organization, which it should never have been allowed to join. China's goal is not just to become the world's largest economy, but to be the world's dominant one as well, and it is willing to do almost anything to achieve this end.

Nowhere is China's undermining of the international order more evident than in this rapacious currency manipulation. China's currency has been undervalued for literally decades.[8] All during this time, cheap Chinese goods have been dumped into the world's markets, flooding into the United States and other countries at alarming rates. As a result, the U.S. trade imbalance with China has reached record—and unsustainable—levels. Unable to compete with these artificially low prices, U.S. factories by the thousands have closed, and the jobs that they provided to middle-class Americans have moved overseas.

The past couple of years have put a twist in this tale of Chinese mercantilism. As Xi's anti-corruption campaign got underway, China's nouveau riche, many if not most of whom are corrupt officials, began bundling money out of China as quickly as they could get their hands on dollars. As a result of this outflow of currency, the yuan has been in free fall since 2014. In 2016 alone, the yuan fell nearly 7 per cent against the greenback.[9] So alarmed was the Central Bank of China by this sudden, sharp decline that it spent over a trillion dollars of its hard currency reserves trying to moderate it. Apologists for China's rapacious economic behavior point to this intervention as proof positive that Beijing is not keeping its currency artificially devalued. It is no such thing.

I grant that this sharp decline in the value of the country's currency, unlike previous declines, was not directly engineered by Chinese officialdom. But this does not mean, as some have suggested, that China's rulers were displeased by this trend. Had they been, they had an additional three trillion in currency reserves they could have used—but did not—to bolster the yuan. Moreover, the capital flight was a direct consequence of the dictatorial actions of Big Daddy Xi, who was busily gathering more and more political, military, and economic power into his own hands. His blatant channeling of Chairman Mao made it obvious—to Chinese if not to naïve foreigners—that the country would never open up its financial markets and allow the yuan to float, as it had agreed to do way back in 2000 as a condition of joining the WTO.

Why didn't China make a more serious and sustained effort to keep its solemn pledge to keep its exchange rate stable? At the time, Beijing may have been calculating (along with nearly everyone else, it must be said) that Clinton would win the election, and would not press them on the devaluation.[10] Instead they got Donald Trump who, during the campaign, vowed to stop China's outrageous "theft of intellectual property," "illegal dumping," and "devastating currency manipulation."[11]

But it wasn't just President Trump complaining. Even international bankers were and are crying foul, asserting that China has violated its pledge to keep its exchange rate stable. Mark Williams, chief China economist at Capital Economics, fumed, "This [devaluation] makes a mockery of the People's Bank of China's suggestion that its policy is to keep the currency's value stable."[12] That promise did not originate with the PBOC, of course, but with China's leaders. It was none other than China's number two, Premier Li Keqiang, who had repeatedly reassured the world that "China will not rely on currency depreciation."[13]

I understand the anger of bankers like Williams. He and others who relied upon Premier Li's empty promises to bet on the stability of the yuan have lost money. But I wonder where they have been for the past thirty years. China has systematically kept the yuan artificially deflated—and systematically lied about it—for a generation or more. The benefits to China have greatly outweighed the costs. Why would it not continue?[14]

The yuan is still undervalued, despite the claims of some Chinese economists to the contrary. By comparing costs in China and elsewhere, economists at the World Bank and the International Monetary Fund have calculated that, under conditions of market equilibrium, the exchange rate should be about 3.5 yuan per USD. This is presumably where the RMB would trade without government meddling.[15] At the time of this writing, however, the actual exchange rate is 6.9. This means that the yuan is undervalued by almost half. Beijing is deliberately making Chinese goods cheap for foreign buyers—and making it almost impossible for American manufactures to compete.

CHINA'S RACE FOR RESOURCES

Everywhere you go in the world, you encounter China Inc.'s voracious appetite for land and resources. A Chinese government–controlled entity now owns the famous Bobbara Station in New South Wales—roughly the equivalent of Beijing taking over the King Ranch in Texas—along with many other prime agricultural properties in Australia. In New Zealand Chinese corporations have been buying up tens of thousands of acres of prime dairy land through local front companies, circumventing laws limiting foreign purchases.[16] In Canada PetroChina bought out its Canadian partner to become the first state-owned Chinese company to wholly own an oil sands development—a development that 75 percent of Canadians opposed. Canada, it should be noted, has the largest proven reserves of oil outside of Saudi Arabia and Venezuela.

These are not isolated events. All over the world, China is snapping up mines, agricultural land, and oil fields at a frenetic pace, often paying more—considerably more—than the going rate. The sheer scale of its purchases is astonishing. According to the American Enterprise Institute's "China Global Investment Tracker," over the past six years, China has spent an estimated $400 billion—about $1 billion per week—on direct investment abroad, most of which has gone towards securing commodities.[17]

From my perspective, China's global buying binge raises serious questions.

It would be disruptive enough if this sudden commodities grab were done with private capital. But it is not. Instead, it is orchestrated and carried out by the Chinese party-state, acting through its vast network of state-owned and state-controlled corporations. If China is determined to deploy the bulk of its foreign reserves, currently estimated at $3 trillion, in this fashion, it will be well on its way to controlling a significant percentage of key global commodities. I am convinced that we need to think long and hard about the security implications of allowing China to corner certain sectors of the commodities market.

A whole host of questions arises: How would China's leaders behave if they were in a position to set prices for, or restrict access to, various key commodities? Would they restrict access for non-economic policy ends? How and under what circumstances would they resort to military force to defend those resources, once they have purchased or otherwise asserted control over them?

China's past behavior gives cause for concern. We have already seen how when Beijing set out to punish Japan for arresting a Chinese fishing boat captain who had violated Japanese territorial waters it immediately imposed an embargo on shipments of "rare earths" to Japan. Since China has a near global monopoly on the production of "rare earths," of which Japan's electronics industry is a voracious consumer, this economic warfare proved very effective. Here we have a major international incident that dragged on for months, attracted enormous press attention, and provides us with a definitive answer to the question of how China will behave when it gains the upper hand in the competition for resources. If anyone doubts that the Chinese party-state will use any monopolies or near-monopolies to achieve political and strategic ends, ask the Japanese.

China also does not hesitate to administer economic punishment on foreign companies operating on its soil for the perceived misdeeds of their governments. The deployment of the THAAD missile defense system in South Korea over Beijing's objections has led China to angrily lash out against South Korean companies operating in-country. Never mind that the North Korean missile threat is real, or that it has been aided and abetted by China. According to South Korean officials, China's illegal targeting and harassment of Lotte, KIA, and other companies has cost these South Korean firms $10 billion to date.[18]

With examples like these, it is not easy to interpret China's drive to achieve market dominance in the coming struggle for the world's resources benignly, although some have tried. Dambisa Moyo, for instance, has argued that, since our "plundered world" is rapidly running out of everything—land, water, energy and minerals—China cannot be faulted for trying to lock up the lion's share of what little remains. In fact, she believes that, "Of all the world's great powers, only one, China, has focused its economic and political strategy on anticipating the considerable challenges presented by a resource-scarce future."[19]

Moyo argues that China, unlike the United States, is a beneficent presence in the world, since it "underwrites schools and hospitals, and pays for infrastructure projects such as roads and railways, catering to the needs of the host nations." All this largesse, she claims, "mak[es] China an altogether more attractive investor than international bodies such as the World Bank, which often tie loans to harsh policy restrictions." These supposedly "harsh policy restrictions," which she does not detail, include commitments from loan recipients to allow such things as freedom of the press, association, and assembly, as well as free and fair elections.

Of course, it is simply not true that aid from China comes with no strings attached. Beijing's aid is anything but altruistic, but rather is aimed at bending as many governments to its will as possible. Take the country of Cambodia, for example, which suffered so much from the Maoist-inspired and Beijing-supported predations of the Khmer Rouge. Cambodian prime minister Hun Sen used to call China "the root of all that is evil in Cambodia." Now he gushes that Phnom Penh's relations with Beijing are "entering into the best stage in history."[20] Hun Sen's transformation from panda hater to panda hugger began when the World Bank threatened to suspend hundreds of millions of dollars worth of assistance because of Phnom Penh's rampant corruption and its crackdown on civil liberties. China rode to the rescue with an April 2006 offer of $600 million worth of grants and loans, which came untied to any "harsh policy prescriptions." Other money has followed, and Cambodia has carried China's water in Association of Southeast Asian Nations (ASEAN) and other international forums ever since.[21]

In Angola, home of the second-largest oil deposits in Africa, the International Monetary Fund tried to force the government "to agree to provisions that would slash graft and improve economic management," as a first step towards moving the country in a democratic direction. Again China stepped in, offering a package of loans and credits worth up to six billion, on condition that Chinese firms carry out the reconstruction of the oil infrastructure. Privileged access to Angola's oil resources may well be another, albeit unpublicized, condition.[22]

When Western aid agencies insist that dictators respect human rights, they are not tying loans "to harsh policy restrictions," but to universal human values. When China rewards bad behavior by bribing those same dictators and turning a blind eye to human rights abuses, this is not accurately characterized as a value-neutral foreign policy. Rather, it is one that rewards tyrants and encourages despotism.

The Chinese party-state has always claimed to be operating from the purest of economic motives, denying charges of neo-colonialism and scoffing at suggestions that it might be tempted to military action in defense of its interests. Whereas the United States intervened in Iraq for its oil, or so Beijing claims, its own pursuit of resources would never, ever lead it to engage in such imperialistic adventures. But China has built a military base in Djibouti and Chinese combat troops are participating in the UN peacekeeping operation in South Sudan—clearly in the region to protect China's oil interests.[23] The bogus Chinese claim also conveniently overlooks one of the biggest resource grabs in history, namely, its insistence that the entire South China Sea—lock, stock, and oil barrel— is its sovereign territory. Not only has China arrogantly rebuffed the competing territorial claims of Vietnam, the Philippines, and several other Southeast Asian countries, it has shown a willingness to back up its claim with military force.

CHINA'S SOFT POWER: A HARD SELL

Since the Tiananmen Square demonstrations of 1989, the Chinese party-state has been fighting a desperate rearguard action against the incursions of Western political and popular culture. While the millions of protesters were ostensibly demonstrating against "bureaucracy and corruption," their real target was the Chinese Communist Party, which in their minds had become synonymous with both bureaucracy and corruption. What was also evident to everyone, up to and including Paramount Leader Deng Xiaoping himself, is that the political inspiration for their disaffection was American democratic ideals. Why else would the students erect a replica of the Statue of Liberty on Tiananmen Square itself? Although the episode ended in a massacre, for the Chinese leadership it was a sobering demonstration of the fact that not all political power grows out of the barrel of a gun.[24] A substantial number of their own citizens had been persuaded to demand radical change by nothing more than the attractive example of ordered liberty presented by the United States. It was an object lesson in the importance of soft power that Central Committee members are not likely to ever forget.

In the years since, China's leaders have repeatedly denounced the inroads of American soft power while seeking to enhance China's own— which is to say its ability to attract foreign support and persuade other countries to follow its lead. In 2012 then-President Hu Jintao warned the Party faithful that they "must clearly see that foreign hostile forces are intensifying the strategic plot of Westernizing and dividing China, and ideological and cultural fields are the focal areas of their long-term infiltration." He went on to decry the fact that "the international culture of the West is strong while we are weak."[25]

His successor, Xi Jinping, also blames "hostile foreign forces"—the West in general and the United States in particular—for any and all dissent from Communist Party rule.[26] "Western hostile forces are doing their best to promote so-called 'universal values,'" Xi told the thousands of Communist cadres in attendance at the August 2013 National Propaganda and Ideology Work Conference. "But they are 'hanging up a sheep's head to sell dog meat,'" he went on, using an idiom to suggest that the United States was being deliberately deceptive. "Their ultimate goal...is to overthrow the leadership of the Chinese Communist Party and China's Socialist system. If we allow [hostile foreign forces] to have their way, those false efforts will lead people astray, which is bound to bring chaos to the Party's hearts and the people's hearts, endanger the Party's leadership and the security of the Socialist national regime." The Communist Party should meet this threat head-on, he made it clear, using every means at its disposal to mold public opinion and ruthlessly quash dissent: "We must dare to arrest, dare to control, and dare to brandish the sword."[27] If Xi's ongoing crackdown on everyone—from pro-democracy activists and human rights lawyers to Falungong practitioners and Christian believers—tells us anything, it is that the "sword" of state power is being actively used to silence anybody and everybody who raises a dissenting voice.

Reflecting Xi's hardline anti-Western views, China's 2014 Defense White Paper also insists that America's soft power constitutes an existential threat to the continued rule of the Chinese Communist Party: "China faces a formidable task in maintaining political security and social stability" because "anti-China forces have never given up their attempt to instigate a 'color revolution' in this country."[28] Among the measures crafted to confront this threat is a tightening of ideological controls on institutions of higher learning. In 2015, then–Minister of Education Yuan Guiren publicly banned the use of textbooks that "disseminate Western values," by which he meant such subversive notions as respect for human rights, the rule of law, and popular sovereignty.[29] Instead, universities were to produce graduates steeped in Marxism, loyal to the Communist Party and, above all, obedient to "core leader" Xi Jinping.[30] Foreign films are another worrisome source of Western values, and so their entry into China is restricted under a quota system. Only thirty-four prescreened and preapproved movies are allowed to compete with China's heavily subsidized—and heavily censored—state film industry each year.[31]

Even as China seeks to exterminate its own nascent civil society, which it apparently regards as a Western-inspired Trojan Horse, it is seeking ways to influence the West's. In 2007 Hu Jintao told the Seventeenth Party Congress that it was time for China to fight back against the West and launch its own soft power offensive. China wanted to attract international support for its foreign policy initiatives by highlighting the success of its development model and showing off its traditional culture, not just by bullying or bribing countries into falling into line.

In the years since, China has spent billions of dollars on extravaganzas like the 2008 Beijing Olympics and the ongoing "Boao Forum for Asia," a Chinese mimicry of the Davos Forum that is held on Hainan

Island each year for some two thousand China-friendly Asian politicians and businessmen.

Aside from such high-profile ventures, Beijing has also steadily—if very, very stealthily—expanded its international media outreach. Such efforts picked up steam in 2013 following Uncle Xi's dicta to "vigorously construct more international communications capacity; Create new ways of doing foreign propaganda; Strengthen our ability to frame discourse.... "[32] Some of this has been done openly. Xinhua and China Central Television (CCTV) have been ramped up into global media outfits, for example.[33] But other efforts have been more clandestine. State-run China Radio International (CRI) is quietly buying or leasing foreign radio stations through front companies, stations that it then uses to broadcast China-friendly news and programming. A 2015 Reuters investigation identified "at least 33 radio stations in 14 countries that are part of a global radio web structured in a way that obscures its majority shareholder"—the Chinese party-state. These stations include a 50,000-watt AM station located near Washington, D.C., whose pro-Chinese slant on the news can be heard at the White House and on Capitol Hill. After CRI gained control of its programming, the station changed its call sign to WCRW, which the station's owner confirmed to Reuters stands for China Radio Washington.[34]

CRI head Wang Gengnian has described Beijing's strategy of paying foreign media outlets to carry Chinese propaganda as "borrowing a boat to go out to sea" (*jie chuan chu hai*).[35] But I would suggest to Wang that another popular Chinese idiom, "to kill with a borrowed sword" (*jie dao sha ren*), better conveys what he is actually about. After all, this disinformation campaign, broadcast from stations whose listeners are unaware that they have been "borrowed" by China, is intended to twist, distort, and indeed kill the truth.

Examples of the way these stations slant the news for their largely unsuspecting foreign audiences are easy to find. When foreign ministers from ten ASEAN countries criticized China for building artificial islands in the South China Sea, WCRW lived up to its name by blaming tensions in the contested region on "external forces" that were attempting "to insert themselves into this part of the world using false claims." Later in 2015, when a U.S. Navy ship steamed close by those same islands in a freedom-of-navigation exercise, WCRW reported that senior Chinese and U.S. naval commanders planned to speak by video "amid the tension the U.S. created this week." The Beijing-scripted broadcast somehow omitted to mention the actual source of the "tension": China's feverish construction of military bases on artificial islands in the South China Sea, intended to cement its outrageous claim that these international waters are actually its own sovereign "blue soil." The borrowed sword had struck again.

CONFUCIUS AS COMMUNIST FRONT MAN

The Chinese party-state has also been hard at work constructing a network of propaganda outposts—called Confucius Institutes or Confucius Classrooms—on the campuses of universities, colleges, and secondary schools around the world. Since the first such institute opened its doors on November 21, 2004, in Seoul, South Korea, hundreds more have been established in dozens of countries around the world, with the highest concentration of Institutes in the United States, Japan, and South Korea.

According to the Chinese government, these Confucius Institutes innocently devote themselves to teaching China's language, history, and culture. As an added bonus for busy university administrators, they come complete with Chinese government funding, teachers, and teaching materials. What could possibly be wrong with an American academic institution, say Stanford University, accepting such a generous gift from the Chinese people?

Well, everything. Do we really want Communist front organizations making panda huggers out of the next generation of Americans— including the next generation of China watchers? Do we really want

Chinese language teachers chosen by Beijing sanitizing China's brutal image, endorsing its global grab for power and, at least in some cases, gathering intelligence and information at America's best universities?[36]

That the mission of the Confucius Institutes is to brainwash American students into accepting Beijing's version of modern history—the line that Chairman Mao was some kind of glorious revolutionary hero and that "Socialism with Chinese characteristics" is the wave of the future—cannot be doubted. After all, the former propaganda chief of the Chinese Communist Party, a man named Li Changchun, has said so. Li, who was also the fifth-ranked member of the Standing Committee of the Politburo at the time—that is, the fifth most powerful man in China—publicly boasted that the Confucius Institutes are "an important part of China's overseas propaganda set-up."[37] I mean, if the CCP's *propaganda chief* has said that the Institutes are all about *propaganda,* they probably are.

Former leader Hu Jintao has gone even further. In remarks made to the senior leadership of the CCP, he admitted that "through many years of effort, we have now found the way to cultivate and prepare [foreign] supporters for our Party.... Establishing and spreading the various Chinese language institutes such as Confucius Institutes around the world increases our Party's influence worldwide."[38]

Those Beijing bureaucrats at the innocuously named Office of Chinese Language Council International—*Hanban*, for short—who run the Confucius Institute network are at pains to deny any subversive intent, of course. They blithely compare the Institutes to France's *Alliance Francaise* and Germany's *Goethe-Institut*, claiming that they exist only to promote the Chinese language and culture, and to facilitate cultural exchanges.

But these comparisons simply don't hold water. Unlike Alliance Francaise, the Confucius Institutes are not independent from their government; unlike the Goethe-Institut establishments, they do not occupy their own premises. Instead, participating universities agree to provide office space on campus in exchange for funding. "That, in itself, is astonishing," says Notre Dame Professor Lionel Jensen, a critic of what he calls these "instruments of propaganda."[39] But even more surprising is that American universities—supposed bastions of academic freedom—actually allow Hanban to dictate whom they will hire to run the Confucius Institute: an Institute director can only be appointed with the approval of the Hanban board. Thus academic control of the Confucius Institutes is effectively ceded to Hanban, which in turn answers to the United Front Work Department of the Chinese Communist Party. Noting this connection, Representative Chris Smith of New Jersey maintains, "U.S. colleges and universities should not be outsourcing academic control, faculty and student oversight or curriculum to a foreign government—in this case a dictatorship."[40] In fact, the current Chairman of the Confucius Institutes is none other than Vice Premier Liu Yandong, who served as the head of this very same United Front Work Department from 2002 to 2007. This is roughly like Joseph Goebbels assuming control of the *Goethe-Institut* network.

The college administrators who are so eager to accept handouts from the Chinese Communist Party should first audit a course in the history of modern China. There they would learn how during the Chinese Civil War the Party successfully used united front tactics to subvert, co-opt, and overthrow the Nationalists.[41] Communist Party members burrowed into universities, unions, and other political parties. Some of the political parties that were co-opted, such as the Chinese Democratic League, were even allowed to continue in existence after the revolution succeeded, albeit as hollow shells, in order to further the illusion of "democracy." That the United Front Work Department has de facto control over the Confucius Institutes means only one thing: that their chief purpose is to subvert, co-opt, and ultimately control Western academic discourse on matters pertaining to China.[42]

I know from personal experience how ruthless the Chinese party-state can be with its overseas academic critics. Following my exposé of forced abortions and forced sterilizations in China's one-child policy in the early eighties, Party officials put tremendous pressure on Stanford University to deny me the doctorate I had earned. Beijing went so far as to threaten to abrogate its *entire* scholarly exchange program with the United States unless I was, in its words, "severely punished" for speaking out. And punished I was, by a cowardly and compromised university administration.[43]

In the years since, the Chinese party-state has gotten considerably more sophisticated in the ways it manipulates and controls foreign academics, promoting the careers of its "friends" while keeping its critics at arm's length—which means out of China. "Friends of China" already enjoy all-expenses-paid travel to China, where they are paid for giving speeches and publishing work there. With the establishment of Confucius Institutes around the globe, the party-state is attempting to get even further ahead of the curve. It is cultivating a new generation of China watchers who will be more favorably disposed towards China and its ruling class than ever; who will collaborate in crafting an academic discourse that praises the economic achievements of the Chinese party-state, rationalizes away its expansionism, and looks away when it crushes dissent.

It is political satire of the first order that China's Communist leaders, who for decades vilified Confucius and attacked all he stood for as feudal, reactionary "rubbish," should now trot him out to serve as their international front man.[44] But it is no mystery why they have done so. Chen Jinyu, vice chairman of the Confucius Institute Headquarters, said that the Party deliberately chose the name of Confucius because "brand name means quality; brand names means returns. Those who have a better brand name will enjoy higher popularity, a better reputation, more social influence, and will be able to generate more support [for the Party] from local communities."

China's ancient sage is undoubtedly the country's best brand name: a universally recognized symbol of traditional Chinese culture. Confucianism, his benevolent philosophy of governance, is far better known—and far more palatable to Westerners—than the brutal Legalism that actually animates the Chinese Communist Party. Moreover, an institute named after Confucius does not evoke the distaste, even revulsion, that an institute named after the founder of the People's Republic of China would. How many universities—other than those in, say, North Korea, Venezuela, and Cuba—would have welcomed an institute named after Chairman Mao Zedong, one of the great mass murderers of the twentieth century?

It is no wonder that his successors, Legalists all, should eschew Mao and instead invoke the time-honored name of Confucius to cloak their purposes and reinvent their brand. Nor, it must be said, are they being particularly original in doing so. As we saw in chapter three, Chinese emperors from the Han dynasty onward have been equally two-faced. Being "Confucian on the outside, Legalist on the inside" (*wairu neifa*) is a political ruse that has been practiced in the Middle Kingdom for a very, very long time.

The ongoing controversies surrounding the operation of the Confucius Institute program go far beyond its name, of course. There have been allegations of Confucius Institutes undermining academic freedom at host universities, monitoring the activities of Chinese exchange students, and even engaging in industrial and military espionage. There is no doubt that the Institutes are being used to actively advance the Chinese party-state's political agenda on such issues as the Dalai Lama and Tibet, the Chinese pro-democracy movement abroad, dissent within China, and Taiwan independence. Peng Ming-min, a Taiwan independence activist and politician, claims that colleges and universities where a Confucius Institute is established are required to sign a contract in which they affirm their support for Beijing's "one China" policy. As a result, Peng says, a whole host of issues, from discussion of Taiwan and Tibetan issues and the Tiananmen Massacre, to China's military expansionism and exchange rate manipulation, have become "untouchables."[45]

Add to this the fact that many of the individuals holding positions within the Confucius Institute system, aside from the chairman herself, have backgrounds in Chinese security agencies and the United Front Work Department. Together these agencies are responsible for a number of activities in foreign countries including propaganda, the monitoring and control of Chinese students abroad, the recruiting of agents among the Overseas Chinese diaspora and sympathetic foreigners, and long-term clandestine operations. The Confucius Institutes provide a perfect cover for this kind of underground activity.[46]

Because of these concerns, a number of countries have banned or restricted the establishment of Confucius Institutes. The Indian Ministry of External Affairs opposed the establishment of Confucius Institutes in universities, arguing that they were nothing more than "a Chinese design to spread its 'soft power'—widening influence by using culture as a propagational tool." The Japanese government has serious reservations as well. It is telling that of the twenty or so Institutes that have been set up in Japan, all were at private colleges. Government-funded public universities in that country have so far refused to play host to what is obviously an ideologically driven political power play. For these same reasons, a number of universities in Western countries have also rejected Hanban's efforts to establish Confucius Institutes on their campuses, including the University of Chicago and the University of Melbourne.

Still, the Chinese party-state is moving ahead with its plans. There are already over six hundred Confucius Institutes and Classrooms around the world, and the goal is to have a thousand in operation by 2020.[47] The biggest concentration of Institutes is in the country that China hungers to overtake and eclipse in both power and prestige: our own. Many American universities, such Stanford, either because of the leftist orientation of their faculties or because they are simply hungry for money, have said yes to these Chinese Trojan Horses quicker than you can say, "Mao Zedong." If they were truly committed to academic freedom, as every American university claims to be, it is clear that they should instead reject them.

As should all Americans. The Chinese party-state does not share our democratic institutions, or our commitment to open markets, or our understanding of human rights. And it is bent on dethroning America and dominating Asia and the world. Should we really be allowing a cruel, tyrannical, and repressive regime that hates everything that America stands for to educate our young people?

While it is true that dozens of countries are engaged in efforts to improve their international image and generate good will, what sets China apart is its lack of transparency. It is blindingly obvious that the Voice of America and Radio Free Asia are funded by the American government, that the United States Information Agency is behind American Public Diplomacy Centers, and so forth. China, on the other hand, seems to delight in being duplicitous, purchasing television and radio airtime through front companies and using the borrowed prestige of both American university campuses and their long-dead Sage to gain access to young Western minds. And should we really be surprised that a communist party, which itself is organized along conspiratorial lines, behaves this way?[48]

HARD POWER WITH SOFT CHARACTERISTICS

So what can we conclude about China's frenzied efforts to generate soft power? Are they working?

The first thing that can be said is that these efforts constitute the most extravagant program of state-sponsored propaganda the world has ever seen, costing China an estimated $10 billion or more a year. By way of comparison, American spent a comparatively paltry $700 million for its public diplomacy in 2016.

It is unclear what Chinese party-state has gotten in return for this huge investment. Beautiful images of ancient temples and imperial tombs may flit across a giant electronic billboard on Times Square, as the Chinese government advertises the "new perspective" of its English-language news channel. But how can this redeem the brand of a Communist Party that, during the ironically misnamed Cultural Revolution, deliberately destroyed much of the country's art, artifacts, and architecture? Even today, the Chinese government does not hesitate to tear down historical structures dating back centuries to make way for the latest government-funded skyscraper or toll road. Behind the sun-drenched paddy fields and the neon-lit skyscrapers of propaganda flicks lurks the Chinese party-state, and no amount of face paint will hide the ugliness of one-party dictatorship.

Hanban, for its part, may buy its way into a few hundred colleges and high schools across America, but does learning conversational Chinese ensure that the attending students will become solid supporters of Beijing's policies? Does donning traditional Chinese robes and bowing to their teachers on Confucius Day—the practice in some of these Institutes—predispose Americans to bow to the Chinese party-state? Perhaps the run-of-the-mill twenty-year-old college student just takes the Institutes at face value and goes away with a vaguely positive attitude towards China—and China wins. But it seems to me equally likely that the sympathy generated by exposure to the Chinese language and culture may well find expression in support for Hong Kong's democracy movement, for Tibetan autonomy, or even for Xinjiang separatism. Certainly independent Taiwan, where one can speak freely—in Chinese—about everything under the sun, will be one of the unintended beneficiaries of Beijing's largesse.

But there is an even deeper problem with the Chinese government's efforts to manufacture soft power under a state plan. Joseph Nye, from whom we get the concept of soft power, *specifically excluded government-run programs from his calculations*. This means that China can build all the roads, railways, and soccer stadiums it wants to gain favor with governments. It can spend billions setting up an international broadcasting network, as well as hundreds of Confucius Institutes, to try to generate popular support. But each and every one of these government-funded initiatives is an expression of hard power, not soft. Genuine soft power—what Professor Nye called the "soft power of attraction"—has to come organically from the natural appeal of a country's culture and its political values, plus the popularity of its foreign policies. Measured against each of these yardsticks, China comes up woefully short.

The "culture" that the party-state is falsely advertising is China's traditional Confucian culture, which was deliberately exterminated in the early decades of the PRC. It has not existed inside of China—outside of museums—for a half century or more. Socialist Realism, a style of art and literary composition that China's propaganda czars borrowed from the Soviet Union, elicits little more than mockery and contempt these days, both within China and without. And yet, even today, "cultural workers"—as the Party clumsily insists on classing artists and writers—are handicapped by the Party's renewed insistence that "art must serve the people," coupled with the censorship of works that do not.

China's propaganda chief, Liu Yunshan, rang in the Chinese New Year in 2017 by visiting prominent "cultural workers" to tell them that they "should promote traditional Chinese culture, revolutionary culture, and advanced socialist culture by enhancing creativity and producing quality works." [49] But by trying to bring creativity itself under its control, the Party has effectively stifled it. Paranoid political systems rarely exert much in the way of cultural soft power.

The international cachet of China's political values is self-limited as well by a party-state that insists that it is practicing a home-grown ideology called "Socialism with Chinese characteristics." This bow to China's authoritarian traditions may appeal to native pride, but it does little to inspire non-Chinese. China's soft power has greatly declined since the decades of Mao's rule, when the Great Helmsmen and his vision of a communist Utopia instigated revolutionary movements around the world. Aside from a tiny handful of Marxist regimes, no one today is interested in emulating the "China model" of governance, which is to say a one-party dictatorship presiding over socialist-fascist system. The trappings of modernity that have accompanied China's impressive economic growth—from the ubiquitous McDonald's to the glass and concrete structures that dominate its cities skylines—can be found in dozens of countries. They are hardly unique to China.

China's foreign policy, which is increasingly heavy-handed and threatening, does not win plaudits abroad either. Beijing has instigated territorial disputes with many of its near neighbors in recent years, some of which I have discussed elsewhere in this book. China's hegemonic ambitions have provoked fear among the peoples of Asia, further reducing its appeal. Farther away, in Africa, where it has not asserted any territorial claims, China is regarded more benignly. But then African dictators like Robert Mugabe of Zimbabwe have far more in common with Uncle Xi than the democratically elected governments of China's neighboring states, from Japan and South Korea in the east to Singapore and India in the south.[50] Who but the most repressive of dictators would want to follow the lead of China's Communist Party leaders on cultural or political matters, however much they might like to emulate China's economic growth by devaluing their own currency, oppressing their own workers, and successfully practicing mercantilism against the West?

President Xi Jinping has accused the West of duplicity in its dealings with China, of "hanging up a goat's head and selling dog meat," but this is *exactly what China is doing* with its "soft power" campaign. It is trying to sell its one-party dictatorship to the world by hanging up the dead head of Confucius. Behind the lifeless visage of the sage, however, lurks the stern countenance of Core Leader Xi. Behind the neon-lit skyscrapers and emerald green paddy fields of Chinese infomercials skulks a ruthless regime that routinely locks up and tortures human rights activists, aborts mothers who are pregnant without permission, oppresses its restive minorities, and each year executes more people than the rest of the world combined. The leaders of the Chinese party-state may believe that "socialism with Chinese characteristics" is superior to Western democracy, chiefly because it allows them to stay in power forever and subvert the international trading system to their advantage. But this is a tough sell to the rest of the world.[51]

10

WHAT AMERICA CAN DO

*"The broader mission is to...chang[e] the course of a
history which at this point appears grimly and inexorably
headed for conflict—and perhaps even a nuclear cliff."*
—PETER NAVARRO, *Crouching Tiger: What China's Militarism
Means for the World*[1]

Big Daddy Xi's dream is the world's nightmare. The Chinese party-state, if allowed to grow unchecked, could prove fatal not only to American preeminence but to a world order based on the rule of law and universally recognized human rights. Too few Americans know how the Beijing regime ruthlessly and routinely persecutes its own citizens. Too few take seriously the Chinese party-state's outrageous demands for territorial concessions from neighboring states, or its frequently voiced threats of war. Even fewer recognize that in numerous arenas from currency manipulation and trading practices to cyberspace and outer space China is already engaging in a kind of nonkinetic warfare with us.

The same voices that insist that we all but declare war on Russia grow strangely quiet when issues concerning China are raised. Some academics, determined to accommodate a rising China, seem to suggest that the United States should ignore China's aggressive rhetoric, understate China's aggressive acts and, *under*react in response to its many provocations. Amitai Etzioni, for instance, has argued that China can and should be placated, and that the alternative is "a strategy that holds that China cannot be accommodated and that it must be contained by any means necessary."[2] But refusing to characterize the Chinese party-state as a threat does not make it any less threatening, nor does mislabelling China's aggressiveness as mere assertiveness make it any less belligerent. It only weakens our resolve to prepare for, and to prevail, in the coming confrontation that China is openly, obviously, and actively seeking.

Some of those who are unwilling to speak ill of the Dragon are simply watching their pocketbooks. Chinese corporations are an important source of advertising revenue for the U.S. media, and they have shown that they are prepared to withhold advertising dollars from any newspaper, magazine, or other media outlet that is too critical of China. Add to this the fact that virtually all of the Fortune 500 companies have made multi-billion-dollar investments in the Chinese market, thus allowing themselves to be held hostage. The American business community well understands that the Chinese party-state will not hesitate to retaliate against their interests in China if U.S.-China relations deteriorate, and so they have become an effective lobby for…not antagonizing the Dragon.

There is no equivalent lobby in the Untied States urging softer coverage of Russia, which is neither an important trading partner of the United States, nor a country where American corporations have invested a lot of money, nor an important source of advertising revenue for media outlets. Add to this the fact that some analysts, particularly at the Pentagon and the three-letter agencies, still seem to be fighting the last war. They appear not to realize that the Cold War ended over a quarter century ago—and we won.[3]

Finally, we cannot overlook the Trump factor. The president is on record as a stern critic of China, repeatedly singling it out for its unfair trading practices, its currency manipulation, and its support of the rogue regime in North Korea. Since the legacy media seem to loathe everything he says and does, their natural inclination is to rush to the defense of the Chinese party-state, or at the very least to mute their own criticism of its heinous behavior. They would far rather talk themselves—and the American public—into exhaustion by speculating endlessly about "Russian collusion."

But Trump is right about China. In fact, he is more right about China than he probably knows. The Chinese party-state is the self-declared mortal enemy of our values, our democratic institutions, and our very way of life. It is even more dangerous than its fiercest critics, such as the University of Chicago's John Mearsheimer, generally give it credit for.

GLOBAL HEGEMONY: CHINA'S IMPOSSIBLE DREAM?

We began our examination of China's intentions by pointing out that the world is an anarchic system in which force is the ultimate arbiter. What this means in practice is that *the only security to be found in this world of insecurity lies in being the biggest badass on the planet.* It is not to be found anywhere else. Not in walls, treaties, alliances, or international organizations—all of which are temporary expedients that will sooner or later fail. Period.

The leaders of the Chinese party-state, well schooled in their country's long history, instinctively understand this. That's why the goal of previous occupants of the Dragon Throne—going back to Chairman's Mao's "ancestral dragon" himself, Qin Shihuang—has been to dominate their known world. And China has in fact been the regional hegemon of its half of Asia for the better part of *two millennia*. It would be strangely out of character, to say the least, if the current leaders of China did not want to reassume that role.

And it would be equally surprising if, as some analysts have suggested, they were willing to stop there. For history to end in a stark,

"China wins, America loses," scenario—as the Chinese believe it will—China must become more than just a regional hegemon. Indeed, the full and complete realization of the "China Dream" requires the establishment of "A World of Great Harmony." And what but a *global* hegemon could possibly work its will on the world in this way?

So far we have hewn very closely to John Mearsheimer's theory of international politics, but here we must part company. For Mearsheimer believes that "It is almost impossible for any state to achieve global hegemony, because it is too hard to project and sustain power around the globe and onto the territory of distant great powers."[4] In his view, there is simply too much landmass to traverse and too many oceans to cross: great walls and giant moats, containing a state's hegemonic ambitions to the region where it is located. "The best outcome that a state can hope for is to be a regional hegemon," Mearsheimer concludes, "and thus dominate one's own geographical area... [while] seek[ing] to prevent other great powers in other regions from duplicating their feat."[5]

The experience of the United States—Mearsheimer's prime example—certainly fits this pattern. Once the United States had established a regional hegemony over the Western Hemisphere in the late 1800s, it acted to constrain other great powers to ensure that no rival great power was able to dominate its own region in the same way. Even in the aftermath of World War II—a time when America alone produced an astonishing 50 percent of the world's GDP as the rest of the industrialized world lay prostrate—it did not attempt to utterly dominate the world. Nor did it seek to do so following the collapse of the Soviet Union, when it enjoyed another span of unparalleled preeminence.

America's hesitance to embrace of hegemony is in part due to its democratic ideals, which include the self-determination of peoples. But more than anything else it is a function of our unique geography. Vast stretches of ocean separate the Americas from the rest of the world. The Atlantic Ocean did indeed serve as a giant moat in the early days of the "Republic"—a natural defensive barrier that served to dissuade other great powers from trying to project power onto its shores. In fact, the last European power to actually invade a country in the Western Hemisphere was France, which carried out what is called the French Intervention in Mexico in 1861.

But the same giant moats that posed such a formidable barrier to potential aggressors also hindered America's efforts to project power outwards into other regions. It took nearly a full year after the United States entered World War I, for example, for the bulk of American Expeditionary Force to reach the front lines in France. American combat units did not land in North Africa until November 1942, eleven months after the United States entered World War II. Even today, it would take a carrier task force two weeks to steam across the Pacific, by which time the latest Taiwan Straits crisis, or whatever it might be, could well have been decided.

All this is to say that the strategy of the United States is partly dictated by its own unique geography, not by immutable strategic principles. America's best course of action after becoming the regional hegemon of the relatively isolated Americas—really its *only* course of action—was to try and prevent any other great power from dominating the eastern or western ends of the Eurasian continent.

But China, which sits at the eastern terminus of the *world-island*, as it has been called, has other options.

CHINA AS "HEARTLAND"

In 1904, when Sir Halford Mackinder first conceived of his "Heartland" theory, China was "the sick man of Asia." It was a "country" barely worthy of the name, on the brink of dynastic collapse and colonial dismemberment. So it is understandable that Mackinder did not give a second thought to its prospects as a great power, which at the time seemed nil. Besides, Mackinder was a geographer, who understandably believed that the geopolitical center of gravity of the Eurasian continent could not be far removed from its geographical center. With Germany and Russia in mind, he stuck a pin in the middle of the map, and wrote a three-part proposition:

1. Who rules East Europe commands the Heartland;
2. Who rules the Heartland commands the World-Island;
3. Who rules the World-Island commands the World.

Mackinder's third proposition is the most defensible. If a single country were able to dominate Eurasia and control its vast population and resources, then the world would arguably have a hegemon. Or something very close to it. He *who ruled the world-island* would indeed command so much of the world that what was left over would more or less be compelled to concede it primacy.[6]

Mackinder's first proposition, on the other hand, has not stood the test of time. Indeed, in picking East Europe as the pivot of Eurasia he seems—with the benefit of hindsight—to have been about half a continent off. He was certainly mistaken from the traditional Chinese perspective. For as the Chinese see it, the Middle Kingdom has always constituted the Heartland of Asia—and always will. The leaders of the modern Chinese party-state certainly believe that whoever rules China commands the Heartland. Or by historical right should.

That leaves Mackinder's second proposition. And here it turns out that the same Chinese party-state that "rules the Heartland" is busily positioning itself to one day "command the World-Island" as well. America needs to start paying a lot more attention to the ways in which it is extending its reach.

Just as America's grand strategy is presupposed by its geography, so is China's. Although the states of the Pacific Rim are within easy reach of China, beyond them lie the vast reaches of the Pacific Ocean, the Middle Kingdom's own "giant moat." To the West, however, the Chinese party-state suffers no such geographical constraint. The deserts and mountains that in earlier times proved such sturdy barriers to expansion have been reduced by modern transport to mere sand lots and foothills, figuratively speaking. A round trip along the ancient Silk Road between China and Rome took approximately two years to complete. The New Silk Road, announced by Xi Jinping in 2013, already features weekly rail freight service between Shanghai and London.[7] An estimated trillion dollars in Chinese-built infrastructure will follow in the next few years.

But the New Silk Road is intended to do more than just facilitate trade. Its larger strategic goal is to remake the map of the global economy to put China at its heart, drawing not just Central Asia, the Middle East, and Russia, but faraway Europe as well, into China's orbit. Just listen to vice minister of commerce Fang Aiqing: "The New Silk Road, which targets growth and *rebalancing the global economy*, is a desirable solution. Most countries along the [Road] are developing nations and eager for better economic performance and *regional economic integration* [emphasis added]."[8] And what economy will these other Eurasian countries be rebalancing towards and integrating with but the one that is now dominant on the Eurasian continent?

China watchers who remain convinced that China's ambitions do not extend beyond its region should take a close look at the map of the New Silk Road. The various rail lines, ports, power plants, and roads that will one day crisscross Eurasia indicate a larger strategic objective. They might also ask themselves why a country that is supposedly only interested in dominating its Asia-Pacific neighborhood should have just built a new military base in Djibouti, Africa.

Geography is not destiny, as some geopolitical theorists once believed, but neither should it be airily dismissed as irrelevant in the twenty-first century.[9] It may not count for much in air warfare—given that, as Christopher Fettweis points out, bombers can take off from Missouri, bomb virtually any place on the planet, and then land back in Missouri. But if a country is driven to expand its global footprint by a potent combination of communist ideology,[10] hypernationalism, and a sense of cultural entitlement—as China clearly is—then having land borders with fourteen other countries clearly facilitates such expansionism. Time, space, and distance may not count for as much as they once did, but in matters of national security geography is still paramount. It is not only a lot easier to put your goods on stores' shelves if your railroad runs right up to the border crossing, it is also easier to engage in subversion, propaganda campaigns, punitive economic measures, and political manipulation. And, of course, propinquity also makes it possible, in the event of open conflict, to put boots on the ground in a hurry.

Before anyone dismisses out of hand the possibility of China gaining a commanding position on the World-Island, recall that this was pretty much accomplished eight hundred years ago—from the back of a galloping horse. The Mongol hordes, starting from the steppes of Central Asia, conquered everything from the Pacific to the Mediterranean. And as lately, as we have seen, the Chinese party-state has appropriated both the empire and the ethnicity of the great khans as its own. The Yuan dynasty is now considered to be a Chinese, not a foreign, dynasty, and the Mongolian people have been elevated to co-descendants of the Yellow Emperor. Does the historical map of the Mongol Empire, the largest empire the world has ever seen, justify a desire among the China Dreamers to expand westward? Given China's propensity to use ancient maps to justify modern borders, it would be surprising if it didn't.

Why cannot modern China accomplish the same end? Not by embarking upon a campaign of military conquest, perhaps, but by slow economic absorption and political encroachment through its New Silk Road initiative and its Shanghai Consortium. Much of the area formerly ruled by the Mongols is sparsely populated and governed by corrupt elites, and so could be drawn closer to China with relative ease. Indeed, this process is already underway. Moreover, each of the countries whose borders contain a part of this territory has a large population of Chinese expatriates, who would prove a very useful Fifth Column. In this scenario, China would not technically be a global hegemon, but it would control a region so vast that it would be by far the most powerful state on the planet.

A Eurasia dominated in large part by the Chinese party-state would be problematic for America, but the reverse is not true. It is largely irrelevant to Beijing's plans whether the United States continues to dominate the Americas or not, since this does not interfere with its main chance, which is to construct an economic empire across as much of the nine-thousand-mile width of the Eurasian continent as it can, extracting the resources there to fuel its giant industrial machine, while dominating its markets with its products. That alone would guarantee China's primacy, almost regardless of America's continued economic and military strength. Moreover, China does not have to convince a single country in the Western hemisphere, or even the countries of the Pacific Rim, to ally with it in order to succeed with this strategy. America, on the other hand, must exert itself to retain its alliances with countries both on the Pacific Rim and on the World-Island itself in order to prevent China from gaining an overwhelming advantage. If it does, it is game over.

All this is to say that China has an innate advantage in the great game of the twenty-first century. While the World-Island will never be America's, it could well fall to China. This in turn would open up to the Chinese party-state the prospect, difficult of execution but by no means out of reach over time, of global hegemony. The best that America can hope for, on the other hand, is to continue to follow its current strategy, which is to remain the regional hegemon of the Western Hemisphere while seeking to prevent China from dominating its own region in the same fashion. For once China becomes a regional hegemon, the path to global hegemony lies open before it.

The profound impact that China as a regional hegemon would have on the world should not be minimized. The leaders of the Chinese party-state feel no obligation to honor the current rules-based international order. They will either restructure its institutions to China's advantage if they can or, failing that, simply ignore them. Existing international agreements and understandings that do not suit China's purposes will be unilaterally rewritten, or simply jettisoned altogether, on the specious grounds that they are "antiquated," "unfair," or "unequal." We catch a glimpse of the arrogant face of Chinese hegemony in the rejection of the Hague Tribunal's ruling on the South China Sea, and in the sneering repudiation of Beijing's legally binding treaty with Britain over Hong Kong.[11] This face of "thuggish and bellicose nationalism," as executed Noble Peace Prize winner Liu Xiaobo called it, is itself a reflection of the Maoist "China at the center of the world" mentality, and will be ever more prominently on display as a self-aggrandizing China gains strength. How dare the barbarians from the fringes dictate terms to the mighty Chinese party-state!

Were China to become *the* hegemon—the globally preeminent power—the world would necessarily be a far different place than it is today. The mild, half-hearted, vacillating, and ultimately benevolent primacy exercised by the United States would be replaced by a hard and unyielding hegemony.[12] The Chinese party-state would narcissistically revel in its newfound power in a way that the United States never did, as what Liu Xiaobo called its "underlying arrogance and self-centeredness" came again to the fore. Once in command, Liu warned, "It will 'wipe out humiliation through acts of revenge,' as the heroes of Chinese opera do, and stand as master of a powerful China at the center of the world stage."[13]

A dominant China would also actively promote its principles of governance—one-party dictatorship, a socialist-market economy, and sharp curbs on fundamental human rights—to the far corners of the world. It would, in short, seek to remake the world in its own image. It would not completely succeed in this endeavor, just as the seeds of liberty that America has sought to plant around the world did not always germinate. But it is safe to say that China's baleful influence would result in the spread of copycat political systems that disdained democracy, the free market, and human rights. A long, dark night of one-party dictatorship would slowly descend upon the planet, and perhaps remain for a long, long time.

We owe it not just to ourselves, but also to the peoples of Asia, Europe, Africa, and Australia—and even to the Chinese people themselves—to ensure that this doesn't happen. But how?

HOW TO DOMESTICATE A DRAGON

Is a rising China good for America and the world?

Clearly it has not been good for America. The trillions of dollars of wealth, technology, and intellectual property that have been transferred across the Pacific—much of it stolen, as we have seen—has been a disaster for American industry and trade, has sent millions of workers to the unemployment lines, and has caused the wages of the middle class to stagnate.

China's effort to extract raw materials from the developing world has generated jobs in export industries in the Third World, but not industrialization. It has kept the harbors full of ships, but has also bred corruption and stifled democratization.

Still, the "rising China good" formula has held sway in Washington since Nixon first stood on the Great Wall, and it remains popular there and on Wall Street even today. It was a view that Barack Obama often championed. "I've been very explicit," the former president remarked on more than one occasion, "in saying that we have more to fear from a weakened, threatened China than a successful, rising China."[14] Obama, who famously wanted to fundamentally transform America, may have welcomed the rich and powerful China that we have largely created *precisely because* it seeks to move the center of the world economy from America to China, undermines Western values that he did not particularly value, and broadly threatens an American pre-eminence that he felt was both dangerous and undeserved.[15] Most Americans, I suspect, would prefer dealing with a "weakened, threatened China," rather than the powerful, threatening, and aggressive one that our feckless policies have helped to create.

Obama's strategic assessment of China was based on the assessment, subscribed to by every president from Nixon on, that China's opening to the West, combined with its increasing prosperity, would painlessly result in its peaceful evolution away from one-party dictatorship towards a more open political system. In the end, if we would all just be patient, China would become a pluralistic democracy not all that much different from our own. Conservatives naturally imagined that this process would be driven by the economics of reform, as increased freedom of choice in the marketplace resulted in popular demands for more latitude in political matters. Liberals and leftists, on the other hand, such as Barack Obama, saw the distances between practices in China and the West shrinking as a result of convergence: as Beijing retreated from dictatorship and Washington socialized medicine and other sectors of the American economy, our two systems would come to look increasingly alike. Both sides thus subscribed to the comforting notion that improving U.S.-China relations, or even integrating China into the existing international order, would not require much effort on America's part. As more Chinese ate Big Macs, watched Hollywood movies, and vacationed in Florida, they would willy-nilly become *just like us*. The dangerous Chinese Dragon would be transformed into a cuddly kung-fu panda.

This pleasant fantasy about China's future was dead wrong—something that should have been obvious to anyone as early as June 4, 1989, when the charming Deng Xiaoping ordered the PLA to massacre thousands of innocent students in and around Tiananmen Square in downtown Beijing. Or if not then, perhaps ten years later, when the ever-smiling President Jiang Zemin ordered a brutal crackdown on the Falungong that led to hundreds of thousands of arrests and tens of thousands of executions, many for the purpose of extracting and reselling the victims' internal organs.[16] For those still skeptical, there were the 2008 demonstrations in Tibet, when the seemingly mild-mannered Hu Jintao ordered peaceful protesters shot. Finally, for the especially hard to convince, there is Big Daddy Xi's ongoing crackdown, which is sweeping up Christians, Tibetans, Uyghurs, human rights activists, dissident lawyers and, well, just about anyone else who questions the People's Democratic Dictatorship over which he—in increasingly dictatorial fashion—presides. Despite this "high tide of Chinese despotism," as China watcher Orville Schell now calls it,[17] the fantasy that China will evolve peacefully continues its Zombie-like existence, decades after it stopped showing any signs of life.

It is long past time to discard the idea that China's rise is anything but a disaster of global proportions. For the disturbing truth is that the China that is rising is the precise opposite of the China of our complacent fantasies. China is changing, all right: it is returning to the template laid down by the Legalists two millennia ago, steadily marching backwards towards the totalitarianism that gave it birth.

The increasingly wealthy, increasingly powerful Chinese party-state is *reverting to type*.

MORE (AND MORE COURAGEOUS) CHINA HANDS

Before anything else—before discussing how China is the key to resolving the North Korean standoff, how Taiwan offers the opportunity of rolling back China's attempted seizure of the South China Sea, and how to form a balancing coalition to counter the growing strength of China—we need to make sure that we fully understand the grim situation that we find ourselves in.

For that, we need more and better China hands. China's history, intentions, and capabilities are increasingly an open book, but we need people who are capable of reading it. There is no reason for us to be taken in by Chinese propaganda, to be swayed by bombastic threats, or to behave on visits to Beijing like awestruck tribal leaders swept away by the magnificence of the imperial court. Mind games only work if you are unaware that you are being gamed. Having more China analysts familiar with the party-state's stratagems would allow us to negotiate more effectively with Beijing.

At present, the relatively small China-watching community in U.S. academic and government circles is constantly being monitored and massaged to ensure that flattering views of the Middle Kingdom predominate. The carrot (as well as the stick) is access. Those China watchers whose writings are especially pleasing to Beijing are given all-expense-paid trips to China, arranged visits to universities and research institutes, and even carefully scripted interviews with high-level officials—all the raw material, in other words, of a successful career in academia or policy-making. Those who refuse to kowtow to Beijing, on the other hand, are denied visas and forced to do their China watching from a distance. Those who focus on the "Three Unmentionables"—Taiwan, Tibet, and Tiananmen—such as Andrew Nathan, Perry Link, and myself, have been shut out for years, even decades, at a time.[18]

All this is an open secret in the China-watching community, many of whose members deliberately trim their sails to avoid antagonizing Beijing. I once invited a well-known China hand, who is on the faculty of a major university, to speak at a conference I was organizing on human rights in China. As soon as he heard the words "human rights," he shot me a look of alarm. "I avoid such meetings," he hastily demurred. "I prefer to keep my channels open to Beijing." This kind of *self*-censorship is disturbing enough, but there are also cases of American organizations and academic institutions censoring their members and publications. The case of Chinese attorney Teng Biao is instructive. At first the American Bar Association (ABA) was enthusiastic about publishing Teng's critique of human rights abuses in China, which the ABA gushed promised to be "an important and groundbreaking book." The project was cancelled after the group began worrying about Beijing's reaction, however, explaining to a disappointed Teng that "There is concern that we run the risk of upsetting the Chinese government by publishing your book, and because we have ABA commissions working in China there is fear that we would put them and their work at risk."[19]

One of the reasons that this kind of barbarian-management works so well for Beijing is that the ranks of China watchers are so thin. Several years ago I gave an address at the Central Intelligence Agency on the challenge posed by China's hegemonic ambitions. I learned that day that we have only a relatively small number of China analysts monitoring the PRC on a full-time basis, most of whom were present for my talk. Compare that to the roughly one thousand CIA analysts we once had keeping a watchful eye on the former Soviet Union, roughly half of whom were following military affairs, while the other half tracked political, economic, and social developments. The disparity is troubling, especially given that the level of threat from China is rapidly approaching that which we faced from the Soviets in the heyday of the Cold War.

To have so few China analysts is to invite unpleasant surprises from across the Pacific. The number of analysts should be tripled—or more—as quickly as we prudently can. And as many as possible of these new hires should be proficient in Chinese. The current crop of analysts apparently is not. During the course of my talk, I asked how many of those present could read, write, and speak Chinese languages. I was dismayed to see only one hand—out of a couple hundred attendees—go up. The other analysts were presumably working with translations provided by the Open Source Enterprise (known before 2005 as the Foreign Broadcast Information Service). According to China expert Michael Pillsbury (who *is* fluent in Chinese), the center's Chinese-language translators deliberately edit out most of the inflammatory anti-U.S. rhetoric emanating from Beijing on the grounds that it is repetitious.[20] It certainly is, which is precisely why we ought to be paying more attention to it. Better language training would not only ensure that less would be lost in translation, it would also weaken China's ability to control the conversation.

Well-trained China analysts could help us understand—and counter—some of the stratagems that China is currently employing against us. Few contemporary China watchers grasp, for example, how Beijing is using its client state, North Korea, to distract Washington's attention from issues involving China's "core interests," such as its attempt to seize the South China Sea. Others are so committed to the "one China policy," that they are reluctant to even consider innovative ways to enlist the help of our allies in Taiwan. While avoiding miscalculations that could result in open conflict, there is much more we could be doing to check China's advances along the Pacific Rim and in South Asia.

IF YOU WANT TO STOP NORTH KOREA, PUNISH CHINA

Imagine Beijing's reaction if South Korea were splashing down missiles off the coast of China, carrying out underground nuclear tests, and regularly threatening to turn Beijing and Shanghai into radioactive dust. China would be demanding crippling international sanctions against Seoul and would probably threaten a unilateral naval blockade of the peninsula as well. But its chief course of action would be to lodge a formal protest with Washington, demanding in no uncertain terms that it rein in its ally.

The Chinese ambassador to the United States would be instructed to inform the U.S. president, *South Korea is a close ally of yours, which you are bound by treaty to defend. We believe that it would not be carrying out these provocative acts and making these outrageous statements without at least tacit U.S. approval. That is why my government has decided, Mr. President, that any attack by South Korea on China will be treated as an attack on China by the United States. Unless, of course, you sever your mutual security treaty with Seoul and join with us in completely isolating it, politically and economically.*

In the real world, as opposed to the above fictional scenario, neither South Korea nor any other U.S. ally would be allowed to behave in such a reckless manner. In fact, as soon as we learned that "South Korea" was attempting to acquire nuclear weapons in violation of the Nuclear

Nonproliferation Treaty we would have taken steps to halt the program, as we did in Taiwan back in the eighties.[21] We would have certainly do everything possible to discourage South Korea from carrying out any nuclear or missile tests, in violation of international treaties and sanctions, and urged it to refrain from any further threatening rhetoric.

Internationally, we would make it clear that we were opposed to "South Korea's" behavior by supporting sanctions against the regime, including everything up to and including a complete trade embargo. Well before matters came to such a pass, we would have concluded that South Korea, as a result of its dangerously destabilizing behavior, had gone from being a strategic asset to the United States to being a strategic liability and withdrawn our troops. Finally, if South Korea persisted in its provocative behavior, we would abrogate our mutual defense treaty. We would not want to be caught up in a war between China and South Korea of our one-time ally's own making. We would, in short, behave like a responsible great power.

Now substitute "North Korea" for "South Korea" in the above paragraphs. Then ask yourself: Has China has done *any* of the things that a responsible great power would do when confronted with such a dangerously unhinged ally?

The answer to the above question is an unequivocal no. But China has not merely done nothing, which would have been irresponsible enough. The evidence shows that Beijing, far from discouraging Kim Jong Un's missile madness, is quietly and deliberately *encouraging* it.

Despite promising to put pressure on Pyongyang, China has privately continued to aid the rogue regime in various ways. This is the primary reason why the six rounds of sanctions imposed by the UN against North Korea have been ineffective. In fact, we now know that, with China's help, North Korea has actually improved its military procurement capability in recent years. And as other countries stop trading with the rogue regime, China is picking up the slack.[22]

"Trade between China and North Korea grew almost 40% in the first quarter," President Trump tweeted out in July 2017. "So much for China working with us—but we had to give it a try!"[23] As U.S. Secretary of State Rex Tillerson highlighted before the UN Security Council, fully nine-tenths of North Korea's foreign trade is now with China, which has become Pyongyang's only lifeline to the wider world.[24] There is no doubt that Beijing could quickly cripple the North Korean economy—and ultimately shut down its missile and nuclear programs—by cutting off trade. But China thus far has refused to "remove the firewood from under the pot" (*Fu di chou xin*) in this way, even though it knows it has the ability to eviscerate Kim Jong Un's ability to wage war.

At the same time that some mouthpiece in Beijing is issuing a mild condemnation of Pyongyang's weapons testing, a steady stream of trucks and trains are rumbling across the Dandong crossing into North Korea, Chinese ships are docking at North Korean ports, and planes from China are landing at North Korean airports. These carry all manner of Chinese-made goods including, in all likelihood, missile components and other high-tech gear. We know that China has sold North Korea the trucks used to carry and launch its long-range missiles.[25] It may even have supplied North Korea with its JL-1 Submarine Launched Ballistic Missile (SLBM), along with access to the military version of its GPS system, *Beidou*, to help improve the accuracy of this and other missiles.[26] As Gordon Chang has noted, Kim Jong Un "can press a button and send three types of missiles to the lower 48 states, the Taepodong-2; the road-mobile KN-08; and the KN-08 variant, the KN-14."[27] Richard Fisher of the International Assessment and Strategy Center has even suggested that the KN-14 that Kim fired in July 2017 might be able to reach the U.S. Capitol.[28]

Aside from supplying economic and military aid to its ally, China has another equally important role to play in this Beijing Opera of its own making: to buy time for its North Korean ally to further upgrade its weaponry. Each time North Korea conducts a nuclear test or fires off a missile, Beijing counsels the United States that the only way to resolve the tension on the Korean Peninsula is to exercise strategic patience, enter into negotiations, and gradually build trust. The statement of Chinese Ambassador Liu Jieyi, made in response to the round of UN sanctions announced on 2 June 2017, was a classic example of this delaying tactic in action. "There is a critical window of opportunity for the nuclear issue of the peninsula to come back to the right track of seeking a settlement through *dialogue and negotiations*," the ambassador somberly intoned. "It is incumbent on all parties concerned to *exercise restraint* and to do more to help *ease the tension and build mutual trust* [emphasis added]."[29]

These words were spoken at a time when Dear Leader Kim was threatening a sixth nuclear test and more missile launches. It is hard to know how the Chinese ambassador was able to keep a straight face. (Perhaps massive injections of Botox?) Americans should be insulted by these brazen displays of Chinese duplicity. Here we find China lecturing us on the need to "exercise restraint" and "build mutual trust" *at the very same time* it is quietly helping North Korea, its closest ally, to increase the inventory and accuracy of its missiles. We know the Chinese leadership believes Americans to be naïve and simple in general, but with regard to North Korea, they have been treating us as complete fools.

From the American point of view past negotiations with North Korea have accomplished nothing. From the Chinese point of view, however, they have accomplished precisely what they were intended to. They have bought North Korea the time—and over a billion dollars in American aid—that it needed to build more missiles and more nukes, and to start learning how to pair them together.

As long as Kim Jong Un is convinced that he enjoys China's quiet support, he has absolutely no reason to change his behavior. Especially not now, when he has missiles that are perhaps capable of reaching the United States.[30] Instead, he will continue to launch every couple of months, this accompanied by a barrage of threats to take out Seattle, San Francisco, or Los Angeles. At the same time he will be demanding, through his Chinese brokers, to be paid protection money in return for his promise to stop. This kind of blatant extortion has worked before. Kim's father received huge bribes from both the Clinton and Bush administrations in return for a promise to halt his nuclear weapons and missile programs—promises he never intended to keep. The younger Kim has no reason to think that this kind of shakedown won't work again.

The only way to deal with North Korea's serial deceit is to put pressure on China to reign in its unhinged client state. Given that Beijing is no slouch at deceit itself—it's a characteristic that People's Democratic Dictatorships have in common—its actions against North Korea would have to be open and dramatic. These days, as the Trump administration ratchets up pressure on China, China's leaders are rather frantically claiming that they have no real leverage over North Korea.[31] But this is obviously not true. If China were to close its border with North Korea, for example, it would ignite an economic crisis that would bring the country to its knees in a matter of weeks. Or if China were to abrogate its mutual defense treaty with North Korea, announcing that it would no longer come to Pyongyang's aid if it were attacked, it would be clear to everyone, not least to Kim Jong Un himself, that he was on his own.[32] Either action would let both Kim and the world know that the Chinese party-state was no longer a willing accomplice in his extortion scheme.

There are several reasons why Core Leader Xi Jinping will refuse to abandon the PRC's closest ally unless he is left with no other options. Like Chairman Mao Zedong before him, Xi sees North Korea as a buffer state between China and U.S.-allied South Korea. Mao often referred to the strategic relationship between China and North Korea as being "As close as lips and teeth," and worried that "If the lips are gone, the teeth will be cold" (*Chun wang chi han*). Today's China is just as worried about the fact that the collapse of North Korea and the reunification of the Korean Peninsula would bring U.S. troops right up to the Yalu River.

Kim Jong Un's hostile rhetoric and saber rattling also enable China to work its "disturbing the water to catch a fish" (*Hun shui mo yu*) stratagem. In this ploy—one of the better known of the famous "36 Stratagems"—you deliberately sow confusion and then, under its cover, secretly pursue your own ends. The confusion, in this case, is caused by the maniacal Kim who, by distracting Washington's attention from Beijing's own adventurism, provides China with the opportunity to assert its "core interests" in the South China Sea and elsewhere. The festering crisis on the Korean Peninsula also works to China's advantage by keeping the attention of our East Asian allies riveted on their own backyard. The prospect of imminent conflict with North Korea makes both Tokyo and Seoul less willing to contribute to more distant American efforts to restrain China.

China's diplomats may quietly admit to being embarrassed by some of Kim's outbursts, but they know that Dear Leader Kim and their own Core Leader Xi are "comrades" in more than name. Both are surrounded by flourishing personality cults—although Kim's is far more elaborate, after three generations of Kim dynastic rule—and both run nuclear-armed, dictatorial regimes known for widespread human rights abuses. North Korea is an international pariah, while China—largely by virtue of its economic might—largely escapes censure. But it wasn't very long ago that China itself sought to terrorize the people of Taiwan by splashing down missiles off the island's coast and threatened to nuke Los Angeles if the U.S. intervened. This and other thuggish behavior by then–Party chief Jiang Zemin back in the nineties may well be where Kim Jong Un's father, Kim Jong Il, first got the idea of engaging in nuclear blackmail against the United States. The leaders of China and North Korea have more in common than most Western analysts give them credit for. Big Daddy Xi is just a taller (but not leaner), older (and probably even meaner) version of the five-foot-seven-inch Korean strongman.[33] After all, although Xi was born a princeling, he had to fight his way to the top, while Kim inherited his position from his father.

This year on the July 11 anniversary of the China-Korea Military Alliance Treaty—as it is called in China—Comrade Xi Jinping sent a personal message of congratulations to "Comrade Kim." "The China–North Korea friendly ties are a mutually precious treasure," Comrade Xi assured him. "It is the steadfast policy of the Chinese party-state to continue to deepen and develop the ties." Comrade Kim replied to Comrade Xi that he would deepen and develop North Korea-China friendly ties "to meet the demands of the time."[34] This doesn't read like a relationship on the rocks to me.

The anti-American conspiracy between China and North Korea is going exactly as planned. There is only one way to convince Beijing that the Pyongyang regime and its continual provocations are no longer a strategic asset but a strategic liability. We must make it clear that we hold China directly responsible for the behavior of its closest ally. From now on, instead of letting ourselves be held hostage to Pyongyang's *bad* behavior, we need to hold China accountable for North Korea's *good* behavior. China must either rein in its erstwhile ally—which is to say force it to end its nuclear program and its provocative missile launches—or it must cut its ties with this rogue nuclear power that threatens the stability of the region.

The good news is that Washington finally seems to be getting it. After twenty years of trying to buy off the Pyongyang regime—which only whets the appetite of its rulers for the next round of extortion—we are at last putting pressure directly on China. As Secretary of State Rex Tillerson said on July 28, 2017, "As the principal economic enablers of North Korea's nuclear weapon and ballistic missile development program, China and Russia bear unique and special responsibility for this growing threat to regional and global stability."[35]

The Trump administration understands that raising the costs to China requires more than rhetoric. Only a tough, no-holds-barred confrontation with China will convince that country to move against North Korea. Sanctions need to be imposed on entities within China itself for the continuing assistance it has given to its ally's nuclear and missile program. An initial step in this direction was taken in June 2017, when the U.S. Treasury Department announced that the Bank of Dandong would be severed from the U.S. financial system.[36] The bank, located on the China–North Korea border, had been acting "as a conduit for illicit North Korean financial activity," the Treasury said. Treasury Secretary Steven Mnuchin was at pains to point out that the United States was not accusing the Chinese government itself of laundering North Korean cash. Beijing, surprisingly, remained silent.[37]

President Trump has rattled China's leaders with his insistence on a quick end to the huge trade surpluses that their government's unfair trading practices have racked up with America.[38] But he has offered to soften his demands on trade if the Chinese party-state uses its leverage to bring North Korea's nuclear and missile programs to an end.[39] Most China analysts believe that this does not go far enough: only by completely dropping his plan to confront China on trade—and offering additional concessions to boot—can China be induced help disarm North Korea. China expert Gordon Chang is more inclined to believe the opposite, "that waging a trade war on China may be the only way to obtain Beijing's cooperation on North Korea."[40]

In addition to using trade as leverage, there is one more thing that America can and should do to put pressure on both China and North Korea. President Trump should demand that China, as a responsible great power, sever its mutual defense treaty with North Korea. It is China, after all, that by guaranteeing to come to the aid of its North Korean ally, has created the space in which that rogue nation has developed both nuclear weapons and intercontinental missiles. Without China's defensive umbrella, without its technology, without its missile and reactor components, without its trade, North Korea would never have become the kind of threat that it is today.

Beijing already has more than enough reasons to end the pact, if it chose to do so. The terms of the treaty require both China and North Korea to "safeguard peace and security," a provision that Pyongyang breaches every time it launches a long-range missile or detonates a nuke.

Moreover, Pyongyang's development and possession of nuclear weapons is a violation of the United Nations treaty on non-proliferation, to which Beijing is a signatory, and so arguably constitutes a second violation of their pact.

If, despite all this, China refuses to distance itself from North Korea, then there is only one thing left to do. We must tell China that we will treat an attack by North Korea on the United States or its allies as an attack by China.

Then we can sit back and count the days until China removes Mad Young Kim from power and shuts down his nuclear and missile programs.

———

FREE TAIWAN

For almost four decades we have engaged in the pretense that—diplomatically speaking—Taiwan doesn't exist. In order to placate China, we abrogated our mutual security treaty with Taiwan, recalled our ambassador, and shut down our embassy in Taipei. We established diplomatic relations with the People's Republic of China in 1979, agreeing to virtually all of Beijing's demands, including acknowledging that there was only "one China." Although we have stopped short of formally acknowledging the PRC's sovereignty over Taiwan, the lack of an embassy in Taipei and the presence of one in Beijing certainly implies that the Chinese party-state is the sole legitimate government of China.

Of course, China may regard Taiwan as its sovereign territory, but the inhabitants of that large island off the Chinese coast beg to differ. And for good reason: they haven't been ruled from Beijing since 1895. The vast majority of the twenty-four million people of the Republic of China (ROC), who have been governing themselves through free and open elections since 1996, say they want to remain free and independent of Communist Party control. Who can blame them?

So what did we get in return for our Faustian bargain with Beijing? Has selling out Taiwan, which had been our loyal ally for decades, proven to be a good deal?

By moving our embassy to Beijing in 1979, we were told, we would be able to play the "China card" against the Soviet Union. But we had already been playing that particular "card" since 1972, when Nixon first went to China. There is no doubt that it was a useful gambit in the great game of geostrategic poker called the Cold War—although it was President Reagan's military buildup, credit freeze, and controls on technology transfers that would ultimately force Moscow to fold. In any event, the "China card" justification for keeping Taiwan out in the cold vanished twenty-five years ago, with the 1991 implosion of that failed state known as the Soviet Union.

We convinced ourselves that we were sacrificing Taiwan for a greater prize: the prospect that the totalitarian People's Republic of China would gradually and peacefully evolve into a country that was at worst authoritarian, even eventually into a nation where basic human rights were respected and civil society would flourish. As we have seen, that comforting vision of China's democratic future died when China's "reform-minded leaders" horrified the world by butchering their own children to stay in power.

But the biggest argument of all was one billion Chinese customers. Nearly all the Fortune 500 companies imagined their goods and services flooding into China.

In fact, the reverse has happened. Instead of dominating the Chinese market, we handed China the keys to the kingdom—membership in the WTO—that it has used to dominate our own markets. Beijing continues to cleverly skew its market against foreign companies through technology theft, unwritten rules, and other machinations. As the *Economist* noted several years ago, "The meddling state lets multinationals in, only to squeeze them dry of their valuable technologies and then push them out."[41]

While our China policy has failed, our Taiwan policy—if we can even be said to have one—has succeeded. Isolated by the international community, largely abandoned by the United States, Taiwan has continued to thrive. Against all odds, it has evolved into a modern democratic state, one that shares our values and institutions. As such, it is an island of democratic hope in a sea of Chinese despotism. Upgrading our de facto alliance with Taiwan would strengthen our position in the Asian-Pacific, secure a vital linchpin in our defenses along the Pacific Rim, and give hope to China's dissidents.

Some of the same China experts who designed our failed China policy—and perpetuated it for three long decades—are now warning us that China's leaders will be angry if we try and change the status quo with regard to Taiwan. Given that the Chinese are already shutting out American businesses, violating currency agreements, and dumping cheap goods on the U.S. market—not to mention carrying out cyber-attacks, making baseless territorial claims, militarizing sandbars in the South China Sea, and protecting Pyongyang—they seem pretty hostile towards us already.

Former UN Ambassador John Bolton, among others, has suggested that "If China won't back down in East Asia, Washington has options that would compel Beijing's attention," and that chief among these would be the "play[ing] the 'Taiwan card.'"[42] So is it in America's interest to distance ourselves from dictatorial China and draw closer to democratic Taiwan at this time? The answer is unequivocally yes, for two reasons, one tactical and one strategic.

As China continues to militarize artificial islands in the South China Sea, we should remember that a real island—250 miles long and ninety miles wide—sits a little over a hundred miles from China's southeast coast. Strategically, no location in the "first island chain," which stretches from Japan down to Australia, occupies such a commanding position.

General MacArthur memorably called Taiwan "an unsinkable aircraft carrier," but even during the Taiwan Straits Crises of the 1950s, the United States never fully capitalized on the island's strategic potential. Until now, past administrations have been more interested in placating Beijing. Given that the Chinese party-state is literally implacable—that is to say, there is no set of concessions that would not whet its appetite for more of the same—that should now change and change quickly.

Within six months of taking office, the Trump administration had approved the sale of $1.42 billion in arms to Taiwan. Like most previous sales, the package was intended to bolster Taiwan's self-defense capability. It included technical support for early warning radar, high-speed anti-radiation missiles, torpedoes, and missile components.[43]

But this should be just the beginning. For decades the United States has let China essentially dictate the quality and the quantity of the weapons that we sold Taiwan. The ROC's requests for more advanced systems, such as diesel submarines, F-16 CDs, and F-35s have been rejected for fear that the PRC would be offended by the sale of these "offensive weapons." Given that any advanced mobile weapons platform can arguably be put to both offensive and defensive uses, this artificial distinction should be discarded. The island's defense depends upon controlling the battlespace around Taiwan, for which modern aircraft and submarines are indispensable. Assisting Taiwan in developing a homegrown undersea warfare program would deter China from attempting to blockade the island.

We should also strengthen strategic cooperation with Taiwan. An initial step in this direction would be to allow U.S. Navy vessels to resume making port calls in Kaohsiung and other Taiwan ports for the first time since 1979. From there we should move to conducting joint military exercises. This is the only way to ensure that the more advanced systems that we will be providing to Taiwan can successfully interoperate with our own to trade communications, intelligence, and other data in the event of a crisis.

On the diplomatic front, we could upgrade the American Institute in Taiwan (AIT), which is what we call our unofficial embassy to Taiwan, to the status of a formal consulate general. After all, we have a consulate general in Hong Kong, which under China's "one country, two systems" formula, is part of China. Why not in Taipei, where Beijing makes similar, albeit currently unenforced, claims? The new consulate general would be headed by a consul general who, like the one in Hong Kong, would serve as our ambassador in all but name.

China will predictably protest each and every one of these moves. Given that it finds our *very presence in Asia* offensive, this should not surprise us. But we should not let Beijing's arrogance dictate our actions. In my view, Americans should be just as offended that an increasingly belligerent China continues to threaten to launch an attack on Taiwan, sink our ships if they enter the Taiwan Straits, or down our planes if they get too close to Chinese airspace. Perhaps we should resolve to pay just as much attention to Beijing's "sensibilities" as it does to ours—which is to say little to none—and simply do right by our ally.

Of course, in terms of strengthening our de facto alliance with Taiwan, we could easily take matters a lot further. Beijing should be made to understand: if you want to play games by militarizing sand bars in the South China Sea, there is a real island with a real democracy not too far away from your shores whose defenses we may want to bolster considerably.

In 2017 the United States began regular Freedom of Navigation Operations (FONOP) in the South China Sea, breaking with the on-again, off-again timidity displayed by the Obama administration. In May the USS *Dewey* sailed within a few miles of China's military base on Mischief Reef, which the Hague Tribunal has ruled is Philippine territory.[44] Such transits, bringing American vessels within the twelve nautical miles of China's illegal bases, are intended as a rebuttal to Beijing's claim of sovereignty. By themselves, however, they will hardly convince the Chinese party-state to retreat from its illegal occupation of these reefs. Playing the Taiwan card right, on the other hand, just might.

In any event, Taiwan's security and de facto independence must be preserved. For as important as Taiwan's military potential is to the future security of Asia, it has an even more critical political role to play in the future of Greater China. For it was here on this island on March 23, 1996, that a Chinese people went to the polls and directly elected their leader for the first time. Taiwan may be an "unsinkable aircraft carrier." But it is as a functioning, indeed flourishing democracy that it poses *an existential threat to the continued rule of the Chinese Communist Party*.

In the fifties and sixties, while China was locked in the grip of a totalitarian regime run by the megalomaniac Mao Zedong, Taiwan was busily gaining experience in local democracy, holding election after election at the county and township level. A successful land reform and the encouragement of foreign trade led to economic progress, which in turn promoted even greater contact with the West. And over the past two decades, as the People's Republic was reverting to a "people's democratic dictatorship," the Republic of China has successfully made the transition from autocratic state to modern democracy.

Cultural and political changes were greatly accelerated in Taiwan not only because it was cut off from the mass of China, but also because it was utterly dependent upon the United States. The American example of ordered liberty and respect for human rights carried the day, overwhelming traditional notions of autocratic rule within a generation. Although the Chinese Communist Party won the military contest in 1949, the Nationalist and Democratic Progressive Parties—the two major parties on Taiwan—have won the peace in the nearly seventy years since. By every measure of human well-being, from per capita GNP to respect for human rights, Taiwan stands head and shoulders above the mainland. There are few on either side of the Taiwan Strait who would deny this.

Taiwan can best be integrated into the common defense against the hegemon not just with the erection of a THAAD missile defense system on the island, the stationing of elements of the Seventh Fleet in Kaohsiung or Su-ao, or assistance to the Taiwanese military in developing a robust submarine fleet. All these are important, and should be considered. But the best defense the PRC's hegemonic ambitions is, quite simply, the continued existence of a stable, democratic, and prosperous Taiwan. By its powerful example of ordered liberty, it contradicts the Communist Party's claim to be the sole alternative to chaos in China. With its first-world living standards and life spans, it exposes the continued poverty of socialism with Chinese characteristics. Taiwan, in short, is not just a parallel universe coexisting uneasily with an evil twin, but rather a road map to what could one day exist in all of China. This is why the Chinese party-state is determined to extinguish this beacon of freedom, and it is also why we must continue to protect it.

Diplomats who are determined that the United States should enjoy "good relations" with the PRC tend to view Taiwan as nothing more than "the flashpoint of Asia," or worse, as a constant irritant to U.S.-China relations. Seen in the larger context, however, Taiwan assumes a much larger, even historic, significance. For the beleaguered democrats and dissidents on the Mainland, the ROC is more than just a success story for democracy. It is a *sister Chinese state* that inspires them to hope that all of China will one day follow a similar path.

It should be clear by now that the Chinese party-state—the political entity I have called the Bully of Asia—is playing for the highest stakes. It seeks to realize the perennial "China Dream" of the Grand Unification of All Under Heaven. It would be a mistake to think that the present conflict between China and the United States is about trade relations, cyber-espionage, or the South China Sea. These are merely the eddies on the surface of a deep underlying clash of values, institutions, and civilizations. The conflict is ultimately about whether America and its allies, or China alone, will dominate the world of the future.

This means that the well-intentioned efforts of some Asia experts to diplomatically contrive win-win solutions to our difficulties are pointless. In Beijing's view—although it sometimes pretends otherwise—U.S.-China relations are a zero-sum game. They are, as the Chinese say, a

"You die, I live" scenario. China's hegemonic ambitions must be taken as a given, and U.S. policy must be consistently and resolutely directed at curbing them. If we can disarm North Korea, foil China's ambitions in the South China Sea, and arm and integrate Taiwan into the common defense of the Pacific Rim, we will have set back the party-state's plans to dominate Asia by a generation. Even if we succeed in these matters, however, we will not have diminished its relentless drive for domination. Only the Chinese people, by overthrowing the current Communist dynasty in favor of democratic rule, can accomplish that.

At the moment, as the Chinese party-state continues to tighten its stranglehold on power, the country's democratic prospects seem vanishingly small. Freedom has always been a relatively rare commodity in human history, but particularly so in China. In the Middle Kingdom "He who has the most force" has always won.

ACKNOWLEDGMENTS

I wish to first acknowledge my intellectual debt to my good friend Professor Zhengyuan Fu. He was the first to argue, explicitly and compellingly, that the political system of the PRC is best understood as a revitalized restoration of Chinese imperial autocracy. His *Autocratic Tradition and Chinese Politics* (Cambridge University Press, 1994) is a tour de force, and should be read by anyone who wants to better understand the historical gestation of the party-state's totalitarian impulses.

It is worth noting that Prof. Fu did his "graduate work"—so to speak—in Beijing's Prison Number One. He was incarcerated there in 1958 for daring to criticize the party-state during the infamous Hundred Flowers episode. He spent the next twenty years working in the prison's print shop, while taking advantage of every spare moment to read through all the volumes in the prison library. There he pondered Chinese history in an environment that was, shall we say, extraordinarily conducive to understanding the decisive role that Legalism had played, and continues to play, in Chinese political institutions.

I am also fortunate not just in my friends, but in my two research assistants, Matthew McGinty and Allen Baldanza. Matthew's years of teaching in China gave him a unique window into the minds of his Chinese students that I have drawn upon more than once in writing these chapters. He often reminds me that young people in China today have been taught to idolize two of the great mass murderers of history, Mao Zedong and the first emperor of the Qin dynasty (*Qin Shihuangdi*, r. 220–210 B.C.), and for the same reason: "They unified China." Nothing else matters.

Allen Baldanza, who studied Chinese in Beijing, also frequently encountered the ultranationalism and xenophobia of which I write. The description of the ruins of the Summer Palace in chapter seven, for example, owes much to his visit there. Both Allen and Matthew were indefatigable in tracking down references and scouring the latest news out of China. I cherish the hope that both will continue their studies in the years to come. Both have much to contribute to the China field.

Earlier versions of chapters two and three appeared in my *Hegemon: China's Plan to Dominate Asia and the World* (Encounter Books, 2000), and appear here with permission.

Throughout the entire process of writing this book, I have received incredible support and encouragement from the directors and staff of the Population Research Institute, including John Delmare, Professor Brian Scarnecchia, Dr. Christopher Manion, Father Linus Clovis, Colonel Vince E. Cruz, USMC (ret.), and Joel Bockrath, as well as long-time colleagues like Chuck DeVore.

Above all, I wish to acknowledge my family: my wife, Vera, and children, Julie, Steven, Matthew, Hannah, Andrew, Moriah, Thomas, Luke, and Chiara. I love you all more than you will ever know.

NOTES

INTRODUCTION

1. Thucydides, *History of the Peloponnesian War* (London: J. M. Dent; New York, E. P. Dutton, 1910), 1:23. Translation by the author.

2. *Book of the Han Dynasty*, Volume 56, Biographies 26, "Biography of Dong Zhongshu" in *Dong Zhongshu Zhuan*, http://ctext.org/han-shu/dong-zhong-shu-zhuan accessed on January 9, 2017. Translation by the author. Also quoted in Xiaobing Li, Patrick Fuliang Shan, eds., *Ethnic China: Identity, Assimilation, and Resistance,* chapter by Xiaoyuan Liu," 32. All translations of Chinese texts, ancient and modern, are by the author.

3. The passage about the "Great Uniformity" is found in the book *Li Yun* ("The Conveyance of Rites") of the *Li Ji* (Book of Rites), in W. T. de Bary, ed., *Sources of Chinese Tradition*, vol. 1. (New York: Columbia University

Press, 1960),176. The "Great Uniformity" has also been translated as the "Grand Union" by the Scottish missionary James Legge and, somewhat less accurately, as the "Great Harmony" or the "Great Tranquility." The Legge translation is available at http://ctext.org/liji/li-yun.

4. Confucian scholar Tu Wei-ming seems to think that "Great Unity" and "Great Harmony" work equally well. But while "Great Harmony" is an authentically Confucian reading of the phrase, with "Great Unity" the later "Legalist" interpretation, it is the Legalist sense that has dominated down through the ages. In fact, the Confucian reading of the phrase imposes a meaning on *datong* that cannot be found in the characters themselves. The *tong* character in *datong* does not mean "harmony" at all, but rather "sameness," "uniformity," "union," or "unity." The Chinese for "harmony"—*he*—is a different character altogether. See Tu Wei-ming, *Humanity and Self-Cultivation: Essays in Confucian Thought* (Berkeley: Asian Humanities Press,1979), 29.

5. Angang Hu and Yilong Yang, *China 2030* (Springer, 2014). See p. 188, n. 8. Hu is generally regarded as one of China's top students of politics and economics.

6. Graham Allison, "The Thucydides Trap: Are the U.S. and China Headed for War? *Atlantic*, September 24, 2015, https://www.theatlantic.com/international/archive/2015/09/united-states-china-war-thucydides-trap/406756/; see also, Graham Allison, *Destined for War: Can America and China Escape Thucydides's Trap?* (Houghton Mifflin Harcourt, 2017).

7. Peter Navarro, *Crouching Tiger: What China's Militarism Means for the World* (Prometheus Books, 2015)

8. John J. Mearsheimer, *The Tragedy of Great Power Politics* (New York: W.W. Norton, 2001).

9. This early meaning of *ba*, or "hegemon," needs to be distinguished from the modern meaning of the term as an all-dominant power. The latter is the sense in which it is generally used in this book. The title, originally meaning something akin to "defender of the realm," was first

conferred upon Duke Huan of the kingdom of Qi by King Hui of the Zhou dynasty. It gave Duke Huan royal authority in military ventures. See Hsu Cho-yun, "The Spring and Autumn Period" in Michael Loewe and Edward L. Shaughnessy, *The Cambridge History of Ancient China: From the Origins of Civilization to 221 BC* (Cambridge: Cambridge University Press, 1990), 545–86.

10. This experience is said to have left the Chinese with a deeply ingrained personal fear of *hunluan*, which is generally translated as "chaos and disorder", but which is also a pretty good synonym for anarchy. The Chinese party-state incessantly plays on this fear by claiming that it, and only it, stands as a bulwark between the people and total anarchy.

1. A DISEASE OF THE HEART

1. Lloyd Eastman, "Nationalist China during the Nanking Decade 1927–1937," in Lloyd Eastman, ed., *The Nationalist Era in China, 1927–1949*," (Cambridge: Cambridge University Press, 1986), 1-52 at 33.

2. Henry Kazianis, "The greatest challenge to Trump: It Isn't ISIS. It Isn't Russia. The Greatest Challenge Is China," *Washington Times*, November 20, 2016, http://www.washingtontimes.com/news/2016/nov/20/donald-trumps-greatest-challenge-will-be-china/ Accessed on August 15, 2017.

3. Sun Yat-Sen, *Xuanji*, 3 vols. (Beijing: Remin Chubanshe, 1956), 188.

4. Mark Manyin and Mary Beth Nikitin, "Foreign Assistance to North Korea," Congressional Research Service, April 2, 2014, https://fas.org/sgp/crs/row/R40095.pdf.

5. There have been serious proposals to reinstate the monarchy and install Putin as Tsar; see Will Stewart, "Russia Should Reinstate the Monarchy and Appoint PUTIN as Royal Emperor, Says Influential Russian Churchman, *Daily Mail*, January 1, 2017, http://www.dailymail.co.uk/news/article-4079962/Russia-reinstate-monarchy-appoint-PUTIN-royal-emperor-says-influential-Moscow-churchman.html.

6.   Following the fall of Constantinople to the Ottoman Turks in 1453, Moscow began styling itself the "Third Rome," the successor to Rome and Constantinople.

7.   Putin has criticized "the excesses of political correctness" in no uncertain terms: "We can see how many of the Euro-Atlantic countries are actually rejecting their roots, including the Christian values that constitute the basis of Western civilisation. They are denying moral principles and all traditional identities: national, cultural, religious and even sexual. They are implementing policies that equate large families with same-sex partnerships, belief in God with the belief in Satan.

       "The excesses of political correctness have reached the point where people are seriously talking about registering political parties whose aim is to promote paedophilia. People in many European countries are embarrassed or afraid to talk about their religious affiliations. Holidays are abolished or even called something different; their essence is hidden away, as is their moral foundation. And people are aggressively trying to export this model all over the world. I am convinced that this opens a direct path to degradation and primitivism, resulting in a profound demographic and moral crisis.... What else but the loss of the ability to self-reproduce could act as the greatest testimony of the moral crisis facing a human society?" "Meeting of the Valdai International Discussion Club," September 19, 2013, http://en.kremlin.ru/events/president/news/19243

8.   Since the Chinese introduced the term "hegemony" into the vocabulary of international relations, it has been elaborated by scholars in various ways. In addition to the original Chinese meaning, scholars now also speak of benign hegemony, regional hegemony, etc. But the Chinese use of the term is the historical antecedent for these refinements. The other uses are derivative.

9. See Steven Mosher, "International Tribunal Decisively Rejects Beijing's Claim to the South China Sea," Breitbart News, 12 July 2016, http://www.breitbart.com/national-security/2016/07/12/international-tribunal-decisively-rejects-beijings-claim-south-china-sea/.

10. 10 Japanese foreign ministry analyst Koro Bessho writes, "The Middle Kingdom was not simply Asia's largest state, but the world itself.... In theory, there were no boundaries between the Empire and neighboring nations, which were seen as little more than 'barbarian' lands owing different levels of allegiance to the Emperor." Koro Bessho, "Identities and Security in East Asia," Adelphi Paper 325 (London: International Institute for Strategic Studies, March 1999).

11. See Edward L. Dreyer, *Zheng He: China and the Oceans in the Early Ming Dynasty, 1405–1433* (Longman, 2006), for a detailed and historically accurate account of these voyages.

12. Ross H. Munro, "Eavesdropping on the Chinese Military: Where it Expects War—Where it Doesn't," *Orbis* (Summer, 1994): 1–17.

13. Lucian W. Pye, "International Relations in Asia: Culture, Nation, and State," The Sigur Center for Asian Studies, George Washington University, July 1998, quotation at p. 9, at https://www2.gwu.edu/~sigur/assets/docs/scap/SCAP1-Pye.pdf.

14. Ross Terrill, *The New Chinese Empire*, (New York: Basic Books, 2003), 63–64.

15. Ibid., 82.

16. Christopher A. Ford, *The Mind of Empire: China's History and Modern Foreign Relations*, (Kentucky: University Press of Kentucky, 2010), 101.

17. Ibid.

18. Richard J. Smith, *Chinese Maps: Images of "All Under Heaven"* (New York: Oxford University Press, 1996), 68, 75.

19. *Ming shizong shilu, juan* 199, 6b–7b. Cited in Terrill, *The New Chinese Empire*, 42.

20. Morris Rossabi, ed. *China Among Equals: The Middle Kingdom and Its Neighbors, 10th–14th Centuries* (Berkeley: University of California Press),1983), 48–49.

21. Peter Gries, *China's New Nationalism,* (Berkeley and Los Angeles: University of California Press, 2004), 39.

22. Yang Lien-sheng, "Historical Notes on the Chinese World Order," in John K. Fairbank, ed., *The Chinese World Order: Traditional China's Foreign Policy* (Cambridge: Harvard University Press, 1968), 28.

23. Harry G. Gelber, *The Dragon and the Foreign Devils, (New York:* Bloomsbury, 2007), 161.

24. Albert Feuerwerker, "Chinese History and the Foreign Relations of Contemporary China," *Annals of the American Academy of Political and Social Science* 402 (July 1974), 4.

25. S. C. M. Paine, *Imperial Rivals: China, Russia, and Their Disputed Frontier* (Armonk, NY: Sharpe, 1996), 245–46.

26. China's tradition of hegemony implies a preexisting claim on the loyalties, if not the territory, of neighboring vassal and tributary states. So even Chiang Kai-shek could write, "After having witnessed the tragedy of the loss of the Liuchiu Islands [Ryukyus], Hong Kong, Formosa [Taiwan], the Pescadores, Annam [Vietnam], Burma and Korea, China was confronted with the great danger of imminent partition of her entire territory." Chiang Kai-shek, *China's Destiny* (New York: MacMillan, 1947), 34; see also 242 n. 19.

27. Christopher A. Ford, *The Mind of Empire: China's History and Modern Foreign Relations,* (Kentucky: University Press of Kentucky, 2010), 93.

28. For these and many similar comments, see Michael Pillsbury, ed., *China Debates the Future Security Environment* (Washington, DC: National Defense University Press, 2000).

29. Song Yimin, "A Discussion of the Division and Grouping of Forces in the World after the End of the Cold War" (in Chinese), *Renmin Ribao*

(People's Daily), April 29, 1996. A longer version of this article originally appeared in the journal *International Studies* (Beijing: China Institute of International Studies) 6, no. 8 (1996): 10.

30. Zbigniew Brzezinski, *The Grand Chessboard: American Primacy and its Geostrategic Imperatives* (New York: Basic Books, 1997), 170. The most accessible translation of Sunzi's thought is by Ralph D. Sawyer, *The Complete Art of War* (Boulder, CO: Westview Press, 1996).

31. *China's National Defense*, white paper issued by the Information Office of the State Council, the People's Republic of China, 27 July 1998, 1. This white paper is available at the Chinese Embassy's web site at www.china-embassy.org.

32. Ibid.

33. This formulation is not new. China has placed itself in opposition to the United States since at least August 1994, when Deng Xiaoping defined China's geostrategic goals as "First, to oppose hegemony and power politics and safeguard world peace; second, to build up a new international political and economic order."

34. "Seven New Members Join NATO," NATO, April 1, 2004, http://www.nato.int/docu/update/2004/03-march/e0329a.htm; "Enlargement," NATO, June 16, 2017, http://www.nato.int/cps/en/natolive/topics_49212.htm.

35. Brzezinski, *The Grand Chessboard*, 172. The *People's Daily* had earlier condemned the increased scope of U.S.-Japan military cooperation as "a dangerous move." "Strengthening Military Alliance Does Not Conform with Trend of the Times" (in Chinese), *Renmin Ribao*, 31 January 1997.

36. *China's National Defense*, 1998, 5.

37. *The Diversified Employment of China's Armed Forces* white paper issued by the Information Office of the State Council, The People's Republic of China, April 16, 2013.

38. *The Diversified Employment of China's Armed Forces white* paper issued by the Information Office of the State Council, The People's Republic of China, April 16, 2013.

39. Ibid.

40. Timothy Heath, "China's Defense White Paper: A New Conceptual Framework for Security," The Jamestown Foundation, *China Brief*, Volume 13, Issue 9 (April 25, 2013), http://www.jamestown.org/programs/chinabrief/single/?tx_ttnews%5Btt_news%5D=40784&cHash=7cdb20872966140532416d3f7eafe6fd#.VLXGIorF-9U.

41. Brzezinski, *The Grand Chessboard*, 172.

42. Ibid., 169. At the same time, there are tactical reasons for China's interest in a "strategic partnership" with America over the short to medium term, among them driving a wedge between the U.S. and its long-standing allies in the region, and providing cover for the transition to Chinese dominance.

43. *Megatrends China* (Beijing: Hualing Publishing House, 1996), cited in Bruce Gilley, "Potboiler Nationalism," *Far Eastern Economic Review*, 3 October 1996. According to several selections in *China Debates the Future Security Environment*, the late Chinese leader Deng Xiaoping was the author of the military strategy of "biding our time and building up our capabilities."

44. These examples come from Pillsbury, ed., *China Debates*.

2. HEGEMON: THE INVENTION OF THE TOTALITARIAN STATE

1. One of Confucius' oft-quoted sayings, this appears twice in *Li ji (Book of Rites)*, in chapters 7 and 30, and once in Mencius, *Mengzi (Book of Mencius)*, in chapter 5a.4. Easily accessible online versions of these Chinese classics include Confucius, *The Book of Rites*, Ed., Dai Sheng (A.D. 80), translated by James Legge (Boston: Intercultural Press, 2013) 249, 320, and *Mencius*, translated by James Legge, (Pantianos Classics, 2016), 80. In *Mencius* the version is slightly altered to "Confucius said:

'Just as there are not two suns in the sky, so there cannot be two emperors on earth.'"

2.   *Zizhi Tongjian* ("*Comprehensive Mirror in Aid of Governance*"), trans. Joseph P. Yap (North Charleston, S.C.: CreateSpace, 2016), 58. The *Zizhi Tongjian* is a chronicle written by the great historian Sima Guang. It is considered to be the pioneering reference work in Chinese historiography. It was also Chairman Mao's favorite book, which he read multiple times throughout his life.

3.   In the following sections I draw heavily upon the seminal work of Professor Zhengyuan Fu, especially his *Autocratic Tradition and Chinese Politics* (Cambridge: Cambridge University Press, 1994) and *China's Legalists: The Earliest Totalitarians and Their Art of Ruling* (Armonk, New York: M. E. Sharpe, 1996). Professor Fu was well acquainted not only with China's totalitarian past, but with its totalitarian present as well, since he spend the years from 1957 to 1979 incarcerated in Beijing Prison Number 1 for speaking out during the Hundred Flowers Campaign.

4.   Cited in Zhengyuan Fu, *Autocratic Tradition and Chinese Politics* (Cambridge: Cambridged University Press, 1993), 15. The traditional way of referring to this passage is *Shang shu* ("*Book of Documents*"): *pan geng, tang shi.*

5.   The traditional citation for this famous passage is *Shi jing* ("*The Book of Odes*"): xiaoya ("The Lesser Court Hymns"), beishan ("North Mountain Decade"), poem 205. It can be found in English in James Legge (1871), trans., *The She King, or the Lessons from the States* (Hong Kong: Hong Kong University Press, 1960), 360.

6.   Despite the influence of their thought on Chinese history, the Legalists have been largely neglected by modern Sinology. John King Fairbank's *China: A New History* (Cambridge: Harvard University Press, 1992), for example, contains not a single reference to this pivotal school of

statecraft, which is key to understanding so much of China's behavior, both past and present.

7.   Cho-Yun Hsu, *Ancient China in Transition* (Stanford: Stanford University Press, 1965), 58.

8.   *Han Fei Zi*, chapters 47, 49, 50 in Fu, *Autocratic Tradition and Chinese Politics* 20. What Professor Fu translates as "force" I translate as "power," which more accurately aligns with modern-day English usage. Among the forerunners of Legalism was a branch of Daoism called the Huang-Lao school (after the legendary Yellow Emperor Huang-di and Daoist philosopher Lao Zi), through which many Daoist prescriptions became Legalist statecraft. This connection came to light with the discovery of the *Huangdi sijing* ("Four Canons of the Yellow Emperor") during a 1973 excavation of a Han dynasty tomb in Hunan province. The views expressed in this ancient document accord with those of the Legalists, for example: "Possessing a large territory, a teeming population, and a strong army, the ruler is matchless in the world." See Fu, *Autocratic Tradition*, 37.

9.   Charles O. Hucker, *China's Imperial Past* (Stanford: Stanford University Press, 1975), 92.

10. *Han Fei Zi*, chapter 14.

11. Max Weber defined power as "the probability that one actor within a social relationship will be in a position to carry out his own will despite resistance, regardless of the basis on which this probability rests." Max Weber, *The Theory of Social and Economic Organizations*, trans. A. M. Henderson and Talcott Parsons (New York: The Free Press, 1947), 152.

12. Those Legalists who successfully implemented their programs thus ran a risk of execution, and at least two Legalist chancellors (Shang Yang and Wu Qi) met their that fate. Hsu, *Ancient China*, 38–52.

13. *Guan Zi*, chapter 16.

14. *Shangjun shu*, chapter 24; *Han Fei Zi*, ch. 45).

15. *Han Fei Zi*, chapter 14.

16. *Shangjun shu*, chapter 7.

17. *Shangjun shu*, chapter 5.

18. *Shi ji*, chapter 68.

19. *Shi ji*, chapter 6.

20. The Great Wall of China as we know it today was built by the Ming dynasty in the sixteenth century, as Arthur Waldron has conclusively shown in *The Great Wall of China: From History to Myth* (Cambridge: Cambridge University Press, 1990). Earlier walls were built by Qin, other Warring States, and later dynasties.

21. Li Si, "Memorial on the Burning of Books," *Shi Ji* 87:6b–7a, translated in Theodore de Bary, Wingtsit Chan, and Burton Watson, *eds., Sources of Chinese Tradition* (New York: Columbia University Press, 1960), 154–55.

22. Derk Bodde, *Cambridge History of China*, volume 1 (Cambridge University Press, 1986) suggests that the 460 (not 463) scholars were not actually buried alive, only murdered, but this is a minority view.

23. There are those who would argue, even in the face of all this evidence, that the Qin state was not truly totalitarian since it was not able to achieve total control over the entire range of human thought and action. But this is like saying that the U.S. is not truly democratic because not everyone votes in elections. Totalitarianism, like democracy, is an ideal type, the real-world iteration of which can scarcely be without deficiencies. Intentions must be weighed alongside results. And the intent of the first emperor of the Qin dynasty, few would dispute, was to dominate his subjects totally. The Legalist system of government that he employed for that purpose came as close to achieving total control over the population as the relatively primitive means of communication and transportation then allowed; it can properly be judged totalitarian.

24. Confucius, *Lun yu*, chapter 13.6.

25. Confucius, *Lun yu*, chapter 2.1.

26. Confucius, *Lun yu*, chapter 12.22.

27. Confucius, *Lun yu*, chapter 17.6.

28. Confucius, *Lun yu*, chapter 15.23, 12.2.

29. Ross Terrill, *The New Chinese Empire* (University of New South Wales Press, 2003), 72.

30. *Han shu*, chapter 9.

31. See H. G. Creel, *Chinese Thought: From Confucius to Mao Tse-tung* (Chicago: University of Chicago Press, 1953), especially chapter 9, and Hsiao Kung-chuan, *Zhongguo zhengzhi sixiang shi* (A History of Chinese Political Thought) (Taipei: Linking, 1982. "By the time the Legalists had completed their work of sabotage," Creel astutely concludes, "the true nature of Confucius had been thoroughly obscured." (237–41) Respect for the inviolability and integrity of the sacred texts of Chinese history had given way before the political exigencies of succeeding dynasties. The official ideology of Imperial China was not Confucianism but Legalism with a Confucian patina.

32. *Zhongyong*, chapter 29.

33. Ibid.

34. Confucius, *Lun yu*, chapter 16.2. Because many elements of Legalist political philosophy are traceable to Daoism through the Huang-Lao school, some Chinese historians assert that traditional Chinese political philosophy is a mixture of Confucianism and Daoism.

35. Fu, *Autocratic Tradition and Chinese Politics*, 35. For most of the past two thousand years, the Chinese state has loudly proclaimed its adherence to moral principles that it rarely observed in practice.

36. Some rulers, of course, were more cunning practitioners of the Confucian-Legalist deceit than others. As PRC historian Fan Wenlan writes, "Following the Qin and Han periods, those emperors of succeeding dynasties who knew how to employ Confucianism on the outside but applied Daoism [of the Legalist variety] on the inside, that

is, blending the Way of Sage Kings with that of the Hegemon, saw their reigns prosper. Those who were not adept at this saw their reigns decline." Fan Wenlan, *Zhongguo tongshi* (A general history of China), vol. 1 (Beijing: Renmin chubanshe, 1978), 248; cited in Fu, *Autocratic Traditions and Chinese Politics*, 62.

37. Swaine and Tellis's book, *Interpreting China's Grand Strategy,* is a heroic effort to tease out of the history of China's domination of East Asia the elements of a "grand strategy" without explicitly acknowledging that it is precisely the primal urge for hegemony and nothing else that is China's grand strategy. While they admit that "a concern with cultural or ideological preeminence has often influenced Chinese security behavior," they do not equate this "concern" with China's grand strategy on the grounds that "the ability of the Chinese state to sustain such preeminence ultimately relies greatly on both internal and external material conditions and power relationships." But this is merely to state the obvious: that China's actual grand strategy— the incessant drive for hegemony—is constrained by other mediating factors.

38. As Mearsheimer writes, "Given the difficulty of determining how much power is enough for today and tomorrow, great powers recognize that the best way to ensure their security is to achieve hegemony now, thus eliminating any possibility of a challenge by another great power. Only a misguided state would pass up an opportunity to be the hegemon in the system because it thought it already had sufficient power to survive." John Mearsheimer, *The Tragedy of Great Power Politics.* (New York: W. W. Norton, 2001), 35. China has never been under any illusions on this point. America, on the other hand, has.

39. Wang Guowei, Shuijing zhujiao (Shanghai: Shanghai renmin chubanshe, 1984), 1150. Cited in Terrill, *The New Chinese Empire*, 37.

40. *Tang da zhaoling ji*, chapter 13, 77.

41. *Jiu Tangshu*, chapter 194, 5162.

42. *Song huiyao jigao*, chapter 7, 6874.

43. See John King Fairbank, "Introduction: Varieties of the Chinese Military Experience," in Frank A. Kierman Jr. and John K. Fairbank, eds., *Chinese Ways in Warfare* (Harvard University Press, Cambridge, Massachusetts: 1974), 1–26.

44. For these figures, see Alastair I. Johnston, *Cultural Realism: Strategic Culture and Grand Strategy in Chinese History* (Princeton University Press, Princeton, New Jersey: 1995), 27.

45. These are the conclusions of Choon Kun Lee in *War in the Confucian International Order* (Doctoral Dissertation, the University of Texas at Austin, August 1988), 210–12, as cited in Swaine and Tellis, *Interpreting China's Grand Strategy* 49. They mesh well with what we know about the military behavior and aggressiveness of the Chinese state in the twentieth century, as we will see in chapter 3.

46. China Proper, as commonly defined, is "a roughly square land mass about half the size of the continental United States, bounded on the north by the Great Wall, on the west by Inner Asian wastelands and Tibetan highlands, and on the south and east by oceans. This is the historical Chinese homeland." Charles O. Hucker, *China's Imperial Past* (Stanford: Stanford University Press, 1975), 2.

47. I offer a population figure with some trepidation. As the eminent Israeli ancient historian Ben Isaac has written, "Demography is one of those topics which are as important as they are frustrating to those interested in the ancient world. The absence of information is such that modern specialists consider any effort at serious study an idle undertaking." Ben Isaac, "Jews, Christians and Others in Palestine: The Evidence from Eusebius," in *Jews in a Graeco-Roman World*, ed. M. Goodman (Oxford: Clarendon Press, 1998), 65. Some scholars have, nevertheless, attempted to estimate the size of the empire's population, and occasionally a figure of 60 million is mentioned. Professor Ian Haynes of Newcastle University has written, "I am pretty convinced that this is

too low. What makes such estimates so doubtful is the basis on which they are calculated and the way in which local studies repeatedly suggest higher population levels than those once suspected. Britain, one of the most intensely studied provinces, offers an example of this phenomenon. Up until recently, scholars tended to imagine that the population stood at around 2 million (approximately twice the generally accepted estimate for the Iron Age population at the beginning of the 1st millennium B.C.). Now scholars talk of figures of 6 to 8 million, after field survey and aerial reconnaissance reveal the existence of much denser settlement patterns. At the same time, prehistorians have started to question their earlier estimates, observing not only much denser settlement, but also that far higher agricultural yields were possible with Iron Age farming methods than was hitherto believed." Personal correspondence with the author, February 29, 2000.

48. For the size of the Roman army, see John Wacher, ed., *The Roman World* (London, Boston: Routledge & K. Paul, 1987), 3.

49. Although summary records of Han dynasty censuses survive intact to the present day, they count only households, so one has to use a somewhat controversial multiplier to reach the generally accepted figure of 59.5 million in A.D. 2. The Han dynasty was able to maintain such a large number of men under arms by practicing conscription, with all able-bodied males in the country obliged to serve for two years. Convicts and volunteers provided additional manpower.

50. The brief Sui dynasty (519–618) was immediately succeeded by the Tang (618–906), without an appreciable interregnum.

51. The legendary Yellow Emperor is said to be the ancestor—in a literal sense—not only of the Han Chinese, but of the Mongols, Manchus, Tibetans, and the Hui Muslims as well.

52.   Alastair I. Johnson, *Cultural Realism: Strategic Culture and Grand Strategy in Chinese History* (Princeton: Princeton University Press, 1995), 195.

53.   *Ming shizong shilu, juan*, 197–200. Quoted in Terrill, *The New Chinese Empire*, 45.

54.   Etienne Balazs, *Chinese Civilization and Bureaucracy* (New Haven: Yale University Press, 1964), 10.

55.   Michael Edmund Clarke, *In the Eye of Power: China and Xinjiang from the Qing Conquest to the 'New Great Game' for Central Asia, 1759–2004* (thesis, 2004, Griffith University, Brisbane: Dept. of International Business & Asian Studies); see also, Fred W. Bergholz, *The Partition of the Steppe: The Struggle of the Russians, Manchus, and the Zunghar Mongols for Empire in Central Asia, 1619–1758* (New York: Peter Lang, 1993) and David M. Crowe, *War Crimes, Genocide, and Justice: A Global History* (Palgrave Macmillan, 2014), 31–32.

3. THE HEGEMON AWAKENS FROM ITS SLUMBERS

1.   Mao Zedong, "The Chinese People Have Stood Up!," opening address at the First Plenary Session of the Chinese People's Political Consultative Conference, September 21, 1949, https://www.marxists.org/reference/archive/mao/selected-works/volume-5/mswv5_01.htm.

2.   Ibid.

3.   Mao Zedong, "Friendship' or Aggression," in *Selected Works of Mao Tse-tung*, vol. 4 (Beijing: Foreign Language Press, 1969), 447–49. This speech was a response to the U.S. State Department's white paper on China, formally called *United States Relations with China,* and Secretary of State Dean Acheson's "Letter of Transmittal" of it to President Truman, both of which were published on August 5, 1949.

4.   Mao Zedong, *Mao Zhuxi shici sanshiqi shi* (Thirty-seven poems of Chairman Mao) (Beijing: Renmin chubanshe, 1964). Translation by the

author. "True hero" is a phrase taken from the famous Chinese novel, *Romance of the Three Kingdoms*, in which Liu Bei says to Cao Cao that "the only true heroes in the world are you and I."

5. Mao, *Selected Works,* vol. 4, 195; cited in Fu, *Autocratic Tradition and Chinese Politics* (Cambridge: Cambridge University Press, 1994), 188. Some sources have forty-six thousand instead of four hundred and sixty thousand.

6. During the Cultural Revolution, PLA Marshal Peng Dehuai told the Red Guards who were persecuting him that "Comrade Mao Zedong is more familiar with Chinese history than anyone else in the Party. The first emperor of a dynastic era was always very wise, and very ferocious." Wang Xizhe, "On Socialist Democracy," in *On Socialist Democracy and the Chinese Legal System,* ed. A. Chan, Stanley Rosen, and J. Unger (Armonk, New York: Sharpe, 1985).

7. Zheng Yongnian, *The Chinese Communist Party as Organizational Emperor* (New York: Routledge, 2010), 16, 22.

8. For example, see Roderick MacFarquhar, *Mao Tse Tung: China's Peasant Emperor* (A&E Biography, 2005).

9. Stuart Schram, ed., *Chairman Mao Talks to the People* (New York: Random House, 1974).

10. V. Holubnychy, "Mao Tse-tung's Materialistic Dialectics," *China Quarterly* 19 (July–September 1964).

11. Mao Zedong and the Chinese Communist Party had adopted a pose as "agrarian reformers" during the last decade of the Chinese civil war, advocating a "New Democracy" in local governance and promising to rule "democratically" when they came to power. But as Nationalist resistance collapsed in early 1949 and a Chinese Communist Party victory appeared certain, Mao decided the time had come to abandon this pretense. The new national government would not be a democracy after all, he declared on 1 July 1949, but a "people's democratic dictatorship."

12. Philip Selznick, *The Organizational Weapon: A Study of Bolshevik Strategy and Tactics* (Glencoe, IL: The Free Press, 1960), especially chapter 1, "The Combat Party," 17–73.

13. Qi ZhiFeng and Wei Zhi, "Wei Jingsheng: Xi Jinping Makes Provocative Moves against Chinese Neighbors to Save His Regime (VOA exclusive)" Voice of America, June 2, 2014 [WJSF A825-W525], http://www.weijingsheng.org/report/report2014/report2014-06/WeiJSon1989DemocracyMovement140622VOAexclusiveA825-W525.htm. Accessed on 15 January 2015.

14. Patrick Tucker, "Here's the Biggest Difference Between US and Chinese Military Policy," Defense One, July 10, 2015, http://www.defenseone.com/threats/2015/07/heres-biggest-difference-between-us-and-chinese-military-policy/117553/, July 15, 2015.

15. The Chinese Communist party led "a counterrevolution against the first Chinese republican revolution of 1911," argues Professor Zhengyuan Fu, and following its victory restored a revitalized traditional autocracy. Fu, *Autocratic Tradition,* 2. Former President Lee Teng-Hui of Taiwan holds a similar view: "What did the Communist revolution accomplish? It did not bring the continent out of stagnation or free the people of stifling, oppressive tradition; what it did do was resurrect "hegemony" and imperialism." Lee Teng-hui, *The Road to Democracy: Taiwan's Pursuit of Identity* (Tokyo: PHP Institute, 1999), 53.

16. Mao was characteristically blunt about his aims. Under the guidance of the Chinese Communist Party, the masses would exercise a "democratic dictatorship," whose first and most important task would be to liquidate bad or "antagonistic" classes, defined as "the running dogs of imperialism—the landlord class [and] the bureaucrat-bourgeoisie, as well as the representatives of those classes, the Kuomintang reactionaries and their accomplices." Eventually all class distinctions would cease to exist, Mao promised, but before that could happen these

two "antagonistic" classes had to be "eliminated." Nor was Mao coy about how this class war was to be prosecuted. "Our present task is to strengthen the people's state apparatus," he wrote. "The state apparatus, including the army, the police and the courts, is the instrument by which one class oppresses another. It is an instrument for the oppression of antagonistic classes." Interestingly, Mao still felt obliged to pay lip service to democracy. "The people" would "enjoy freedoms of speech, assembly, association," and would have the right to vote and "elect their own government." But only on one condition: none of this was to interfere with the primary task of the new government, which was to exercise a dictatorship over the enemies of the people. It did not take a political philosopher to see that, even if the rights enumerated by Mao were inalienable, the right to membership in "the people" was not. Those who vigorously exercised their freedom of speech (or assembly, or association), or took seriously their right to "elect their own government," would run the risk of being declared "enemies of the people" by the state apparatus, which would then punish, imprison, or execute them with impunity. Mao Zedong, "On the People's Democratic Dictatorship," in *Selected Works*, vol. 4, 417–18.

17. Liu Xiaobo "The Roots of Chinese 'Patriotism,'" *No Enemies, No Hatred*, Selected Essays and Poems (Cambridge: Harvard University Press, 2012), 67.

18. Personal conversation, August 28, 1998. The more things change the more they remain the same: while Southeast Asia is no longer shown as being within China's borders on Chinese maps today, virtually the entire South China Sea now is.

19. This was not the only time that Stalin attempted to restrain Mao. At the end of 1947, when the Red Army had swept the field in North China, Stalin suggested to Mao that he not cross the Yangtze to finish off the Nationalist armies in the south. "Stalin wanted to prevent China

from making revolution," Mao later recalled, "saying we should not have a civil war and should cooperate with Chiang Kai-shek, otherwise the Chinese nation would perish. But we did not do what he said. The revolution was victorious.... After the victory of the revolution [Stalin] next suspected China of being a Yugoslavia, and that I would become a second Tito." Here Mao must have had his tongue firmly in cheek, for he had always been "a Tito." Despite his public posture of deference to Stalin, he was privately determined not to allow Soviet bases or troops on Chinese soil. Mao Zedong, "Speech at the Tenth Plenum of the Eighth Central Committee," September 24, 1962, reprinted in Schram, *Chairman Mao Talks,* 191.

20. Edgar Snow, *Red Star Over China* (New York: Grove Press, 1961), 110.

21. Mao Zedong, "Talks at the Chengdu Conference," March 1958, reprinted in Schram, *Chairman Mao Talks,* 101. Mao also complained about the Soviets' two "colonies" of the Northeast and Xinjiang. Although these two border regions were under Chinese control, the Soviets had insisted upon retaining special privileges in them, where people of any third country were not allowed to reside.

22. Stalin seems to have taken a softer line with China than in Eastern Europe, deciding in the end not to bind it to the Soviet Union by force but by economic aid and compromise. Still, given Mao's assertive nationalism, even Stalin's uncharacteristically velvet-glove approach would have failed within a few years had it not been for the outbreak of hostilities on the Korean Peninsula, which reforged the Sino-Russian alliance in the crucible of war, delaying for the Sino-Soviet split for a decade.

23. Samuel Wells, "The Lessons of the Korean War," in *The Korean War: A 25-Year Perspective,* ed. Francis Heller (Kansas, 1977). Although Russia was in the process of giving back much of this territory, other irritants remained. Outer Mongolia, which had been detached from

China in the twenties, remained a Soviet puppet state. Much of the Russian Far East and Central Asia had also once been Chinese territory.

24. Those who believe that the Communist Party Chairman was frightened by the thought of American forces reaching his borders should consider that those forces at the time numbered only 200,000, scarcely enough to undertake the conquest of a continent guarded by four million battle-hardened PLA troops. Even at its peak strength in July 1953, the UN Command stood at 932,539 ground forces. Republic of Korea (ROK) Army and Marine forces accounted for 590,911 of that force, and U.S. Army and Marine forces for another 302,483. By comparison, other U.N. ground forces totaled some 39,145 men, 24,085 of whom were provided by British Commonwealth Forces (Great Britain, Canada, Australia and New Zealand) and 5,455 of whom came from Turkey. See Harry G. Summers, "The Korean War: A Fresh Perspective," *Military History* 13 (April 1996), 1.

25. Schram, *Chairman Mao Talks*, 128. Even today, PLA generals boast of their "victories" over the United States. Take Lieutenant General Li Jijun, vice-president of the PRL's Academy of Military Science, who has written, "To fight against a superior force and win victory is the highest honor for our army. From the end of the Second World War to the Gulf War, the United States fought two local wars, the Korean War and the Vietnam War, and in both suffered defeat. In both, its opponent was China. In the Korean War, it was the direct opponent, and in the Vietnam War, it was the indirect opponent.... To fight against a superior force and win victory is the highest honor for our army." Li Jijun, "Notes on Military Theory and Military Strategy,' in *Chinese Views of Future Warfare*, ed. Michael Pillsbury, 2d ed. (Washington, D.C.: National Defense University Press, 1998), 230.

26. John Gittings, *The World and China*, 1922–1975 (London: Eyre Methuen, 1974), 236; Mao Zedong, "Talks at the Chengdu

Conference: On the Problem of Stalin," March 1958, in Schram, *Chairman Mao Talks*, 98–99. Mao also began quietly questioning the way the Soviet "Elder Brothers" treated other countries within the Communist bloc. When unrest broke out in Poland and Hungary following Khrushchev's anti-Stalin speech, Mao initially urged Khrushchev to withdraw all Soviet troops from these and other Eastern European countries. He mediated Polish-Soviet tensions following the election of reformer Wladyslaw Gomulka as party first secretary, helping to prevent Soviet armed intervention. Lowell Dittmer, "China's Search for Its Place in the World," in *Contemporary Chinese Politics in Historical Perspective*, ed. Brantly Womack (Cambridge: Cambridge University Press, 1991), 213, based on a 1985 interview by the author with a member of the Institute of Soviet and Eastern European Studies in the Chinese Academy of Social Sciences in Beijing.

27.   As Liu Xiaobo has written, "The economic program of the Mao era has sometimes been described as a planned economy, and sometimes as an attempt to overtake the Western democracies, but in fact it is probably most accurately viewed as dedicated to preparing for war." "The Roots of Chinese 'Patriotism," *No Enemies, No Hatred*, Selected Essays and Poems (Cambridge: Harvard University Press, 2012), 67.

28.   Jung Chang and John Halliday, *Mao: The Unknown Story* (London: Random House, 2005), 484.

29.   Strobe Talbot, ed., *Khrushchev Remembers: The Last Testament* (Boston: Little, Brown, 1974), 269. Mao's pleasure over the signing of this agreement perhaps explains his mid-November visit to Moscow—his last. The occasion was a conference of leaders from Communist countries to commemorate the fortieth anniversary of the October Revolution. Mao, not given to self-effacing remarks, declared at this event, "Our camp must have a head, because even a snake has a head. I would not agree that Chinese should be called head of the camp, because we do not merit this honor and cannot maintain this role, we

are still poor. We haven't even a quarter of a satellite, while the Soviet Union has two.... The socialist camp is headed by the USSR." Quoted by Enver Hoxha, in *The Artful Albanian: Memoirs of Enver Hoxha*, ed. Jon Halliday (London: Chatto and Windus, 1986), 215.

30. Indeed, just two months before he had told a meeting of the Military Affairs Commission that Chinese military theory and experience (which is to say, Mao's own) were superior to those of the Soviets.

31. For years leftists and Maoists, including some American China watchers, denied reports that Chairman Mao had ever made such callous comments. They preferred to believe that no leader, especially not a Communist one who claimed to put the well-being of the people above all else, could possibly say such a thing. Recently, however, Chinese state television, in a series on Mao, broadcast an episode entitled "The One Above All", which contained actual footage of Mao speaking at the World Communist Representative Meeting in Moscow in November 1957. In the course of giving his speech, "American Imperialism Is a Paper Tiger," he can clearly be heard to say "I'm not afraid of nuclear war. There are 2.7 billion people in the world; it doesn't matter if some are killed. China has a population of 600 million; even if half of them are killed, there are still 300 million people left. I'm not afraid of anyone." The original document from China can be found on page 106 at http://www.usc.cuhk.edu.hk/PaperCollection/webmanager/wkfiles/6693_1_paper.pdf. A CIA document on the speech that was obtained via a FOIA request is available at http://www.foia.cia.gov/sites/default/files/document_conversions/89801/DOC_0000246535.pdf. The *Epoch Times* has also reported on Mao's speech in Ariel Tian, "Mao's 'Nuclear Mass Extinction Speech' Aired on Chinese TV," *Epoch Times*, March 5, 2013, http://www.theepochtimes.com/n3/4758-maos-nuclear-mass-extinction-speech-aired-on-chinese-tv/.

32. Strobe Talbot, ed., *Khrushchev Remembers: The Last Testament* (Boston: Little, Brown, 1974), 269.

33. Mao, "Speech at the Enlarged Session of the Military Affairs Committee and the External Affairs Conference," 11 September 1959, in Schram, *Chairman Mao Talks*, 151.

34. At the Tenth Plenum of the Central Committee in 1962, Mao recalled his escalating troubles with Soviet leaders: "In 1958 Khrushchev wanted to set up a Soviet-Chinese combined fleet in order to seal us off [from attacking the offshore islands held by Taiwan]. At the time of the border dispute with India, he supported Nehru. At the dinner on our National Day he attacked us.... Today...we are called 'adventurists, nationalists, dogmatists.'" Mao's speech became public knowledge in the West only after it was published in 1969. Laszlo Ladany, *The Communist Party of China and Marxism: A Self-Portrait, 1921–1985* (Stanford: Hoover Institution Press, 1988), 267–68. Added to these insults was a real injury: Khrushchev's suspension of all technical assistance to China. Perhaps because Mao did not want to appear the supplicant, he did not mention that in 1960 Soviet engineers and technicians in China had rolled up their blueprints and returned home, cutting China off from its only source of modern technology.

35. Ibid., 321. At the end of his speech, Lin Biao quoted Mao's great 1962 prophecy that within fifty to a hundred years the world would go through a great transformation. Mao had not specified what the transformation would bring about, but it is likely that he meant China's return to greatness and centrality in world affairs. Putin should remember that Chinese leaders have in the past rejected the current border between China and Russia as the result of an "unequal treaty," and are virtually certain to do so again at some point in the future. For Lin Biao's speech, see Lin Biao, "Report to the Ninth National Congress of the Communist Party of China," April 1, 1969, https://www.marxists.org/reference/archive/lin-biao/1969/04/01.htm.

36. Beijing had been forced to take these steps, Zhou Enlai explained at the time, because Tibetan officials had "colluded with imperialism, assembled rebellious bandits, carried out rebellion," and—most incredible of all—"put the Dalai Lama under duress." Zhou's claims were treated with the scorn they deserved. On March 28 the U.S. State Department accused Communist China of a "barbarous intervention" and of attempting to "destroy the historical autonomy of the Tibetan people." On March 30 even the normally placid Indian prime minister Jawaharlal Nehru charged that the Chinese Communists had broken pledges to allow Tibet "full autonomy." India sympathized with the Tibetan rebels, he said, and would admit refugees from Tibet on an individual basis.

37. The Dalai Lama and his party of eighty officials, after an arduous three-hundred-mile journey over the southern mountains of Tibet, reached India on March 31, 1959. He charged that Communist China was bent on the "complete absorption and extinction of the Tibetan race," and that sixty-five thousand Tibetans had been slain since 1956. T. N. Schroth et al., *China and U.S. Far East Policy,* 1946–1967 (Washington, D.C.: Congressional Quarterly Series, 1967), 74–75, 92.

38. The problem with these stories was that "there has been no systematic serfdom in Tibet for centuries. In 1879, an Indian scholar who had spent his life in the Himalayan area, Sarat Chandra Das, traveled to Lhasa and studied the social order. He found no trace of bonded servitude. He described a place (unlike caste-ridden India) where 'the rich may bestow their daughters on the poor; the daughter of a poor man may become the bride of the proudest noble in the country.'" Barbara Crossette, "The Shangri-la that Never Was," *New York Times,* 5 July 1998, 3.

39. In April 1955, the Prime Ministers of Burma, Ceylon, India, Indonesia, and Pakistan invited representatives of a total of twenty-nine countries to an Asian-African Conference at Bandung in Indonesia. In addition to

the sponsoring countries, there were Afghanistan, Cambodia, China, Egypt, Ethiopia, the Gold Coast, Iran, Iraq, Japan, Jordan, Laos, Lebanon, Liberia, Libya, Nepal, the Philippines, Saudi Arabia, Sudan, Syria, Thailand, Turkey, North Vietnam, South Vietnam, and Yemen. The list included countries allied with the Western powers, Communist countries, and neutral countries, but not include the Republic of China (that is, Taiwan), North and South Korea, and Israel, which were regarded as being too controversial, and South Africa, which was barred on the grounds of its racial policies. The conference provided a platform for the expression of anti-colonial sentiments, and several Asian leaders also made strong public statements against Communist imperialism.

40. This theory of *yuan jiao jin gong* was advocated by the Legalist scholar-strategist Fan Sui of the state of Qin during the Warring States period (481–221 B.C.).

41. See Thomas J. Christensen, *Worse Than a Monolith: Alliance Politics and Problems of Coercive Diplomacy in Asia* (Princeton University Press, 2011).

42. Qiang Zhai, *China and the Vietnam Wars, 1950–1975* (Chapel Hill, NC: University of North Carolina Press, 2000), 135.

43. Christensen, *Worse Than a Monolith*.

44. Cited in H. C. Hinton, *China's Turbulent Quest* (New York: MacMillan, 1970), 67.

45. D. D. Eisenhower, *Mandate for Change, 1953–56* (New York: Doubleday, 1963), 462–63.

46. The Jinmen complex comprises Jinmen (Quemoy), Little Jinmen (Liehyu) and twelve islets. The total area of the Jinmen complex is 176.37 square kilometers. As of 1971, Jinmen had a population of 61,008, not including military personnel. The Mazu Islands comprise Nangan and eighteen other islets and have an area of 27.1 square kilometers. As of 1971, the civilian population was 17,057.

47. Eisenhower's advisers were divided in their response to the Jinmen crisis. Some felt that the U.S. should pledge itself to defend the offshore islands and launch preemptive strikes. Of the members of the Joint Chiefs of Staff, Admiral Arthur W. Radford, Chairman of the Joint Chiefs of Staff; Admiral Robert B. Carney, Chief of Naval Operations; and General Nathan F. Twinning, the Air Force Chief of Staff urged that American and Nationalist Chinese planes be used to bomb Communist bases. General Matthew B. Ridgway, the Army Chief of Staff, opposed any such action, saying it was likely to involve the United States in full-scale war. President Eisenhower sided with Ridgway. See N. M. Blake and O. T. Barck, *The United States in Its World Relations* (New York: McGraw Hill, 1960), 751.

48. The Joint Resolution on the Defense of Formosa was passed by the House on a vote of 409 to 3 on February 26, and by the Senate two days later on a vote of 85 to 3. The resolution gave Eisenhower precisely what he wanted. Both the threat faced by Taiwan and the vital American interest at stake were specified with admirable clarity: "[C]ertain territories in the West Pacific under the jurisdiction of the Republic of China are now under armed attack, and threats and declarations have been and are being made by the Chinese Communists that such armed attack is in aid of and in preparation for armed attack on Formosa and the Pescadores.... the secure possession by friendly governments of the Western Pacific Island chain, of which Formosa is a part, is essential to the vital interests of the United States and all friendly nations in or bordering upon the Pacific Ocean." Joint Resolution on Formosa, January 29, 1955, 84th Congress, 1st Session. *United States Statutes at Large,* vol. 69 (Washington, D.C.: Government Printing Office, 1955), 7.

49. The concept of "escalation dominance" was developed by U.S. national security experts during the Cold War. Generally speaking, it is a strategy of deterrence that posits that the United States can avoid

escalation by being dominant at each successive rung up the "ladder of escalation," up to and including the top rung of nuclear weapons. Proponents argue that escalation dominance, based in balance-of-power calculations, can be successfully used to avoid escalation and contain conflicts. "Escalation dominance" resonates with an important strategic lesson from China's Warring States period, namely, that a rising power should avoid challenging the reigning hegemon before the balance of forces has shifted decisively in its direction. That is a lesson that is not lost on current Party supremo Xi Jinping and his small circle of military and party hardliners, who can be counted on to avoid making this classic Chinese strategic blunder. See, for instance, Dean A. Wilkening and Ken Watman, "Nuclear Deterrence in a Regional Context," http://www.rand.org/pubs/monograph_reports/MR500. html on July 18, 2016.

50. Dulles responded on April 26 by indicating his willingness to talk with the Chinese Communists about a cease-fire in the Taiwan Strait. He stressed that these talks would not imply official diplomatic recognition of the Chinese Communist regime, nor would the U.S. discuss the interests of the ROC "behind its back."

51. Eisenhower, *Mandate for Change*, 482. The Geneva talks were upgraded from consular to ambassadorial level halfway through 1955, largely on the strength of a speech that Zhou Enlai had made all but promising to release forty-one Americans detained by the PRC as "spies" and to renounce the use of force against Taiwan. Twelve were released over the months the followed, but Beijing sought to use the remaining twenty-nine as bargaining chips. On September 10 Ambassador Wang Pingnan told Ambassador Johnson that all Americans would be released if the U.S. agreed to higher-level discussions. Johnson replied that the U.S. would consider the matter only after the Americans had actually been released. Schroth et al., 74–75.

52. D. D. Eisenhower, *Waging Peace: The White House Years, 1956–1961* (New York: Doubleday & Co., 1963), 556.

53. President Eisenhower preferred that the Seventh Fleet merely patrol the Taiwan Strait rather than provide escorts for conveys. He assented to escort, however, with the proviso that American vessels should halt three miles off the unloading beaches, remaining in international waters. Frustrated in his plan to seize Jinmen by force, Mao fell back once more on political maneuvers and requested talks with the U.S. Eisenhower, anxious to avoid a repetition of the explosive confrontation of September 7, agreed. On September 15 talks between the U.S. and the PRC were resumed in Warsaw after a hiatus of nearly a year. Dulles told a press conference that the odd and partial truce proved that "the killing is done for political purposes and promiscuously," and that the Communists "are trying to save themselves from a loss of face and a defeat in the effort which they had initiated but had been unable to conclude successfully." The ROC armed forces acquitted themselves well in the conflict. Thirty-one MIG-17s were shot down, 16 torpedo boats and gunboats were sunk, and a large number of PLA artillery batteries were destroyed. A total of 576,636 rounds of high explosives had fallen on Jinmen by November 22, resulting in some 3,000 civilian and 1,000 military casualties, and destroying many thousands of homes.

54. The Great Leap Forward was actually part of a larger political campaign called *sanhongqi*—three red banners—referring to the general line of the Chinese Communist Party, the great leap forward, and the people's communes.

55. Eisenhower undertook a tour of East Asia, including the Republic of China on his itinerary. During his stay in Taipei, which began on June 18, 1960, he met twice with Chiang. The conversation ranged from ongoing security cooperation under the Sino-American Mutual Defense Treaty of 1954 to the international situation following the recent

collapse of the Paris summit. Chiang emphasized the high priority that Soviet planners gave to East and Southeast Asia, which they viewed as the Achilles heel of the free world. The talks were satisfying and reassuring, with Eisenhower pledging the "steadfast solidarity" of the U.S. with the ROC. Eisenhower also gave a public address to a crowd of sixty-five thousand people. The U.S. did not recognize the claim of the "warlike and tyrannical Communist regime" in Beijing to speak for all the Chinese people, he affirmed to thunderous cheers, promising that the U.S. would stand fast behind free China in resisting Communist aggression. As Eisenhower spoke, the Communist Chinese were saluting him in their own inimitable way. During the twenty-four hours Eisenhower was in Taipei, Quemoy was given its heaviest pounding ever by the PLA artillery batteries. An incredible 174,854 rounds fell upon the island. Eisenhower, *Waging Peace,* 564–65.

56. Jonathan Wilkenfield, Michael Brecher, and Sheila Moser, eds., *Crises in the Twentieth Century,* vol. 2 (Oxford: Pergamon Press, 1988–89), 15, 161. Samuel P. Huntington, *The Clash of Civilizations and the Remaking of World Order* (New York: Simon & Shuster, 1996), 258.

57. William A. Callahan, *China Dreams: 20 Visions of the Future* (New York: Oxford University Press, 2013), 43.

4. THE DIMINUTIVE HEGEMON: DENG XIAOPING

1. Samuel P. Huntington, "The Clash of Civilizations?" *Foreign Affairs* 72:3 (Summer 1993), 22–49.

2. "Memorandum of Conversation between Chairman Mao Zedong and Secretary of State Henry Kissinger on 12 November 1973" in *The Kissinger Transcripts: The Top Secret Talks with Beijing and Moscow,* ed. William Burr (New York: The New Press, 1998), 187. This was not the only time that Mao protested Russian land grabs to Kissinger. At an earlier meeting, he spoke of how the Russians "didn't fire a single shot and yet they were able to grab so many places." While Premier Zhou

Enlai chuckled ruefully in the background, he went on, "They grabbed the People's Republic of Mongolia. They grabbed half of Xinjiang. It was called their sphere of influence. And Manchukuo, on the northeast, was also called their sphere of influence." Ibid., 91.

3. We can ignore here the hapless Hua Guofeng, a placeholder whom Deng soon side-lined after returning from exile.

4. The poll was conducted by the *Global Times*, which of course is a mouthpiece for the party-state, so Mao's popularity may well have been exaggerated. See: Zhang Yiwei, "85% say Mao's Merits Outweigh His Faults: Poll", *Global Times*, December 24, 2013, http://www.globaltimes.cn/content/834000.shtml.

5. See, for instance, David S. G. Goodman, *Deng Xiaoping and the Chinese Revolution: A Political Biography* (London and New York: Routledge, 1994), 75.

6. John Gittings, "New Material on Teng Hsiao-p'ing," *China Quarterly* 67 (September 1975): 489.

7. As James Mann has written, "[I]n 1989, the Chinese Communist Party was choosing a fundamentally different path from that of its counterparts in Eastern Europe and the Soviet Union. Rather than resort to violence, most of the other regimes were willing to share or, ultimately, give up power. The rulers of China were not." "Debunking the Myths behind Tiananmen Crisis," *Los Angeles Times*, 2 June 1999.

8. See, for example, Richard Baum, *Burying Mao: Chinese Politics in the Age of Deng Xiaoping* (Princeton: Princeton University Press, 1994).

9. Jiang's differential handling of the two issues remains a befuddling inconsistency to some, leading editors to write subheads such as, "Who Is China's president? For All Jiang's Courage in Securing the WTO Deal, His Handling of Falun Gong Suggests Fear Is Getting the Better of His Appetite for Political Reform." Susan V. Lawrence, "Jiang's Two Faces," *Far Eastern Economic Review*, 2 December 1999, 16–17.

10. The English edition, published by Simon and Schuster, was translated and edited by Renee Chiang and Adi Ignatius. The original Chinese edition, entitled *The Process of Reform* (*Gaige Licheng*), was published in Hong Kong by New Century Media. It was, of course, banned in China.

11. Perry Link, "The Tiananmen Diaries", *Washington Post*, May 17, 2009, http://www.washingtonpost.com/wp-dyn/content/article/2009/05/15/AR2009051503122.html.

12. Kerry Brown, *The New Emperors: Power and the Princelings in China*, (New York: I.B. Tauris & Co. 2014), 44.

13. Andrew J. Nathan, "Zhao's Version", *London Review of Books*, vol. 31 no. 24, December 2009.

14. Perry Link, "The Tiananmen Diaries," *Washington Post*, May 17th, 2009, http://www.washingtonpost.com/wp-dyn/content/article/2009/05/15/AR2009051503122.html

15. Cited in William McGurn, *Perfidious Albion: The Abandonment of Hong Kong, 1997* (Washington, D.C.: Ethics and Public Policy Center, 1992), 37. McGurn's book remains the best single account of the Hong Kong handover.

16. "China's Town," *Asian Wall Street Journal*, 10 July 1990.

17. "Press Freedom Under Siege: Grave Threats to Freedom of Expression in Hong Kong", The Hong Kong Journalists Association, 2014 Annual Report, http://www.hkja.org.hk/site/Host/hkja/UserFiles/file/annual_report_2014_Final.pdf.

18. "Full text of NPC decision on universal suffrage for HKSAR chief selection", Xinhua, 31 August 2014, http://news.xinhuanet.com/english/china/2014-08/31/c_133609238.htm. The decision states that for the 2017 Chief Executive election, a nominating committee similar to the present Election Committee system will be formed to nominate two to three candidates, each of whom must receive the support of

more than half of the members of the committee. Since Beijing will stack the committee, no democratic candidates need apply.

19. Chinese State Council white paper on 'One Country, Two Systems' policy in Hong Kong, June 10, 2014, http://www.scmp.com/news/hong-kong/article/1529167/full-text-practice-one-country-two-systems-policy-hong-kong-special.

20. Ben McGrath, "Hong Kong Protests Denounce Beijing's Anti-Democratic Plans," September 3, 2014, http://www.wsws.org/en/articles/2014/09/03/hong-s03.html.

21. Stuart Schramm, *Mao's Road to Power: Revolutionary Writings, 1912–1949*, vol. 1, illustrated ed. (M.E. Sharpe, 1997), 369.

22. King C. Chen, *China's War Against Vietnam, 1979; A Military Analysis,* Occasional Papers/Reprints Series in Contemporary Asian Studies, no. 5 (Baltimore: University of Maryland School of Law, 1983). Nie Rongzhen, "Report to the Central Military Affairs Commission, February 1980," cited in *Inside China Mainland,* July 1980, 11. Chen Yun, "Speech to World Conference, April 1979," in *Inside China Mainland*, September 1979, 3.

23. Rongzhen, "Report," 11. Chen Yun, "Speech," 3. Daniel Tretiak, "China's Vietnam War and Its Consequences," *China Quarterly* 80 (December 1979): 740–67, especially 752–53.

24. Henry Kissinger, *Years of Upheaval* (Boston: Little Brown, 1982), 50.

25. Burr, ed., *The Kissinger Transcripts*, 309. Since China and the U.S. lacked common values and institutions, Kissinger was forced to rely on an essentially negative inducement—the Soviet threat—to draw China closer to the United States. Lucien W. Pye, "An Introductory Profile: Deng Xiaoping and China's Political Culture," *China Quarterly* 135 (September 1993): 412.

26. Burr, ed., *The Kissinger Transcripts*, 313–15.

27. Ibid., 384–85.

28. Ibid., 371.

29. For twenty years the official position of the U.S. government had been that Taiwan's future could only be determined through negotiations between Beijing and Taipei. In their very first meeting Kissinger told Zhou Enlai to ignore the official position and spontaneously pledged that America would oppose an independent Taiwan. And he did so without extracting any concessions—such as the renunciation of the use of force—in return. See James Mann, *About Face: A History of America's Curious Relationship with China from Nixon to Clinton* (New York: Knopf, 1999).

30. See, for example, Goodman, *Deng Xiaoping*, 100.

31. For Deng himself, this marked a radical turnabout. In 1977, shortly after his return from political exile, Deng could still say, "In almost no likelihood will my generation or the generation of Comrade Hua Guofeng and Wang Dongxing or even the following generation ever re-establish close contact with the Communist Party of the Soviet Union." Yet in subsequent years he laid the groundwork for the restoration of ties between the Chinese Communist Party and the CPSU. "Speech at 3rd Plenum of the 10th Central Committee," 20 July 1977, *Issues and Studies* (July 1978): 103.

5. HEGEMONY UNDER JIANG ZEMIN, GENERAL SECRETARY OF THE CHINESE COMMUNIST PARTY, 1989-2002

1. New China News Agency, 31 July 1997. Quoted in Willy Wo-lap Lam, *The Era of Jiang Zemin* (New York: Prentice-Hall, 1999), 161.

2. *South China Morning Post*, January 20, 1995, Cited in Willy Wo-Lap Lam, *The Era of Jiang Zemin* (Singapore, Prentice Hall: 1999), 81.

3. The most complete and insightful description of Jiang Zemin comes from veteran China watcher Willy Lam. See ibid. Lam describes a dozen other occasions on which Jiang staged photographs, or even entire journeys, to emulate the first Red Emperor. It was a form of political mimicry that made many Chinese whose memories of Mao are not all that pleasant nervous.

4. Ibid., 39

5. *People's Daily*, 13 September 1997, quoted in Lam, *The Era of Jiang Zemin*, 96.

6. Anne-Marie Brady, *Making the Foreign Serve China: Managing Foreigner's in the People's Republic*, (Oxford: Rowman & Littlefield Publishers, 2003), 238.

7. Lam, *The Era of Jiang Zemin*, 48–49

8. Andrew Nathan and Bruce Gilley, eds., *China's New Rulers: The Secret Files*, 2nd rev. ed. (New York: New York Review of Books, 2003), 111, 191. This figure means that China accounts for fully 97 percent of the world's executions each year. Moreover, it is the only country to sell the harvested organs of executed prisoners.

9. This phrase is from Jiang's speech on 1 July 2000, the 80th anniversary of the founding of the Chinese Communist Party. For a discussion of the "Three Represents," see Stig Thogersen, "Parasites or Civilizers: The Legitimacy of the Chinese Communist Party in Rural Areas, *China: An International Journal* (University of Singapore), vol. 1, no. 2., 200–223.

10. I served as a Commissioner on the 1991–1992 joint presidential-congressional Commission on Broadcasting to the People's Republic of China, which was instrumental in recommending the establishment of a "Radio Free Asia" modelled upon Radio Liberty and Radio Free Europe.

11. Lam, *The Era of Jiang Zemin*, 161.

12. *South China Morning Post*, October 28, 2000. The episode is recounted in Ross Terrill, *The New Chinese Empire*, (University of New South Wales Press, 2003) 221–22.

13. *South China Morning Post*, October 28, 2000. The episode is recounted in Terrill, 222.

14. New China News Agency, July 31, 1997. Quoted in Lam, *The Era of Jiang Zemin*, 161.

15. On December 10, 1998, Republican Representative Dana Rohrabacher of California travelled to Mischief Reef in the South China Sea on a fact-finding tour. He discovered evidence of a Chinese military build-up on the disputed islands, which form part of the Spratly Islands. The Associated Press reported on January 7, 1999, that China was altering its air force doctrine. On August 2, 1999, the Chinese state media first reported a successful test of the DF 31 (https://www.highbeam.com/doc/1P3-45738834.html).

16. The story about Jiang and his generals is in Arthur Waldron, "Clinton's China Policy Invites Disaster," *Wall Street Journal*, January 26, 1999, A18.

17. "Taiwan Strait 21 July 1995 to 23 March 1996," Global Security, http://www.globalsecurity.org/military/ops/taiwan_strait.htm GlobalSecurity.org.

18. See Andrew Scobell, "Show of Force: The PLA and the 1995–1996 Taiwan Strait Crisis," January 1999, *http://aparc.fsi.stanford.edu/sites/default/files/Scobell.pdf*

19. Richard D. Fisher Jr., "China's Missiles over the Taiwan Strait: A Political and Military Assessment," in James R. Lilley and Chuck Downs, eds., *Crisis in the Taiwan Strait* (Ft. McNair, Washington, D.C.: National Defense University Press, 1997), 167. Iain Johnston's research reveals that Chinese military strategists have openly discussed the use of tactical nuclear weapons. Alaistair Iain Johnston, "China's New 'Old Thinking': The Concept of Limited Deterrence," *International Security* vol. 20, no. 3 (winter 1995–1996), 5–42.

20. "People's Liberation Navy—Offshore Defense," Global Security, http://www.globalsecurity.org/military/world/china/plan-doctrine-offshore.htm.

21. *Wen Wei Po*, 24 September 1997. Cited in Lam, *The Era of Jiang Zemin*, 354.

22. Xin Ziling, former director of China's Defense University Press, told Voice of America that Hu Jintao was subordinate to Jiang Zemin even after the latter held no formal office. Hu Jintao, he said, "cannot speak" to the military. The orders had to come from Jiang Zemin. See "Jiang Zemin at Dead End after Xu Caihou's Downfall," which was originally broadcast on New Tang Dynasty television, and is available on YouTube at https://www.youtube.com/watch?v=V1tjVly4ozQ.

23. Jim Yardley, "Violence in Tibet as Monks Clash with the Police," *New York Times*, March 15, 2008, http://www.nytimes.com/2008/03/15/world/asia/15tibet.html?mcubz=1.

24. This material on recent dissent in China is based on my official Congressional testimony before the House Committee on Foreign Affairs, Subcommittee on Africa, Global Health, and Human Rights on May 13, 2011.

25. Smith is a writer and researcher with the Tibetan Service of Radio Free Asia (RFA). RFA's broadcasts into China, which focus on domestic happenings in that country, are routinely jammed by the Chinese authorities.

26. See Blake Kerr, "Witness to China's Shame," *Washington Post*, February 26, 1989, https://www.washingtonpost.com/archive/opinions/1989/02/26/witness-to-chinas-shame/d1862427-84f9-4209-9e15-ec7c6dcd3f0e/?utm_term=.363f6a20a07d; see also, Steven W. Mosher, "U.N. Population Fund Targets Minorities in China," July 1, 2009, https://www.pop.org/content/un-population-fund-targets-minorities-china-new-pri-investigation-reveals-manchus-are-under.

27. Ben Blanchard, "Almost 100 Killed during Attacks in China's Xinjiang Last Week," August 2, 1014, http://www.reuters.com/article/2014/08/03/us-china-attacks-xinjiang-idUSKBN0G301H20140803.

28. Xin Lin, "China Bans 'Extreme' Islamic Baby Names among Xinjiang's Uyghurs," April 20, 2017, Radio Free Asia, http://www.rfa.org/english/news/uyghur/names-04202017093324.html.

29. Gulchehra Hoja, "China Embeds Cadres in Uyghur Homes during Ramadan," Uyghur Human Rights Project, June 8, 2017, http://uhrp.org/news/china-embeds-cadres-uyghur-homes-during-ramadan.

30. Allen Baldanza, who studied Chinese in Beijing, noted that his Chinese language tutor was from Inner Mongolia, and that she was racially Mongolian. Nevertheless, she considered herself and her family to be not just Chinese but Han Chinese. This is like a Native American proclaiming that she is not just an American, but a White American. That is to say it represents not only the adoption of a common national identity, but the total rejection of one's own ethnicity in favor of the dominant one.

31. Willy Wo-Lap Lam, *Chinese Politics in the Hu Jintao Era: New Leaders, New Challenges* (New York: East Gate, 2006), 31.

32. See, for example, "China's Military Strategy," The State Council Information Office of the People's Republic of China, May 2015 which, in an obvious reference to the U.S., warns of "new threats from hegemonism, power politics and neo-interventionism," http://eng.mod.gov.cn/Press/2015-05/26/content_4586805.htm.

33. The 2015 Defense White Paper cited above also assures the world that China pursues "a national defense policy that is defensive in nature, opposes hegemonism and power politics in all forms, and will never seek hegemony or expansion." Japan, for one, has repeatedly warned China over its "territorial aggression." See Agence France–Presse, "Japan Warns China over Territorial Aggresion," Defense News, August 2, 2016, https://www.defensenews.com/global/asia-pacific/2016/08/02/japan-warns-china-over-territorial-aggression/.

34. John Pomfret, "U.S. Takes a Tough Tone with China," *Washington Post*, July 30, 2010. http://www.washingtonpost.com/wp-dyn/content/article/2010/07/29/AR2010072906416.html.

35. Esther Pan, "The Promise and Pitfalls of China's 'Peaceful Rise'" Backgrounder, Council on Foreign Relations, April 14, 2006, https://www.cfr.org/backgrounder/promise-and-pitfalls-chinas-peaceful-rise.

6. MOVE OVER, GREAT HELMSMAN, "BIG DADDY" XI IS HERE

1. In his now-famous December 2012 internal talk on the factors behind the demise of the Communist Party of the Soviet Union, Xi laid the blame on "traitors" such as Mikhail Gorbachev and Boris Yeltsin. Xi's more colorful language has been translated into English as, "When the Soviet Party was about to collapse, there was not one person who was man enough to turn back the tide," Ming Pao [Hong Kong] February 16, 2013, BBC Chinese Service, February 16, 2013. See also Willy Lam, "Xi Jinping wants to be Mao but will not learn from the latter's mistakes," AsiaNews.it, January 1, 2014. http://www.asianews.it/news-en/Xi-Jinping-wants-to-be-Mao-but-will-not-learn-from-the-latters-mistakes-31787.html But my translation is more faithful to the original.

2. Long-time China watcher Bill Gertz has pointed out that Xi Jinping's doctorate—and there are some questions about its authenticity—is in "scientific socialism," a fact which helps explain his drive for Maoist-style hegemony both at home and abroad. Personal communication with the author, September 4, 2017.

3. Francis Fukuyama, "China's 'Bad Emperor' Problem," http://www.the-american-interest.com/2012/05/28/chinas-bad-emperor-problem/, *The American Interest*, February 13, 2015.

4. Politically well-connected apologists for one-Party dictatorship such Hu Angang, the Director of the Center for China Studies at the Chinese Academy of Social Sciences in Beijing, predictably disagree with this assessment. But then Hu also maintains such absurdities as, "Many in

the West still mistake China for a Stalinist totalitarian state. But the truth is, arguably, the distribution of power and accountability within China's "Collective Presidency" is more sophisticated than the separation of power between legislative, executive and judiciary branches in the western political context." See Hu Angang, "Is China More Democratic Than The U.S.?" *Huffington Post* http://www. huffingtonpost.com/hu-angang/china-us-democracy_b_5310800.html, which can be read in Chinese at http://www.guancha.cn/HuAnGang/2014_05_14_229346.shtml. One suspects that members of the collective leadership who have been purged would have a somewhat different view of the matter.

5. Bo Zhiyue, "Is China's PLA Now Xi's Army?," *The Diplomat*, January 12, 2016 http://thediplomat.com/2016/01/is-chinas-pla-now-xis-army/.

6. Evan Osnos, "Born Red: How Xi Jinping, an Unremarkable Provincial Administrator, Became China's Most Authoritarian Leader since Mao," *New Yorker*, April 6, 2015, http://www.newyorker.com/magazine/2015/04/06.

7. Chris Buckley, "From Political Star to 'a Sacrificial Object' in China," *New York Times*, July 22, 2017, https://www.nytimes.com/2017/07/22/world/asia/china-xi-jinping-sun-zhengcai-chongqing-.html?mcubz=1.

8. Tom Phillips, "Man Tipped as China's Future President Ousted as Xi Jinping Wields 'Iron Discipline'" *Guardian*, July 25, 2017, https://www.theguardian.com/world/2017/jul/25/china-future-president-ousted-xi-jinping-iron-discipline-sun-zhengcai.

9. Zheng Yangwen, *The Social Life of Opium in China*. (Cambridge: Cambridge University Press, 2005), 18–19.

10. Had Mao Zedong's eldest son, Mao Anying, not been killed in action by an air strike during the Korean War, a Mao dynasty might well reign in China today, like the Kim dynasty that reigns in North Korea and the Lee dynasty that holds power in Singapore. After all, Mao Anying, at twenty-eight years of age, had already been promoted by his

father to the rank of lieutenant general when he was killed while serving as PLA commander Peng Dehuai's aide-de-camp at the outset of the Korean War. Mao's other son, Mao Anqing, suffered from mental illness and was never active in politics. But Mao Anqing's son—the sole surviving male member of Mao line—has done well for himself. In 2009 the corpulent Mao Xinyu, Mao's grandson, was promoted to major general, making him at the age of forty the youngest general in the People's Liberation Army.

11. David Barboza, "Billions in Hidden Riches for Family of Chinese Leader," *New York Times*, October 25, 2012, http://www.nytimes. com/2012/10/26/business/global/family-of-wen-jiabao-holds-a-hidden-fortune-in-china.html?pagewanted=all&_r=0. The timing of these reports, coming as they did immediately prior to his leaving office, suggests that they were deliberately leaked by Xi Jinping's faction to reduce Wen's influence as the Chinese leadership met to decide the next generation of Chinese leaders.

12. In Chinese they are referred to as the "princeling party, or *taidz dang,* which is a way of saying that they are "a party within a party," or a powerful faction of the Chinese Communist Party.

13. Zhiyue Bo, *China's Elite Politics: Governance and Democratization* (World Scientific, 2014), 141.

14. Hailing from Fengyang did not hurt Li's name recognition either, since it is one of the most famous counties in China. Fengyang's most famous native son, Zhu Yuanzhang (1328-1398), was the founder of China's Ming dynasty. He is known as the Hongwu Emperor and reigned from nearby Nanjing.

15. The Central Commission for Discipline Inspection (CCDI) is responsible for enforcing internal rules and regulations and combating corruption and malfeasance in the Party. Since the vast majority of officials at all levels of government are also Communist Party members, the commission is in practice the top anti-corruption body in China.

The overseas Chinese news agency, Boxun, reported on December 8, 2014, that around $13.4 billion worth of gold, calligraphy works, and antiques had been confiscated from Ling Lihua's estate, characterizing these as bribes to Ling by those who wanted to obtain official positions. This is a number so large that it is scarcely credible.

16. Jamil Anderlini and Simon Rabinovich, "Ex-President Jiang Urges Beijing to Curb Anti-Corruption Crive," *Financial Times*, 31 March 2014. http://www.ft.com/intl/cms/s/0/1bc9c892-b8c7-11e3-a189-00144feabdc0.html#axzz3U6tWnSra.

17. Xi delivered his speech at the laboriously named "Commemoration of the 70th Anniversary of the Victory of the Chinese People's War of Resistance against Japanese Aggression," for example, in full Maoist regalia. See "Full Text of Chinese President's Speech at Commemoration of 70th Anniversary of War Victory," Xinhua, http://news.xinhuanet.com/english/2015-09/03/c_134583870.htm.

18. For details of the book's publication, see "Book of Xi Jinping's Remarks on Party Discipline Published," Xinhua, January 2, 2016, http://www.chinadaily.com.cn/china/2016-01/02/content_22900957.htm and Wei Pu, "Xi Jingping: Is China on the Road to Total Dictatorship?" Radio Free Asia, February 8, 2016, http://www.rfa.org/english/commentaries/xi-jinping-is-china-on-the-road-to-total-dictatorship-02082016112759.html.

19. According to the China Media Project of the University of Hong Kong, Xi Jinping dominates the pages of the *People's Daily*. See "Xi Jinping Most Mentioned in People's Daily since Mao, Researchers Find," *South China Morning Post*, July 29, 2014, http://www.scmp.com/news/china/article/1561414/xi-jinping-most-mentioned-peoples-daily-mao-researchers-find.

20. While the song was not, as far as we know, written by state propagandists, it has certainly been vigorously promoted by the state media. The song can be heard, in Chinese with English subtitles, at

"New Hit 'Xi Dada Loves Peng Mama' Goes Viral Online," CRIENGLISH, November 24, 2014, http://english.cri. cn/12394/2014/11/24/2361s853616.htm.

21. People's Daily, China, "How Should I Address You—an Affectionate Song for Our Xi Dada", YouTube Video, February 12, 2016, https://www.youtube.com/watch?v=ByMTB6n6HVU.

22. "Xi's Wife to Play Role in Chinese Charm Offensive", Financial Times, March 13, 2013, https://www.ft.com/content/d83a8ed4-8bbf-11e2-8fcf-00144feabdc0.

23. The shawl "incident" was instantly covered up in the Chinese media, since it would tarnish Xi's image for his people to think that he was careless about his wife's well-being. The Russian media played it up, however, in an attempt to show how much of a "gentleman" Putin was. "Putin's Shawl Chivalry Gets Blanket Coverage from Western Media, Chinese Censors," RT, November 11, 2014, https://www.rt.com/news/204547-putin-xi-peng-shawl/; Bethany Allen-Ebrahimian, "Putin Hits on China's First Lady, Censors Go Wild", *Foreign Policy*, November 10, 2014, http://foreignpolicy.com/2014/11/10/putin-hits-on-chinas-first-lady-censors-go-wild/.

24. See Lauretta Brown, "China Censors Winnie the Pooh Because of Comparisons to President Xi Jinping," Townhall, July 17, 2017, https://townhall.com/tipsheet/laurettabrown/2017/07/17/china-censors-winnie-the-pooh-because-of-comparisons-to-president-xi-jinping-n2356086?utm_source=thdaily&utm_medium=email&utm_campaign=nl&newsletterad.

25. In 1956 a political commissar suggested to Peng, who was then serving as minister of defense, that "The East Is Red" to be taught to Chinese troops. Peng rejected the idea out of hand, reportedly declaring, "That is a personality cult! That is idealism!" His outburst was undoubtedly reported to Mao and helped to seal his fate. Jurgen Domes, *Peng*

Te-huai: The Man and the Image (London: C. Hurst & Company, 1985), 72.

26. See Liu Yanwei, *Zhongguoren bi Eguo Minzong Ai Pujing* ("Chinese people love Putin more than the Russian people"), March 22, 2014, http://view.news.qq.com/original/intouchtoday/n2740.html.

27. For example, *Global People*, a magazine run by the *People's Daily*, featured an article by Chinese Academy of Social Sciences (CASS) researcher Wu Wei praising Putin for "defending democracy" by welcoming National Security Agency defector Edward Snowden into the open arms of Russia's intelligence service. David Gitter, "Why China's Love for Putin Is Dangerous," The Diplomat, August 6, 2014, http://thediplomat.com/2014/08/why-chinas-love-for-putin-is-dangerous/.

28. Guo Jinyue, "The Different Images of Putin in China and America," China Institute of International Studies, June 27, 2014, http://www.ciis.org.cn/chinese/2014-06/27/content_7014488.htm.

29. Bao Tong, "The Communist Party's 'Magic Spell of Obedience' in China," Radio Free Asia Commentaries, September 16, 2013, http://www.rfa.org/english/commentaries/baotong/spell-09162013105548.html.

30. And sometimes eaten. One of the more heinous practices of the Cultural Revolution was what could be called "political cannibalism." See, for example, Beth Duff-Brown, "Scholars Continue to Reveal Mao's Monstrosities: Exiled Chinese Historians Emerge with Evidence of Cannibalism and up to 80 million Deaths under the Communist Leader's Regime," *Los Angeles Times*, November 20, 1994.

31. This event was covered in the Western press, but its larger significance was missed. See Dexter Roberts, "Echoing Mao, China's Xi Says Art Must Serve the People and the Socialist Cause," Bloomberg Business News, 6 October 2014, http://www.bloomberg.com/bw/articles/2014-10-16/chinas-xi-to-artists-follow-the-party-line.

32. See Colin MacKerras, *Chinese Theatre: From Its Origins to the Present Day* (University of Hawaii Press, 1983), 170–71, for a discussion of the 1982 decision.

33. See Shao Jiang, "A Nightmarish Year Under Xi Jinping's 'Chinese Dream: 2013 Annual Report on the Situation of Human Rights Defenders in China", Amnesty International, March 6, 2014, http://www.amnesty.org.uk/blogs/countdown-china/nightmarish-year-under-xi-jinping%E2%80%99s-%E2%80%9Cchinese-dream%E2%80%9D-2013-annual-report.

34. 34 There are *zero* references to Charles Xue's high-profile case on Chinese state television's English-language service, which is careful to showcase only "positive" news about the Chinese party-state.

35. See: Martin Patience, "Charles Xue 'Confession' Highlights China's Blogging Backlash" BBC, October 1, 2013.

36. To avoid public scrutiny, Tie Liu was shipped to Chengdu for his trial, which took place six months after his arrest. The original vague charge was dropped, and he was given a suspended two-and-a-half-year sentence on the equally fabricated charge of "running an illegal business." See "China Sentences 81-Year-Old Dissident", CBS News, February 25, 2015, http://www.cbsnews.com/news/china-sentences-dissident-huang-zerong-81-for-criticizing-communist-party/.

37. For an accessible summary of recent work on the famine that followed the Great Leap Forward, see Ian Johnson, "China: Worse Than You Ever Imagined," *New York Review of Books*, November 22, 2012, http://www.nybooks.com/articles/archives/2012/nov/22/china-worse-you-ever-imagined/

38. Readers will note that I use the term hegemon to refer to both the "country" of China, and its more dominant leaders, such as Mao Zedong and Xi Jinping. Indeed, in a highly centralized hegemonic state operating on Legalist principles, Louis XIV's famous exclamation,

"L'etat, c'est moi!" is perfectly appropriate. One can almost hear Xi Jinping proclaiming, "The hegemon, it is I!"

7. GREAT HAN CHAUVINISM: THE NEW RELIGION OF A NATION OF NARCISSISTS?

1. Liu Xiaobo, "Bellicose and Thuggish: The Roots of Chinese 'Patriotism,'" *No Enemies, No Hatred* (Cambridge, Massachusetts: Harvard University Press, 2013), 66. In the preceding paragraph Liu also notes that the term "foreign devils" survives in use in China even today.

2. Joseph Campbell, "Chinese Dissident Liu Xiaobo Dies in Custody, Struck by Liver Cancer," Reuters, July 13, 2017, http://www.reuters.com/article/us-china-rights-idUSKBN19Y1MV.

3. The Nobel Peace Prize 2010—Prize Announcement, Nobel Prize, October 8, 2010, http://www.nobelprize.org/nobel_prizes/peace/laureates/2010/announcement.html.

4. Liu Xiaobo, "Behind the Rise of Great Powers," *No Enemies, No Hatred* (Cambridge Massachusetts: Harvard University Press, 2013), 236.

5. As Chinese dissident Yang Jianli testified during a congressional hearing on "The Tragic Case of Liu Xiaobo," held on July 14, 2017, "The denial of medical care lead to Liu Xiaobo's advanced liver cancer, and at its core was a disguised death sentence." See "The Tragic Case of Liu Xiaobo," House Foreign Affairs Committee testimony, https://foreignaffairs.house.gov/hearing/subcommittee-hearing-tragic-case-liu-xiaobo/.

6. "Policy Outline," Section 1, Item 2. Barme, *In the Red*, 339–40.

7. Liu Xiaobo, "Bellicose and Thuggish: The Roots of Chinese 'Patriotism,'" *No Enemies, No Hatred*, 76. Bellicose nationalism is only one of several similar phrases that Liu uses to describe the aggressive self-worship of the Chinese party-state.

8. Liu argued that China's ruling group capitalized on this psychology: "In the state media, China's military, economic, scientific, and even

athletic successes since 1949 are all spun as signs China is on its way to world domination." Liu, "Bellicose and Thuggish," 79.

9.   Ibid., 75.

10.   As Callahan writes, "the current patriotic nationalist form of Chinese identity is much more than the outcome of an instrumental manipulation of cultural nationalism than the party elite. This expression of national pride and national humiliation flourishes because it resonates with a complementary structure of felling—the civilization/barbarian distinction—that preceded the PRC." Throughout his book Callahan shows how the civilization/barbarism distinction keeps being reproduced in new ways to meet new political situations. William A. Callahan, *China: The Pessoptimist Nation* (Oxford: Oxford University Press, 2010), 195.

11.   Ibid., 25.

12.   Ibid., 9.

13.   Ian Baruma, *Bad Elements: Chinese Rebels from Los Angeles to Beijing* (New York: Random House, 2001), 385–86.

14.   One of Callahan's key theses. See for example Callahan, *China*, 28.

15.   Orville Schell and John Delury, *Wealth and Power: China's Long March to the 21st Century,* (Random House, 2013), 372–73.

16.   Callahan, *China*, 21.

17.   "China Passports Claim Ownership of South China Sea and Taiwan," *Guardian*, November 23, 2012, https://www.theguardian.com/world/2012/nov/23/china-passports-ownership-sea-taiwan.

18.   Jullia Lovell, "China's Conscience", *Guardian,* 12th June 2010.

19.   Bo Yang, *The Ugly Chinaman and the Crisis of Chinese Culture,* trans. and ed. by Don J. Cohn and Jing Qing (Sydney: Allen & Unwin, 1992).

20.   Yan Fu, quoted in Jonathan D. Spence, *The Search for Modern China* (W. W. Norton & Company, 1991), 301.

21.   Ian Baruma attended a play in Beijing just after the Belgrade bombing. As the patriotic performance reached its anti-Japan climax, the mostly

young audience erupted in shouts, hoots, and clapping. Baruma was surprised that the outburst appeared to be genuine and not an ironic protest against the government's attempt to stir up patriotic fervour. As he describes it, "it was like a high point in a revivalist church, a religious, crescendo, a kind of orgasmic release." His companion, the Chinese professor Mao Haojian, soon enlightened him about the depth of patriotic fervour in China, telling of the legacy of Social Darwinism in China. Baruma, *Bad Elements*, 385–86.

22. William A. Callahan, *China Dreams: 20 Visions of the Future* (New York: Oxford University Press, 2013), 107

23. Quoted in Callahan, *China Dreams,* 107. Originally from Xi Jinping, ed. *Kexue yu aiguo: Yan Fu sixiang xintan* [Science and patriotism: New explorations of Yan Fu's thought]. (Beijing: Qinghua daxue chubanshe, 2001).

24. Frank Dikotter, "Racial Theories in The China Critic," *China Heritage Quarterly* (The Australian National University) 30/31 (June/September 2012), http://www.chinaheritagequarterly.org/features. php?searchterm=030_dikotter.inc&issue=030. A longer analysis appears in Dikotter's book, *The Discourse of Race in Modern China* (Stanford: Stanford University Press, 1992).

25. Sun Longji (Lung-kee), *Qingji minzu zhuyi yu Huangdi chongbai zhi faming* ("Qing-period nationalism and the invention of the worship of Huangdi"), *Lishi yanjiu ("Historical Research"*), 2000 (3): 68–79, at 69.

26. The restoration of Confucius himself to the Chinese pantheon of cultural heroes follows the same pattern: China's ancient sage was rehabilitated so that he in turn could help rehabilitate the same Chinese Communist Party that had earlier condemned him.

27. Allen Baldanza, personal communication, December 13, 2016. The video, which should come with a "racist" warning attached, is available at DailyNation, "Racism in a Chinese Laundry Detergent

Advertisement" YouTube, May 27, 2016, https://www.youtube.com/
watch?v=Few8kJ0zfnY.

28. Emma Graham-Harrison, "Black Man Is Washed Whiter in China's
Racist DetergentAadvert," *Guardian*, May 28, 2016, https://www.
theguardian.com/world/2016/may/28/china-racist-detergent-advert-
outrage. The company itself belatedly apologized. "Shanghai-based
Qiaobi said it had 'no intention of discriminating against people of
color' by making the commercial. 'The color of one's skin is not the
standard by which we should judge each other. We strongly oppose and
condemn racial discrimination,' the company said late Saturday on its
official Weibo account, the Chinese equivalent of Twitter." See Hannah
Gardner, "Chinese Company Apologizes, Sort of, for Racist Ad," *USA
Today*, May 29, 2016, http://www.usatoday.com/story/news/
world/2016/05/29/chinese-detergent-maker-sorry-harm-done-
racist-ad/85121362/. This disclaimer notwithstanding, the commercial
itself obviously appealed to the generally held prejudice of the Chinese
people that dark-skinned people are inherently dirty and smelly and
need a good soaking to be cleaned up.

29. Andrew Marr, *A History of the World*, (BBC, 1996), 38.

30. Callahan, *China Dreams*, 105.

31. Callahan, *China*, 8.

32. As William C. Kirby wrote, "There were several ways of preserving
conceptions of Chinese 'centrality' to the modern world even during a
century of consistent defeat and humiliation. One lay in the realm of
national (and international) myth and ideology. Another had to do with
the endurance of certain traditional Chinese diplomatic methods—
what we might call centrality in practice—in a modern world in which
China was in fact reduced to peripheral status." Perhaps the most long-
lived myth of Chinese centrality to the modern world is that of "the
China Market." The notion of the indispensability of China to global
capitalism was always as much a Chinese as a Western myth. How

international capitalism survived while China was unable to realise its famed potential "remains a mystery." William C. Kirby, "Traditions of Centrality, Authority, and Management in Modern China's Foreign Relations," *Chinese Foreign Policy: Theory and Practice* (New York: Oxford University Press, 1994).

33. Jung Chang and Jon Halliday, *Mao: The Unknown Story* (London: Random House, 2005), 485.

34. Christopher A. Ford, *Mind of Empire: China's History and Modern Foreign Relations* (University Press of Kentucky, 2010), 176.

35. Geoff Dyer, 'China's Glass Ceiling', *Foreign Policy,* March 28, 2013.

36. Wang, a boyhood friend of Xi Jinping's, is the Secretary of the Central Commission for Discipline Inspection and the Leader of the Central Leading Group for Inspection Work. As such, he has served Xi loyally and well by dispatching teams to the provinces and state-owned enterprises with the goal of rooting out and purging Xi Jinping's political enemies—always on charges of corruption. After Xi himself, he is the second most powerful man in China today.

37. Edward Luttwark, *The Rise of China vs. the Logic of Strategy* (Cambridge Massachusetts: Harvard University Press, 2012), 86. Luttwark contends that while leaders of all large countries, because of their many internal distractions, are prone to make decisions on foreign affairs on the basis of highly simplified, schematic representations of complex realities, the tendency is more prone for Chinese leaders who already see the world through the narrow chauvinism and legacy of the "all under Heaven" (tianxia) system.

38. James Kynge, *China Shakes the World: The Rise of a Hungry Nation*, (Phoenix, 2006), 204.

39. Isaiah Berlin, "Kant as an Unfamiliar Source of Nationalism" in *The Sense of Reality: Studies in Ideas and Their History* (New York: Farrar, Straus and Giroux, 1998), (first pub. 1996), 232–48, at 248.

40. Eric Beckett Weaver, *National Narcissism: The Intersection of the Nationalist Cult and Gender in Hungary* (Oxford: Peter Lang, 2006), 63.

41. Huajian Cai and Peter Gries, "National Narcissism: Internal Dimensions and International Correlates," *PsyCh Journal*, 2013. DOI: 10.1002/pchj.26.

42. Americans reported much lower levels of anxiety in response to national symbolic losses than did the Chinese, and the Chinese were more than twice as sensitive to gain and loss as Americans were, with regard to national pride, although the study can't tell us if American levels were low or Chinese high. Unfortunately carrying out this type of political psychology experiments is extremely difficult in China. Peter Gries, Kaiping Peng, and H. Michael Crowson, "Determinants of Security and Insecurity in International Relations: A Cross-National experimental Analysis of Symbolic and Material Gains and Losses," in Vaughn P. Shannon and Paul A. Kowert, *Psychology and Constructivism in International Relations: An Ideational Alliance*, (Michigan: The University of Michigan Press 2012), 187.

43. "Rio Olympics: How China Charmed the World "*Shanghai Daily*, August 22, 2016 http://www.shanghaidaily.com/sports/Rio-Olympics-How-China-charmed-the-world/shdaily.shtml. Sina, the Chinese online media company, chimed in consolingly that China's younger generation values "charisma, fun as well as victory." "At Rio Games, China's New Generation Values Charisma, Fun as well as Victory," Sina English, August 21, 2016. http://english.sina.com/sports/o/2016-08-22/detail-ifxvcsrn8856661.shtml.

44. While at the time of Margaret Thatcher's death much of the world praised her toughness and willingness to stand up against tyranny and her defence of free markets, and individual liberty, the Chinese press coverage instead noted her submission to China's unbending will in 1982, after, emboldened by the Falklands victory, she had tried to push

China for a deal that would have allowed for a continued British role in Hong Kong after 1997. As we have seen, she was forced to capitulate to Deng Xiaoping. In an online review of her career the *Beijing Times*, included pictures of her fall down the steps of the Great Hall of the People after her rebuff by Chinese leaders. The *Global Times* noted that since Thatcher had left office there had been no more iron men or iron ladies—partly because of a "decline in European power,", which made it impossible to maintain so rigid a stance. "The World's Reaction: Opinions Divided," *Economist*, April 13, 2013.

45. Ross Terrill, *The New Chinese Empire* (University of New South Wales Press, 2003), 304.

46. Lucien W. Pye *The Spirit of Chinese Politics: A Psychocultural Study of the Authority Crises in Chinese Development* (MIT Press, 1968), 50. Ford later reached the same conclusion.

47. David Shambaugh, *China Goes Global: The Partial Power* (New York: Oxford University Press, 2013), 266.

48. For an excellent account of this long tradition see Orville Schell and John Delury, *Wealth and Power: China's Long March to the Twenty-First Century* (New York: Random House, 2013).

49. C. P. Fitzgerald, *The Chinese View of their Place in the World*, (Oxford: Oxford University Press, 1964), 40.

50. Callahan, *China Dreams,* 105.

51. Christopher A. Ford, "'If China Ruled'—a Thought Experiment', *New Paradigm Forum*, www.newparadigmsforum.com/ NPFtestsite/?p=1731.

52. Yan Xuetong, "The Rise of China in Chinese Eyes," *Journal of Contemporary China* 10:26 (2001), 33–39. Yan, it should be noted, is one of China's top scholars.

53. Martin Jacques, author of *When China Rules the World*, spends many pages explaining why China's superior culture will vault it into global domination. At the same time, he spends an entire chapter complaining

about China's superiority complex and pervasive racism, which I happen to think are not signs of China's coming strength at all, but signs of weakness that may prevent China from achieving the kind of global domination that the CCP elite obviously dream of.

54. Reading Chinese blogs, one gets the impression the U.S. is jealous of China's presence in Africa, jealous of its space program, jealous of China's long history, and of much more, as well as more generally of its rise.

55. David Wertime, "Chinese Expert: Obama—Dalai Lama Meeting Shows U.S. 'Jealous,'" *Foreign Policy*, February 21, 2014.

56. As the Olympics opening ceremony's deputy director announced, "I really hope that the people of the world can get to know the Chinese culture through [the Opening Ceremony], to get to know China, to understand China, to love China, and to desire China. This Olympics is the best opportunity.... What will they see about China? I think the most important thing is to see that Chinese people are happy." Interview with Zhang Jigang, Deputy Director of the Beijing Olympics Opening Ceremony," *Liberation* Daily, August 1, 2008, translated for *China Digital Times*, August 6, 2008. Quoted in Callahan, *China: Pessoptimist Nation*, 4.

57. If you ask taxi drivers in Beijing about the Olympics now they tend to be a bit muted, just saying it was good. You can see the disappointment that the Olympics didn't change much in terms of the foreign perception of China. The many foreigners visiting Beijing may remark about what a great games it was, but it hardly shifted underlying attitudes to China, as the Chinese so fervently expected.

58. Callahan, *China*, 9.

59. In what is only one of many examples of Chinese double standards, or doublethink.

60. Warren W. Smith Jr. *Tibet's Last Stand? The Tibetan Uprising of 2008 and China's Response* (Plymouth: Rowman and Littlefield, 2010), 266.

8. THE SUM OF ALL CHINA'S FEARS

1. "U.S.-China Economic and Security Review Commission Annual Report, 2002," July 15, 2002, http://china.usc.edu/ShowArticle. aspx?articleID=686#below.

2. See my *A Mother's Ordeal: One Woman's Fight Against China's One-Child Policy* (New York: Harper Collins, 1993)

3. "China Bans Internet News Reporting as Media Crackdown Widens," July 25, 2016, Bloomberg News, available at http://www.bloomberg. com/news/articles/2016-07-25/china-slaps-ban-on-internet-news-reporting-as-crackdown-tightens. See also Peng Pai, Beijing shi Wangxinban zeling Xinlang, Souhu, Wangyi, Fenghuang, xianqi gaizheng weigui xingwei. ("The Beijing Cyberspace Administration Orders Xinlang, Souhu, Wangyi, Fenghuang to Correct their Illegal Behavior Within Deadline."), July 24, 2016, available at http://www. thepaper.cn/newsDetail_forward_1503393.

4. Quoted in Lionel M. Jensen, "Culture Industry, Power, and the Spectacle of China's "Confucius Institues," in Lionel M. Jensen, eds., *China in and Beyond the Headlines* (Rowman and Littlefield, 2012), 271–96. Quotation at 280.

5. For this definition, see Liu Hong et al., eds., *Zhongguo guoqing*, restricted circulation (Beijing: Zhonggong zhongyang dangxiao chubanshe, 1990), 3–8, cited in Geremie Barme, *In the Red: On Contemporary Chinese Culture* (New York: Columbia University Press, 1999), 446 n. 15. Emphasizing Chinese exceptionalism also helps to insulate the Middle Kingdom from subversive foreign ideas, such as universal human rights. It enables the Party to rebuff Western criticism of its human rights record by saying, in effect, that "here we have different standards." This was the tack taken by the official white paper on human rights published in 1991. See Guowuyuan Xinwen Bangongshi, *Zhongguode renquan Zhuangkuang* (The human rights situation in China) (Beijing: Zhongyang wenxian chubanshe, 1991).

6. See "Aiguozhuyi jiaoyu shishi gangyao" (Policy outline for implementing patriotic education), *Renmin ribao*, September 6, 1994.

7. Zhao Suisheng puts it somewhat differently. He identifies the four major themes of the Patriotic Education campaign as (1) China's unique national condition (teshu guoqing), (2) continuity between the communist state and China's noncommunist past, (3) the communist state as the defender of China's national interests, and (4) national unity as a theme against ethnic nationalism. See Zhao Suisheng, *A Nation-State by Construction: Dynamics of Modern Chinese Nationalism.* (Stanford, California: Stanford University Press, 2004). See also Peter Hays Griess, *China's New Nationalism: Pride, Politics, and Diplomacy.* (Berkeley and Los Angeles, California: University of California Press, 2004.)

8. Based on Churchill's paraphrase of *Mein Kampf*, as contained in his *The Second World War*, vol. 1 (New York: Houghton Mifflin, 1948).

9. *Mein Kampf*, Vol. 2, "Conclusion."

10. Bear in mind that China's Planned Birth campaign includes a strong eugenics component, designed to improve the "quality" of the Chinese race.

11. "U.S.-China Economic and Security Review Commission Annual Report, 2002."

12. Michael Pillsbury, *The Hundred-Year Marathon: China's Secret Strategy to Replace America as the Global Superpower* (New York: Henry Holt, 2015), 106.

13. "WSJ Archives: Goddess of Democracy Is Erected in Tiananmen Square," May 30, 2014, http://blogs.wsj.com/chinarealtime/2014/05/30/wsj-archives-goddess-of-democracy-is-erected-in-tiananmen-square/.

14. Mao Tse-tung, "'Friendship' or Aggression?" *Selected Works of Mao Tse-tung*, Volume IV (Beijing: Foreign Languages Press, 1961).

15. As Michael Pillsbury reports in *The Hundred-Year Marathon*, the website of the Chinese Academy of Social Sciences posted an online editorial about the book's reprinting on its website. Wang Chun, *A History of U.S. Aggression in China* (Beijing Worker's Press, 1951). The Chinese version of the CASS website is available at http://www. cssn.cn/. The English version can be found at http://bic.cass.cn/english/ index.asp. By the time I checked the website, the online editorial had disappeared. China's leaders go to extraordinary lengths to conceal their defamation campaign against the United States from us.

16. Mao, "'Friendship' or Aggression?" 450.

17. Pillsbury, *The Hundred-Year Marathon*, 104.

18. Mao, "'Friendship' or Aggression?" 449.

19. Pillsbury, *The Hundred-Year Marathon*, 104–5

20. Tang Qing, "U.S. Policy toward Japan Before the Outbreak of the Pacific War," in *Jiangnandaxue Xuebao* [*Jiangnan University Journal*] (April 1997): 105–9. Cited in Pillsbury, *The Hundred-Year Marathon*, 106.

21. See Stefan Verstappen, *The Thirty-Six Strategies of Ancient China* (San Francisco: China Books and Periodicals, 1999). For the application to those strategies to what Chinese analysts see as Roosevelt's scheme to dominate China, I am indebted to Michael Pillsbury.

22. Zhao Suisheng, "Foreign Policy Implications of Chinese Nationalism Revisited: The Strident Turn," in *Construction of Chinese Nationalism in the Early 21st Century: Domestic Sources and International Implications,* Ed. Zhao Suisheng, (London and New York: Routledge, 2014), 25. The strategy finds its origin in the Three Kingdoms period, when Zhu Geliang served as the prime minister of the Kingdom of Shu. The Kingdom of Wei in the North was the strongest of the three kingdoms, so Zhu allied himself with the Kingdom of Wu in the East to resist Wei in the North.

23. "Letter to the Emperor of China from the President of the United States of America, July 12, 1843" at http://www.chinaforeignrelations.net/node/231. Accessed on August 2, 2016.

24. John Schrecker, "'For the Equality of Men—for the Equality of Nations': Anson Burlingame and China's First Embassy to the United States, 1868," *Journal of American-East Asian Relations* 17.1 (2010): 11.

25. Bishop Favier, who organized the defense of Beitang Catholic Cathedral, estimated that close to twenty thousand members of his Beijing Chinese Catholic community were killed during the uprising. Most of the nearly four thousand people who sought sanctuary in the church survived. See *Annals of the Propagation of the Faith* LXIV: 18–19. See also Arthur Judson Brown, *New Forces in Old China: An Inevitable Awakening*, 2nd ed. (1904), 199.

26. The Flying Tigers are justly famous in China. In fact, representatives of the Flying Tigers were invited to attend China's September 2015 World War II Victory Parade held on the fiftieth anniversary of the end of that conflict. But they are portrayed in the Chinese media as simply a group of American aviators who selflessly volunteered their service to the Chinese resistance. The fact that they were there on a mission encouraged and funded by their president goes largely unmentioned.

27. Pillsbury, *The Hundred-Year Marathon*, 108.

28. For a recent discussion of the "Patriotic Education" program, see Wang Zheng, *Never Forget National Humiliation: Historical Memory in Chinese Politics and Foreign Relations* (New York: Columbia University Press, 2012), and his shorter article by the same name at http://iias.asia/sites/default/files/IIAS_NL59_3233.pdf, accessed on July 29, 2016.

29. Leslie Chang, "In China, History Class Means an 'Education in National Shame,'" *Wall Street Journal*, 23 June 1999, A1.

30. He Peiling, "Preface," Zhang Zangzang et al., *Zhongguo Keyi Shwo Bu* ("China Can Say No"), (Beijing: China Industrial and Commercial Joint Press, 1996).

31. As Lucian Pye has observed, "Modern Chinese intellectuals have shown a passion for patriotism which has at each critical movement hobbled their political judgment" and "because they do not wish to seem unpatriotic, Chinese intellectuals have become more the lackeys of their political rulers than have the intellectuals in any other Asian countries." Lucian Pye, *Asian Power and Politics* (Cambridge: Harvard University Press, 1985), 193. This is not to suggest that China has completely lacked intellectuals who able to think independently and challenge authority, but rather that, because they have been relatively few in number, they have been easy to isolate and destroy when the government is intent on doing so. In Mao's China, intellectuals who breathed a hint of criticism paid a terrible price. Only the sychophants were left standing.

32. Edward Wong, "In New China, 'Hostile' West Is Still Derided," *New York Times*, November 11, 2014, http://www.nytimes.com/2014/11/12/world/asia/china-turns-up-the-rhetoric-against-the-west.html?_r=0.

33. Amy Qin, "Undermining China, One Knockout at a Time," *New York Times*, July 17, 2014, http://sinosphere.blogs.nytimes.com/2014/07/17/undermining-china-one-knockout-at-a-time/?_r=1.

34. "Evildoers Doomed to Meet Destruction" (in Chinese), *Renmin Ribao*, 15 May 1999. *Renmin Ribao,* 19 May 1999.

35. *Beijing Qingnian Ribao* (Beijing youth daily), 19 May 1999. Lest one think that these sentiments owe their origin solely to the embassy bombing, a 1996 poll conducted by the China Youth Research Center showed that 90 percent of all Chinese youth—and 96 percent of college students—think the U.S. tries to dominate China. Eighty-four percent of Chinese youth believe that U.S. censure of China for human rights

violations is "based on malice." See "China Can Say No to America," *New Perspectives Quarterly* 14., no. 4 (Winter 1996).

9. AS CHINA ADVANCES, AMERICA MUST NOT RETREAT

1. Bill Gertz, *iWar: War and Peace in the Information Age* (New York: Threshold Editions, 2017), 114.

2. Office of the Secretary of Defense, *Military and Security Developments Involving the People's Republic of China 2016*, April 26, 2016, https://www.defense.gov/Portals/1/Documents/pubs/2016%20China%20Military%20Power%20Report.pdf.

3. Of course, China also continues to scavenge the world looking for pieces of U.S. military hardware, such as parts of the military helicopter that crashed during the raid that took out Bin Laden, or the drone that went down in Iranian territory in 2011. See Catherine Herridge, "Iran Making Overtures to China on Access to US Drone Technology," Fox News, April 23, 2012, http://www.foxnews.com/politics/2012/04/23/officials-challenge-iran-claims-on-us-drone-despite-concerns-about-working-with.html. But reverse engineering is obviously more difficult than the straightforward engineering that stealing the original designs and technical data allows.

4. "China's Military Built with Cloned Weapons," U.S. Naval Institute, October 27, 2015. https://news.usni.org/2015/10/27/chinas-military-built-with-cloned-weapons. See also, Robert Farley, "5 Lethal Chinese Weapons of War (Stolen or Copied from Russia and America)" *National Interest*, August 7, 2016, http://nationalinterest.org/blog/the-buzz/5-lethal-china-weapons-war-stolen-or-copied-russia-america-17275. In what is something of a rarity, a Chinese agent was actually arrested and sentenced to prison for assisting Chinese military hackers seeking to illegally access information about the F-35. See "Chinese Businessman Sentenced to Prison for Hacking U.S.

Contractors", *New York Times*, July 13, 2016, https://www.nytimes.com/2016/07/14/us/chinese-businessman-hacking-prison.html?_r=0.

5. Mearsheimer has proposed that we could "strangulate" the Chinese economy by denying it access to the U.S. market, but while such an approach might have succeeded some years ago, the Chinese economy is probably too large, and too resilient, for it to succeed today. Peter Navarro, "Crouching Tiger: John Mearsheimer On Strangling China And The Inevitability of War," March 10, 2016, http://www.realcleardefense.com/articles/2016/03/10/crouching_tiger_john_mearsheimer_on_strangling_china_and_the_inevitability_of_war_109127.html.

6. As the 2016 Pentagon report notes, "Chinese leaders have characterized modernization of the People's Liberation Army (PLA) as essential to achieving great power status and what Chinese President Xi Jinping calls the 'China Dream' of national rejuvenation. They portray a strong military as critical to advancing Chinese interests, preventing other countries from taking steps that would damage those interests, and ensuring that China can defend itself and its sovereignty claims." Office of the Secretary of Defense, *Military and Security Developments*.

7. The 2016 Pentagon report noted, "The long-term, comprehensive modernization of the armed forces of the People's Republic of China (PRC) entered a new phase in 2015 as China unveiled sweeping organizational reforms to overhaul the entire military structure. These reforms aim to strengthen the Chinese Communist Party's (CCP) control over the military, enhance the PLA's ability to conduct joint operations, and improve its ability to fight short-duration, high-intensity regional conflicts at greater distances from the Chinese mainland." Office of the Secretary of Defense, *Military and Security Developments*.

8. Prior to June 2005, the exchange rate was fixed at 8.27 yuan per dollar for more than a decade, massively undervaluing the yuan. The Chinese

gradually appreciated their currency to as high as 6.1 RMB per dollar in 2015, but even at this level, it was still undervalued by 8 percent or so. Chinese economists deny this, of course, but that is not surprising since nearly all work, directly or indirectly, for the government.

9.   Cathy Zhang, "Yuan Ends 2016 with Biggest Annual Loss since 1994," *South China Morning Post*, December 30, 2016, http://www.scmp. com/business/article/2058260/yuan-ends-2016-biggest-annual-loss-1994.

10. After all, the Clintons have taken millions of dollars in Chinese money over the years. See Mike Flynn "Chinese Government Paid Bill Clinton Massive Speaking Fee 10 Days Before Hillary Made 'Asia Pivot,'" June 23, 2016, http://www.breitbart.com/big-government/2016/06/23/trump-media-spar-clintons-china-cash/. Clinton's main concern was that China "keep buying our debt," in effect subsidizing her plans to continue to spend beyond our means. See Aaron Klein, "Hillary Email on China: 'I Just Hope They Keep Buying Our Debt!'" May 17, 2016, http://www.breitbart.com/jerusalem/2016/05/17/hillary-emails-china-just-hope-keep-buying-debt/.

11. Eamonn Sheridan, "World Faces Deflation Shock as China Devalues at Accelerating Pace," ForexLive, July 7, 2016, http://news.forexlive. com/!/world-faces-deflation-shock-as-china-devalues-at-accelerating-pace-20160707. It was in response to this devaluation that Donald Trump issued a stern warning to the Beijing regime in his acceptance speech at the Republican National Convention. He said he would stop China's "outrageous theft of intellectual property," "illegal dumping," and "devastating currency manipulation." See "Donald J. Trump Republican Nomination Acceptance Speech," https://assets. donaldjtrump.com/DJT_Acceptance_Speech.pdf.

12. Hudson Lockett, "Rmb Falls 'Make a Mockery' of PBoC Stability Aim: Capital Economics," *Financial Times,* July 6, 2016. https://www. ft.com/content/6beff5f0-12a0-34af-a7cc-dd52edbf68bb.

13. "Premier Li: China Will Not Rely on Currency Depreciation," China. org, March 22, 2016, http://www.china.org.cn/video/2016-03/22/ content_38082020.htm.

14. Critics suggest that while China definitely suppressed the rise of the renminbi from 2000 to 2014 to maintain a competitive advantage for its exports, they sold dollars to prop up the yuan thereafter. The primary yardstick they use is whether China is buying or selling dollars and whether its foreign currency reserves are expanding or contracting. But China is able to keep its currency undervalued by other means as well, and does. See Eduardo Porter, "Trump Isn't Wrong on China Currency Manipulation, Just Late," April 11, 2017, https://www. nytimes.com/2017/04/11/business/economy/trump-china-currency-manipulation-trade.html.

15. Most PPP conversion rates fall in the range of 3.5 per USD, suggesting that the RMB should be worth almost twice as much as it actually trades for. The IMF, the World Bank, and the OECD give this number in their most recent data on Purchasing Price Parity (PPP), which date from 2015–16. See OECD, "PPPs and Exchange Rates", https://stats. oecd.org/Index.aspx?DataSetCode=SNA_TABLE4; IMF, "Download entire World Economic Outlook Database," http://www.imf.org/ external/pubs/ft/weo/2017/01/weodata/download.aspx; World Bank "PPP conversion factor, GDP (LCU per international $)," http://data. worldbank.org/indicator/PA.NUS.PPP?end=2015&start=1990. The World Bank also reports what it calls the "price level ratio of PPP conversion factor (GDP) to market exchange rate." It gives a value of .57 in 2014, and .55 in 2015, which means that the Yuan is devalued by nearly half. http://databank.worldbank.org/data/reports.aspx?source=2 &type=metadata&series=PA.NUS.PPPC.RF#. Another economist pegs the PPP conversion rate at 5.7 RMB per USD. But even this would mean that the yuan is 21 percent devalued. See Farok J. Contractor, "Does China Manipulate Its Currency as Donald Trump Claims?" June 13,

2016, http://theconversation.com/does-china-manipulate-its-currency-as-donald-trump-claims-60148.

16.   A leading New Zealand developer assured me in 2012 that a new law requiring government approval for foreign land purchases over five hectares would solve the problem. He was flabbergasted when the next China deal—for twenty thousand acres of prime dairy land—went through anyway.

17.   "China Global Investment Tracker," American Enterprise Institute, http://www.aei.org/china-global-investment-tracker/.

18.   Ankit Panda, "China Hits Back at South Korea's THAAD Deployment Following North Korea's Latest ICBM Test," *Diplomat*, August 18, 2017. The $10 billion figure comes from conversations that Bill Gertz had with Korean Embassy officials in Washington, D.C., in August 2017. Personal communication with the author, September 4, 2017.

19.   Dambisa Moyo, *Winner Take All: China's Race for Resources and What It Means for the World* (Basic Books, 2012).

20.   Quoted in Joshua Kurlantzick, *Charm Offensive: How China's Soft Power is Tranforming the World* (New Haven: Yale University Press, 2007), 133.

21.   Yun Samean, "Hun Sen Hails Beijing for Aid without Strings," *Cambodia Daily*, April 12, 2006, https://www.cambodiadaily.com/archives/hun-sen-hails-beijing-for-aid-without-strings-53594/.

22.   Kurlantzick, *Charm Offensive*, 174.

23.   Over a thousand Chinese combat troops are currently deployed in the South Sudan. "Summary of Contributions to Peacekeeping by Mission, Country and Post," United Nations, http://www.un.org/en/peacekeeping/contributors/2017/may17_5.pdf.

24.   Mao Zedong famously—or infamously, if you prefer—insisted that "All political power grows out of the barrel of a gun."

25. See Joseph S. Nye Jr., "Why China is Weak on Soft Power," *New York Times*, January 17, 2012, http://www.nytimes.com/2012/01/18/opinion/why-china-is-weak-on-soft-power.html?mcubz=1.

26. Chinese Communist and Western values are totally antithetical, according to Xi Jinping. At his National Propaganda and Ideology Work Conference, held in August 2013, Xi warned that "Western anti-China forces" were seeking "to overthrow the leadership of the Chinese Communist Party and China's Socialist system." He seemingly presented a choice between infiltration and total refusal, with the latter the only option open to loyal Chinese communists.

27. Xi Jinping's unpublished August 19, 2013, speech was first revealed in the *China Digital Times* on November 4 of that same year. It is available in translation at https://chinacopyrightandmedia.wordpress.com/2013/11/12/xi-jinpings-19-august-speech-revealed-translation/. "Brandish the Sword" (*Liangjian*) is a reference to one of the most popular television series ever broadcast in China. It was produced by a People's Liberation Army propaganda unit and follows the exploits of a crude and ruthless Red Army commander during the Chinese civil war. Since the series first aired in 2005, the "spirit of brandishing the sword" (*liangjian jingshen*) has become something of a catch phrase in China. It means to win at all costs.

28. People's Republic of China, State Council Information Office, "China's Military Strategy," May 2015, http://news.usni.org/2015/05/26/document-chinas-military-strategy.

29. *Yuan Guiren: gao xiao jiaoshi bixu shou hao zhengzhi, falu, daode, san tiao di xian,* ("Yuan Guiren: University instructors must keep to the three basic [Party] lines in politics, law, and virtue."), January 29, 2015, http://news.xinhuanet.com/edu/2015-01/29/c_1114183715.htm

30. On January 19, 2015, the General Office of the Central Committee of the Chinese Communist Party issued the turgidly named "Guidelines Concerning the Further Strengthening and Improvement of Ideological

and Propaganda Work in Higher Education under the New Situation."
(*Guanyu jin yi bu jiaqiang he gaijin xin xingshi gaoxiao xuanchuan sixiang gongzuo de yijian*) The "new situation" is an oblique reference to Xi Jinping's rule, as is the document's use of the phrase, the "great restoration of the Chinese race under the China Dream." http://news.xinhuanet.com/2015-01/19/c_1114051345.htm. For Xi Jinping as "core leader," see Michael Martina and Benjamin Kang Lim, "China's Xi Anointed 'Core' Leader, on Par with Mao, Deng," Reuters, October 27, 2016, http://www.reuters.com/article/us-china-politics-idUSKCN12R1CK.

31. From 1994 to 2002 the import quota was ten films per year. In 2002, as China sought to gain entry into the World Trade Organization, it doubled the quota to twenty films per year and promised to end the quota altogether in the near future. The present import quota dates from 2012, after a long-delayed WTO ruling demanded that China end the restrictions. China did not comply, but agreed to increase the quota to thirty-four. See Jonathan Papish, "Foreign Films in China: How Does It Work?" China Film Insider, March 2, 2017 http://chinafilminsider.com/foreign-films-in-china-how-does-it-work/.

32. Xi Jinping's full instruction reads, "We must vigorously construct more international communications capacity; Create new ways of doing foreign propaganda; Strengthen our ability to frame discourse; Strive to forge new concepts, new categories and new expressions for foreign consumption; Tell China's story well; Magnify China's voice; Strengthen the international influence of what we say." In other words, increase China's soft power where international communications are concerned. Xi Jinping's unpublished August 19, 2013, speech was first revealed in the *China Digital Times* on November 4 of that same year. It is available in translation at https://chinacopyrightandmedia.wordpress.com/2013/11/12/xi-jinpings-19-august-speech-revealed-translation/.

33. Xinhua, short for the New China News Agency, is the PRC's ministry of propaganda. It is a ministry-level organization, headed by a Central Committee member, responsible for disseminating the press releases and pronouncements of the Chinese party-state. In recent years, as part of China's effort to manufacture soft power, Xinhua has greatly expanded its international presence. It currently operates more than 170 bureaus worldwide, while aiming for 200 by 2020. It owns a dozen magazines and twice as many newspapers, which it publishes in eight different languages.

34. Koh Gui Qing and John Shiffman, November 2, 2015, "Special Report: Exposed—Beijing's Covert Global Radio Network," Reuters, http://www.reuters.com/article/us-china-radio-idUSKCN0SR1KM20151102.

35. Wang laid out his vision in a 2009 article in *Chinese Journalist* (*Zhongguo Jizhe*) entitled "Constructing a First Class International Media Organization: Actively Fight for Power in International Discourse" (*Jianshe Guoji Yiliu Meiti, Jiji Zhengchu Guoji Huayu Quan*). The article was reprinted in the CCP's theoretical journal, *Qiushi*, in 2011, indicating its importance. See *QS Theory*, October 9, 2011, http://www.qstheory.cn/special/2011dd/gjcbnl01/xz/hyq/201110/t20111009_114870.htm.

36. See, for instance, Eamonn Fingleton, "Is Stanford Collaborating with Chinese Propaganda? Just Asking," Forbes, October 5, 2014, https://www.forbes.com/sites/eamonnfingleton/2014/10/05/is-stanford-collaborating-with-chinas-espionage-program/#7ede2f3332b3. See also, Fabrice de Pierrebourg and Michel Juneau-Katsuya, *Nest of Spies: The Startling Truth about Foreign Agents at Work within Canada's Borders* (HarperCollins Canada, 2009), 160–62.

37. See "A Message from Confucius: New Ways of Projecting Soft Power," *Economist*, October 22, 2009, http://www.economist.com/node/14678507.

38. Omid Ghoreishi, "Beijing Uses Confucius Institutes for Espionage, Says Canadian Intelligence Veteran," *Epoch Times*, October 14, 2014, http://www.theepochtimes.com/n3/1018292-hosting-confucius-institute-a-bad-idea-says-intelligence-veteran/.

39. Lionel M. Jensen, "Culture Industry, Power, and the Spectacle of China's "Confucius Institues," in Lionel M. Jensen, eds., *China in and beyond the Headlines* (Rowman and Littlefield, 2012), 271–96, especially 292. "Because the CIs are instruments of propaganda, they are necessarily controversial and should be anathema to college and universities," Jensen maintains.

40. Smith is the chairman of the Subcommittee on Africa, global Health, Global Human Rights and International Organizations of the House Committee on Foreign Affairs. Quoted in Nicole Gaudiano, "House Panel investigates 'Confucius Institutes,'" *USA Today*, December 4, 2014, https://www.usatoday.com/story/news/politics/2014/12/04/house-china-confucius-institutes/19909507/.

41. When I visited the League's small office in Guangzhou, panic broke out among the staff, who were undoubtedly afraid that they would be accused of conspiring with the enemy.

42. China is trying to influence American universities in even more blatant ways as well, by simply giving them large sums of money. As Bill Gertz has recently pointed out, "China is providing Harvard with $360 million that a former military intelligence analyst says appears to be part of an effort to influence one of America's most important educational institutions." See Bill Gertz, "China's $360 million gift to Harvard," *Washington Times*, August 16, 2017, http://www.washingtontimes.com/news/2017/aug/16/inside-the-ring-chinas-360-million-gift-to-harvard/.

43. I have told this story elsewhere. See my chapter in *Academic License: The War on Academic Freedom*, edited by Les Csorba III (UCA Books, 1989).

44. During the "Criticize Lin Biao, Criticize Confucius" (*Pi Lin Pi Kong*) campaign of 1974, Chairman Mao's one-time heir apparent Lin Biao was accused of being "an out-and-out disciple of Confucius. Like all reactionaries in history on the verge of extinction, he worshipped Confucius and opposed the Legalist school, attacked Qin Shihuang, the first emperor of the Qin dynasty, and used the doctrine of Confucius and Mencius as his reactionary ideological weapon." Mao "repeatedly criticized Confucianism and the reactionary ideas of exalting Confucianism and opposing the Legalist school." "Carry the Struggle to Criticize Lin Biao and Confucius Through to the End," *Beijing Review* 17:8 (February 8, 1974): 5–6. An English-language version can be accessed at "Carry the Struggle to Criticize Lin Piao and Confucius Through to the End" *Peking Review*, February 8, 1974, https://www.marxists.org/subject/china/peking-review/1974/PR1974-06f.htm.

45. Peng Ming-min, "China Picks Pockets of Academics Worldwide," *Taipei Times*, May 31, 2011, 8, http://www.taipeitimes.com/News/editorials/archives/2011/05/31/2003504575.

46. Pierrebourg and Juneau-Katsuya, *Nest of Spies*, 160–62

47. This is the goal announced by Hanban, the Chinese government agency responsible for the Confucius institute initiative, but it may prove difficult to achieve. There were 659 Confucius Institutes in existence in 2010, but that number has since declined. According to Hanban, here were only 611 in existence in 2017, perhaps because the institutes have become increasingly controversial. Still, there are 157 Confucius Institutes and Classrooms in the Americas. See http://english.hanban.org/node_10971.htm.

48. The above material is based on testimony I presented to the U.S. Congress. "Confucius Institutes: Trojan Horses with Chinese Characteristics," Testimony Present to the Subcommittee on Oversight and Investigations of the House Committee on Foreign Affairs, March

28, 2012, http://archives.republicans.foreignaffairs.house.gov/112/ HHRG-112-FA17-WState-MosherS-20120328.pdf.

49. Liu Yunshan is a member of the Standing Committee of the Politburo and the top official in charge of ideology and propaganda work. See "Senior Official Visits Cultural Workers," Xinhua, January 17, 2017, http://news.xinhuanet.com/english/2017-01/17/c_135990831_2.htm.

     Imagine the reaction if a senior White House staffer visited, say, Meryl Streep, and asked her to promote traditional American culture and advanced capitalist culture.

50. Pew found that China's neighbors are quite wary of Asia's largest economic and military power, especially given its propensity to instigate territorial disputes with many of them. See "Chapter 4: How Asians View Each Other" http://www.pewglobal.org/2014/07/14/chapter-4-how-asians-view-each-other/. Accessed on July 13, 2017.

51. Center for Strategic and International Studies, "How Are Global Views on China Trending?" July 13, 2017, http://chinapower.csis.org/global-views/.

10. WHAT AMERICA CAN DO

1. Peter Navarro, *Crouching Tiger: What China's Militarism Means for the World* (New York: Random House, 2015), 18.

2. Amitai Etzioni, "How Aggressive Is China?" *Korean Journal of International Studies* 14:2 (August 2016), 291–307 at 301, https://icps.gwu.edu/sites/icps.gwu.edu/files/downloads/Etzioni_How%20Aggressive%20is%20China.pdf. Etzioni is the Director of the institute for Communitarian Policy Studies at the George Washington University.

3. As Bill Gertz points out in *iWar*, "…Beijing regards [America] as its most important strategic enemy. Yet American leaders remain lost in a Cold War political gambit that once saw China as covert ally against the Soviet Union. Today the Soviet Union is gone but China remains a

nuclear-armed communist dictatorship on the march. Bill Gertz, *iWar: War and Peace in the Information Age* (New York: Threshold Editions, 2017), 114.

4. John J. Mearsheimer, "China's Unpeaceful Rise," *Current History*; April 2006; 105, 160, 690, http://johnmearsheimer.uchicago.edu/pdfs/A0051.pdf.

5. Ibid.

6. Yale University professor Nicholas Spykman turned Mackinder's geopolitical theory on its head, arguing that the "Rimland"—the Eurasian littoral—rather than the Heartland was key to controlling Eurasia. But he agreed that "Who rules Eurasia controls the destinies of the world." Nicholas J. Spykman, *The Geography of Peace* (New York: Harcourt & Brace, 1944), 43. Spykman became known as the "godfather of containment," and his ideas became the intellectual basis for "containing" the Soviet Union to prevent it from overrunning Eurasia.

7. Jonathan Josephs, "All aboard the China-to-London Freight Train," BBC News, January 18, 2017, http://www.bbc.com/news/business-38654176. Under discussion is a prospective high-speed rail line between Moscow and Beijing that would make it possible to move passengers and freight between the two capitals in only two days.

8. "China Focus: A Modern Silk Road in the Making," Xinhua, May 12, 2017, http://news.xinhuanet.com/english/2017-05/12/c_136276995.htm.

9. Christopher Fettweis, writing in 2000, believed that "the notion that an imbalance of power in Eurasia (even if it were conceivable) would somehow threaten the interests of the United States is not tenable." Unfortunately, the imbalance of power that seemed so inconceivable just a few years ago has now materialized, and is already threatening our allies and our interests. Christopher Fettweis, "Sir Halford Mackinder, Geopolitics, and Policymaking in the 21st Century,"

Parameters, Summer 2000, 58–71 at 71, http://ssi.armywarcollege.edu/pubs/parameters/Articles/00summer/fettweis.htm.

10. However one wishes to characterize the Chinese party-state's governing ideology—I think its "socialism with Chinese characteristics" more closely resembles Fascism than anything else—the Chinese Communist Party proudly insists that it is still, after all, communist. This enables it to claim it represents and acts on behalf of the masses in exercising its "people's democratic dictatorship."

11. On June 30, 2017, China's Foreign Ministry repudiated the 1984 Sino-British Joint Declaration once and for all. According to spokesman Lu Kang, "Now that Hong Kong has returned to the embrace of the motherland for 20 years, the Sino-British Joint Declaration—as a historical document—no longer has any practical significance." "China Says Sino-British Joint Declaration No Longer Has Meaning," Reuters, June 30, 2017, http://www.reuters.com/article/us-hongkong-anniversary-china-idUSKBN19L1J1?il=0. In the Joint Declaration, China had promised to honor the principle of "One Country, Two Systems" for at least fifty years following the handover, that is, until 2047. The citizens of Hong Kong were to continue to enjoy the civil liberties and fundamental rights that they had enjoyed in the British colony, such as political freedom, free elections, press freedom, freedom of speech, and an independent judiciary.

12. "Benevolent American hegemony" was a phrase popularized by Bill Kristol and Robert Kagan in their 1996 essay, "Toward a Neo-Reaganite Foreign Policy," *Foreign Affairs*, July/August 1996, https://www.foreignaffairs.com/articles/1996-07-01/toward-neo-reaganite-foreign-policy.

13. Liu Xiaobo, "The Roots of Chinese Nationalism," in *No Enemies, No Hatred* (Cambridge, Massachusetts: Harvard University Press, 2013), 72.

14. James Fallows, "China's Great Leap Backward," *Atlantic*, December 2016, https://www.theatlantic.com/magazine/archive/2016/12/chinas-great-leap-backward/505817/.

15. Certainly, many of Obama's followers, if not he himself, believed that America was a racist, sexist, homophobic, imperialistic, capitalist society that deserved to be punished for its many sins. What better way humiliate the country that you so despise than to ensure that its socialist rival will one day eclipse it?

16. Ethan Gutmann estimates that some sixty-five thousand imprisoned Falungong practitioners were killed for their organs. See *The Slaughter: Mass Killings, Organ Harvesting,* and *China's Secret Solution to Its Dissident Problem* (Prometheus Books, 2014), 322.

17. Orville Schell, "Crackdown in China: Worse and Worse," *New York Review of Books*, April 21, 2016, http://www.nybooks.com/articles/2016/04/21/crackdown-in-china-worse-and-worse/. Schell draws striking parallels between the "factionalism, intrigue, paranoia, intimidation, fratricide, and extrajudicial ruthlessness" of today's China and the Ming dynasty in the fifteenth century. I would go back even further, to the elaborate network of internal surveillance and harsh punishments that characterized the very first and formative Chinese empire, that of the brutal Qinshihuang.

18. Perry Link, Professor Emeritus of East Asian Studies at Princeton University, has been banned from China since 1996. Andrew Nathan, Professor of Political Science at Columbia University, has been banned since the publication of the English version of *The Tiananmen Papers* in January 2001, which he, along with Perry Link and Orville Schell, edited and translated. Andrew J. Nathan, "The Tiananmen Papers," *Foreign Affairs*, January/February, https://www.foreignaffairs.com/articles/asia/2001-01-01/tiananmen-papers.

19. Teng Biao, "The West Kowtows to China through Self-Censorship," *Washington Post*, July 28, 2016, https://www.washingtonpost.com/opinions/global-opinions/the-west-kowtows-to-china-through-self-censorship/2016/07/28/6d2e4ebe-49f8-11e6-bdb9-701687974517_story.html?utm_term=.76da267db06e.

20. Michael Pillsbury, *The Hundred-Year Marathon: China's Secret Strategy to Replace American as the Global Superpower* (New York: Henry Holt, 2015).

21. After the U.S. learned that its ally Taiwan was attempting to acquire nuclear weapons, it brought pressure on Taipei to halt its secretive program. William Ide, "How the US Stopped Taiwan's Bomb," Taipei Times, October 14, 1999, http://www.taipeitimes.com/News/local/arch ives/1999/10/14/0000006401/3.

22. A recent analysis by John Park of Harvard University and Jim Walsh of MIT concluded that sanctions imposed by the United Nations Security Council "have not worked" and were at times counterproductive.

    "In some ways, the sanctions have had the net effect of actually improving (North Korean) procurement capabilities," Park and Walsh wrote. While North Korean trade with nations other than China has come to a virtual halt, its trade with China is growing apace. North Korean state-run companies have opened branches on Chinese soil, have hired better Chinese middlemen, and have expanded their nuclear procurement operations in Hong Kong, Southeast Asia, and North Korean embassies around the world. See John Park and Jim Walsh, "Stopping North Korea, Inc.: Sanctions Effectiveness and Unintended Consequences," MIT Studies Program, https://www.scribd.com/ document/323470624/Stopping-North-Korea-Inc.

23. Kristina Wong, "Trump: 'So Much for China Working with Us' on North Korea," Breitbart, July 5, 2017, http://www.breitbart.com/ national-security/2017/07/05/trump-so-much-china-working-us-north-korea/. It may have been Xi Jinping himself who convinced President Trump that China was the key to curbing North Korea. The Chinese leader went out of his way to claim a proprietary interest in the Korean Peninsula. As Trump later recounted the conversation to the *Wall Street Journal*, "[Xi] then went into the history of China and Korea.... And you know, you're talking about thousands of years...and many wars.

And Korea actually used to be a part of China." Joseph Campbell, "Trump Says 'Korea Used to Be Part of China'...Twitter Goes Ballistic and S. Korea Investigates," Reuters, April 20, 2017, https://www.rt.com/usa/385409-trump-china-part-korea/.

24. Rex Tillerson, "Remarks at the United Nations Security Council Ministerial Session on Democratic People's Republic of Korea," April 28, 2017, https://www.state.gov/secretary/remarks/2017/04/270544.htm.

25. James Pearson and Jack Kim, "North Korea Appeared to Use China Truck in ICBM Test," Reuters, July 4, 2017, https://www.reuters.com/article/us-northkorea-missiles-china-truck-idUSKBN19P1J3 As Bill Gertz has pointed out, the latest sanctions imposed on China did not include punitive action against CASIC, the company that makes the missile transporter-erector-launchers for new North Korean long-range mobile missiles. See "U.S. sanctions Chinese, Russians for illicit trade with North Korea," *The Washington Free Beacon*, August 23, 2017. http://freebeacon.com/national-security/u-s-sanctions-chinese-russians-illicit-trade-north-korea/

26. "Just looking at the JL-1 and the North Korean SLBM, they're looking exactly the same," noted one analyst. See https://sputniknews.com/asia/20160905/1044996747/expert-china-north-korea-missile.html. On the use of China's *Beidou* for targeting, see Peter J. Brown, "Is North Korea Using China's Satellites to Guide Its Missiles?" *National Interest*, May 23, 2017, http://nationalinterest.org/blog/the-buzz/north-korea-using-chinas-satellites-guide-its-missiles-20810.

27. Gordon G. Chang, "To Disarm North Korea, Wage Trade War on China," *Forbes*, November 27, 2016, http://www.forbes.com/sites/gordonchang/2016/11/27/to-disarm-north-korea-wage-trade-war-on-china/#2e3d69a12864.

28. "U.S. Officials Sound Alarm over North Korea," CNN, November 24, 2016, http://www.cnn.com/TRANSCRIPTS/1611/24/cnr.19.html.

29. Michelle Nichols, "U.N. Expands North Korea Blacklist in First U.S., China Sanctions Deal under Trump," Reuters, June 2, 2017, http://www.reuters.com/article/us-northkorea-missiles-un-idUSKBN18T2X3.

30. "North Korean ICBM Appears Able to Reach Major US Cities," Union of Concerned Scientists," July 28, 2017, http://www.ucsusa.org/press/2017/north-korean-icbm-appears-able-reach-major-us-cities#.WX3-3a3Mwvp.

31. China is predictably apoplectic that the U.S. is no longer willing to turn a blind eye to its machinations. In fact, when this new policy was announced, Beijing's spokesman went on a long rant, shouting "enough with" blaming China for North Korea." See Frances Martel, "Beijing Spokesman Rants: 'Enough with' Blaming China for North Korea," Breitbart, July 11, 2017, http://www.breitbart.com/national-security/2017/07/11/china-north-korea-isnt-our-fault/.

32. The 1961 treaty is commonly referred to in China as the "China–North Korea military alliance treaty" (*zhongchao junshi tongmeng xieyi*), following the military obligations laid out in Section II. That is to say, it is a mutual defense treaty, with both countries obligated to come to the aid of the other if attacked. The importance of this defense treaty to both China and North Korea is underlined by the fact it is the *only* formal military alliance that either country has. The other treaties that China earlier signed with, for example, the former Soviet Union, have been rescinded. An editorial published in China's state-run *Global Times* argued that "China should make it clear that if North Korea launches missiles that threaten U.S. soil first and the U.S. retaliates, China will stay neutral." "Reckless Game over the Korean Peninsula Runs Risk of Real War," Global Times, August 10, 2017, http://www.globaltimes.cn/content/1060791.shtml. Western news outlets interpreted this to mean that China was backing away from its mutual defense treaty with North Korea, but this is wrong on two counts. First, the *Global Times* has a history of writing hyperbolic editorials

that do not represent official policy, and that are often significantly different from the government's actual position. Second, the mutual defense treaty was never intended to obligate China to defend North Korea if it launched an attack on the United States.

33. China even sanitizes the image of the North Korean dictator, blocking unflattering descriptions of him as "Kim Fatty the Third" on social media. Mary Bowerman, "People in China Are Calling Kim Jong Un Fat, and North Korea Isn't Happy About It," *USA Today*, November 16, 2016, https://www.usatoday.com/story/news/nation-now/2016/11/16/people-china-calling-kim-jong-un-fat-and-north-korea-isnt-happy/93950570/.

34. Lee Seong-hyon, China–N. Korea Defense Treaty," *Korea Times*, November 19, 2016, http://www.koreatimes.co.kr/www/news/opinon/2016/11/197_210355.html.

35. Rex Tillerson, "On the Latest DRNK Provocation," July 28, 2017, U.S. Department of State, https://www.state.gov/secretary/remarks/2017/07/272936.htm.

36. *Agence France*–Presse, "US Sanctions Chinese Bank for Laundering North Korean Cash," Breitbart, June 29, 2017, http://www.breitbart.com/news/us-sanctions-chinese-bank-for-laundering-north-korean-cash/.

37. Since the small bank was not owned and operated by the Chinese party-state, this was technically true. But given the level of corruption in China, combined with the degree of oversight that nominally private banks must submit to, it is virtually certain that high-ranking Chinese officials knew perfectly well that much of the bank's business came from across the Yalu River. And given the way things work in China, they were probably well compensated to look the other way.

38. The idea that the Chinese party-state, with its five-year plans and huge state-owned sector of the economy, could ever be induced to practice free trade is delusionary. Repeated promises by Beijing to reduce market

interventions, reform state-owned enterprises, protect intellectual property, and move towards a market economy have not been kept, and never will be. The only way to bring trade between the U.S. and China back into balance is to demand strict reciprocity where exports and imports are concerned. Japan manages its trade with China in precisely this way; whenever a trade imbalance in one or the other country's favor arises, trade representatives from Beijing and Tokyo quietly enter into negotiations to rebalance it. This kind of managed trade is not ideal, but it would be a vast improvement over the rapacious mercantilism currently practiced by Beijing.

39. In an April 12, 2017 interview with the *Wall Street Journal*, Trump revealed that he had offered Xi Jinping a better trade deal in return for bringing North Korea to heel. "We have tremendous trade deficits with everybody, but the big one is with China…and I told them, 'You want to make a great deal?' Solve the problem in North Korea. That's worth having deficits. And that's worth having not as good a trade deal as I would normally be able to make." Gerard Baker, Carol E. Lee, and Michael C. Bender, "Trump Says He Offered China Better Trade Terms in Exchange for Help on North Korea," *Wall Street Journal*, April 12, 2017, https://www.wsj.com/articles/trump-says-he-offered-china-better-trade-terms-in-exchange-for-help-on-north-korea-1492027556.

40. Chang, "To Disarm North Korea."

41. "Shades of Grey: Ten Years of China in the WTO," *Economist*, December 10, 2011, http://www.economist.com/node/21541408.

42. John Bolton, "The U.S. Can Play a 'Taiwan Card,'" *Wall Street Journal*, January 17, 2016, http://www.wsj.com/articles/the-u-s-can-play-a-taiwan-card-1453053872.

43. David Brunnstrom and Arshad Mohammed, "U.S. Plans to Sell Taiwan about $1.42 Billion in Arms," Reuters, June 29, 2017, https://www.reuters.com/article/us-usa-taiwan-arms-idUSKBN19K2XO.

44. Patricia Lourdes Viray, "Challenging China, US Launches First South China Sea Operation under Trump," *Philippine Star*, May 25, 2017, http://www.philstar.com/headlines/2017/05/25/1703487/challenging-china-us-launches-first-south-china-sea-operation-under.

INDEX